Limited Edition# 3912

Rich Tomaskie

A Guide Book of
Franklin and Kennedy
Half Dollars

If you enjoy *A Guide Book of Franklin and Kennedy Half Dollars*, you'll also enjoy these books in Whitman's Bowers Series of numismatic references.

A Guide Book of Morgan Silver Dollars (Q. David Bowers)

A Guide Book of Double Eagle Gold Coins (Q. David Bowers)

A Guide Book of United States Type Coins (Q. David Bowers)

A Guide Book of Modern United States Proof Coin Sets (David W. Lange)

A Guide Book of Shield and Liberty Head Nickels (Q. David Bowers)

A Guide Book of Flying Eagle and Indian Head Cents (Richard Snow)

A Guide Book of Washington Quarters (Q. David Bowers)

A Guide Book of Buffalo and Jefferson Nickels (Q. David Bowers)

A Guide Book of Lincoln Cents (Q. David Bowers)

A Guide Book of United States Commemorative Coins (Q. David Bowers)

A Guide Book of United States Tokens and Medals (Katherine Jaeger)

A Guide Book of Gold Dollars (Q. David Bowers)

A Guide Book of Peace Dollars (Roger W. Burdette)

A Guide Book of the Official Red Book of United States Coins (Frank J. Colletti)

A Guide Book of Civil War Tokens (Q. David Bowers)

A Guide Book of Hard Times Tokens (Q. David Bowers)

A Guide Book of Mercury Dimes, Standing Liberty Quarters, and Liberty Walking Half Dollars (Q. David Bowers)

A Guide Book of Half Cents and Large Cents (Q. David Bowers)

A Guide Book of Barber Silver Coins (Q. David Bowers)

A Guide Book of Liberty Seated Silver Coins (Q. David Bowers)

A Guide Book of Modern United States Dollar Coins (Q. David Bowers)

A Guide Book of the United States Mint (Q. David Bowers)

A Guide Book of Gold Eagle Coins (Q. David Bowers)

THE OFFICIAL RED BOOK®

A Guide Book of
Franklin and Kennedy
Half Dollars

History • Rarity • Values • Grading • Varieties

3RD EDITION

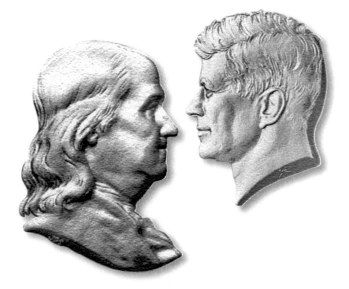

Rick Tomaska

Foreword by
Q. David Bowers

Whitman
Publishing, LLC
PUBLISHING SINCE 1934

A Guide Book of
Franklin and Kennedy Half Dollars
3rd Edition

© 2018 Whitman Publishing, LLC

1974 Chandalar Drive • Suite D • Pelham, AL 35124

The WCG™ grid used throughout this publication is patent pending.

Correspondence concerning this book may be directed to the publisher, Attn: Franklin-Kennedy Half Dollars, at the address above.

ISBN: 0794845290

Printed in the United States of America

Dedicated to my beautiful Ilona, who has stuck with me all these years!
All my love to you, Honey.

Disclaimer: Expert opinion should be sought in any significant numismatic purchase. This book is presented as a guide only. No warranty or representation of any kind is made concerning the completeness of the information presented. The author is a professional numismatist who regularly buys, trades, and sometimes holds certain of the items discussed in this book.

Caveat: The price estimates given are subject to variation and differences of opinion. Before making decisions to buy or sell, consult the latest information. Past performance of the rare-coin market or any coin or series within that market is not necessarily an indication of future performance, as the future is unknown. Such factors as changing demand, popularity, grading interpretations, strength of the overall coin market, and economic conditions will continue to be influences.

For a complete catalog of numismatic reference books, supplies, and storage products, visit Whitman Publishing online at **www.whitman.com**.

CONTENTS

FOREWORD

Franklin and Kennedy half dollars are two of the most popular series in American numismatics—and by reading the second edition of *A Guide Book of Franklin and Kennedy Half Dollars*, by Rick Tomaska, you can become an expert on these widely collected coins!

Q. David Bowers

When the Franklin half dollar debuted in the slow market of 1948, it received little attention. Two years later, when the Mint reintroduced Proof sets after a 35-year hiatus, the Franklin half was included. Collector interest rose a bit, but the general market didn't heat up much until 1953, when Proof-set popularity truly took off. Then, in 1955 and 1956, it came to light that the 1955 half dollar circulation mintage out of Philadelphia had been just 2,498,181—the smallest in the series. It was a collector's dream come true: a low-mintage issue available for a modest premium or even at face value. On top of that came the discovery of the "Bugs Bunny" variety, in which a die defect on Franklin's upper lip somewhat resembled the famous cartoon rabbit's teeth. This stirred even more interest.

Franklin half dollars remained in regular production through 1963 and today are avidly collected. Premium coins with Full Bell Lines can sell for hundreds or thousands of dollars—but a basic set of dates and mintmarks in a high grade such as MS-65, without Full Bell Lines, can be had relatively easily. Proofs can provide a separate collection to go with the circulation strikes.

In 1964 the half dollar design changed, now featuring the profile of the recently assassinated President John F. Kennedy on the obverse and, on the reverse, the Great Seal of the United States. Collector interest was keen when, in March 1964, the first pieces struck at the Philadelphia and Denver mints were released. This reception was in stark contrast to that for Franklin half dollars. Soon, however, the rising price of silver bullion made the cost of producing coins in that metal greater than their face values; and in 1965 the half dollar was struck in a new "clad" composition, in which a small amount of silver was combined with copper and nickel. After 1970, silver was removed entirely except in certain silver strikes made for collectors.

Meanwhile, numismatists were continually improving upon their standards for grading the coins they collected. Simple descriptors like "Good" and "Fine" were replaced by Dr. William H. Sheldon's system of numerical grades in the 1950s; since then, grading has evolved even further, becoming highly technical and somewhat controversial in the process. Today, the Mint State and Proof categories alone use every number from 60 through 70 (inclusive), as well as stars and other superlatives. Franklin half dollars may have "Full Bell Lines," and certain Proofs may have designations like "Cameo," which indicates a frosted head. (These terms are explained in detail in this book.) In the late 1980s, companies like Professional Coin Grading Service and Numismatic Guaranty Corporation began to offer coins enclosed in plastic "slabs" and marked with expert grade designations and other information.

Grading, however, is an art, not a science, and even sophisticated graders often disagree. Thus, although a certified MS-66 coin is nearly always better than one certified as 63, cherrypicking for quality and extra value—something this book will aid you in doing—can lead you to a 65 that can be certified as a much more valuable 66.

This book gives details of all the Franklin and Kennedy issues, values in multiple grades, certified populations, and more. Between these two covers is just about everything you ever wanted to know, and more than you ever imagined existed. Enjoy!

Q. David Bowers
Wolfeboro, New Hampshire

Q. David Bowers became a professional numismatist as a teenager in 1953. Actively involved in the hobby since then (including as a dealer, auctioneer, researcher, and writer), today he is chairman emeritus of Stack's Bowers Galleries, numismatic director of Whitman Publishing, research editor of the *Guide Book of United States*, and senior editor of *Mega Red* (the deluxe-edition Red Book). He is the author of more than 60 books; hundreds of auction and other catalogs; and several thousand articles, including columns in *Coin World* (now the longest-running by any author in numismatic history), *The Numismatist*, and other publications.

President John F. Kennedy   United States Founding Father Benjamin Franklin.

AUTHOR'S PREFACE

It was around 1982 or 1983 that my career in cameos began. I had been a full-time coin dealer since early 1981, having started out as a wholesaler selling prooflike Morgan dollars. I originally became interested in prooflike Morgan dollars around 1979, when I walked into a coin shop in La Jolla, California, and saw a book on the shelf by Jim Osbon, *The Silver Dollar Encyclopedia*.

Reading through the book, I became fascinated with the coins called *prooflike*. It was the practice during that era to polish commercial dies in a manner that early strikes off these dies would display deeply mirrored fields with frosted cameo devices, very similar in appearance to Proof Morgan dollars. The prooflike dies were not polished to the same degree as those used for Proof coins, so the resulting coins' mirrors were not quite the quality of Proofs, and the prooflikes also did not display the razor-sharp strike of Proofs. Prooflikes also had bagmarks, since the coins were intended for commercial use and were dumped into Mint bags, where they were abraded as they rubbed against other coins during shipping.

They seemed like a series with tremendous potential for collectors, with the finest examples offering the best possible eye appeal along with a high degree of rarity, for a most reasonable cost—at that time, a superb gem prooflike 1880-S Morgan dollar could be acquired for under $100.

And that was what really attracted me. Aside from the fact that I was just beginning and was on a very limited budget, it seemed a no-brainer that the combination of *exceptional eye appeal*, *rarity*, and *affordability* offered tremendous potential for future price appreciation for the collectors of the day.

If I took the time to scour enough dealers' inventories, occasionally a prooflike that ranked among the earlier strikes off a polished die, and had relatively few bagmarks—a "gem"—would turn up. Usually the date would be a common 1879-S or, more often, an 1880-S. But they were stunning. I really loved owning those finest prooflike Morgan dollars.

It was always a little disturbing when I sold a prooflike coin to another dealer, because I never had the opportunity to sell it to a collector who would actually enjoy and appreciate the coin as much as I did. So in 1981 I started selling directly to the public.

I was doing a pretty good business in those early days specializing in exceptional prooflike Morgan dollars. It was the early 1980s, and Morgans were red-hot in general. I quickly built a dedicated clientele who appreciated the quality of the prooflikes I was able to offer.

But I began having a little problem. While there were plenty of prooflikes still available in the marketplace, I noticed a gradual but steady deterioration of the quality. Even the most common date, 1880-S, was getting difficult to find in minimally marked "black-and-white" cameo condition. I could find 1880-S Morgans in prooflike, but the really deep-mirrored pieces had more bagmarks than the coins I had been selling, and the prooflikes that were true gem quality did not have the same depth of mirror as before. Astute collectors were wisely salting away the finest prooflikes, and, like most collectors, when they sold coins from their collection they would rarely part with their finest pieces. They would instead sell their second- and third-finest examples of a given date. That is what I felt was generally available on the market: quality that was less than the best.

And that presented a problem for a coin business that I had built around the philosophy of offering collectors the finest, most visually appealing coins of a series. When the finest was no longer available, what was I to do?

It was at a Long Beach coin show in the early 1980s that the answer came. At that time, "The Beach," held three times a year, ranked among the biggest shows in the country. I was roaming the aisles looking for something to catch my eye, perhaps a splendid dream Morgan like a black-and-white gem 1889-P prooflike, when a 1967 Special Mint Set caught my eye.

At that time a Special Mint Set (SMS) from the 1965–1967 era ranked pretty much near the bottom of the desirability spectrum among collectors. The government had discontinued the sets after only a three-year run because of declining sales, and nothing had changed since. An SMS coin wasn't really a Proof, but it wasn't exactly a circulation strike either.

But the 1967 SMS set I was looking at seemed to me to be a truly *special* Mint set. Most SMS coins I had seen to that point displayed a fully brilliant, mono-colored look, with no cameo contrast between the fields and devices. This was unlike the most recent Proof coins of the time, all of which displayed fabulous black-and-white cameo contrast featuring snow-white devices and the deepest possible fields, which gave them a black appearance when viewed straight on. But the set I was looking at contained a Kennedy half dollar that looked very much like the most modern cameo Proofs of the early 1980s.

The difference, of course, is that virtually all Proof Kennedy half dollars from 1977 onward display this ultimate level of cameo contrast. It was apparent to me that the 1967 Kennedy was quite rare in this condition— I had never seen such a spectacular coin before. The devices offered exceptional icy-white frost. And the coin was a superb gem, with only the most minimal surface ticks to disturb its otherwise flawless surfaces.

I needed to own that coin.

The typical 1967 SMS set at that time sold for around $5. I asked the dealer how much he wanted for his, thinking he might ask a premium, given the quality of the half dollar, and I was prepared to pay him $15 or $20 if I had to.

"Seventy-five dollars," he shot back. Seventy-five? That was quite a bit more than I was prepared to pay. Who would I sell the coin to? Who would be willing to give me a profit on this coin, when the typical 1967 SMS Kennedy could be acquired for around $5?

Well, I bought it anyway. Even if I couldn't sell it for a profit, it seemed a good coin to hold onto, one that would someday be worth more than what I had paid.

That stunning cameo 1967 SMS Kennedy was not as difficult to sell as I had thought it would be. I gave the coin a good write-up, explaining in detail the rarity and quality it offered, and pointing out that at this price level it offered tremendous opportunity for a collector willing to tuck it away. My philosophy has always been to buy the finest, most visually appealing rare coins possible so that I could sell them simply by telling their stories, feeling that the rest would take care of itself.

So it was with the 1967 SMS Kennedy, a coin that today, in MS-68 DC/UC condition, sells for $6,000 to $12,000.

In the weeks, months, and years that followed, I hunted out the very finest cameo Franklin and Kennedy half dollars, Washington quarters, Roosevelt dimes, Jefferson nickels, and Lincoln cents. I could once again offer my clientele coins that boasted the finest possible quality and eye appeal, that were very rare, and that were affordable.

But that first SMS Kennedy half was the coin that started it all, that first stirred my passion in a field that ranks among the most significant areas of collector interest today.

The *Guide Book of Franklin and Kennedy Half Dollars* could not have been achieved without the significant contributions of those listed in the acknowledgments. This book was truly a team effort. Nevertheless, it might not be the last word on the Franklin and Kennedy half dollar series. The collector base is growing for these coins by leaps and bounds—just witness the number of participants in the PCGS and NGC set registries if you need confirmation. And there is more work to be done. Both series are still in their collecting infancy.

Now is the perfect time for the release of this expanded and updated third edition. Virtually all known deposits of Mint State Franklin and early Kennedy half dollars have already been plundered for their precious gems. Virtually every Proof and Special Mint Set from the 1950–1970 era has been inspected, not once but five or ten times over, for the possibility of a high-quality coin. And so we are now at a point where we have very good, reliable data on the true rarity of these coins.

The Franklin and Kennedy half dollars represent the end of the era when superb gem Proof coins coming from the U.S. Mint were the rare exception, not the rule, as they are today—and when Mint State coins actually were meant for circulation. Whether your coin budget is $50 a month or $50,000, these series offer challenges and rewards like few others in numismatics.

Rick Tomaska
Solana Beach, California

PUBLISHER'S PREFACE

I first met Rick Tomaska (virtually, through email and phone conversations) in the early weeks of 2005, not long after I came aboard at Whitman Publishing. Editorial work was under way on the 59th edition of the *Guide Book of United States Coins* (the hobby's popular "Red Book"), and Rick shared his knowledge of Special Mint Sets, cameo designations, and coin pricing. He had recently contributed to David W. Lange's *Guide Book of Modern United States Proof Coin Sets*. We kept in touch over the years on various numismatic book projects. Then in 2008 we started talking about Franklin half dollars, and the growing collector interest in these coins, especially in high grades. Rick had already written two editions of his *Complete Guide to Franklin Half Dollars*, published by DLRC Press. That May, after our conversations turned toward the potential of Rick writing a book for Whitman, I envisioned him in our Bowers Series lineup. In this format his work would be published in full color in our standard six-by-nine–inch trim.

I talked with Q. David Bowers (Whitman's numismatic director) and with our sales team, studied the market and collector demand, and looked at activity in auctions and set registries. Would a book dedicated solely to Franklin half dollars be big enough for our publishing needs? Such a book would have been our first Bowers Series volume devoted to a single relatively short modern coinage series. (In 2007 we had covered Jefferson nickels, but we combined them with Buffalo nickels into a 288-page volume.) I began to wonder if we might broaden the scope of Rick's book by including Kennedy half dollars. To gauge the strength of this idea I conducted an informal poll of 146 novice, intermediate, and advanced coin collectors. About one-third of them actively collected Kennedy half dollars—that included hobbyists who were constantly upgrading their sets, those who were filling holes in an album or folder, and enthusiasts who sought every Fivaz-Stanton die variety. Another 13 percent identified themselves as *casual* collectors of the coins ("Yes, I collect them, but not actively"). Another one-third said they owned some Kennedy half dollars but considered them more of an accumulation than a carefully assembled collection. And about one-quarter of the hobbyists I polled didn't collect Kennedy half dollars at all. This information painted a picture of a coin with many passionate fans, a robust presence in the hobby community, and the potential to continue growing in popularity.

I asked Rick what he thought of covering Kennedy half dollars in his book. "An interesting proposition," he opined. "The two series are closely tied together and they complement each other." Dave Bowers agreed. "I think this is a dandy idea," he emailed me in June. (Yes, conversations that started in early May were still ongoing in June! Decision-making in the publishing world can take a while.) "These are very popular," Dave said, "and Rick Tomaska is a tried, tested, and true name."

We moved forward. Rick tackled the million moving parts involved in putting together a book manuscript—researching, writing, photographing coins, gathering data—and the *Guide Book of Franklin and Kennedy Half Dollars* debuted in December of 2010 as volume 15 in the Bowers Series. It was the first book devoted substantially to the Kennedy half dollar, while also showcasing the author's extensive knowledge of the Franklin series. It was immediately popular in the hobby, and our inventory sold out by the end of 2011. Rick updated the book in a second edition that came out in early 2012. It went through several printings over the next five years.

Since then much has happened in the world of Franklin and Kennedy half dollars. The latter coins were highlighted in William Rice's acclaimed *The Kennedy World in Medallic Art*, a study of John F. Kennedy and his family in coins, tokens, medals, and other collectibles. The United States Mint issued, to great fanfare and excitement, a special gold Kennedy half dollar and several silver versions that celebrated the coin's 50th anniversary. This brought national mainstream news coverage to the hobby. Meanwhile, collector interest has climbed for both series. The number of registry-set collections of Franklin half dollars has more than doubled since the first edition of this book was published. Auction records have continued to be broken, and numismatic research has been ongoing.

In this newly expanded third edition of the *Guide Book of Franklin and Kennedy Half Dollars*, Rick Tomaska has updated the market commentary, the pricing, auction records, and other details about each coin. He has increased the catalog to include more recent coins, added a section on Proof Liberty Walking half dollars (precursors to the Proofs of the Franklin series), and included new photographs. Longtime collectors will appreciate the new information in this volume, while beginning collectors will benefit from an immersion in its two very popular and historically significant coin series.

I'm pleased that Rick's book has accomplished so much, resonated with so many collectors new and old, and taken a significant position in the body of important numismatic literature.

Dennis Tucker
Publisher, Whitman Publishing

HOW TO USE THIS BOOK

To research individual coins by date and mintmark, see chapters 4 and 5. Each begins with biographical and historical information, then proceeds to individual listings: circulation-strike coins first, then Proofs. (*Note:* The 1964 and 1998-S Special Mint Set half dollars are listed with the circulation-strike Kennedy halves; the 1965, 1966, and 1967 SMS coins are listed with the Proofs. Significant varieties are listed within their respective date-mintmark entries.)

Each entry is organized as follows: 1.5x enlargements of each coin, with the illustrated grade given in the caption; a general discussion of that issue's history, strike quality, availability, and other collector information; a certified-population chart; a discussion of the population of coins in each grade or range of grades, including typical appearance and availability; and typical values for coins in that grade, including the rationales behind the values and commentary on exceptional and highly toned specimens.

Certified populations are from the Numismatic Guaranty Corporation of America (NGC). The distribution of grades tends to be similar from one grading service to the next, so the charts serve as "thumbnail sketches" of the proportional distribution of grades in the general population of certified coins. A quick-reference mintage and valuation chart is in appendix B, which also gives additional values for Franklin coins graded below Mint State. Lower-grade values may move with changes in silver's bullion value (~$16/ounce at press time).

MINTING PROOF AND SPECIAL MINT SETS

EVOLUTION OF THE MINTING ART

A coin collection is rarely complete without a segment devoted to the coin minter's art: Proofs. These special coins were never intended for inclusion as pocket change, but rather were struck as souvenirs or for numismatic purposes. The word *Proof* is sometimes misconstrued as indicating a grade or a level of quality, but it does not—it describes the method of manufacture. When its abbreviation, PF or PR, is included with a numeric grade, it is merely there to distinguish the coin from those that were struck for circulation (often called circulation strikes or "business-strike" coins). Historically, Proofs were struck to check the quality of the dies, and for archival purposes.

Proofs were struck before the mid-1800s, with many Proofs crafted to demonstrate a new design prior to production. The process itself involved the use of highly polished dies and the hand-feeding of special blanks (planchets) into the press.

In 1973, the Mint began sandblasting Proof dies to enhance the cameo effect (i.e., the contrast between the frosty design elements and the shiny, flat field around them); in addition, to help the dies retain the cameo effect longer, they were chrome-plated to protect the cameo surfaces. Over time this process was improved even further, so that by the late 1970s Proof dies could retain a heavy cameo effect for more than a thousand planchet strikes.

However, as technology improved, the rarity of cameo Proofs decreased. Today, you can easily purchase a post-1977 Proof set with five coins of gem PF-65 quality or better, all with a heavily frosted cameo effect. But with a production run of nearly three million sets yearly, where is the rarity of owning a 1982 cameo PF-67 Kennedy half dollar?

THE BRIDGE BETWEEN TWO WORLDS: RARITY AND BEAUTY

In my opinion, one of the most fascinating series in U.S. Proof history is that of 1950 to 1970, including the short-lived Special Mint Set (SMS) series of 1965 to 1967 (the SMS coins were of better quality than Mint State, but not as good as Proof). During my research, I had the opportunity to interview active and retired Mint personnel who were involved with the Proof-making process. In the course of my conversations, one crucial point emerged that helped explain the rarity of the high-quality cameos minted from 1950 to 1972.

This time period was a transitional one for the Mint, as it moved from using long-established minting techniques to producing coins using modern technology. During this "bridge" period—before the advent of the technological advances of the early 1970s—Proofs were produced more like those of an earlier era, by craftsmen of varying skill levels. What this means to collectors is that the quality of the coin was dependent on the human factor. Skilled craftsmen simply produced higher-quality Proofs than their less-skilled colleagues.

To further illustrate this bridge period, let's look at the four basic phases of Proof manufacturing to see how they were performed in the past and present, and to learn about the problems encountered during earlier periods. These phases are *die preparation, planchet preparation, press operation and die maintenance,* and *packaging.*

EXPLORING THE FOUR PHASES OF PROOF-MAKING

DIE PREPARATION

While some phases of the minter's art have changed little, die preparation itself has undergone dramatic improvement since 1970. Interestingly, changes in die preparation came not from within the Mint, but from the numismatic community.

For decades, collectors had treasured the eye appeal of the cameo Proofs more than that of typical non-cameo Proofs. To meet that demand, when the Mint resumed Proof production in 1968 following a three-year hiatus, it began developing techniques to allow more cameos and fewer brilliant (i.e., completely shiny) Proofs per die.

At the end of the 1970s, the sandblasting and chrome-plating processes described previously became standard. The sandblasting etched the frost deeply into the devices of the die while the mirrored field of the die was protected with tape. However, these techniques were not employed on the coins minted from 1950 to 1970.

So how did die preparation affect the production of cameos in this period?

Pre-1971 Die Preparation

All Proof dies have started life as regular-production dies, and all production dies have always been made at the Philadelphia Mint. While there are scant Mint records from 1950 to 1964, evidence suggests that the commercial dies selected for Proof manufacture went through several processes not routinely used on their commercial counterparts.

These additional steps included the following:

1. Cleaning the die with a solvent oil to remove contaminants.
2. Creating a frosted texture over the entire surface by dipping the die into a "pickling bath" of 5% nitric acid and 95% alcohol.
3. Hand-checking the frost for irregularities or unevenness, then cotton-swabbing with the pickling solution to add frost to weak areas. (I believe this step accounts for some of the more interesting cameo variations from this period.)
4. Polishing and buffing the die's surface with a diamond-dust compound, first with a wooden *mandrel* (a hand-sized drill with a wooden bit) and then with a felt-tipped mandrel. As in post-1970 die preparation, polishing did not reach the recessed portions of the die.

At this point in the die preparation process, the Proof die had a two-tone effect, with the recessed portions displaying a frosted cameo, contrasted with the mirrored finish of the fields. Unfortunately, the frost of the pickled 1950–1970 Proof die was so fragile that it could be picked off with a fingernail. (Contrast that to the extreme durability of the sandblasted and chrome-plated cameos made after 1972.)

An anomaly in this process was the treatment of the Special Mint Set (SMS) coins of 1965 through 1967. Although pickled, they did not receive the fine polish of the Proofs. You can see this most clearly on the 1965 SMS Kennedy half dollars. Even the earliest strikes from 1965 lacked the deeply mirrored fields that can sometimes be found on the 1966 and 1967 SMS Kennedys.

Factors Affecting Durability of 1950–1970 Cameos

Imagine the impact caused by double-striking the planchet with 160 to 200 or more tons of pressure from a steel die, and you'll understand why, in some years, as few as 5 to 10 high-quality cameos were produced before the frost began to wear.

The striking of metal on metal quickly smoothed the surfaces of the devices to the same mirror finish as the surrounding fields. In contrast, a sandblasted and chrome-plated die of today can strike hundreds of cameos without perceptible signs of wear.

I find it interesting to note the factors that determined how many cameos a die struck during this bridge period. For example, a shorter time than normal in the pickling bath resulted in a less intense frosting. If you look at some of the cameo Franklins from the 1950s, you'll see how this factor could easily account for the rarity of high-mintage issues.

Throughout the late 1950s, the cameo effect of Franklin Proofs decreased at successively faster rates each year. For collectors, this means the 1957 cameo Franklins are rarer than the 1956 vintage, 1958s are rarer than 1957, and 1959s even rarer. As a result, you'll find far more 1956 cameo Franklins than you will 1959s, even though there were one-third fewer Franklins minted in 1956 than 1959.

Why the difference?

1. Acid Bath Time. Look closely at an exceptional early-strike 1956 Franklin cameo and you'll see that the frost has a granular appearance compared to a 1959 cameo, which has a much smoother appearance. This could possibly have been caused by the 1956 vintage taking a longer acid bath.

Why would the Mint have shortened the pickling time of the Franklin dies as the 1950s wore on?

I believe it was due to the noticeable deterioration of the Franklin master die. When you compare a 1950 Proof Franklin to a 1959 one, you can see a softening of detail, particularly in Franklin's hair. This softening is evident even though the 1959 Proof is as fully struck as the 1950.

If the master die was wearing out, a longer acid bath would have only worsened the situation. I believe that the Mint made a logic-based decision to shorten the bath each year to retain as much detail as possible on the dies.

My theory seems to be supported by the 1960 reworking of the master die with sharpened detail and the production of more cameos that year. Having a reworked die would allow the Mint to give the new dies a longer bath without damaging the die detail.

2. Die Material. Although steel suppliers assured the Mint that the quality of steel used for dies was of the required grade, different batches of steel produced different results.

In addition, Philadelphia die makers didn't always temper the steel correctly. This inconsistency in tempering (a heating process used to harden steel) caused some dies to be soft, shortening their life, and others to be so brittle they would crack under the pressure of the presses.

It's also my belief that some Proof dies made in the 1950–1970 period never went through the pickling process, as evidenced by the rarity or nonexistence of highly contrasted cameos for many dates in the nickel and cent series.

Planchet Preparation

From the 1950s through the 1970s, planchet preparation remained virtually unchanged. The one notable exception was a new annealing process introduced in the mid-1970s.

Historically (at least from 1950 to 1970), planchets—both commercial and Proof—were struck from strips about six feet long and several inches wide. The resulting blanks then underwent *upsetting*, the process in which the rims of the planchet were contoured, which transformed the blanks into planchets.

Next, the planchets underwent annealing, a heating process that left the metal soft enough to allow further refinement. In our interesting 1950–1970 era, commercial and Proof blanks went through the same annealing process. First, planchets were fed into a tube called a *retort*, which ran horizontally through a 22-foot-long oven. The interior perimeter of the retort was set with corkscrew grooves that spiraled in a forward direction.

Once the planchet dropped into the retort, it lay flat inside a groove and moved forward as the retort rotated, while being subjected to temperatures from 1,100 degrees Fahrenheit (for silver) to 1,600 degrees (for nickel). This process lasted about an hour.

For planchets intended for commercial purposes, the process was then complete, and they were ready for striking.

The planchets intended for Proofs underwent additional polishing and cleaning, a process known as *burnishing*. Burnishing consisted of mixing and rotating planchets for 24 hours with a mixture of 3/16-inch metal beads in a stainless steel barrel resembling a cement mixer. It was this metal-on-metal process that helped produce the mirrored surfaces of the Proof coin.

If the planchet was properly prepared, the strike could produce deeply mirrored, nearly flawless cameos. This transitional period, however, saw a large number of planchets receiving too short an annealing time and at too low a temperature, resulting in a planchet that was too hard. Small batches of these (10 to 20) quickly abraded away the delicate cameo effect of a new Proof die.

Even more of a problem were striations. Where these ran to the edge of the rim or device, that was an indication that the lines were there before striking. This problem continued through the 1950s and '60s, and was finally addressed in the mid-1970s. At that time, a new annealing process was introduced whereby Proof planchets were placed on a stainless steel belt that kept them stationary as they moved through the oven. This was an innovation over their former sliding movement through the retort tube, a process that set up the "perfect storm" of conditions for picking up striations.

Press Operation and Die Maintenance

Perhaps nowhere in the Proof production process of 1950 to 1970 did human error come into play as much as it did during the press operation phase. It was here that the skill of the press operator could critically impact the quality of Proof coins.

Once planchets were burnished, it fell upon the press operator to inspect each planchet before placing it into the press. If any contaminant was left on the planchet, it would produce an imperfect Proof as well as damaging the die surface. Typically, a press operator would wash planchets in an Ivory soap bath and towel-dry them.

I believe an incomplete towel-dry was the cause of silver Proof issues from 1958 to 1964 displaying white spots (sometimes called *milk spots*) on the surface. The spots are leftover soap, and they are impossible to remove without damaging the coin. Once a trace of soap is subjected to 200+ tons of pressure, the residue becomes a permanent part of the coin.

(The milk-spot problem was addressed in 1968, when soap-washed planchets underwent an additional bath into muriatic or similar acid to remove any residue. A side benefit of the extra bath is a more brilliant planchet. Now planchets are inspected again, both before and after striking, to ensure that only the most perfect planchets are struck. As a result, modern Proofs with milk spots are virtually never found.)

Let's return to the responsibilities of the press operator. In addition to the duties previously mentioned, he is also responsible for maintaining the press itself. It's here that the paths taken by commercial and Proof planchets diverge yet again. Planchets destined for the shops and banks of the world are oiled to increase die life. Conversely, any buildup of oil on Proof and SMS dies would quickly dull the mirrors, decreasing die life.

A typical procedure in the 1950–1970 era was to use alcohol and cotton to clean the die every 20 to 30 coins. The only anomaly was the 1965–1967 SMS years; as these sets were not considered Proof quality, die cleaning was infrequent.

The die-cleaning process was one more area where the press operator's skill affected final quality. Some operators weren't as conscientious as others, and missed recommended cleaning intervals.

In addition, an occasional cotton strand would remain on the die after cleaning, with the result that an impression of the strand was struck onto the next planchet fed into the press. Cotton-strand impressions could be minor, although some left a large knot-like imprint.

A fascinating bit of press history reveals that operators in 1950 to 1970 did not maintain the obverse and reverse dies in the same manner. When a die needed replacing, the operator would replace only the more worn die—either the obverse or the reverse, but usually not both—resulting in many so-called one-sided cameos, most notably in 1957, 1958, 1959, and 1963.

What else impacts a die's durability, and thus the durability of the new cameo effect? The amount of pressure during striking is one such factor. This amount is ruled by the size of the planchet, as larger planchets require more pressure.

For example, during the 1950–1970 era, a Proof half dollar planchet is struck two to four times under 160+ tons of pressure; compare that to the 125 tons needed for a quarter, 45 tons for a dime, 90 tons for a nickel, and only 30 tons for a cent. A half dollar Proof die may be able to strike only 1,200 to 1,400 coins, while a cent die can sometimes strike more than 5,000 coins.

Lastly, a cameo's durability in the 1950–1970 period was influenced by the metal content of the planchet. Quarters and dimes minted from 1965 to 1970 contained cupronickel (an alloy of copper that contains nickel and strengthening impurities, such as iron and manganese), which was harder than silver and quickly wore the frosted cameo devices of a new die. This resulted in very few high-quality contrasted quarters per die. Because of the dime's smaller size (for which less pressure was needed), the wear on the dies was far less.

Repolishing of Proof Dies

Part of the press operator's responsibilities for die maintenance was repolishing the die. Proof half dollar dies are repolished in today's Mint an average of every 500 to 1,000 strikes. Smaller coin dies are repolished after striking two to five times this number.

During repolishing (known as *recycling*), the die is removed and inspected for wear. If the die appears to be worth saving, the chrome plating is removed and the die is once again sandblasted and chrome plated, just as if it were a new die.

In the 1950s, recycling was a new and untried procedure, one born of the higher demand for Proof coins. Before 1950, Proofs had last been made in 1942, when 21,120 Proof sets were struck. In 1950, with the resumption of Proof sets, more than twice the old number was required—51,000 sets. I'm unconvinced that the dies were repolished in 1950, as many Proofs struck in this year look like commercial uncirculated coins (BUs). After examination of these coins, it's my guess that some of the half dollars came from a die with more than 5,000 strikes.

In my interviews of Mint personnel involved in the manufacture of Proof sets, I've yet to determine why the Mint resorted to using worn dies. Perhaps it was overwhelmed with the demand for 51,000 sets, and one should also remember that recycling was not yet a standard process. In addition, only a certain number of dies were allotted for production, probably forcing Mint personnel into continuing to use worn dies.

Fortunately, in 1951, worn dies were routinely repolished; unfortunately, repolishing techniques were crude, to say the least. From 1951 to 1955, the recessed portions of the dies were wire-brushed with a diamond-dust compound. While this helped to recreate the cameo effect, the roughness of the wire-brushed die's devices, when transferred to the silver planchet during striking, gave the devices a whitish cast because it diffused the reflective nature of the silver.

After the devices were wire-brushed, the fields were repolished and rebuffed (with diamond dust compound) to restore their mirror finish.

It's important for collectors to note that this two-step process resulted in two types of cameos from this era: one struck from original dies and one struck from repolished ones. The latter coins are distinguished by wire-brushed die lines on their devices. On some repolished dies, the lines extend into the fields surrounding the devices. Under magnification, you can see the lines; these are distinguishable from hairlines because die lines appear raised, while hairlines are recessed.

It is fascinating that some of the frostiest, most attractive cameos, as well as some of the ugliest cameos from this period, came from repolished dies. Whether attractive or ugly cameos were produced was due to the repolishing skill of the operator.

Franklin dies were badly overused from 1950 to 1953, with shallow mirrored effects an indication of over-repolishing. This process was phased out by the mid-1950s, as finer brushes were used for repolishing, and a typical die underwent only one to three repolishes.

I believe the 1965 dies were used much longer than the 1966 and 1967 ones, as many 1965 SMS coins have no mirror finish and look like ordinary BUs.

In 1968, with the resumption of Proof production, the Mint repolished the fields of used dies, as well as remaking the cameo using the pickling-bath process. After a light wire brushing and acid dipping, the fields were polished and buffed; however, I'm unsure whether this process was used on all denominations, owing to the scarcity of cameos of some of the smaller denominations.

Packaging

While improvements in die preparation caused the most significant improvements in Proof quality, improved packaging ensured that the Proof received by the collector looked as good as it had when it left the Mint.

While coins destined for general circulation were simply dumped into bins after being struck, Proofs were treated far differently.

After striking, Proofs were handled individually, typically with large tweezers. Early-1950s Proofs were packaged using the same technique as coins of the 1936–1942 period:

Each coin was placed in a small, brittle Mylar-type envelope. The five envelopes of a Proof set were then stapled together, one on top of another, then placed in a cardboard box and sealed with paper tape.

In mid-1954, the Mint began packaging Proofs in soft plastic pouches. However, neither the plastic nor the Mylar-type envelopes could adequately protect the Proof coin. The old brittle envelopes would eventually crack open, exposing the Proof to air. And if that cracking wasn't enough, the coin could also suffer damage from rusting staple particles or envelope glue.

Because of their size and heft, the Franklins suffered more than other denominations. Almost all Franklins from 1950 to 1954 have hairlining that was often caused by packaging.

Although a slight improvement, the soft pouches used from mid-1954 through mid-1955 were not inert; over time, silver Proofs housed in these pouches developed a purple cast. If the purple coins were dipped in a commercial dip in an attempt to remove the toning, the surface of the coin would turn from purple to brown—not an improvement.

In mid-1955, the Mint began using the *flat pack*, which was used through 1964 and during the 1965 SMS production. Instead of being stacked, all five coins lay flat, each in its own sealed compartment, in a single Mylar envelope, which was then placed in a brown paper envelope with cardboard on either side for protection. Coins from this packaging era have generally undergone minimal if any toning. The major damage is done when the surface of the packet abrades the coins.

Snap-lock holders were used in 1966 and 1967; these containers protected coins from abrasion, but they were not airtight. By 1968, packaging similar to today's came into use, with Proofs shipped in sealed inert hard plastic cases. The cases are durable, protecting the coins from abrasion. Unfortunately, some are not airtight, and the majority of Proofs from this time have oxidization and heavy toning.

UNDERSTANDING THE RARITY OF THE 1950–1972 PROOFS

After reading about the four factors that made the production of 1950–1970 Proofs so distinctive, you can easily see why "ultimate" cameos from this era are so rare.

The technology that has been in place since the late 1970s helps create the extraordinary cameo Proof coins we all love to collect, but it was simply not available for those prior decades. In addition, the possibility of human error in that time period held significant sway over ultimate quality.

Moreover, as grading standards have become more exact, the minor imperfections that were insignificant 40 years ago are no longer acceptable in today's marketplace. That even a few of those 1950–1972 Proofs have survived in cameo condition that rivals the quality of today's Proofs is a miracle.

Now you see why I call this one of the most fascinating eras in the history of coin collecting.

GRADING THE PROOF: FACTORS THAT DETERMINE GRADE

THE GRADING ART

While superb cameo Proofs and SMS coinage may be among the best numismatic values in the marketplace today, it's critical that the coin you're buying is graded correctly. No one wants to pay top dollar for a PF-69 DC/UC when what he or she is actually getting is a PF-68 DC/UC.

Part of the problem lies with some coin dealers' lack of knowledge or experience in assessing a Proof or cameo Proof. It's nearly impossible to grade a coin by reading books alone; hands-on experience truly is a necessity.

Fortunately, there are several professional grading services that collectors within our hobby can turn to, all of which grade coins for a nominal fee. But can you trust that the grade one service awards is the same grade you'll get from another service? Frequently, the answer is yes, though each service uses its own criteria when establishing a grade, for both brilliant Proofs and cameo Proofs.

Let's take a look behind the curtain and examine the factors used to establish Proof grade, and then learn how the cameo grade is determined.

AN OVERVIEW OF GRADING PROOFS

In my experience, establishing a grade in modern Proofs is easier than grading BU coins. For example, strike, luster, and bagmarks are not as critical in judging 1950–1970 cameo and brilliant Proofs as in BUs, for the following reasons:

> Proofs are double-struck under higher pressure than BUs, so they generally are fully struck.

> Proofs are struck from relatively fresh, highly polished dies, adding to their luster and deep mirrors.

> Proofs are individually handled and placed in individual containers, alleviating the issue of bagmarks.

There are always exceptions to these guidelines, but as a rule of thumb I've found the grading philosophy of Proofs versus BUs to be true.

What exceptions might you find?

A Proof not fully struck

Heavy toning due to improper storage

Bagmarks on SMS coinage

Proof surface damaged by abrasion

All of these factors will affect grade, but rather than relying on those general benchmarks, I encourage you to study as many pregraded coins as possible—particularly those graded by a respected grading service. This way, you'll be in a much better position to accurately assess whether that coin of interest really *is* the grade assigned by the dealer.

As you move forward with your grading education, you'll notice the surface imperfections on Proof or SMS coins. Those imperfections can most often be divided into two categories: imperfections occurring at the Mint, either before or during striking, and imperfections occuring after the coin is struck.

IMPERFECTIONS DURING MINTING

The three most common problems that occur during the Minting process are *pitting*, *striations*, and *milk spots* or *glue spots*.

PITTING

Seen most commonly on Proofs of the early 1950s, pitting typically occurs on the high points of the Proof planchet. This imperfection is caused by inadequate metal flow into the deepest recesses of the die during striking.

Among Franklin half dollars, the worst victims of pitting are the 1950 issues. (Also in 1950, Jefferson nickels and 1950 Lincoln cents frequently show pitting.) Other Franklins from the 1950s will show minor pitting, most often on the high point of Franklin's cheekbone, and on the Liberty Bell on the reverse.

How does pitting affect grading? This depends on both the degree of pitting and how distracting it is. A beautiful frosted Proof with minor pitting can grade PF-67 or even PF-68. However, if the pitting is so heavy that it detracts from the coin's beauty, the grade will decrease accordingly.

HAIRLINES DURING MINTING

Hairlines can result from mishandling after the coin is struck, but some are actually struck into the coin during the minting process.

Hairlines can occur during the annealing process (when the planchet is sliding along through the retort tube) or during the burnishing phase.

Typically, all but the deepest hairlines are struck out under the pressure of the press. However, the lines can generally be seen under high lighting conditions.

As discussed in the previous chapter, the press operator would clean the die every 20 to 30 strikes, using cotton dipped in alcohol. Occasionally, a small strand of cotton would break off and remain on the die, resulting in a coin's being struck with an imprint of the cotton fiber. It takes excellent light and a magnifying glass to distinguish a cotton fiber imprint from a scratch.

MILK SPOTS AND GLUE SPOTS

There is a debate among coin dealers about the cause of milk spots. Most often found on the silver Proof issues from 1958 to 1964, milk spots can be as tiny as a pinhead or cover 25% of the surface or more.

Some dealers believe milk spots were caused by improperly prepared Proof dies. In my opinion, if this were true, then the milk spot would appear in the same position on each coin struck by the affected die. This isn't true, as the position of milk spotting on Proofs from a particular die is random on individual coins.

Like several Mint employees I interviewed, I believe milk spots are the result of residue left from a cleaning solution used on the planchet during preparation for striking.

How does milk spotting affect grade? It depends on the degree to which spotting occurs and the location of the spot. For example, if your coin has a tiny pinhead spot tucked away in the lettering, it won't be as distracting as a spot clearly seen in front of Kennedy's or Franklin's nose. The more distracting the spot, the less desirable the coin.

Removing milk spots can be an iffy proposition: tiny spots can generally be removed with commercial coin dips, but larger ones cannot be removed without damaging the Proof surface.

Glue spots were a major problem of 1950 Proofs and are similar to milk spots in color. These spots were caused by residue from the sealant used for the Mylar-like packets of the era.

In the image shown here, you'll see the white milk spot over Franklin's bust on the 1963 Franklin half dollar.

IMPERFECTIONS AFTER MINTING

The four most common problems that occur after the Minting process are *hairlines*, *toning* or *discoloration*, *carbon spots*, and *bagmarks*.

Hairlines After Minting

Other hairlines are typically caused by mishandling after striking. Hairlines occur in the center portion of the fields, where the field is the area least protected by the raised portions of the coin, and on the high points of the devices.

Hairlines were a particular problem on Proofs prior to the development of the flat packs in 1955. Almost all Proof Franklins, in particular virtually all of the 1950–1953 Proof Franklins, have hairlines (see the discussion of striations earlier in this chapter).

Toning or Discoloration

This is an interesting category of imperfections. While certain toning enhances the value of a Proof, other toning (discoloration) decreases the value. What's the difference?

A Proof that displays dull brown or black toning over its surface is considered an undesirable coin. However, a Proof with light blue toning or peripheral light burgundy toning—an attractive appearance we will call *color toning*—is considered desirable by most collectors.

Buyer beware: some coins are artificially toned to enhance eye appeal. However, once you've seen hundreds or thousands of naturally lustrous and toned coins, an artificially enhanced one can be easier to pick out.

Carbon Spots

If you find small, pinprick-sized black spots on your coin's surface, they are probably carbon spots. On silver Proofs or SMS coinage, the spots are typically caused by an impurity in the metal, or by some foreign object (dust, saliva, chemical) on the surface.

If carbon spots remain on the surface, they can grow to the point that they are a major distraction, which will affect the grade.

Copper coins and mirrored Proofs are particularly susceptible to carbon spotting.

BAGMARKS

Bagmarks are rarely a problem on Proof coins, as they are individually handled and packaged. However, they can suffer "roll rub," which means the high points—usually Franklin's and Kennedy's cheekbones—have rubbed against another object. This rubbing could occur against another coin in a stack, or the holder itself.

You will, however, see bagmarks on the SMS coins of 1965 to 1967, as they were not handled individually, but rather dumped into bins. The exception is Proof cents from the 1968–1976 era, which, for some mysterious reason known only to the Mint, often suffer from bagmarks.

THE GRADER'S TOOLS

Now that you know what imperfections to look for, I'd like to discuss the numerical Proof (or Mint State) grade for your coins. Hopefully, this will provide you with basic benchmarks for grading your own coins.

First, let's look at two pregrading factors: *lighting* and *magnification*.

LIGHTING

Accurately appraising coins requires excellent lighting. In my experience, two incandescent 75-watt bulbs located three to four feet above my working surface will give good lighting conditions. But even better is a halogen light, although it will cost a little more than an incandescent bulb, of at least 100 watts.

By all means, avoid fluorescent lighting and direct sunlight. Fluorescent light isn't sharp enough to reveal certain flaws; direct sunlight is too harsh, resulting in exaggeration of minor flaws. Fluorescent light can make your coins look better than they are, while direct sunlight can make them look worse.

MAGNIFICATION

The choice of using a magnifying glass is up to you, particularly when viewing large coins like Franklin and Kennedy halves. However, you will need magnification of 4x, 8x, or 16x for small cents and dimes, or when examining for surface irregularity.

THE SUBJECTIVITY OF GRADING PROOFS

Uncirculated Proof grades (or MS grades for SMS series) range from a low of PF-60 to a high of PF-70. A PF-60 coin will show gross mishandling, with many obvious flaws. A PF-70 is a "perfect" coin, the highest grade. A *gem* Proof or SMS coin is at least PF- or MS-65.

What does a gem Proof or SMS coin look like? For me, these are the two important factors: excellent overall eye appeal and no obvious, distracting imperfections.

Keep in mind that a PF-65 coin will have imperfections, but they should be relatively minor and not distract from the visual impact of the coin.

Here are some examples:

You may own a 1963 Proof Franklin half dollar. Look at it carefully. If the first thing you notice are the scratch lines running through the fields, you're probably not holding a gem-quality coin.

If the coin has a tiny (1/8 inch) milk spot in front of Franklin's nose, it can be gem quality.

On the other hand, if your coin has a few hairlines that can only be seen when the coin is held at a certain angle, and perhaps a tiny milk spot near the rim, you probably can award a PF-65 or higher grade to the coin.

A PF-65+ Cameo or brilliant Proof will be virtually flawless, save for a light milk spot or a few light hairlines, noticeable only under excellent light and magnification.

A coin without obvious imperfections will be a PF-67 or higher. Note, though, that the differences between PF-67, PF-68, and PF-69 are subtle. The best way to learn these subtleties is to purchase several Proofs ranging from PF-64 to PF-69 so you can study the nuances.

As far as grading Special Mint Sets, use the same approach as grading BUs; bagmarks are almost always present on SMS coins—they are Mint State, not Proofs—and are a major factor in granting a grade. Again, I recommend studying examples of graded coins. Remember, too, that the size and location of an imperfection do affect grading: a bagmark located at 7:00 on the reverse will not affect grade as much as the same mark on the obverse portrait.

Although handling marks would represent a major flaw on a Proof coin, they are expected on an SMS coin—it is just a question of degree.

HOW TO DETERMINE CAMEO CONTRAST

As in collecting anything—from baseball cards to fly-fishing lures—it's critical to know what was typical and what was exceptional for a certain date. If, for example, you've never seen an exceptional 1952 cameo Franklin, it's going to be impossible for you to appraise lesser examples.

Plus, in the case of the Franklins, there were so few superb gem cameos in the 1950–1963 era that few collectors have an accurate reference point for grading.

The good news is that several grading services have adopted cameo grading standards; the bad news is that each service has a slightly different cameo grading standard. If you're interested in buying a cameo via a long-distance auction or an ad, it helps to be up to date on the grading practices of whichever service certified the coin.

Even though grading services' standards vary, it's still important for you to learn as much as possible about variances in cameos. My best advice is "buy the coin, not the holder"; for me this means the value of your collection is dependent on the coin itself, not the grade stamped on the holder. Obviously, the more educated you can be in terms of cameo grading, the better eye you'll have for the coin, not the grade on the holder.

I also recommend using a grading service with the absolute highest grading standards, which will provide you an exemplary point of reference. And of course, view as many cameos as possible. Remember, though, to view coins under good lighting conditions to determine the level of cameo contrast. Poor lighting can lead to an inaccurate assessment of the cameo because it can appear less or more frosted than it really is.

What if you're somewhere that doesn't have proper lighting? I always suggest bringing a few cameos from your own collection for comparison. If your coin's grade isn't certified, this won't help in grading the cameo of interest, but it will help in determining its contrast.

TURN TO THE EXPERTS

While you are learning the craft of grading Proofs and cameos, I recommend the use of a major grading service, particularly if you want to learn the craft of grading. The Professional Coin Grading Service (PCGS) and Numismatic Guaranty Corporation of America (NGC) are the two most respected coin-grading services in the world. PCGS was founded in 1986, in response to perceived inconsistencies in the appraisal of rare coins. NGC, founded a year later, is today the official grading service of the American Numismatic Association.

Many coin experts credit PCGS as the pioneer in formal, professional third-party coin grading. PCGS introduced to professional numismatics the "slabbing" revolution, in which a coin is encapsulated with an accompanying tamper-resistant certification of its grade. This transformed subjectively appraised coins to numerically valued commodities.

In 2002, the Professional Numismatists Guild surveyed members on the quality of the various certification services, and the results saw PCGS and NGC both scoring the highest.

In addition to seeking the expertise of industry leaders like these two services, I recommend that you purchase coins of various grades, then use them to assess your own coins; I think you'll be pleasantly surprised how this hands-on process will greatly enhance your ability to differentiate the Proof grades and cameo contrasts.

THE UPGRADE FACTOR

I know there are many collectors who still believe that all MS-65s are the same, that a cameo is a cameo, and that a deep cameo is a deep cameo.

These are often the same collectors who ask, "Why should I pay one dealer $1,100 for a 1961-D Franklin MS-65 FBL when another dealer is offering one for only $875?" or "Why should I pay a dealer $850 for a 1956 Franklin Proof MS-68 DC when I can buy one on eBay for only $575?"

As we have already seen, grade alone doesn't necessarily give a full picture of a coin's value. (See also the cameo grading standards in chapter 3 to learn how two cameo coins may be very different.) Cheaper isn't always better, and it definitely doesn't mean that you're getting a killer deal. Believe it or not, when a reputable dealer tells you that a coin is a resubmission candidate or high end for the grade, it might not be just a sales pitch. It may be true.

Savvy collectors know that they reap the rewards when they buy the best quality they can afford. To illustrate this, I'd like to share a success story about a 1950 Franklin NGC PF-67 Cam.

This cameo was purchased by a client of mine many years ago. I had paid a significant amount for this coin because it was an exceptional example of the date. Not only was it a PF-67 (a very high grade for a 1950), but it was a superior cameo and (in my opinion) conservatively graded. In fact, it was a very early strike off the same cameo die that the lone 1950 PCGS PF-66 DC was struck from.

As the years passed, I suggested to this collector that he consider resubmitting his 1950 for grading. I thought the coin was undergraded when he purchased it. Since then, many years had gone by, and in all that time neither NGC nor PCGS had had any truly superb 1950 cameo Franklins of the caliber of this coin submitted to them.

My client resubmitted the coin, and the results speak for themselves.

His 1950 Franklin NGC PF-67 Cam, originally priced at $15,000, upgraded to a PF-67 UC and is the highest-graded Ultra Cameo by two grade points (no other 1950 has graded higher than PF-65★ UC at NGC). It is now the most valuable Proof Franklin ever certified by NGC, and is probably worth between $75,000 and $100,000.

I believe that if my client had originally taken his 1950 Franklin NGC PF-67 Cam to his local coin dealer or placed it on eBay, he would have received only about 25% of

his original purchase price. Why? Because those buyers lacked expertise and wouldn't have known the difference between his coin and a less impressive specimen.

Cheaper definitely isn't always better, and developing an eye for quality can really pay off over the long term—as regrading may demonstrate.

There are many examples of this phenomenon, but I've chosen to list just 10 here. All of these coins were purchased by me and submitted for regrading by my clients. Due to their upgrades, these 10 coins show a total increase in value from $150,000 to $200,000.

Coin	Initial Grade	Grade After Resubmission
1950 Franklin half dollar	NGC PF-67 Cam	NGC PF-67 UC
1955-P Franklin half dollar	PCGS MS-66 FBL	PCGS MS-67 FBL
1959-D Franklin half dollar	PCGS MS-66 FBL	PCGS MS-67 FBL
1883 Morgan dollar	PCGS PF-65 Cam	PCGS PF-66 Cam
1890 Liberty Seated half dollar	NGC PF-67 UC	NGC PF-68 UC
1953 Roosevelt dime	NGC PF-67 Cam	NGC PF-67 UC
1957-D Franklin half dollar	PCGS MS-66 FBL	PCGS MS-67 FBL
1950-D Franklin half dollar	PCGS MS-65 FBL	PCGS MS-66 FBL
1952 Franklin half dollar	NGC PF-65 UC	NGC PF-66 UC
1966 SMS Kennedy half dollar	NGC MS-67 UC	NGC MS-68 UC

Additionally, over the last few years, clients have reported a total increase in lower-valued coins that have been resubmitted and upgraded at between $400,000 and $500,000. What's even more mind-boggling is that this increase in value is from an upgrade only, and does not include the increase caused by simple appreciation.

Each item offers quality and eye appeal that place them in the top tier of coins of that date and grade. I've found that often, with the passage of time, these coins consistently upgrade when resubmitted.

What does this mean for you, the collector? The most knowledgeable collector places a high value on a coin with superior eye appeal over its same-grade counterpart. Over time, this superb coin appreciates more and more, and stands a high chance of upgrading in the future. There is no typical upgrade factor, but I have seen resubmitted upgrades increasing in value more than 500%. That possibility alone means that resubmitting for an upgrade can increase your collection's value many times over.

THE DEPLETION OF RARE-COIN RESERVES

In 2009, consumers took a roller-coaster ride at the gas pump, as the price of gas increased substantially, then decreased. These price changes didn't reflect any change in the world's oil supply, however.

In the world of oil, price is dictated by supply and demand, as well as the cost associated with accessing the planet's oil reserves. As deeper exploration is required, higher-priced technology will be employed, raising the price per barrel even more.

What does this have to do with coins? The answer is simple: a lack of reserves.

No matter what the cost of oil exploration, over time, new oil and shale reserves will be accessed. However, no amount of new technology or underground drilling will open up rare-coin reserves—save for the boxes in granny's attic.

Simply put, there are no vast rare-coin reserves to temper future value appreciation.

THE IMPACT OF PCGS AND NGC POPULATION NUMBERS

Back in the 1980s, when PCGS and NGC first came into being, there were rare-coin reserves the like of which we'll never see again.

Dealers and collectors quickly realized that their PCGS and NGC-certified coins could command far higher prices in the marketplace than noncertified coins. Like manna from Heaven, fresh supplies of high-quality coins were submitted for certification.

If you were collecting rare coins in 1990, I'm sorry to say that the PCGS or NGC population number for that coin was probably not an indication of its rarity. Why? Because there was still a large reserve of coins that had yet to be certified.

Of course, as the decade progressed, more reserve pockets were "drilled," more coins were certified, and the rare-coin reserves began to dry up. Today's collector has a tremendous advantage over the collector of 30 years ago, because the PCGS and NGC population numbers are a fairly accurate indicator of a coin's rarity, with the exception of the most modern coins (from the early 1970s to the present). It has been estimated that the vast majority of finer coins have now been certified, unlike in 1988, when only 5% of the best coins had gone through certification.

Like all things in coin collecting, making population estimates of the world's rare coin reserves requires experience, working with a dealer you trust, and consulting the PCGS and NGC numbers. Combine those three, and you'll have a far better idea of a coin's true rarity.

Franklin half dollars in PCGS and NGC slabs.

THE CAMEO, DEEP CAMEO, AND ULTRA CAMEO DESIGNATIONS

Have you ever seen or owned a Proof Liberty Seated, trade, or Morgan dollar designated cameo or deep cameo by PCGS, or ultra cameo by NGC? Or a Barber coin with one of these designations? Or a modern State quarter designated deep cameo (by PCGS) or ultra cameo (by NGC)?

As you look at the Proof coins being graded today by both PCGS and NGC, with all the Proof moderns being graded (*moderns* here refers to Proof coins struck after 1976), most have either a *cameo* or a *deep cameo* (if PCGS) or an *ultra cameo* (if NGC) designation on their holders.

For a new collector, it may be hard to believe that there was a time when there was no cameo, deep cameo, or ultra cameo designation for Proof coins. Both PCGS and NGC gave a Proof coin a numerical grade and did not even address the issue of cameo contrast.

That is especially difficult to understand when one of the most obvious differences between a cameo Proof and a non-cameo Proof is the two-toned cameo effect of one coin versus the mono-toned non-cameo surface of the other.

The Mint has always understood the difference. Going back to the mid-1800s, one can occasionally find a phenomenal deep cameo Proof from that era. Those coins were not made by accident. Mint personnel have always gone to extra trouble to create Proof coins that represented the state of the art. In the 1800s, they took tremendous pride in the eye appeal and beauty of their specially struck Proof coins.

One of the most fascinating aspects of the history of Proof coin production is the fact that Proof coins from the 1950s and early 1960s were made in much the same manner as Proof coins struck 100 years earlier. As a result, only the earliest strikes from Proof dies of the 1950s and 1960s display exceptional cameo contrast. And many of these coins are mismatched—they may exhibit exceptional cameo contrast on one side, but little or no cameo contrast on the other. This is because the Mint, in an effort to preserve their limited number of working dies, would only replace that half of the die pair that exhibited significant wear. If the other half still had some life left, even though it may have lost its cameo effect thousands of strikes ago, it remained in the press.

To the Mint's credit, it responded to the collector enthusiasm and preference for cameo coins over non-cameo coins in Proof sets. In 1970, one collector would order his Proof set and would find a lovely cameo contrast half dollar, quarter, dime, nickel, or cent in his set, while another collector might order 10 sets from the Mint and not find a single cameo coin. Beginning in 1973, the Mint incorporated new die preparation techniques to create more cameo coins. That process has been improved to the point that, since the late 1970s, virtually every Proof coin struck by the Mint is a deep or ultra cameo.

But how about those Proof coins struck in the mid-1970s and earlier? How is one to grade those for their cameo quality, when most Proof coins had no cameo contrast, many had a little, others had exceptional cameo contrast on one side but not the other, and so on?

Enter the PCGS Cameo Grading Set.

HOW THE PCGS CAMEO GRADING SET CAME ABOUT

The year was 1991. I had just released my first book, *Cameo and Brilliant Proof Coinage of the 1950 to 1970 Era*, and sent a copy to PCGS founder David Hall, suggesting it might be time for PCGS to begin offering cameo designations for their coins. Up until then, no such designation existed. David called me a week later. We had several meetings thereafter, establishing appropriate cameo and deep cameo standards for every series.

Issues we discussed were whether to have two or three cameo standards, what should constitute a designation of cameo, and what should constitute deep cameo.

It was eventually decided that standards similar to what had informally been in place among cameo collectors should be adopted. Until then, as noted in my book, we had used three standards: Proof, cameo, and ultra cameo. Because PCGS was using the term *Deep Mirror Prooflike* (abbreviated DMPL) for their Morgan dollars, it was decided that a term similar to that would be applied to the heaviest cameo Proof coins: *deep cameo Proof*, DCAM (or DC) for short.

While PCGS offers only three Proof designations on its holder for Proof coins, there are actually seven cameo designations in the PCGS Cameo Grading Set. The set comprises several dozen coins purchased by PCGS, most of which I supplied, to help guide present and future graders at PCGS in maintaining a permanent, consistent, and constant standard that will be the same 50 years from now as it is today.

The cameo grading set is used by the graders at PCGS to help determine what designation should go on the holder: PR for Proof, CAM for Cameo, or DCAM for Deep Cameo. It has the following seven comparison categories to aid graders:

1. PR+ **(Proof-plus)**	These are coins that exhibit some cameo contrast, but not quite enough on either obverse or reverse to earn a cameo designation. One side may even be deep cameo. However, the other side does not meet the minimum cameo standard. These coins are simply designated PR, for Proof.
2. CAM– **(Cameo-minus)**	These are coins that exhibit the minimum standard for cameo contrast on both their obverse and reverse. These coins are designated CAM, for cameo.
3. CAM	A "dead center" cameo with slightly more contrast than CAM– coins.
4. CAM+ **(Cameo-plus)**	These are coins with exceptional contrast, approaching deep cameo status, but with at least one side that does not meet the minimum DCAM standard. These coins also receive a CAM designation.

5. DCAM–
(Deep Cameo–minus)

These coins display considerable cameo contrast on both their obverse and reverse. Quite striking in appearance, though not quite the "black-and-white" variety, with slightly more contrast than a CAM+—just enough to earn a DCAM designation on the holder. On other coins, one side can even be DCAM+, but again, the other has just enough contrast to earn a DCAM.

6. DCAM
(Deep Cameo)

A "dead center" deep cameo. This is a black-and-white. The devices offer the snow-white cameo effect, the mirrors the jet-black look, that cameo collectors lust for. There is exceptional contrast, though not at the level of a DCAM+, as there may be a frost break or two on the devices.

7. DCAM+
(Deep Cameo–plus)

The ultimate. Very, very few pre-1972 Proof coins exhibit this level of contrast. On a DCAM+ coin, devices are intensely frosted, with little if any frost break, on both obverse and reverse. From this earlier era, only the very first strikes from a matching die pair that was perfectly prepared ever display this level of contrast, and few dies of any year were prepared this perfectly. These coins also receive a DCAM designation on the holder.

Today, the PR, CAM, and DCAM standard is applied not only to Proof coins struck after World War II, but to all Proof coins struck by the U.S. Mint. Hence, one can find Morgan dollars, Barber half dollars, and Liberty Head nickels all graded cameo and deep cameo.

NGC has had a cameo designation in place since the late 1980s. After the PCGS standards were established, I contacted NGC. Soon thereafter, NCG began offering their cameo and ultra cameo standards for Proof coins as well.

The Proof Franklin images shown here approximate the original coins in the PCGS Cameo Grading Set in their degree of cameo contrast.

Proof	Proof-plus	Cameo-minus	Cameo
Cameo-plus	Deep Cameo–minus	Deep Cameo	Deep Cameo–plus

FRANKLIN HALF DOLLAR ANALYSIS BY DATE, MINTMARK, AND VARIETY

INTRODUCTION

BIOGRAPHY OF BENJAMIN FRANKLIN

For the numismatist, Benjamin Franklin is not only a famous individual in American history, but also one of significant importance in our hobby. While the Franklin half dollar 1948-1963 epitomizes him, medallic portraits as well as images on paper money date back into the early 1800s. An entire book, *The Medals of Franklin, a Catalog of Medals, Tokens, Medallions and Plaques Issued in Honor of Franklin*, by Philip Greenslet, is devoted to his tokens and medals alone. No text has ever been written on images of Franklin on bank notes, but many were issued in the general period from the 1820s through the 1860s on state-chartered bills, and, in our own time the $100 note has his portrait. Beyond that, Franklin is associated in other ways with numismatics, such as being the originator or proponent of certain mottoes on early coins and paper money, including the 1776 Continental dollar, 1787 Fugio copper, and many different Continental Currency notes produced from 1775 through 1779. In our sister field of philately Franklin's portrait can be found on many stamps.

Benjamin Franklin was one of 17 children fathered by Josiah Franklin, who married twice. He married his first wife, Anne Child, about 1677 in Ecton, Northamptonshire, England, and came with her to Boston in 1683 with their three children. In America the couple had four more. After Anne died, Josiah married Abiah Folger, a native of Nantucket, Massachusetts, on July 9, 1689. Benjamin was their eighth child and Josiah Franklin's fifteenth child and tenth and last son.

Benjamin was born on Milk Street, Boston, on January 17, 1706, on the old calendar (January 6, 1705, on the new) and was baptized at the Old South Meetinghouse. His father's Puritan values, including Bible study and a relationship with God, self-determination, and personal independence, helped shape Benjamin's philosophies and life. Benjamin had a very limited formal education, including some studies at the Boston Latin School, which he attended but did not graduate from. His last formal education ended at the age of ten. Afterward he worked for his father in the tallow and related businesses, then at age 12 apprenticed to his brother James, a printer, where he learned a trade that would be important in the rest of his life. When Benjamin was 15 his brother established *The New-England Courant,* remembered today as the first really independent paper in the British colonies. Benjamin was forbidden from writing letters to the editor, so devised a pseudonym, Mrs. Silence Dogood, said to have been a widow of middle age, who sent in her astutely worded opinions that were published, and became widely discussed, with no one the wiser until James discovered the truth.

Franklin then left the print shop without permission of his brother-master, and fled to Philadelphia, seeking a new life. He worked with several printers in that city, and, soon, heeded the advice of Governor Sir William Keith to go to London to find equipment necessary for Keith to establish another journal in Philadelphia. In the meantime, when he was 17 years old, he proposed to Deborah Read, a 15-year-old girl living in the home where he was a boarder. Her mother, whose husband had recently died, was against the idea and it did not move forward. The backing of Keith turned out to be meaningless, no purchases were made, and Franklin went to work setting type in a shop in London. In 1726 he returned to Philadelphia under the sponsorship of Thomas Denham, who employed him as a clerk, bookkeeper, and shop keeper.

Franklin, at age 21, established the Junto, a discussion group for trades people and artists who hoped to improve themselves and to be a credit to the community. Reading was a desirable pursuit for the members, but books were elusive and expensive, so the group created its own small library. This inspired Franklin to go further, resulting in the establishment of the Library Company of Philadelphia, chartered in 1731, the first in America. After Denham died, Franklin went back to the printing trade.

Deborah married a John Rogers, who turned out to be a wastrel and fled to Barbados, taking her dowry with him and abandoning Deborah in Philadelphia. The couple was still married under law. On September 1, 1730, Franklin took Deborah as his wife under common-law marriage. The couple had two children. Deborah died of a stroke in 1774. By 1730 Franklin had his own shop, and set about publishing *The Pennsylvania Gazette,* a forum for essays, observations, and opinions. His thoughts were well expressed and caused much favorable comment in Philadelphia, giving him a degree of fame.

Franklin was a Renaissance man, a polymath, with success in many fields. He was well known as a politician, author, printer, statesman, inventor, and diplomat. As an inventor he devised the lightning rod, the Franklin stove, bifocals, an odometer for carriages, the tuned glass "armonica" that could play melodies, and more. Similar to his library, the fire department he established in Philadelphia was the first in America. Publishing *The Pennsylvania Gazette* and *Poor Richard's Almanac* added to his fame. He was important in establishing the University of Pennsylvania and was the first president of the American Philosophical Society. He took the lead in America to try to persuade the British Parliament to repeal the Stamp Act, one of the situations that led to the American Revolution. He was postmaster general under the Continental Congress from 1775 to 1776, and from 1785 to 1788 was the governor of Pennsylvania (officially the president of the Supreme Executive Council of Pennsylvania).

Franklin served as ambassador to France 1776 to 1785. In 1787 he was a delegate to the Constitutional Convention. In the meantime, starting in 1771 he worked on his autobiography, which was completed in 1788. Even after he achieved much recognition and fame, his letters were signed modestly as "B. Franklin, Printer." His activities were far-ranging and included involvement in many of the societies, organizations, and movements in Philadelphia.

In 1787 several ministers in Lancaster, Pennsylvania, proposed that a college be named in his honor, to which Franklin donated £200. It is now known as Franklin and Marshall College. In 1787 and 1789 he was prominent in abolition and in 1790 was president of the Pennsylvania Abolitionist Society. Franklin died on April 17, 1790, at age 84, and was widely mourned. An estimated 20,000 people attended his funeral services. Today he is remembered as a great leader among the Founding Fathers.

HISTORY OF THE FRANKLIN HALF DOLLAR

The Benjamin Franklin half dollar, produced from 1948 until 1963, was designed by U.S. Mint Chief Engraver John R. Sinnock, who had also designed the Roosevelt dime. A right-facing bust of Franklin appears on the obverse, and the Liberty Bell is depicted on the reverse. Before World War II, there had been talk of putting Franklin on the dime, replacing Miss Liberty. However, when President Franklin D. Roosevelt died in 1945, the Treasury Department decided instead to use the late president's profile, given his close association with the March of Dimes campaign to eradicate polio.

Mint Director Nellie Tayloe Ross, long a proponent of memorializing Franklin in coinage, accomplished that goal in 1948. Sinnock, who based Franklin's image on a bust by Jean-Antoine Houdon, died in office in 1947 before finishing the design. The reverse was completed by Gilroy Roberts, who succeeded Sinnock as chief engraver. In an odd example of anti-communist hysteria, Sinnock's initials (JS), which appear below the shoulder, were briefly rumored to have stood instead for Joseph Stalin.

LIBERTY appears above Franklin's image, and IN GOD WE TRUST arcs along the bottom. The year is to the right, on the level of Franklin's neck. To comply with an obscure requirement by the Mint Act of 1837, a small eagle with spread wings was added to the right of the Liberty Bell on the reverse. UNITED STATES OF AMERICA appears at the top of the reverse, and HALF DOLLAR along the bottom. E PLURIBUS UNUM ("Out of many, one") is on the left. The coin has a reeded edge. Among numismatic aficionados, the design of the Franklin half dollar is not revered for its artistry.

The coin was initially manufactured in relatively small numbers, but its production increased beginning in 1957 until it was replaced shortly after the assassination of President John Kennedy in 1963. At the time of Kennedy's death the only coin denominations eligible by law for a new design were the Jefferson nickel, the Washington quarter, and the Peace silver dollar. Due to political considerations (Franklin was not associated with any political party), the half dollar was chosen to carry the new design.

FULL BELL LINES ILLUSTRATED

The "Full Head" Standing Liberty quarter. The "Full Split Bands" Mercury dime. The "Full Bell Lines" Franklin half.

Most collectors of these series in Mint State understandably desire their coins to be the finest possible quality within their budgetary guidelines.

Bagmarks, luster, and strike all must be considered when determining the relative quality of a coin. The Full Head (FH), Full Split Bands (FSB), and Full Bell Lines (FBL) designations are given to those coins in their respective series that display a full or nearly full strike, with all or nearly all of their design detail struck up as originally intended by the Mint.

Since Proof coins are typically double struck (or more) under higher pressure than that used for Mint State coins, strike is not the issue for these coins, as it is for Mint State coins. For that reason, the FSB and FBL designations are not used for Proof coins of those series. (Proof coins were not struck for the Standing Liberty quarter series.)

It is important to remember that grading will always be somewhat subjective. Of the coins submitted to grading services, 10% to 15% will grade differently on a given day.

The same holds true for the FBL designation. There are some Mint State Franklin half dollars that fall into that gray area—they may or may not grade FBL on any given day.

The grading set shown in this sidebar will help as a guideline when determining whether your Mint State Franklin is FBL.

continued on next page

Full Bell Lines Illustrated

1. Non-FBL   2. Non-FBL

3. Non-FBL   4. Borderline FBL

Coin 1. This coin is an obvious non-FBL. Note the lack of bell lines along the bottom set.

Dates most typically found with this strike: 1949-S, 1951-S, 1952-S, 1953-P, 1953-S, 1954-S, 1957-P, 1958-P, 1959-P, 1961-P, 1962-P, 1963-P.

Coin 2. This coin more nearly approaches having the necessary definition in both the top and bottom sets of lines. To be FBL, both sets, top and bottom, need to be clear and easily distinguished by the naked eye. Additionally, there are several significant, large cuts on the lines. While minor ticks are to be tolerated on Mint State Franklin half dollars, given the fact that Mint State Franklin halves are generally very baggy coins and that they almost always have some tiny ticks on the lines (even on MS-67 coins), the coin in the picture has deep cuts on the lines that fully interrupt the bell lines.

Coin 3. It's a close thing on this 1958-D, but bell lines are just a little mushy near the crack.

Other dates similarly struck: 1951-P, 1955-P, 1956-P, 1960-D, 1961-D, 1962-D.

Coin 4. This 1960-D is so close to FBL. The lines blend in just a bit on the bottom set near the crack. This is a borderline FBL.

UNCIRCULATED FRANKLIN HALF DOLLARS

A View of the Decade: The 1940s

U.S. Mint production in the 1940s felt the impact of World War II, as the demands of the war effort required changes in both coin production and coin content. The production of Proof coins, for example, was suspended after the release of the 1942 Proofs due to wartime exigencies. Proof coinage would resume in 1950. The composition of the nickel five-cent piece was changed in 1942 to 1945 to eliminate nickel, which was a critical war material. Similarly, a shortage of copper in 1943 led to the use of zinc-coated steel for cents.

FULL BELL LINES ILLUSTRATED

5. Borderline FBL

6. FBL

7. FBL

8. FBL

Coin 5. This 1958-D has a great strike with excellent bell lines. There is a cut through the upper set near the crack that may kick the coin out of FBL, but this would be a judgment call by the service.

Coin 6. Nice complete lines on this 1959-P. There are some very minor ticks on the lines that are not a problem.

Coin 7. Similar to the 1959-P, this 1961-P has good distinct bell lines. A couple of minor, shallow cuts can be seen on the top set.

Coin 8. Excellent strong bell lines with the usual light ticks and scrapes, most noticeable on the top set.

After the war's end, changes continued to take place. In 1948 the design of the half dollar changed from the Liberty Walking design by Adolph A. Weinman to the Benjamin Franklin portrait by Chief Engraver John R. Sinnock, whose portrait of Franklin D. Roosevelt had been adopted for the dime just two years before. (The Roosevelt portrait replaced the Winged Liberty Head or "Mercury" dime design, which had been in place since 1916.) This decade also saw the debut of two cornerstone numismatic publications, the *Handbook of United States Coins* (1942) and R.S. Yeoman's *Guide Book of United States Coins* (1946).

⊷⊜ 1948-P, MINT STATE ⊜⊷

MS-67 FBL

The first year of issue for the series, the 1948-P and 1948-D Franklin halves are note-worthy for their sharp design details and bold strikes. As the years went by, the master die used to create the working dies gradually softened in the finer details of this design, so that by the mid- and late 1950s, even fully struck Franklin half dollars do not exhibit the sharp detail of the finer 1948 specimens. This trend would reverse in 1960, when the Mint, aware of this problem, reworked (recut) the master die, restoring most of the detail that had been lost over the past decade-plus.

Original rolls of this date are now quite rare, and seldom surface anymore. When such a roll is available, the quality is usually quite good, with several coins grading MS-64 FBL and maybe one or two at MS-65 FBL. When found in Mint sets, the 1948-P typically features unattractive subdued golden brown or tan coloration. Attrac-tively toned Mint set coins are very rare.

As the 1948-P and all circulation-strike dates are relatively abundant in circulated condition, grades below MS-60 will not be analyzed for this series.

NGC CERTIFIED POPULATION *(from a total mintage of 3,006,814)*   (WCG™)

MS-64	MS-65	MS-66	MS-67	MS-68
429	434	37	1	0
MS-64 FBL	MS-65 FBL	MS-66 FBL	MS-67 FBL	MS-68 FBL
749	724	97	6	1

MS-60–MS-63 and MS-60 FBL–MS-63 FBL. This is a common grade for Uncir-culated 1948-P Franklin halves. Most examples have full bell lines. The typical brilliant Uncirculated 1948-P has considerable abrasion over the high points of the obverse and reverse. Most examples also have excellent bell lines, but bagmarks that disrupt the lines often knock these coins from FBL consideration.

Valuation—**Non-FBL** examples can currently be acquired for $20 to $30; **FBL** examples are in the $25–$35 range.

MS-64 and MS-64 FBL. The 1948-P can be difficult to locate in MS-64 non-FBL simply because most MS-64 specimens do have full bell lines.

The 1948-P used to be readily available in MS-64 FBL. *That is no longer the case.* As more Franklin collectors aspire to assemble MS-64 FBL sets, this date has become quite elusive. When located, this date is about evenly split between brilliant and toned specimens. Mint set coins typically feature lackluster tan-and-gray toning. *Exceptional color-toned coins are rare, and worth a strong premium.*

Valuation—In **MS-64**, these trade at around $25 to $35. This date has seen considerable appreciation in the **MS-64 FBL** grade, with examples now generally trading between $60 and $125, depending on the brilliance. Exceptional color coins have exploded in value in recent years and may sell for multiples of that range.

MS-65 and MS-65 FBL. The 1948-P is more difficult to find in MS-65 than MS-65 FBL. As most examples exhibit bold bell lines, the typical 1948-P that does *not* qualify for FBL will have a serious nick or two that interrupts the bell lines, eliminating them from FBL consideration.

Brilliant examples rank among the most attractive issues in the series, given their bold strikes and sharp detail definition. About the only critique one can make, a minor one, is that the typical MS-65 exhibits very slight pitting on the high point of Franklin's jaw—the result of incomplete metal flow of the planchet into the deepest recesses of the die.

This is a great type coin in MS-65 FBL. Not only is it desirable in being the first year of issue, but the detail of these coins is second to none. Franklin's hair is in sharp focus on virtually every coin, as is the Liberty Bell, with "Pass and Stow" and the bell lines almost always fully struck up.

If looking for a brilliant specimen, seek out those fully lustrous examples. *Most* brilliant 1948-P Franklins actually exhibit a light film (haze) from many years' storage in a roll or coin album.

Again, high-point pitting on Franklin's cheek is a very minor critique of this date. These are, after all, circulation strikes—not Proofs.

Locating an attractively toned specimen of the 1948-P is quite another matter. These coins are very rare. Virtually every 1948-P that originated in a Mint set exhibits very dull gray-brown or tan discoloration. Iridescent toned gems do exist, but comprise perhaps 1% of the total gem population. Be prepared to pay a strong premium for a color coin—the prettier the color, the higher the premium.

Valuation—In **MS-65** without full bell lines, and with average color or brilliance, expect to pay $75 to $125. Most examples have good bell lines that are complete even though the coins have not earned the FBL designation. This coin is surprisingly elusive and a tremendous opportunity when found at these levels.

For **MS-65 FBL** coins, there is a big spread, depending on eye appeal. Average hazy-toned examples, or coins with average Mint set toning, bring about $100 to $150; superb, fully brilliant 1948-Ps, $250 to $350. A few spectacular color-toned 1948-Ps have sold for close to $2,000. In the more attractive Mint State conditions these coins are very highly recommended.

MS-66 and MS-66 FBL. While increasingly elusive in attractive MS-65 and MS-65 FBL condition, the 1948-P is *extremely* scarce in MS-66 and higher grades. Given that the 1948-P is normally a boldly struck date, and that MS-66 coins offer minimally marked surfaces, most MS-66–grade 1948-Ps are also FBL, because the one culprit that normally eliminates the 1948-P from FBL status—bagmarking—is usually not an issue for the higher MS-66 grade.

As with lower grades of this date, most examples in MS-66 display hazy-toned or mottled gray-brown Mint set–toned surfaces. Be willing to pay a premium for a really attractive, fully brilliant or attractive color-toned coin. The latter are especially rare.

This is a great date in MS-66 FBL if you can find it fully brilliant or attractively toned. Given the sharply defined features of this date when fully or nearly fully struck (which it almost always is), the 1948-P ranks as an ideal type coin. About the only detraction is the usually slight pitting along Franklin's jawbone.

Rainbow-toned or other attractively toned examples of this date are very rare. Of the examples certified in MS-66 FBL to date, I would estimate that fewer than 5% offer exceptional color.

Valuation—An extremely scarce coin in **MS-66**, and very reasonably priced considering the rarity: starting around $250 on up, depending on the eye appeal—if you can find one.

Examples in **MS-66 FBL** with the typical light haze, or with average mottled Mint set color, may trade for as little as $300. Most MS-66 FBL 1948-Ps fall into this unfortunate category. Be willing to opt for either the really premium quality blazer, or the superb color coin. The former trades in the $900–$1,500 range. The finest color coins have traded for upwards of $3,000, given their rarity and eye appeal.

MS-67 and MS-67 FBL. When the first two editions of this book were published, all but one of the MS-67 examples had also been designated FBL.

The 1948-P is rare in MS-67 FBL. All known examples graded by PCGS and NGC, with two notable exceptions, have toning, with at least three of the examples I have handled offering outstanding obverse and reverse color.

For the collector assembling that ultimate set, the goal should be to acquire a 1948-P in MS-67 FBL. Considering the rarity of the date in this highest Mint State grade, the most recent NGC-graded example I handled and sold for under $10,000 would seem to offer tremendous future potential.

Valuation—If an **MS-67** non-FBL did surface, eye appeal would be the determining criterion for the value—anywhere from $2,000 to $5,000.

Rare in **MS-67 FBL**, most examples exhibit average color toning. These toned specimens typically sell between $5,000 and $10,000. A fully brilliant **MS-67 FBL**, or a spectacularly toned example, may sell higher into the five figures, $10,000 to $20,000. An **MS-67★ FBL** that last traded around 2004 would likely sell closer to the higher point of the range, should it enter the market again.

At the current time there is but a single MS-68 FBL in the entire series. I have handled this coin. It is a 1948-P and it is spectacular. The coin is graded MS-68★ FBL by NGC. This exceptional 1948-P was pictured on the cover of the first two editions of this book.

While its recent sale price was kept confidential, the coin sold well into five figures.

⋙ 1948-D, MINT STATE ⋘

MS-65 FBL

As with the 1948-P, this first-year-of-issue Franklin half is noteworthy for its sharp design detail and bold strike. The master die used to create the working dies gradually wore down as the years passed, softening the finer design details, so that fully struck Franklin halves of the mid- and late 1950s lack the sharp detail of the finer 1948 specimens. As mentioned previously, the Mint reworked the master die in 1960, restoring most of the detail that had been lost over the years.

Original rolls of the 1948-D are essentially nonexistent at this time. When a roll does surface, it usually has been put together from other rolls.

The 1948-D is easily obtainable in circulated condition.

NGC CERTIFIED POPULATION *(from a total mintage of 4,028,600)*   (WCG™)

MS-64	MS-65	MS-66	MS-67	MS-68
514	508	17	1	0
MS-64 FBL	**MS-65 FBL**	**MS-66 FBL**	**MS-67 FBL**	**MS-68 FBL**
732	552	30	0	0

MS-60–MS-63 and MS-60 FBL–MS-63 FBL. As with the 1948-P, MS-60 to MS-63 (with or without bell lines) is the most common grade for Uncirculated 1948-D Franklin halves. The typical 1948-D is actually baggier than the typical 1948-P, and this is reflected in the lower population numbers for high-grade 1948-D coins compared to the 1948-P.

While most 1948-Ds have excellent bell lines, severe marks on the bell lines drop many of these lower-grade specimens into non-FBL status. The bell lines of the 1948-D normally rank among the boldest in the series.

Valuation—Available for modest premiums over melt. Not recommended, except as a bullion investment.

MS-64 and MS-64 FBL. The 1948-D is difficult to locate in MS-64 non-FBL, primarily due to the fact most MS-64 specimens have full bell lines.

The 1948-D coins are roughly equal in availability at this time to the 1948-P in MS-64 FBL. Both dates are now elusive in *attractive* MS-64 FBL, as many display haze or streaky toning over the surfaces.

Attractive brilliant examples are worth a premium. The 1948-D with exceptional color-toning is quite rare and worth a *strong* premium!

Valuation—Coins in **MS-64**, with average eye appeal, trade at around $25 to $35. Fully brilliant **MS-64 FBL** coins trade in the $90–$175 area, but pretty color coins will be multiples of that price range.

MS-65 and MS-65 FBL. The 1948-D is roughly equal in rarity to the 1948-P. Both dates share many similar characteristics—bold strike, great rarity with exceptional color—but the 1948-D follows in the tradition of all Denver-minted Franklin half dollars in the series in that they typically come with a preponderance of bagmarks.

For the brief life of the Franklin series, of the three mints, the Denver Mint's coins earn the reputation of ranking among the best struck in the series, with the Philadelphia Mint second, and the San Francisco Mint's coins usually weakly struck. Unfortunately, these boldly struck D-Mints usually have severe bagmarks—far more than typically found in the Liberty Walking half dollar series that precedes it.

Minimally marked 1948-D Franklin half dollars in MS-65 are very elusive. Once again, FBL specimens outnumber non-FBL, as nearly all 1948-D Franklin half dollars were struck with full bell lines. The examples that do not earn the designation typically exhibit a serious bagmark or two on their lines.

When found in MS-65, most 1948-Ds exhibit either subdued, hazy luster or dull Mint set toning. Bright, brilliant specimens are worth the modest premium they usually command. And if you can find a fabulous color coin, though it may be priced several times that of the typical MS-65, get it. These coins are *rare*.

The 1948-D is a great coin in gem FBL if you can pick one up with exceptional brilliant surfaces, or exceptional color-toning. The latter coins are particularly elusive. An MS-65 FBL example with exceptional color that I handled recently traded for more than $1,500!

Valuation—The 1948-D exhibits a big price spread in **MS-65**, depending on the eye appeal. Average hazy-toned examples, or coins with average Mint set toning, will bring about $100 to $150; superb fully brilliant 1948-Ds, $150 to $250. As with the 1948-P, spectacular color-toned 1948-Ds in MS-65 have sold for up to $1,000.

As with the 1948-P, a large price spread exists for the 1948-D in **MS-65 FBL**. It all depends on the eye appeal. Average hazy-toned examples, or coins with average Mint set toning, generally trade for between $125 and $225. Superb fully brilliant 1948-Ds, on the other hand, typically sell for $300 to $450. Should a 1948-D MS-65 FBL surface with exceptional color-toning (a rare occasion), be prepared to dig a little, or a lot, deeper—the few spectacular color-toned 1948-Ds that have been on the market the past few years have traded anywhere from $800 to $1,500. The 1948-D is very highly recommended in the more attractive Mint State conditions, as these coins are tougher to locate with each passing year.

MS-66 and MS-66 FBL. The 1948-D, even more than its P-Mint counterpart, is especially elusive in MS-66 or MS-66 FBL, as it is rarely found with the near-flawless surfaces required for an MS-66 grade. (Once again, bagmarks are the culprit.) Being a boldly struck coin, when it does achieve the 66 level, it usually has full bell lines. Despite its sharp strike, however, the date is especially tough to find in *attractive* MS-66 (FBL), as this is a grade in which average eye appeal and dull, mottled-tan Mint set toning predominate. Attractive, fully brilliant specimens are worth a premium, as are attractively color-toned coins.

While the 1948 P-Mint and D-Mint halves are close in rarity at MS-65 FBL, the 1948-D is considerably rarer in MS-66 FBL, due to the bagmark issues endemic among Denver-minted Franklin halves in general.

Valuation—This is a fairly rare coin in **MS-66**, and very reasonably priced considering the rarity: starting around $300, depending on the eye appeal. Beware of "mistake" coins—I have seen a couple of examples in MS-66 holders that exhibited more bagmarks than one would expect at this grade. While these coins exhibited some attractive color-toning, an MS-66 coin should have minimal bagmarks, irrespective of the eye appeal, or lack of it.

The 1948-D in **MS-66 FBL** with the typical light haze, or average mottled Mint set color, may trade for as little as $600 to $900. As with the 1948-P, most 1948-Ds at MS-66 FBL fall into this unfortunate category. Be willing to opt for either the really premium quality blazer or the superb color coin. The former may trade in the area of $2,000 to $3,000. The finest color coins have traded for upwards of $4,500, given their rarity and eye appeal.

MS-67 and MS-67 FBL. *Extremely* rare. To date, only six examples have been certified in MS-67 FBL. Most are toned.

Valuation—A 1948-D with the virtually mark-free, fully struck surfaces necessary for the **MS-67** grade is a most rare coin. The general price range is $9,000 to $20,000, with differences in price being due to eye-appeal factors.

⟐ 1949-P, MINT STATE ⟐

MS-66 FBL

The second year of issue, the 1949-P, was not hoarded as was the 1948-P. Original rolls of this date have always been extremely elusive. It has been many years since I handled a true original roll of this date, though put-together rolls sometimes surface. When an original roll does surface, expect to find several MS-64 FBL coins.

Mint set–toned 1949-P Franklin halves are marginally better in eye appeal than the 1948-P. Examples with attractive color toning do exist, but they are extremely scarce.

The 1949-P is easily obtainable in circulated condition.

NGC CERTIFIED POPULATION *(from a total mintage of 5,614,000)* (WCG™)

MS-64	MS-65	MS-66	MS-67	MS-68
332	245	21	1	0
MS-64 FBL	MS-65 FBL	MS-66 FBL	MS-67 FBL	MS-68 FBL
433	279	39	1	0

MS-60–MS-63 and MS-60 FBL–MS-63 FBL. This is the most common grade range for this date, about evenly split between non-FBL and FBL examples. The 1949-P is very similar to the 1948-P in its strike characteristics—most coins are boldly struck with bold bell lines. When found in brilliant condition, luster is exceptional. The big negative are bagmarks—the 1949-P ranks among the baggiest P-Mint halves in the series.

Valuation—The 1949-P is among the tougher dates to find in brilliant Uncirculated condition, with low-grade examples currently trading in the $35–$55 range, with or without the FBL designation.

MS-64 and MS-64 FBL. As with the 1948-minted coinage, the 1949-P is difficult to locate in MS-64 non-FBL, primarily because most MS-64 specimens have full bell lines. Many examples are from Mint sets and display average toning.

The 1949-P is very elusive in MS-64 FBL. Whether in brilliant or toned condition, the 1949-P is many times rarer than the 1948-P in MS-64 FBL, though this date has a higher mintage. A 1949-P in MS-64 FBL with attractive color toning is even rarer. Most toned examples are from Mint sets and feature average color.

Valuation—$40 to $70 for non-FBL coins in **MS-64,** though attractive color pieces will of course sell for more. Superb brilliant specimens are elusive and have appreciated to the $125–$250 range, while the average Mint set–toned coins might trade for under $100, due to the lack of eye appeal. Superbly toned pieces may trade for upward of $500 to $800. The latter are quite rare.

MS-65 and MS-65 FBL. Over the past several years the 1949-P in either or MS-65 FBL has become a very elusive coin. Most examples in MS-65 have some degree of toning. These coins typically also have excellent bell lines, though a serious nick or two on the lines drops them from FBL consideration.

Fully brilliant examples in MS-65 are extremely scarce, as are attractively toned pieces. In either condition, the 1949-P is worth a significant premium over average bid levels.

Currently this is a very elusive coin in any condition of MS-65 FBL. Most examples display average Mint set toning. *The 1949-P is especially scarce in fully brilliant MS-65 FBL.* I recall that even during the mid-1980s, before PCGS and NGC were launched, the 1949-P was extremely difficult to find in minimally marked gem condition.

Beautifully toned 1949-P MS-65 FBL Franklin halves are rarer still, and worth a significant premium—if you can find them.

Valuation—The typical dull Mint set–toned piece can usually be acquired for around $100 in **MS-65**. Superb color toned pieces may be two to three times those levels.

Most **MS-65 FBL** 1949-P Franklins have average Mint set toning and trade for as little as $100 to $200. On the other hand, fully brilliant, haze-free blazers have been selling for up to $500 to $800. Given the rarity and eye appeal of gem FBLs with spectacular color toning, it is no surprise that these rarities may change hands for $1,000 and more—on the rare occasion that such a coin surfaces.

MS-66 and MS-66 FBL. Any examples graded MS-66 are likely to have complete bell lines, but lose the designation due to a tick or two on the bell lines. Virtually every example in MS-66 features average Mint set toning. Attractively toned MS-66 1949-P Franklin halves are very rare.

The 1949-P is very scarce in MS-66 FBL, though the PCGS and NGC population numbers do not give a complete picture of this date's true rarity in MS-66 FBL with either exceptional color toning or fully brilliant surfaces. About 90% to 95% of existing MS-66 FBL coins are Mint set toned, and most of these coins feature average toning about on a par with that of the 1948-P. Spectacular color-toned coins are very, very rare. *Fully brilliant* MS-66 FBL 1949-P Franklin halves are *very rare* as well! I have handled perhaps seven or eight such coins going back to the mid-1990s when PCGS and NGC first began offering the FBL designation.

Valuation—Most superb gems are Mint set coins with average color in **MS-66** and are also **FBL**. Some trade for as little as $600 to $900 despite their rarity, due to the uninspiring toning. Any exceptional brilliant blazers or color coins can be expected to sell for many times that figure. Superb untoned brilliant specimens are extremely rare. The last specimen sold for almost $5,500. Superb color coins are in strong demand as well.

MS-67 and MS-67 FBL. *Extremely* rare. Only three examples have been certified in MS-67 FBL to date. The rarity of the 1949-P in this condition is not a surprise to any experienced Franklin collector, and is further evidence of the tremendous rarity of high-grade Mint State Franklin halves in general. Over the past 30-plus years I have had the opportunity to look at thousands of Mint State 1949-P Franklin half dollars. To a coin, they are *all* bagmarked, with most examples grading MS-63 and lower. I have never in that time been so fortunate as to stumble upon a 1949-P with the near-perfect surfaces that would merit an MS-67 FBL grade.

Valuation—One of the three examples known in **MS-67** sold in a Heritage auction in 2008 for $14,950— a tremendous buy given the rarity of the date in this lofty grade.

ᐁ═ 1949-D, Mint State ═ᐅ

MS-66 FBL

As with the 1949-P, original rolls of the 1949-D have always been extremely elusive. This date is much more difficult to locate in average brilliant Uncirculated condition than the 1948-D, though the mintage figures are very similar.

An original roll of 1949-D Franklin halves is generally of low quality. There may be a few MS-64 FBLs, but the chance of finding a gem MS-65 FBL is small.

This is another date that is generally very unattractive in Mint set–toned condition. Once again, dull brown, tan, and gray tones are generally the rule for a Mint set 1949-D. On the bright side, there is a reasonably good chance that a 1949 Mint set will contain at least one 1949-D in MS-64 FBL.

The 1949-D is easily obtainable in circulated condition.

NGC CERTIFIED POPULATION *(from a total mintage of 4,120,600)*   (WCG™)

MS-64	MS-65	MS-66	MS-67	MS-68
587	100	2	0	0
MS-64 FBL	MS-65 FBL	MS-66 FBL	MS-67 FBL	MS-68 FBL
603	136	1	0	0

MS-60–MS-63 and MS-60 FBL–MS-63 FBL. The most common grade for this date. The 1949-D. The 1949-D is another well-struck Denver Mint coin. Nearly all examples are struck with complete bell lines, though severe bagmarks on the bell lines on the lower-grade specimens kick many out of FBL consideration.

The average brilliant Uncirculated 1949-D is quite typical in appearance to the Denver minted coins from this era. Most examples are very seriously bagmarked and grade MS-63 or lower.

Valuation—Because of the scarcity of this date in brilliant Uncirculated, even the scruffiest, ugliest 1949-D in **MS-64** Uncirculated condition sells in the $50–$60 range.

MS-64 and MS-64 FBL. As with the early Franklin issues, the 1949-D is difficult to locate in MS-64 non-FBL primarily because most MS-64 specimens have full bell lines. Many examples are from Mint sets and display average toning.

Brilliant 1949-D Franklin halves in MS-64 FBL, while scarce, are actually not as elusive as the 1949-P in this condition. The current higher premium for the 1949-D compared to the 1949-P is due primarily to the fact that MS-65 FBL 1949-D Franklin half dollars are rarer than MS-65 FBL 1949-Ps.

Many 1949-D Franklin halves in MS-64 FBL are Mint set toned, and they typically are among the ugliest toned coins in the series! Dull speckled tan and gray toning is the rule. Spectacular color-toned examples are *extremely* rare, and worth a considerable premium—*if you can find one.* Good luck.

Valuation—$50 to $75 in **MS-64.** Anything with exceptional color will sell for many times that range. **MS-64 FBL** coins usually trade for between $150 and $300, depending on the eye appeal for brilliant examples. Superbly toned pieces may be four or five times those levels.

MS-65 and MS-65 FBL. The 1949-D ranks among the rarest dates in the series in gem condition. The typical brilliant Uncirculated 1949-D Franklin almost looks as if it had been run over by a tank. Gems with minimal marks are seldom encountered, and when they are, they are usually of the dull Mint set–toned variety with poor eye appeal. FBL examples outnumber non-FBL 1949-Ds in MS-65.

It is worth holding out for a bright, haze-free brilliant example of this date, or a superb color coin. The latter are especially rare, though, as many a Franklin color aficionado has spent years trying to hunt down a rainbow MS-65 1949-D to no avail.

MS-65 FBL is the grade to shoot for in attractive brilliant condition. Most examples rank at the lower end of the MS-65 spectrum, one tick away from an MS-64 FBL grade. Hold out for a premium quality MS-65+. This is a beautiful coin when found in brilliant condition, without the usual ticks and scrapes on Franklin's cheek and jawbone or on the Liberty bell. There will be a premium attached to a 1949-D of this caliber, but an MS-65 FBL 1949-D of this caliber is many times rarer than the garden-variety gem.

If the goal is to assemble a superb gem color-toned Franklin set, the challenge is greater still. Most of the existing toned 1949-D Franklin half dollars have their origins from Mint sets, and the Mint set toning found on 1949-D is almost, without exception, very dull and unattractive. A beautifully toned gem 1949-D Franklin half is an extremely rare coin.

Valuation—Due to the poor Mint set–toned eye appeal of 1949-D Franklin halves in **MS-65,** most examples are very modestly priced, given their great scarcity, and usually trade for between $300 and $500. Exceptional color coins will sell for five to ten times more, but are extremely rare.

Most **MS-65 FBL** 1949-D Franklin halves are unattractive, and as a result, despite their rarity, can sometimes be purchased for as little as $500 to $700. Wait patiently for the superb haze-free 65+ blazer: they are far more attractive, far more elusive, and far more valuable—typically selling in the $1,000–$2,000 range. Exceptional color coins are extremely rare, and may trade anywhere from $1,500 to $5,000 or more, depending on the color!

MS-66 and MS-66 FBL. *Rare.* Forget the MS-66 only (non-FBL) grade. Every MS-66 1949-D I have ever seen has also been FBL. While few 1949-D Franklin halves have been graded in MS-66 FBL, most of the examples that have been certified are, once again, average in eye appeal, with ordinary, dull Mint set toning, as if the coins had been buried in a swamp for 40 years.

All of this makes the hunt for a 1949-D MS-66 FBL with either attractive color toning or fully brilliant surfaces that much more daunting a task. Patience is in order, as this will likely be a hunt that spans many years. Since the inception of PCGS and NGC,

I have handled two 1949-D Franklin halves in MS-66 FBL with fully brilliant surfaces, and two examples with exceptional color toning.

Valuation—Of the examples that have been graded, about half exhibit uninspiring Mint set toning, and may trade for as little as $2,500 to $5,000. There are a few examples in **MS-66 FBL** with fully brilliant or almost fully brilliant surfaces. An example sold at auction in 2011 for almost $11,500. An exceptional color coin would be expected to sell in the low five figures as well, if such a coin were to surface.

MS-67 and MS-67 FBL. Perhaps a fantasy coin. None have been graded by either of the major services, and one wonders if they ever will be. If only one had been employed at the Denver Mint in 1949 and had the foresight to pluck one of the newly struck Franklins as it was ejected from the die, that coin would be an MS-67 FBL today. Unfortunately, that is very unlikely to have happened, and so the Franklin collector is left to choose from a selection of 1949-D Mint State Franklin halves most of which appear to have spent their trip from the Mint to the nearest bank bouncing around loose in a pickup truck. One will not find this date without easily visible bagmarks.

Valuation—Wouldn't it be nice! This is a true fantasy coin. Good luck—call me if you get one.

⤚⟹ 1949-S, MINT STATE ⟸⤚

MS-65★ FBL, Prooflike

MS-66 FBL

Original rolls of the 1949-S are the most elusive of all. This issue was formerly referred to as the "king of the series," due to its key-date status in brilliant Uncirculated condition. That title was dropped with the advent of the PCGS and NGC grading services, when their evolving population reports revealed that the 1949-S, while scarce in MS-65, is not the rarest date in the series in MS-65 condition.

If an original 1949-S roll does surface, most coins will likely exhibit the typical soft S-Mint strike, with few if any examples displaying full bell lines. On the positive side, bagmarks will be fewer than average. There may be a couple of MS-65s in the roll.

Most toned 1949-S Franklin halves originated in Mint sets. These coins are usually average to below average in eye appeal. Exceptional color coins are rare.

NGC CERTIFIED POPULATION *(from a total mintage of 3,744,000)* (WCG™)

MS-64	MS-65	MS-66	MS-67	MS-68
693 (a)	932	165	4	0
MS-64 FBL	MS-65 FBL	MS-66 FBL	MS-67 FBL	MS-68 FBL
69 (b)	113 (c)	16 (d)	1	0

a. Includes three graded MS-64 PL. b. Includes one graded MS-64 FBL-PL. c. Includes 10 graded MS-65 FBL-PL.
d. Includes two graded MS-66 FBL-PL.

MS-60–MS-63 and MS-60 FBL–MS-63 FBL. These are the most common grades for the 1949-S, though while most lower-grade 1949-P and 1949-D Franklin halves are FBL, most 1949-S Franklin halves are not. The 1949-S is a very elusive coin in any Mint State grade in FBL.

Valuation—Because it is an S-Mint issue and is typically softly struck without bell lines, an **FBL** will command a premium even in these lower grades, selling for $75 to $150. Anything with attractive color will sell for more.

MS-64 and MS-64 FBL. While relatively readily available in MS-64 non-FBL, the 1949-S is very scarce in MS-64 with the FBL designation. In recent years this date in this grade has witnessed considerable appreciation, as demand far exceeds supply at current price levels. On the plus side, most examples are relatively brilliant. When found in toned condition, most 1949-S Franklin halves display average Mint set toning, slightly better than the 1949-D in eye appeal, and comparable to the 1949-P. Attractive color-toned 1949-S Franklin half dollars are extremely scarce in any grade.

Valuation—Under $100 in **MS-64** depending on the eye appeal for brilliant examples. Superbly toned pieces may be two to three times those levels. **FBL** examples with average Mint set toning can usually be acquired for around $200 to $300 when they are available. Brilliant specimens have appreciated quite a bit of late, and generally now trade at levels of $400 to $700. Superb color coins may sell for even more. They are quite rare.

MS-65 and MS-65 FBL. As the typical 1949-S is very softly struck, most examples graded in MS-65 are not FBL. Many examples are very flat struck in the area of the bell lines and in the hair over Franklin's ear. On the plus side, most 1949-S Franklin halves in MS-65 grade have attractive brilliant surfaces.

On occasion the 1949-S will surface with a full bold strike, almost comparable to a well-struck 1949-D in its definition. These coins are extremely scarce. Fortunately, they usually possess attractive brilliant surfaces. Superb color-toned examples of the 1949-S are rare. I would be fortunate to handle a single example in any given year.

Most intriguing is the existence of a small group of 1949-S Franklin halves in proof-like condition. Early strikes exhibit deeply mirrored fields with heavy die-polishing similar to deep mirror prooflike Morgan dollars. Additionally, almost every 1949-S prooflike that I have encountered possesses an extremely bold, sharp strike, lending some credence to the speculation at one time that these coins might actually be clandestine branch-mint Proofs. That is doubtful, though the majority of examples from this die do exhibit an unusually sharp strike for this normally softly struck issue.

Most 1949-S Franklin halves in MS-65 FBL exhibit lackluster Mint set toning, though fully brilliant examples are occasionally available. Attractive color-toned 1949-S Franklin halves are rare.

Valuation—$125 to $250 in **MS-65.** Mint set–toned MS-65 FBL coins with average eye appeal can usually be acquired for $300 to $500, while fully brilliant blazers often sell for $1,000 to $2,000. A few of the finer known prooflikes have sold for more than $3,000. Exceptional color coins? Very few exist. If you locate one, be prepared to pay a strong premium.

MS-66 and MS-66 FBL. Extremely scarce. Most examples are once again Mint set toned with average or below-average eye appeal. The 1949-S is quite rare in MS-66, and rarer still in MS-66 FBL with fully brilliant surfaces. I have handled only five or six fully brilliant MS-66 FBL 1949-S Franklin halves since 1990. Attractive color-toned specimens are equally elusive. The 1949-S is worth a considerable premium in fully brilliant or attractive color-toned MS-66 or MS-66 FBL.

Valuation—A great date in **MS-66. Non-FBL** examples with average color are usually only $300 to $400—a steal considering the rarity. Brilliant examples rarely surface, but are also surprisingly inexpensive, generally trading in the $400–$800 range.

MS-66 FBL 1949-S Franklins of the drab Mint set–toned variety are surprisingly inexpensive considering their rarity, trading in the $600–$1,000 range. Exceptional color coins will sell at multiples of that price range—$3,000 or more. Superb brilliant examples are highly prized, as well. The last example I handled sold for $3,000.

MS-67 and MS-67 FBL. *Extremely* rare. To date, only a handful of examples have been certified at this lofty level. All known examples are toned. The color of these specimens, most of which I have seen or handled at one time, are average in appearance.

Valuation—The 1949-S is a $2,000–$3,000 coin in **MS-67,** though it has been several years since the last example surfaced. The next could sell for more. **MS-67 FBL** examples have all sold for upward of $10,000. Again, a 1949-S in MS-67 FBL has not appeared on the market for several years—the last time I handled an attractive example was around 2005. This could be a $15,000–$20,000 coin before very long.

A View of the Decade: The 1950s

The 1950s saw the growth of the numismatic hobby in some important ways. The monthly periodical *Numismatic News* was launched in 1952 by Chet Krause of Iola, Wisconsin. Florida United Numismatists and the Professional Numismatists Guild were founded (both in 1955). Also in 1955, the famous doubled-die Lincoln cent emerged from the Mint, and became greatly sought after by collectors. The popularity of Proof sets increased dramatically, and in 1957 for the first time more than one million sets were sold.

The decade also saw some losses in the numismatic world. The original series of commemorative coins, which had begun in 1892, ended in 1954; it would be 28 years before another U.S. commemorative coin was struck. In 1955 the San Francisco Mint ended its coin production. In 1957 the nation said goodbye to legendary numismatist B. Max Mehl, author of the *Star Rare Coin Encyclopedia*, and saw the final edition of the *Standard Catalogue of United States Coins*.

Other events that marked the decade in numismatics include the legislation in 1955 that mandated that all coins carry the inscription "In God We Trust." In 1959 the Lincoln cent received a new reverse design by Chief Engraver Frank Gasparro; his depiction of the Lincoln Memorial replaced the earlier design of wheat ears, which had been in place since 1909.

⇒ 1950-P, Mint State ⇐

MS-67 FBL

Among the most attractive dates in the series when found in minimally marked brilliant Uncirculated condition, most examples of the 1950-P are very well struck with well-defined highlights and exceptional lustrous semi-prooflike surfaces. Original brilliant Uncirculated rolls of this date are extremely elusive. It has been many years since I handled such a roll. However, if one does have the good fortune to stumble across a truly original (not put-together) 1950-P roll, the quality of the coins will generally be exceptional. Expect many MS-64 FBL and MS-65 FBL coins.

What makes the 1950-P especially elusive in Mint State is the fact that Mint sets were not issued for the year 1950. As a result, attractively toned 1950-P Franklin halves are quite rare, especially in gem condition.

NGC CERTIFIED POPULATION *(from a total mintage of 7,742,123)* (WCG™)

MS-64	MS-65	MS-66	MS-67	MS-68
346	388	26	1	0
MS-64 FBL	MS-65 FBL	MS-66 FBL	MS-67 FBL	MS-68 FBL
261	247	39	2	0

MS-60–MS-63 and MS-60 FBL–MS-63 FBL. The 1950-P is actually unusual to find in the lowest MS-60–MS-62 grades. The typical uncirculated 1950-P usually grades at least MS-63. Most examples are well struck with full bell lines. Even in these lower grades, the 1950-P ranks among the more elusive issues in the series in Mint State.

Valuation—$30 to $50 with or without bell lines.

MS-64 and MS-64 FBL. The 1950-P ranks among the more elusive issues in the Franklin series in MS-64 and MS-64 FBL. When located, most examples display above-average eye appeal with brilliant surfaces. Attractive color-toned specimens are extremely scarce.

Valuation—For **MS-64** examples with brilliant surfaces, $40 to $60. Expect to pay $100 to $200 for **MS-64 FBL** coins depending on the eye appeal. Superbly toned pieces may be three to five times those levels!

MS-65 and MS-65 FBL. Extremely scarce with or without full bell lines—but, when located, these can rank among the loveliest gems in the set. The master die used to create all the working dies for the series was only in its third year of use, and the wear and softening of detail that would soon become evident on Franklin halves struck in subsequent years had only begun to set in. Design detail on most 1950-P Franklin halves is quite sharp, though a surprising number are softly struck in the bell line area. The luster of the typical 1950-P is outstanding and semi-prooflike. As Mint sets were not issued in 1950, superb color-toned 1950-P Franklin halves are rare.

Valuation—Superb brilliant specimens are currently quick sellers in the $350–$450 range, but the demand far exceeds the very limited supply. Expect values to go up for this popular date. Exceptional color coins are extremely rare and worth strong premiums—if you can find them. Beautiful color-toned 1950-Ps are almost never seen. The premiums paid for them can be many times the price of a brilliant example!

MS-66 and MS-66 FBL. Extremely scarce. Occasionally the 1950-P can be found in MS-66 FBL in fully brilliant condition. If one's goal is to assemble a top set of brilliant coins, a superb 1950-P MS-66 FBL will be one of the centerpieces. The luster, strike, and detail are second to none in the series.

Because Mint sets were not issued in 1950, beautifully toned 1950-P Franklin halves are very rare in MS-66 FBL. While brilliant specimens rank among the most captivating brilliant dates in the series, color-toned examples are generally average or slightly above average in color and eye appeal. A spectacular color-toned 1950-P MS-66 FBL is worth a considerable premium.

Valuation—$350 to $500 for brilliant or lightly toned coins in **MS-66**. Superb blazers in **MS-66 FBL** are now $1,500+ coins, when they are located, which is seldom. Given the rarity of color coins, expect to pay premiums above these ranges.

MS-67 and MS-67 FBL. *Very* rare. Only 22 examples have been certified by PCGS and NGC combined. One of these examples was almost brilliant—light surface haze was all that kept the coin from being fully brilliant. Had it been fully brilliant, it would have been the only Mint State Franklin known in brilliant MS-67 FBL.

Valuation—**MS-67 FBL** specimens with average eye appeal have sold for $7,000 to $10,000. A couple spectacular color coins have sold for more than $15,000.

⋙ 1950-D, Mint State ⋘

MS-66 FBL

The 1950-D exhibits surfaces quite different from those of the 1950-P: more satiny in texture, and usually with less luster. Additionally, like all the early Denver Mint halves, the 1950-D tends to be extremely baggy.

This is another very tough date to locate in roll quantities. Original rolls, on the rare occasion that they are encountered, offer typical Denver Mint quality—solid strikes, good luster, and plentiful bagmarks. There should be several MS-64 FBL coins in a roll, though there may not be an MS-65 FBL.

The 1950-D ranks among the rarest issues in the series in superb color-toned condition. The fact that Mint sets were not issued in 1950 is the primary cause.

NGC CERTIFIED POPULATION *(from a total mintage of 8,031,600)* (WCG™)

MS-64	MS-65	MS-66	MS-67	MS-68
500	193	5	1	0
MS-64 FBL	MS-65 FBL	MS-66 FBL	MS-67 FBL	MS-68 FBL
382	142	7	0	0

MS-60–MS-63 and MS-60 FBL–MS-63 FBL. Bagmarks are a serious problem for this date. If one is fortunate enough to locate an original roll of this date, about half the coins will likely grade MS-60 to MS-62, another five or six MS-63, and the remainder MS-64. Most would have full bell lines.

Valuation—The 1950-D is a $30–$50 coin in these lowest grades, with or without bell lines.

MS-64 and MS-64 FBL. The 1950-D is elusive in MS-64 FBL at this time. Bell lines are almost never a problem. Many brilliant Uncirculated examples have ticks and gouges that drop them into MS-64 status or lower.

The 1950-D is elusive in MS-64 FBL with exceptional color toning. Interestingly, early Denver Mint examples tend not to tone well. Most D-Mint halves from the 1948–1954 period (no Denver Mint coins were struck in 1955 and 1956) that toned are quite unattractive. The 1950-D is no exception. A superb color-toned 1950-D is a rare coin, and worth a very strong premium in any grade.

Valuation—Under $100 for **MS-64** coins without full bell lines, $100 to $200 for **MS-64 FBL** coins in brilliant condition. Superbly toned pieces may be three to five times those levels.

MS-65 and MS-65 FBL. This is the grade in which the 1950-D becomes a rare coin. I recall the days before the advent of PCGS and NGC, and how difficult it was to locate gem brilliant examples of this date. It seemed that when the obverse was gem, the reverse was baggy. And when the reverse was gem, the obverse was baggy. Of course, most examples were baggy on both sides.

Minimally marked MS-65 examples that are fully gem on both sides are extremely elusive, whether in brilliant or toned condition. The toned examples are typically average or below average in eye appeal. Because of generally poor eye appeal, these coins usually do not bring the premiums their rarity should command.

Valuation—This date is surprisingly inexpensive in **MS-65,** usually selling for between $200 and $400. **FBL** coins are very scarce in MS-65, and average between $375 and $575. This is a very low price considering the rarity, but the low value is partially also a function of eye appeal: most gems in this price range display either subdued brilliance or toning with average eye appeal. Premium-quality examples should sell for close to double the range given here.

Exceptional brilliant coins in MS-65 usually sell for considerably more, generally trading for between $800 and $1,500. MS-65★ FBL Franklins with exceptional color are extremely rare and trade for large premiums.

MS-66 and MS-66 FBL. Rare. As this is normally a very baggy date, most examples that do grade MS-66 fall at the lower end of the MS-66 spectrum. An extremely choice solid 66 in either brilliant condition or with superb color toning is extremely rare. Be willing to pay a premium.

Valuation—Most examples exhibit eye appeal no better than that of a premium-quality MS-65 FBL. Solid **MS-66 FBL** 1950-D Franklin halves with brilliant surfaces and good eye appeal have recently sold for between $4,000 and $6,000.

MS-67 and MS-67 FBL. Only one has been graded to date. There are just too many bagmarks!

1950-D REPUNCHED MINTMARK VARIETY, D/S OR D/D
It is still up for debate whether this variety is an overmintmark (OMM) or repunched mintmark (RPM). The Wexler Files list it as an overmintmark (WOMM-001), whereas CONECA lists it as a repunched mintmark (RPM-001). South of the primary D there appears to be remnants of either an S or a D. Inside the D appears to be the section of a secondary mintmark. There were no San Francisco Franklins struck in 1950, so it is possible that a die was prepared for this facility and later diverted for use at Denver. An early die state example will need to be found before any more study can be done on this variety. Die markers include diagonal die scratches through the I of LIBERTY, and a long die scratch coming off the E and going through the R. Minor doubling can be seen on the date.

⊰⊷ 1951-P, MINT STATE ⊶⊱

MS-67 FBL

This issue is scarce in any Uncirculated grade. Original brilliant Uncirculated rolls are extremely scarce, and are essentially nonexistent at this time. If you do find one, the typical roll offers above-average quality for the series.

A large percentage of Uncirculated examples have their origins in the Mint sets issued for that year. Most examples offer average eye appeal, though spectacular color coins are occasionally encountered.

The 1951-P is a generally attractive coin in brilliant Uncirculated condition, with most examples displaying good luster and a solid strike, though a significant percentage do not have full bell lines. Bagmarks are generally less prevalent than average for the series.

A distinct softening of the design detail begins to be evident on the 1951-P Franklin, compared to the 1948–1950 Philadelphia Mint examples. This softening is due to the gradual wearing down of the master die—the die that was used to strike all the subsequent working dies, for both the commercial and Proof coinage.

NGC CERTIFIED POPULATION *(from a total mintage of 16,802,102)* (WCG™)

MS-64	MS-65	MS-66	MS-67	MS-68
576	734	72	3	0
MS-64 FBL	**MS-65 FBL**	**MS-66 FBL**	**MS-67 FBL**	**MS-68 FBL**
133	80	14	1	0

MS-60–MS-63 and MS-60 FBL–MS-63 FBL. Most examples that fall into these lower grades have light scuffing. Heavy gouges and the like are more typical of the Denver-minted Franklin halves of this era.

Valuation—This is a $20–$40 coin in these lowest grades, with or without bell lines.

MS-64 and MS-64 FBL. Elusive. The 1951-P offers great value in MS-64 either with or without full bell lines at current levels. Stick with either brilliant, nearly brilliant, or attractively toned examples. The latter are worth a significant premium, as attractive color-toned 1951-P Franklin halves are rare in any grade. Most Mint set–toned pieces are average or below average in color.

Valuation—$35 to $45 for **MS-64s** in average brilliant condition. **FBL** coins in this grade are now trading for between $100 and $200 in brilliant condition. Superbly toned pieces may be two to three times those levels.

MS-65 and MS-65 FBL. A great date in either MS-65 or MS-65 FBL at current levels. Attractively toned or brilliant 1951-P Franklin halves in MS-65 or MS-65 FBL are far more elusive than current valuations might suggest. Luster and strike are very similar to the 1950-P, though the design detail of the obverse and reverse portrait does begin to evince some softening of definition. This is not an indication of a poor strike, but a sign that the master die used to create the working dies was slowly wearing down.

This date is especially rare in MS-65 or MS-65 FBL with exceptional color toning.

Valuation—A great buy in **MS-65**—these coins are usually $75–$125 with either brilliant surfaces or reasonably attractive color toning. **MS-65 FBL** coins are extremely scarce and sell for between $300 and $600 for the more attractive brilliant variety. Dull Mint set examples can be acquired for under $250, but even these coins are tough to come by.

MS-66 and MS-66 FBL. This date is extremely scarce in either MS-66 or MS-66 FBL, and rare in either condition with exceptional color or fully brilliant surfaces. The majority of MS-66 specimens exhibit average, unspectacular Mint set color. A fully brilliant blazer, or a superb color-toned MS-66/MS-66 FBL, is worth a significant premium.

Valuation—**MS-66** coins with average color typically sell for between $200 and $500. The 1951-P is a hot date in **MS-66 FBL,** and even the ugliest coins usually command close to $1,000. Exceptional color coins, or superb brilliant pieces, have continued to rise in value, occasionally selling for more than $3,000!

MS-67 and MS-67 FBL. Extremely rare. The finest known example, a PCGS MS-67 FBL, placed with a client in the early 2000s, displays spectacular multicolored rainbow toning.

Valuation—Establishing a price level for a coin that may appear on the market only every three or four years is difficult. I have handled only three 1951-Ps in **MS-67,** PCGS examples also certified **FBL.** The finest of these coins exhibited beautiful Mint set toning, and it was placed with a client for more than $20,000.

1951-D, MINT STATE

MS-65 FBL

Scarce in any uncirculated grade. Original brilliant Uncirculated rolls are rarely encountered. The typical 1951-D exhibits the usual Denver Mint bold strike, with outstanding bell lines. Luster is generally good. Bagmarks are once again a D-Mint problem.

Most 1951-D Franklin halves found in Mint sets are low-grade coins, with below-average eye appeal—the toning is typically quite dull and lifeless, with browns, tans, and grays predominating.

NGC CERTIFIED POPULATION *(from a total mintage of 9,475,200)*   (WCG™)

MS-64	MS-65	MS-66	MS-67	MS-68
280	144	2	0	0
MS-64 FBL	MS-65 FBL	MS-66 FBL	MS-67 FBL	MS-68 FBL
496	244	11	0	0

MS-60–MS-63 and MS-60 FBL–MS-63 FBL. Most brilliant Uncirculated 1951-D Franklins fall into these lower Mint State grades. The majority will be FBL, but will exhibit many nicks and scuffs consistent with the low grade.

The 1951-D is rare with exceptional color toning in any Mint State grade.

Valuation—These are roll coins, and can be acquired for around $35 to $45 at current roll bid levels. The exception would be a 1951-D with attractive color toning, which could sell for several times more than the more typical example.

MS-64 and MS-64 FBL. Most MS-64 specimens will also be FBL. A majority will be primarily brilliant, though significant opaque hazy toning will detract from the eye appeal. Good luck finding a superb color coin.

Valuation—$100 to $200 depending on the eye appeal for brilliant examples in **MS-64 FBL. Non-FBL** coins bring slightly less. Superbly toned pieces may be three to five times those levels.

MS-65 and MS-65 FBL. Elusive in gem condition, most MS-65s will be FBL, and they will be unattractive as well. Dull, lifeless Mint set–toned gems are the rule. Seek out those superb gems with either fully brilliant, haze-free surfaces or exceptional color toning. While the former are extremely elusive, the latter are extremely rare and worth a very strong premium, depending on the color.

Valuation—The typical toned **MS-65 FBL** is quite inexpensive, considering the rarity—usually selling in the area of $225–$350. This is due to the poor eye appeal. On the other hand, exceptional color examples continue to rise in value, with some selling for upward of $1,500. This is still a great price—these coins are *rare*. Split the difference for exceptional brilliant 1951-D Franklin halves in MS-65 FBL. Also quite rare, and highly prized due to the generally excellent striking characteristics, these usually trade in the $400–$800 range.

MS-66 and MS-66 FBL. A *great* coin in MS-66 or MS-66 FBL in fully brilliant or attractive color-toned condition. These are *rare*. When an MS-66 FBL does appear on the market (it would be very unusual to find this date in MS-66 without the FBL designation), it typically exhibits the usual unattractive Mint set toning commonly seen for the date.

Valuation—The typical lifeless Mint set–toned **MS-66 FBL** 1951-D can be acquired for under $2,000—still not a bad price when one considers the rarity factor. A much better value is the 1951-D with either fully brilliant surfaces or attractive color toning. Such coins are extremely rare, and have been known to trade for anything from $3,500 to $7,000. I have handled only six or seven fully brilliant 1951-D Franklin halves in MS-66 FBL since the inception of the FBL designation at PCGS and NGC.

MS-67 and MS-67 FBL. Only one has been graded, a PCGS example.

1951-S, Mint State

MS-66 FBL

Scarce in any uncirculated grade, 1951-S halves, like the 1951-D original brilliant Uncirculated rolls, are rarely encountered. The typical 1951-S is very softly struck, lacking bell lines. Luster is generally good. As with most of the San Francisco Mint issues, bagmarks are fewer than average for the series.

Most 1951-S Franklin halves found in Mint sets are MS-63 to MS-65 coins, with below-average eye appeal—the toning is typically quite dull and lifeless, with browns, tans, and grays predominating. They are usually not FBL.

NGC CERTIFIED POPULATION *(from a total mintage of 13,696,000)*   (WCG™)

MS-64	MS-65	MS-66	MS-67	MS-68
547	931	138	6	0
MS-64 FBL	MS-65 FBL	MS-66 FBL	MS-67 FBL	MS-68 FBL
59	44	13	1	0

MS-60–MS-63 and MS-60 FBL–MS-63 FBL. Most brilliant Uncirculated 1951-S Franklins fall into these lower Mint State grades. The majority are not FBL.

The 1951-S is rare with exceptional color toning in any Mint State grade.

Valuation—$30 for **non-FBL** coins. **FBLs** in **MS-63** will command slightly more—$50 to $100.

MS-64 and MS-64 FBL. Go for the FBL. On the plus side, the 1951-S is typically a relatively mark-free date—one does not usually see these coins with the deep cuts and digs typical of the 1951-D. Lower grades are usually due to light surface abrasions that often go unnoticed by novice collectors.

Another tough date to find with superb color.

Valuation—Around $50 for brilliant examples in **MS-64**. The 1951-S is very scarce in **MS-64 FBL**, especially with fully brilliant surfaces. These coins have appreciated quite a bit of late, typically selling in the $225–$325 range.

MS-65 and MS-65 FBL. This is a tough coin to locate in MS-65. The population is about evenly split between brilliant coins and Mint set–toned coins with average appeal. This is an extremely scarce coin in MS-65 with full bell lines. The typical 1951-S displays the usual S-Mint strike—soft and mushy. A sharply struck haze-free blazer, or superb color-toned jewel, should be highly prized.

Valuation—$50 to $125 for **MS-65s. MS-65 FBL** coins with dull Mint set toning or hazy surfaces can sometimes be acquired for as little as $400 to $600. Go for the fully brilliant, bright blazer or the exceptional color coin. When one does surface, it can sell for anything from $500 to $1,200 or more, but will be worth the extra investment over the long term.

MS-66 and MS-66 FBL. When found in MS-66, the 1951-S is usually of the Mint set–toned variety, with very clean surfaces and average color and eye appeal. Exceptional color coins are rare, as are fully brilliant specimens in MS-66. The 1951-S in MS-66 FBL follows the same pattern: most examples display average, uninspiring Mint set toning. Superb brilliant specimens, or lovely color-toned Van Goghs, are definitely the exceptions.

Valuation—**MS-66** 1951-S Franklin halves with average eye appeal can be acquired for as little as $200 to $300. Brilliant blazers, or superb color coins, may be two to three times that range, for good reason: in addition to having superior eye appeal, they are extremely scarce. **FBL** coins in MS-66 with brilliant surfaces, when located, are most desirable. They usually trade for between $2,000 and $4,000. Exceptional color coins in MS-66 FBL are rarer still. Expect to pay a similar premium.

MS-67 and MS-67 FBL. *Extremely* rare, with only eight professionally graded. The finest known example, an NGC MS-67★ FBL (the star designating exceptional eye appeal), ranks as the finest example I have handled. The coin features magnificent iridescent rainbow color on the obverse and reverse.

Valuation—A superb **MS-67 FBL** that appeared on the market several years ago (the aforementioned star coin) sold for more than $20,000 in 2008.

1951-S Doubled-Die Reverse Variety (FS-002)

Strong doubling is seen on E PLURIBUS UNUM and the eagle. There are some doubled dies similar to this one but with the doubling not as strong. Die markers include scratches visible off the bottom of the L and TY of LIBERTY. Die scratches also appear to the left and right and below the bell.

⊷⇒ 1952-P, MINT STATE ⇐⊶

MS-66 FBL

The 1952-P is very similar to the 1951-P in luster and bagmark characteristics, though the 1952-P has a bolder, more consistent strike than the 1951-P.

When found in minimally marked condition, the 1952-P ranks among the most attractive brilliant Franklin dates in the series. The one negative—a small one—is the further softening of detail on both the obverse and reverse devices, as the master die for the series progressively wore down. The 1952-P is scarce in any Uncirculated grade. Original brilliant Uncirculated rolls are extremely scarce. A large percentage of Uncirculated examples have their origins in the Mint sets issued for that year.

Mint set–toned coins are generally unattractive, through at least the MS-63 grade with full bell lines. On rare occasions an attractive color coin will be found in a Mint set.

NGC CERTIFIED POPULATION *(from a total mintage of 21,192,093)* (WCG™)

MS-64	MS-65	MS-66	MS-67	MS-68
549	552	91	9	0
MS-64 FBL	MS-65 FBL	MS-66 FBL	MS-67 FBL	MS-68 FBL
240	220	70	2	0

MS-60–MS-63 and MS-60 FBL–MS-63 FBL. Most examples that fall into these lower grades have light scuffing. Heavy gouges and the like are more typical of the Denver-minted Franklin halves of this era.

Valuation—These roll coins can usually be acquired for $20 to $30, and offer nominal investment potential.

MS-64 and MS-64 FBL. This is a scarce coin even in MS-64 or MS-64 FBL. The 1952-P offers exceptional value in these grades at current price levels. Seek out either fully brilliant examples or superbly toned pieces. The 1952-P with exceptional color toning is rare in any grade. Most examples from Mint sets exhibit average color and eye appeal.

Valuation—$75 to $175 depending on the eye appeal for brilliant examples. Superbly toned pieces may be two to three times those levels.

MS-65 and MS-65 FBL. Almost as difficult to find as the 1951-P in either exceptional gem brilliant or color-toned condition, the 1952-P is also usually priced about 30% less than the former date, *making it an extremely attractive value at today's prices*. Most examples in MS-65 are also FBL. While the 1952-P is elusive in MS-65 and MS-65 FBL, when encountered it is usually less than fully brilliant, typically displaying average, subdued Mint set coloration. Exceptional rainbow-toned examples are rare and worth a significant premium. Superb gem brilliant coins are highly prized as well, and rank among the more attractive coins in a brilliant set.

Valuation—Among my favorite type coins in fully brilliant condition, the best-struck examples display a combination of strike and luster that few dates in the series can match. While examples with average toning in **MS-65** can be acquired for around $50 to $75, and similar toned coins in **MS-65 FBL** for as little as $125 to $175, beautiful bright blazers are now trading in the $300–$500 range, on the infrequent occasions when such coins surface. Superb color coins will command even more.

MS-66 and MS-66 FBL. Over the past several years the 1952-P has become quite elusive in the higher Mint State grades of MS-66 and MS-66 FBL. The majority of MS-66 and MS-66 FBL coins offer drab, disappointing Mint set–toned surfaces. The 1952-P is very rare in MS-66 or MS-66 FBL with fully brilliant surfaces or with exceptional color toning.

Valuation—The average Mint set–toned 1952-P in **MS-66** is a $200 coin. **FBL** examples are little more—$300 to $500. Far more elusive, and desirable, is the fully brilliant blazer or the exceptional color coin. Both are extremely rare. The last examples I handled traded for between $1,500 and $3,000.

MS-67 and MS-67 FBL. Rare, with 32 graded. I have handled only five or six attractive examples in this highest grade going back to 1991. All were Mint set toned with better-than-average color.

Valuation—An **MS-67** in non-FBL can be acquired for under $3,000—if you can find one. **MS-67 FBLs** sell for $8,000 to $15,000.

⤙ 1952-D, MINT STATE ⤚

MS-66 FBL

The 1952-D has the fourth-highest mintage in the Franklin series, barely edged out by the 1954-D for third place by a mere 50,000 coins. And yet the 1952-D is far more difficult to find in roll quantity than the 1954-D. When an original 1952-D roll does surface, the majority of the coins are typical Denver Mint quality: very well struck with excellent bell lines and generally good luster, though many may have water spotting and *plentiful* bagmarks. It would be unusual to find a single MS-65 coin in an original roll.

As is typical of the early Denver Mint coins, Mint set pieces are typically quite unattractive—among the ugliest in the series. Dull gray, tan, brown, and similar shades dominate. Color coins are extremely rare. Most coins also grade quite low—MS-63 and below.

NGC CERTIFIED POPULATION *(from a total mintage of 25,395,600)*   (WCG™)

MS-64	MS-65	MS-66	MS-67	MS-68
370	253	11	2	0
MS-64 FBL	**MS-65 FBL**	**MS-66 FBL**	**MS-67 FBL**	**MS-68 FBL**
478	238	13	0	0

MS-60–MS-63 and MS-60 FBL–MS-63 FBL. This is the typical grade for a Mint State 1952-D. If a 1952-D is not FBL, it is only because of bagmarks on the bell lines, as the 1952-D ranks among the most boldly struck dates in the series.

Valuation—Most examples are **FBL,** and can be acquired for $20 to $40.

MS-64 and MS-64 FBL. The 1952-D is elusive in the MS-64/MS-64 FBL grade. Most examples are FBL. The typical 1952-D in MS-64 FBL exhibits hazy surfaces with subdued luster. Mint set–toned pieces are among the least attractive in the series, generally offering a witches' brew of dull gray, tan, and brown. A fully brilliant MS-64 FBL 1952-D is worth a premium, and a lovely color-toned coin is worth a significant premium.

Valuation—The **1952-D** with unattractive Mint set toning can be acquired for as little as $50. Superb brilliant pieces will sell for considerably more—$100 to $200. Exceptional color coins? I have paid more than $300 for some of the prettier examples. They are rare.

MS-65 and MS-65 FBL. The 1952-D is very scarce in this higher Mint State grade. Again, most MS-65 coins are also FBL. Strike is not a problem. Bagmarks are, as is generally unattractive Mint set toning. Most fully brilliant gems fall in the low end of MS-65, with an above-average number of light ticks—typical of Denver Mint Franklin half dollars. Superb color-toned gems are almost never encountered.

Valuation—Most **MS-65s** are either dull Mint set–toned coins or hazy, semi-brilliant pieces, and sell for as little as $100. Even though these coins are deficient in eye appeal, the price is quite cheap when one factors in the scarcity of this date in gem condition. The typical Mint set–toned **MS-65 FBL** example is roughly double the price- $150 to $300. Most quality-conscious collectors opt for fully brilliant examples, which are usually quite attractive, for $300 to $600. Outstanding color coins are extremely rare in gem. *Expect to pay upward of $1,000 for any 1952-D with color that might be considered beautiful.*

MS-66 and MS-66 FBL. The 1952-D is rare in MS-66 non-FBL. Most coins are of the unattractive Mint set–toned variety. When found in MS-66 the 1952-D is also usually FBL. Again, these coins, while rare, are generally also quite unattractive Mint set–toned coins. Fully brilliant 1952-D Franklin halves in MS-66 FBL are very rare, as are examples in this grade with attractive color toning.

Valuation—If one is budget minded, an **MS-66 FBL** 1952-D can be acquired for as little as $1,000 to $1,500. However, the eye appeal will be less than satisfying. This is a date it is wise to be patient for—seek out the superb brilliant specimen or the beautiful color coin. These coins are extremely rare, but worth the $3,000–$6,000 price tag they usually command.

MS-67 and MS-67 FBL. Extremely rare. Only three examples have been graded to date: two by NCG, and one, with full bell lines, by PCGS.

Valuation—Four have been graded in **MS-67 FBL**. The last example I handled, a golden-toned coin graded by PCGS, sold for close to $20,000.

⊷⊷ 1952-S, MINT STATE ⊷⊷

MS-66 FBL

With a low mintage of just over 5.5 million coins, the 1952-S was also not a heavily hoarded date. Original rolls rarely surface, and when they do they command among the highest premiums in the Franklin half series. In original rolls, most of the coins display excellent luster with only modest abrasions. Typical of San Francisco Mint coins from this era, the strike usually presents a problem. Most 1952-S Franklin halves are not well struck and do not have full bell lines.

When found in Mint sets, the 1952-S has fewer than average bagmarks and will quite often grade MS-65. That's the good part. The bad part is that these coins are almost always softly struck, with below-average eye appeal.

NGC CERTIFIED POPULATION *(from a total mintage of 5,526,000)*   (WCG™)

MS-64	MS-65	MS-66	MS-67	MS-68
501	846	248	13	0
MS-64 FBL	**MS-65 FBL**	**MS-66 FBL**	**MS-67 FBL**	**MS-68 FBL**
34	17	2	0	0

MS-60–MS-63 and MS-60 FBL–MS-63 FBL. Most brilliant Uncirculated 1952-S Franklin half dollars do not fall into the lowest grades, MS-60–MS-62. The average grade in an original roll is about MS-63. Several coins may be MS-64, and there may even be an MS-65 or two. The problem for this date is that it is highly unlikely that any of those coins will also be FBL. While many 1952-S Franklin halves are well struck, there is usually not enough delineation of the bell lines to earn these coins an FBL designation.

Valuation—This is a tough date in any Mint State grade—even the scruffiest **1952-S** is at least $40 to $50. An **FBL** coin in these lower grades will command at least triple the non-FBL price.

MS-64 and MS-64 FBL. While not difficult to locate in MS-64, the 1952-S is extremely scarce in MS-64 with full bell lines. Over the past several years, the 1952-S has witnessed considerable appreciation in value in this latter grade, especially in brilliant condition, as collectors attempt to complete their MS-64 FBL sets.

Most 1952-S Franklin halves in toned condition were originally from Mint sets. While the toning is not quite as dull as on the 1952-D, it is usually not considered attractive either. Superb color-toned pieces are rare and worth a premium.

Valuation—This date has seen tremendous appreciation the past several years as collectors intent on building an FBL set have found the 1952-S to be quite a challenge. Even dull Mint set–toned pieces have risen in value, now selling for $400 to $600 in **MS-64 FBL**, about double the price listed in the first edition of this book, compared to a non-FBL **MS-64** 1952-S, which normally sells for around $50. Fully brilliant examples have been selling for $1,000 or more of late. Expect to pay similar premiums for a superb color toned coin.

MS-65 and MS-65 FBL. The 1952-S is scarce in MS-65. Most examples are Mint set toned with average color. Fully brilliant coins are far more elusive and offer tremendous value at current low levels. They are far rarer than current asking prices might suggest. Full bell line coins are extremely scarce. Again, most coins are toned with average, uninspiring color toning. For this reason, blazers command a strong premium. Bagmarks are usually fewer than average for the grade, and the luster can be exceptional. MS-65 FBL 1952-S Franklin halves with attractive color toning are very rare. Of all the 1952-S Franklin halves certified in MS-65 FBL to date, a guesstimate would be that no more than 1% to 2% of these coins display superb color, and 10% to 20% may be of the superb brilliant variety.

Valuation—Unattractive Mint set–toned coins in **MS-65** are usually under $100. Fully brilliant examples offer far better value; they are extremely scarce and surprisingly cheap—usually under $200. Of course, most collectors want the well-struck **FBL** coin if they can find one. This date is so hot that even unattractive Mint set coins are now selling for $1,500 to $2,500—more than double their values from when the first edition of this book was published! Fully brilliant blazers typically trade in the $1,500 to $3,500 range. Color coins command similar premiums.

MS-66 and MS-66 FBL. Very scarce in MS-66, and very rare in MS-66 FBL. Most examples in MS-66 non-FBL are Mint set toned with average color. An MS-66 1952-S with either brilliant surfaces or exceptional color toning is *rare*. And a 1952-S in MS-66 with full bell lines in fully brilliant condition or with exceptional color toning is *extremely* rare. Few such examples exist.

Valuation—The typical average toned **MS-66** 1952-S can be purchased for $200 to $300. Far more elusive is the MS-66 brilliant blazer—a great buy at any price under $1,000. Virtually all 1952-S Franklins in **MS-66 FBL** are Mint set–toned coins with average eye appeal, and can usually be acquired for around $2,500 to $3,000. Again, the 1952-S MS-66 FBL with fully brilliant surfaces, or exceptional color toning, is extraordinarily rare. I have handled only a few of each since the inception of the FBL designation at PCGS and NGC. I have been able to place a few examples for only around $6,000.

MS-67 and MS-67 FBL. A handful of 1952-S Franklin halves have been certified in MS-67 without full bell lines, and only three in MS-67 FBL.

Valuation—The last **MS-67 FBL** to appear, a reasonably attractive Mint set color coin, sold for approximately $20,000.

1953-P, Mint State

MS-66 FBL

A low-mintage issue in the series, the 1953-P is elusive in any Mint State grade. *The 1953-P bears the distinction of producing the most weakly struck Philadelphia issues in the series.* Many examples are flat struck to the point that Franklin's ear detail is nearly nonexistent, with almost no definition visible on the Liberty Bell as well. Interestingly, 1953-P Franklin halves exist at the opposite end of the strike spectrum, exhibiting full, bold strikes and with excellent bell lines, though these coins are certainly in the minority within the series.

The typical 1953-P Franklin found in Mint sets is very softly struck with fewer than average bagmarks. On occasion these coins will have attractive color toning.

NGC CERTIFIED POPULATION *(from a total mintage of 2,668,120)* (WCG™)

MS-64	MS-65	MS-66	MS-67	MS-68
676	542	38	1	0
MS-64 FBL	**MS-65 FBL**	**MS-66 FBL**	**MS-67 FBL**	**MS-68 FBL**
69	34	2	0	0

MS-60–MS-63 and MS-60 FBL–MS-63 FBL. Most brilliant Uncirculated 1953-P Franklin half dollars are MS-60 to MS-63 due to light abrasions and very poor strikes. This date is scarce in MS-63 with full bell lines. On the positive side, most FBL specimens are also brilliant. Mint set–toned examples are almost universally flat struck. Mint set–toned 1953-P Franklin halves with full bell lines are rare in any grade.

Valuation—If you are going after a 1953-P in this lowest Mint State grade, the FBL is the choice. A reasonably attractive **MS-63 FBL** can be acquired for under $100.

MS-64 and MS-64 FBL. Semi-scarce in MS-64, but very scarce in MS-64 with full bell lines. Most examples are brilliant with good eye appeal. Attractive color-toned examples are *rare* and worth a significant premium.

Valuation—Not a highly desirable date in **MS-64;** the 1953-P is fairly common in this grade. However, it is *highly recommended* in **MS-64 FBL.** When located, an attractive brilliant example can still be acquired for around $175 to $300. Superb color coins are rare in any grade. So be willing to pay a significant premium—they are definitely worth it!

MS-65 and MS-65 FBL. The 1953-P is scarce in MS-65. Most examples are Mint set toned and very flatly struck, with average eye appeal. Fully brilliant examples in MS-65 are extremely scarce, and a tremendous value at current price levels. MS-65 examples with attractive color toning are rare.

The 1953-P in MS-65 FBL is a rare coin with or without toning. Most examples are relatively brilliant, though fully brilliant, haze-free examples are rare. Rarer still is the 1953-P in MS-65 FBL with exceptional color toning. Over the past 15+ years I may have handled but two or three examples that could be described as having beautiful color.

Valuation—A great date in either MS-65 or MS-65 FBL. When found in **MS-65** the 1953-P is usually a Mint set coin with average toning. *Fully brilliant examples are a tremendous value when located—usually only $300 to $400.* The 1953-P in **MS-65 FBL** with average Mint set toning can usually be acquired for under $700. Superb brilliant blazers are currently trading in the $900–$1,500 range—in my opinion, very undervalued at this level. The 1953-P ranks among my favorite dates in the series in superb MS-65 FBL.

MS-66 and MS-66 FBL. The 1953-P is extremely scarce in MS-66. Almost every example I have handled has been Mint set toned. While most are extremely clean, as one would expect from an MS-66-graded Franklin, most are also softly struck.

The 1953-P is very rare in MS-66 FBL. Virtually all are Mint set toned. A few of these gems exhibit exceptional color toning. *A beautifully toned MS-66 FBL 1953-P is the rarest Philadelphia issue of the 1948-1958 era in the Franklin series,* when the government issued Mint sets in the cardboard holder that was the catalyst for most of the superbly toned coins in the series. Fully brilliant blazers are extremely rare in MS-66 FBL; I have handled only a couple such coins over the past 15 years.

Valuation—**MS-66** examples with average color can be acquired for as little as $300 to $600. Superb color-toned coins may command two to three times that level, or more. The 1953-P in **MS-66 FBL** is a real challenge. Once again, *because of the typical average Mint set color,* prices are a still relatively modest $1,500 to $3,000. *Exceptional color coins, or fully brilliant coins, can be expected to command two to three times those levels.* A couple spectacularly toned specimens have sold for more than $15,000 in recent months!

MS-67 and MS-67 FBL. One has been graded to date.

⊷⊶ 1953-D, MINT STATE ⊷⊶

MS-67 FBL

The 1953-D is among the highest-mintage issues in the series, though about 5 million fewer were struck than of the 1952-D. This is also among the best-struck dates in the series, with virtually all examples sufficiently boldly struck to rate as FBL. Once again, the problem with the Denver Mint releases is bagmarks.

When found in Mint sets, the 1953-D mirrors the 1952-D. Most examples are very baggy, with poor color characteristics.

NGC CERTIFIED POPULATION *(from a total mintage of 20,900,400)*   (WCG™)

MS-64	MS-65	MS-66	MS-67	MS-68
577	377	5	1	0
MS-64 FBL	**MS-65 FBL**	**MS-66 FBL**	**MS-67 FBL**	**MS-68 FBL**
561	269	15	2	0

MS-60–MS-63 and MS-60 FBL–MS-63 FBL. Most brilliant Uncirculated examples fall into this grade range. Virtually all examples are boldly struck and would grade FBL but for excessive marks on a large percentage of coins in this grade range. Deep gouges and scrapes are the common types of markings on this date. Water spots are also a problem.

Valuation—The 1953-D is not recommended in these lowest Mint State grades except as a bullion investment. The only exception would be an attractive color coin.

MS-64 and MS-64 FBL. The 1953-D is semi-scarce in this grade range with attractive surfaces. Most 1953-Ds in MS-64 and MS-64 FBL are water spotted with hazy toned surfaces. Mint set–toned specimens are typically unattractive, with dull tan and gray surfaces. Fully brilliant pieces are worth a small premium. 1953-D Franklin halves in MS-64 or MS-64 FBL with attractive color toning are rare, and worth a strong premium. A few examples have sold for upwards of $500.

Valuation—Avoid the dull Mint set–toned coins in **MS-64 FBL**. A bright, spot-free blazer is a solid $100+ coin. They are scarce. True color coins are rare. It is easier to find an 1880-S MS-67 Morgan dollar with rainbow color—for a couple thousand dollars—than a 1953-D MS-64 FBL with color.

MS-65 and MS-65 FBL. This issue is very scarce in MS-65 and MS-65 FBL, with most examples in the MS-65 grade also FBL. The majority of 1953-D Franklin halves in this grade range are average or below average in eye appeal. The typical 1953-D from an original roll exhibits some water spotting, along with hazy toned surfaces. Mint set–toned examples are usually dull gray and/or tan with below-average eye appeal. Fully brilliant examples typically fall into the lower end of the MS-65 grade, with several minor ticks and scuffs, just few enough to make the gem grade. Fully brilliant MS-65+ gems are extremely elusive and worth a premium. Gems with exceptional color toning are rarer still, and worth a very strong premium.

Valuation—In **MS-65**, $100 to $200. Color coins will command substantially more. There is a wide range for **MS-65 FBLs** as well: from $150 to $250 for average, dull Mint set toners to $500 and more for superb MS-65+ brilliant blazers. Outstanding color coins may be double that price—*or more*.

MS-66 and MS-66 FBL. The 1953-D is extremely scarce in MS-66 and MS-66 FBL, with most examples in the MS-66 grade also meriting FBL. As with the MS-65s, most 1953-D Franklin halves in this grade offer disappointing eye appeal, with dull, fairly colorless toning. Fully brilliant blazers in MS-66 FBL or examples with exceptional color toning are very rare, and worth a significant premium over the typical example.

Valuation—Only $300 to $500 for **MS-66s**—a good value considering the rarity, if the coin is attractive. Most in demand in **MS-66 FBL** are the exceptional haze-free blazers or the spectacular color coins. These coins are typically found for around $1,000. Depending on the quality of the specimen, however, these coins can trade for between $3,000 and $6,000.

MS-67 and MS-67 FBL. *Extremely* rare. Only five have been certified. Few 1953-D Franklin halves exist with the near-flawless surfaces required of an MS-67 coin. I have handled only a single example in this grade range. Certified by PCGS, in addition to the unusually clean surfaces, this gem features beautiful multicolored Mint set toning on the obverse and reverse.

Valuation—The finest 1953-D I have handled in **MS-67 FBL**, with great color, sold at auction for approximately $33,000.

⊷⊷ 1953-S, Mint State ⊷⊷

MS-67

The 1953-S is a very low-mintage issue. Brilliant Uncirculated rolls sell for high premiums, not because of their scarcity but due to the rarity of this date in FBL. The 1953-S is the weakest-struck date in the series; while most examples are minimally bagmarked, they are also very softly struck.

NGC CERTIFIED POPULATION *(from a total mintage of 4,148,000)*   (WCG™)

MS-64	MS-65	MS-66	MS-67	MS-68
695	2,523	464	8	0
MS-64 FBL	**MS-65 FBL**	**MS-66 FBL**	**MS-67 FBL**	**MS-68 FBL**
1	4	0	0	0

MS-60–MS-63 and MS-60 FBL–MS-63 FBL. A very common coin in MS-63, the 1953-S is a very rare coin in MS-63 with full bell lines. I have never personally found a 1953-S with full bell lines in an original brilliant Uncirculated roll, though apparently a few lucky people have in the past.

Interestingly, the 1953-S is far rarer in MS-63 FBL than in MS-64 FBL or MS-65 FBL. Bagmarks are not a problem with this date; strike is. As with certain S-Mint coins in other series of the 20th century, the 1953-S is rarely seen with surfaces struck well enough to be FBL.

Valuation—Not of interest in the lower grades except as a roll coin—unless it is FBL. An **MS-63 FBL** is at least a $5,000–$10,000 coin on today's market.

MS-64 and MS-64 FBL. Very common in MS-64, and extremely rare in MS-64 with full bell lines. FBL examples have exploded in value over the past decade as collectors vying to complete an all-FBL set compete for the occasional example that surfaces.

On the plus side, this date typically does not exhibit the deep scrapes and gouges usually found on the Denver Mint issues from this period. Most coins are also quite brilliant, with excellent luster. Superbly toned 1953-S Franklin halves are another matter: these coins are rarer in any grade.

Valuation—$40 to $65 depending on the eye appeal for brilliant **MS-64** examples. Superbly toned pieces may be two to three times those levels. *MS-64 FBL examples are now trading between $15,000 and $25,000!*

MS-65 and MS-65 FBL. The 1953-S ranks among the most common dates in the series in MS-65. It is also far and away the rarest date in MS-65 with full bell lines. For the record, while a couple dozen 1953-S Franklin halves combined have been certified as MS-65 FBL by NGC and PCGS to date, I personally submitted only one 1953-S that subsequently graded MS-65 FBL, and that was back in the mid-1990s.

Most examples in brilliant non-FBL and FBL are brilliant. The occasional Mint set–toned 1953-S in MS-65 is average in eye appeal, devoid of significant color. Attractive color-toned MS-65 1953-S Franklin halves are rare and worth a strong premium.

As most MS-65 FBL examples are brilliant or mostly brilliant, the 1953-S in MS-65 FBL with exceptional color toning as well must be considered an ultra rarity.

A very popular alternative for many collectors is the 1953-S in MS-65 with nearly full bell lines, or 95% FBL. These coins exhibit most of the well-struck characteristics of the FBL 1953-S, but for about 1% of the price. These coins typically exhibit excellent bell lines up to about 1/16 of an inch from the crack in the Liberty Bell.

Valuation—A great coin, and very popular in **MS-65,** given the tremendous rarity of FBLs. A nice MS-65 is currently a $100–$200 coin and rising, due to demand. One lightly toned MS-65 FBL recently sold at auction for $25,300. I personally acquired a lightly toned **MS-65 FBL** for a client for $33,000 in 2009, and later sold it for a bit less than 10% more—a record price paid by a dealer to date. More recently a brilliant MS-65+ FBL sold for $49,000.

MS-66 and MS-66 FBL. The 1953-S in MS-66 non-FBL is another attractive alternative to the 1953-S in MS-65 FBL. A large percentage of 1953-S Franklin halves in this grade are lovely brilliant coins with reasonably well-struck surfaces, though not struck sharply enough in the bell lines to earn the FBL designation. These coins are quite scarce and obviously in very high demand.

The typical toned 1953-S will be from a Mint set. These coins are usually best described as uninspiring in their eye appeal. Attractive color-toned 1953-S Franklin halves in MS-66 are quite rare, and worth a strong premium.

To date, there is but a single 1953-S certified in MS-66 FBL. This is a coin I originally handled and placed with a client for around $15,000 in the late 1990s. The coin exhibited lovely gold and sky-blue color toning in addition to the boldly struck MS-66 FBL surfaces. The story of the subsequent sale of this famous Franklin rarity is quite interesting.

A couple of years after the original sale, the owner of the coin called me and explained that he wished to sell the coin back to me, as he was in the process of restoring his Victorian-era home in New England and needed additional funds. My response was that, while I would love to get the coin back, I would be offering him only around $25,000 for the coin—what I considered a fair price, as I would be selling the coin for about 10% more than that amount. However, Franklin halves had been exploding in popularity in recent years, and it might be better if he were to consign the coin in a major auction, where the coin could conceivably realize considerably more.

The rest, as they say, is history. The collector took my advice and consigned his 1953-S MS-66 FBL to a Heritage auction at the annual Florida United Numismatists (FUN) coin convention. The coin world was abuzz. Needless to say, the consignor was extremely pleased when his 1953-S realized $69,000 in that auction! The Franklin half dollar series had gained considerable respect among many previously skeptical rare coin dealers.

Since that day, the Franklin half dollar series, in both Mint State and Proof, has continued to grow in popularity, with many more record auction prices realized, cementing its position among the most popular collector series in U.S. coinage.

Valuation—A red-hot date in **MS-66,** with exceptional specimens easily selling for $250 to $500. Color will sell for even more. One **MS-66 FBL** sold for $69,000 at auction around the year 2000. Only three examples have been certified in MS-66 FBL, by NGC and PCGS combined.

MS-67 and MS-67 FBL. *Extremely* rare in MS-67. Only a few examples have been certified by NGC, and two have been certified by PCGS. These coins offer the typical, relatively soft strike for the date, although the surfaces can best be described as immaculate in terms of bagmarks. All these coins have attractive color toning.

The 1953-S is unknown in MS-67 FBL.

Valuation—The few gorgeous color-toned **MS-67s** to surface, given their rarity and desirability, have sold for between $4,000 and $7,000.

1953-S Repunched Mintmark Variety (FS-001)

A secondary S can be seen northwest of the primary S. This is a scarce RPM and the only one known for this date. Die markers include various horizontal die scratches seen through the mintmark.

❧ 1954-P, MINT STATE ❧

MS-65+ FBL

Original brilliant Uncirculated rolls are now far more elusive than they were 15 or 20 years ago. When a roll does surface, the general quality of the coins is good, with the average grade MS-63 to MS-64, and many coins FBL, though a surprising percentage may be less than FBL. Luster is excellent for this date.

NGC CERTIFIED POPULATION *(from a total mintage of 13,188,202)* (WCG™)

MS-64	MS-65	MS-66	MS-67	MS-68
903	1,160	58	0	0
MS-64 FBL	**MS-65 FBL**	**MS-66 FBL**	**MS-67 FBL**	**MS-68 FBL**
294	219	8	0	0

MS-60–MS-63 and MS-60 FBL–MS-63 FBL. Brilliant Uncirculated 1954-P Franklin halves generally do not fall into the lowest MS-60–MS-62 grade range, as bagmarks are slightly less prevalent than average for Philadelphia Mint coins. Approximately half the coins may be FBL.

Valuation—Roll bid in this grade.

MS-64 and MS-64 FBL. The 1954-P is elusive in this Mint State grade. About 50% of Mint State examples will grade FBL. A large percentage will have good luster and eye appeal for the date and grade, though many brilliant examples possess moderate water spotting. Toned coins from Mint sets are usually average in eye appeal. Beautiful color-toned pieces do exist but are very, very scarce, and worth a strong premium.

Valuation—$75 to $150 depending on the eye appeal for brilliant **MS-64 FBL** examples. Superbly toned pieces may be three to five times more!

MS-65 and MS-65 FBL. A date increasingly elusive in superb gem condition, with or without bell lines. Brilliant and toned examples are about equal in number. When found toned, the 1954-P offers average eye appeal. Exceptional color pieces are very rare. Brilliant coins often evidence light water spotting. Quite often this can safely be removed through careful conservation.

Valuation—There is great upside (potential for appreciation) for the **MS-65 FBL,** with attractive brilliant specimens still selling in the area of $275+, and non-FBL **MS-65s** for about half that number.

MS-66 and MS-66 FBL. The 1954-P is an extremely scarce coin in MS-66 or MS-66 FBL. Fully brilliant MS-66s and MS-66 FBLs are extremely rare, and represent perhaps only 10% of the meager MS-66/MS-66 FBL population. The balance (approximately 90%) offer toning ranging from average to stunning. Unfortunately, most have only average eye appeal. A 1954-P in MS-66 or MS-66 FBL with exceptional color toning is an *extremely rare* coin.

Valuation—$300 to $500 for the average toned **MS-66.** As most **MS-66 FBL** coins are average in eye appeal, with subdued Mint set toning, they often sell for as little as $1,000 to $2,000. However, a superb, haze-free brilliant coin may go for $3,000 to $5,000, and the finest color-toned coins have sold for close to $10,000.

MS-67 and MS-67 FBL. The 1954-P is extremely rare at this level, with only three graded in MS-67 FBL.

⊸⊸⇒ 1954-D, MINT STATE ⇐⊸⊸

MS-67

If one is seeking out original brilliant Uncirculated Franklin rolls, the 1954-D will rank among the easier dates to locate. Virtually all examples will be boldly struck, with well-cut bell lines. Unfortunately, the coins will also likely be extremely baggy, typical of Denver Mint Franklin halves throughout the life of the series, while also displaying serious water spotting that often cannot be removed.

NGC CERTIFIED POPULATION *(from a total mintage of 25,445,580)* (WCG™)

MS-64	MS-65	MS-66	MS-67	MS-68
976	930	22	1	0
MS-64 FBL	MS-65 FBL	MS-66 FBL	MS-67 FBL	MS-68 FBL
883	527	23	1	0

MS-60–MS-63 and MS-60 FBL–MS-63 FBL. The most common condition for this date. Bagmarks, bagmarks, and more bagmarks—that is basically the story of this date.
Valuation—Roll bid.

MS-64 and MS-64 FBL. Most examples of the 1954-D that grade MS-64 are also FBL. Among the most common dates in the series in MS-64 FBL, most are brilliant but for the aforementioned water spots, which can be quite distracting. A brilliant, spot-free MS-64 FBL 1954-D is a scarce coin. Attractively toned 1954-D Franklin halves in MS-64 FBL are rare.
Valuation—Like all nice **MS-64 FBL** Franklins, this is a date in great demand, and a tremendous value at $50 to $100 for spot-free blazers—substantially more for color coins, though!

MS-65 and MS-65 FBL. Moderately scarce in gem condition, the 1954-D can rank among the most attractive dates in the series when found in fully brilliant condition. *The bold strike of the typical 1954-D, the brilliant, often semi-prooflike surfaces, and the sharp detail make this an exceptional type coin—when found without the aforementioned water spotting.*

When found in toned condition, the 1954-D MS-65 or MS-65 FBL is typically of average eye appeal, relatively colorless. Exceptional color-toned examples are very rare.

Valuation—**MS-65s** can still be acquired for around $100 to $125—a bargain at current levels. Superb, spot-free **MS-65 FBL** gems are $350 to $500 and rising. Color coins? Good luck finding one with superb color. I paid more than $1,000 for a gorgeous piece in MS-65 FBL around the year 2004.

MS-66 and MS-66 FBL. While scarce in MS-65 condition, the 1954-D is extremely scarce in MS-66 or MS-66 FBL condition—especially with eye appeal. Of the handful of examples certified in this grade, most exhibit average toning. Brilliant examples are typically less than fully brilliant, with light haze. A 100% blast-white or attractively toned 1954-D is a rare coin.

Valuation—The **MS-66** is a $400–$600 coin with brilliant surfaces, and attractive color coins are in the same range, unless the color is really extraordinary. Given the mediocre eye appeal of the typical Mint set–toned **MS-66 FBL,** these coins usually trade in the $500 to $1,000 range. On the other hand, superb color coins may sell for even more, up to $2,000 to $4,000 for the most beautiful specimens. Superb brilliant coins can bring $1,000 to $2,000.

MS-67 and MS-67 FBL. Extremely rare. A mere four examples have received this grade to date in FBL by PCGS and NGC combined. All examples display some degree of toning.

Valuation—A good starting point for an **MS-67 FBL** is $15,000; depending on the coin, it may sell for a little less than that amount, or a little more.

⇒ 1954-S, MINT STATE ⇐

MS-66 FBL

The 1954-S is among the lowest-mintage issues in the series. When an original brilliant Uncirculated roll is encountered, most coins will be relatively mark free, grading MS-63 to MS-65. On the downside, as is typical of S-Mint Franklin halves, most examples are also very softly struck, without bell lines.

NGC CERTIFIED POPULATION *(from a total mintage of 4,993,400)* (WCG™)

MS-64	MS-65	MS-66	MS-67	MS-68
1,148	4,591	380	11	0
MS-64 FBL	**MS-65 FBL**	**MS-66 FBL**	**MS-67 FBL**	**MS-68 FBL**
39	45	6	0	0

MS-60–MS-63 and MS-60 FBL–MS-63 FBL. It is unusual to find a Mint State 1954-S in the lowest Mint State grades. An average brilliant Uncirculated roll is likely to contain at least a couple of MS-65s, with most examples grading MS-63 and MS-64. Unfortunately, it is unlikely any of the coins will be FBL.

Valuation—Roll bid for **non-FBL** coins. An **MS-63 FBL** sells for $40 to $70.

MS-64 and MS-64 FBL. While relatively easy to locate in MS-64, the 1954-S is scarce in MS-64 with full bell lines. Most examples are relatively brilliant. Attractively toned examples are very scarce with or without bell lines.

Valuation—Little over roll bid for **MS-64** non-FBL coins. This date is in great demand in the marketplace in **MS-64 FBL**, and in short supply, and is currently trading in the $100–$160 range and rising.

MS-65 and MS-65 FBL. The 1954-S ranks among the most common dates in MS-65 condition, but among the rarer dates in MS-65 with full bell lines. Most examples in MS-65 or MS-65 FBL are brilliant or nearly so. Mint set–toned pieces with full bell lines are extremely rare, as most 1954-S Franklin halves pulled from Mint sets are softly struck. Superb color-toned 1954-S Franklin half dollars in gem, or gem with full bell lines, are rare, with perhaps only 1% of certified MS-65s exhibiting exceptional color.

Valuation—The last of the S-Mints, this is a red-hot date in **MS-65**: still only $60 to $100 a coin. **MS-65 FBL** coins with solid bell lines are between $300 and $600 in brilliant condition.

MS-66 and MS-66 FBL. Semi-scarce in MS-66, most examples are brilliant and fairly well struck, though not quite FBL. The 1954-S is extremely scarce in MS-66 FBL, and is rare in MS-66 FBL with either fully brilliant haze-free surfaces or attractive color toning.

Valuation—$300 to $600 for the typical brilliant specimen. **MS-66 FBL** coins with below-average eye appeal may sell for under $1,000. Exceptional brilliant coins or color coins, with strong bell lines, have recently sold for $2,000 to $4,000.

MS-67 and MS-67 FBL. Extremely rare. Only a handful of examples have been certified in MS-67, with only three examples certified in MS-67 FBL.

Valuation—The finest PCGS **MS-67 FBL** I've handled sold for more than $20,000 around the year 2000. More recently, an example was listed for more than $30,000.

⤙⤙ 1955-P, Mint State ⤚⤚

MS-67 FBL

This is the lowest-mintage issue in the series. When original brilliant Uncirculated rolls are encountered, the coins are typically quite baggy. Most examples will exhibit considerable scruffiness on the high points of Franklin's cheek and lower jaw. Strike is generally excellent, and a majority of examples will have complete bell lines. It is unlikely that one will find a single MS-65 gem 1955-P in an original roll.

NGC CERTIFIED POPULATION *(from a total mintage of 2,498,181)* (WCG™)

MS-64	MS-65	MS-66	MS-67	MS-68
1,451	1,320	111	2	0
MS-64 FBL	MS-65 FBL	MS-66 FBL	MS-67 FBL	MS-68 FBL
767	372	35	2	0

MS-60–MS-63 and MS-60 FBL–MS-63 FBL. This is the most common grade range for this date. As noted, the 1955-P in brilliant condition is noteworthy for the high-point scruffiness on Franklin's cheek and lower jawbone. Mint set-toned examples generally grade a point higher, and typically feature darker, subdued colors.

Valuation—Roll bid for this date in **non-FBL** or **FBL**.

MS-64 and MS-64 FBL. Semi-scarce. Most examples are brilliant, though usually spotted. Fully brilliant, spot-free, haze-free 1955-P Franklin halves in either MS-64 or MS-64 FBL are more elusive and worth a premium over the typical MS-64. Attractively toned 1955-P Franklin halves in MS-64 or MS-64 FBL are extremely scarce and and worth a strong premium, representing at most 1 or 2 percent of the MS-64 population.

Valuation—Roll bid for an **MS-64**. This date is in strong demand in **MS-64 FBL**, especially when brilliant or attractively toned. These coins will trade for between $65 and $150—and knockout color coins have sold for more than $500!

MS-65 and MS-65 FBL. These are scarce and a tremendous value at current price levels when found with above-average eye appeal. Again, the majority of 1955-P Franklin halves in MS-65 or MS-65 FBL exhibit either dark, subdued Mint set toning or brilliant, spotted surfaces. Attractively toned examples or fully brilliant, haze-free, spot-free examples are extremely elusive and worth a premium.

Valuation—$50 to $75 in **MS-65.** Given the scarcity of fully brilliant **MS-65 FBL** coins, these coins are in strong demand in the $200–$400 range. Beautiful color coins can be even more—I recently purchased a gorgeous rainbow MS-65 FBL for $1,100. Again representing perhaps 1% of the MS-65 FBL population, a couple of the prettiest examples recently sold for almost $2,000!

MS-66 and MS-66 FBL. This is a tough coin to find in MS-66 or MS-66 FBL. Again, most examples display disappointing eye appeal. Most are Mint set toned, and the toning is usually dark and subdued, lacking the iridescent brilliance often seen on Mint set–toned Franklin halves from 1956 through 1958. Examples with exceptional color toning are rare and worth a strong premium. Fully brilliant 1955-P Franklin halves in MS-66 and MS-66 FBL are extremely rare—I have handled just two or three such examples in the past 15 years.

Valuation—$100 to $200 for the typical Mint set **MS-66.** Most **MS-66 FBL** coins trade for between $300 and $500—these are the coins whose toning has average eye appeal. At the other end of the spectrum, the occasional rainbow-color coin may sell for over $2,000. Rarest of all are the 1955-P MS-66 FBLs in fully brilliant condition. Given their extreme rarity, representing perhaps 2 to 3% of the MS-66 FBL population, they are easy sellers for upward of $5,000.

MS-67 and MS-67 FBL. Extremely rare. Only a few examples have been certified in MS-67 FBL by NGC and PCGS. All are Mint set toned with attractive color.

Valuation—The last **MS-67 FBL** I handled, in the year 2005, sold for $10,000.

1955-P "Bugs Bunny" Variety

Known as the "Bugs Bunny," this is probably the most sought-after Mint State Franklin variety. Only a tiny percentage of the 1955-P population is this variety, perhaps 1% to 2%. Most are very low quality, with considerable scruffiness on the high points. Weak strikes are the rule.

MS-66 FBL CAC

Brett Parrish offers the following information on this variety:

The Bugs Bunny is probably the most popular and best-known variety in the Franklin series. It is so named because it appears as if there are teeth protruding from Ben's mouth. These "teeth" are the result of a die clash. A die clash occurs when the obverse and reverse dies strike each other without a planchet between them. When this happens, some of the design elements are transferred from one die to the other. In this case, the eagle's wings left a toothlike impression in the mouth area.

Bugs Bunnys can be found on a number of different years, with 1955 being the most common. Other dates known with this anomaly are the following: 1949, 1951, 1952, 1953, 1954, 1954-D, 1954-S, 1956, 1959, and 1963. Some of these are very scarce and command high premiums. There very well may be more dates yet to be discovered. This is a neat variety, and a lot of collectors putting together a complete set of Franklins are now including this variety.

MS-60–MS-63 and MS-60 FBL–MS-63 FBL. Most Bugs Bunny 1955-P Franklins fall into this grade range.

Valuation—Non-FBL **MS-63** coins will command about double roll bid. **MS-63 FBL** coins are now up to $50 to $100 a coin.

MS-64 and MS-64 FBL. The Bugs Bunny is elusive in this grade, especially in MS-64 FBL. Water spots are very common on MS-64 FBL coins.

Valuation—**MS-64s** currently sell for $75 to $150 and rising! **MS-64 FBL** coins are now up to $250 to $400 in brilliant condition and rising.

MS-65 and MS-65 FBL. A tough coin in this grade. Most examples feature unattractive, lifeless toning. Attractive blazers are rare, and stunning color coins rarer still.

Valuation—Unattractive **MS-65s** will still command $150 to $300, about double that in FBL. Haze-free brilliant coins in MS-65 are currently $250 to $500, and **MS-65 FBLs** are $700 to $1,000—and climbing. Magnificent color coins are so rare that the price is generally negotiated between buyer and seller.

MS-66 and MS-66 FBL. Very rare. Virtually every example is toned, and most have average eye appeal.

Valuation—I sold a magnificent color coin in **MS-66** in early 2010 for $2,500. The finest color coins in **MS-66 FBL** have sold for $4,000 to $6,000.

MS-67 and MS-67 FBL. None have been graded.

1956-P, MINT STATE

MS-67 FBL

Brilliant Uncirculated rolls of the 1956-P are typically slightly above average in quality for Philadelphia issues. Bagmarks are moderate. Many examples will be FBL, though at least half of the coins may be too weakly struck for FBL status.

NGC CERTIFIED POPULATION *(from a total mintage of 4,032,000)* (WCG™)

MS-64	MS-65	MS-66	MS-67	MS-68
2,239	1,783	514	36	0
MS-64 FBL	MS-65 FBL	MS-66 FBL	MS-67 FBL	MS-68 FBL
1,057	402	96	3	0

MS-60–MS-63 and MS-60 FBL–MS-63 FBL. The most common grade range for this issue. It is unusual to find a 1956-P in the lowest MS-60–MS-61 grades.

Valuation—Roll bid, unless it has nice color.

MS-64 and MS-64 FBL. The 1956-P is easily obtainable in MS-64, though much more elusive in MS-64 with full bell lines. Brilliant examples with light spotting are the rule. Fully brilliant spot-free examples can be surprisingly difficult to locate. Most of the toned 1956-P Franklin halves originate from Mint sets. While most toned examples are average in eye appeal, on occasion superb color coins do surface. Deep purple and blue are a couple of the lovelier colors found on the prettier examples.

Valuation—This issue is much in demand in **MS-64 FBL** with brilliant surfaces or attractive color. The former have appreciated into the $75–$120 range; exceptional color coins may be four to five times that range, or more, depending on how exceptional the toning.

MS-65 and MS-65 FBL. Semi-scarce in MS-65, this issue is increasingly elusive in MS-65 FBL. Most examples are lightly spotted brilliant coins. *Fully brilliant, problem-free specimens can be a challenge to locate. Superb color coins are even more elusive, and worth a strong premium.*

The gradual wearing of the original master die—the die used to create all the subsequent working dies for both the Mint State and Proof Franklin half dollars, and in use since 1948—is evident on the 1956-P Franklin. Even fully struck examples of this date will not have the high-point definition found on Franklin's hair and the Liberty Bell of Franklin halves struck in the early 1950s and before. The master die, now almost a decade old, was simply wearing out. It would be another three years before the Mint would decide to do something about this problem, at which point it would rework the master die for the 1960 Franklin coinage.

Valuation—Brilliant **MS-65s** typically are in great demand. Their limited supply has pushed these halves to around $100 (still a great bargain!). **MS-65 FBLs** with fully brilliant surfaces are $250 to $400. Color coins can be more than $1,000.

MS-66 and MS-66 FBL. The 1956-P in MS-66 or MS-66 FBL is now very, very scarce. Most are average in eye appeal, though occasionally a superb color coin will surface. *These latter coins are extremely elusive on today's market, and worth a strong premium*. Rarer still is the 1956-P MS-66 FBL with fully brilliant surfaces. I would be fortunate to handle even one such example a year.

Valuation—As little as $50 to $120 for an average color piece in **MS-66**. Below-average toners are now trading for between $150 and $300 in **MS-66 FBL**. Attractive color coins in **MS-66 FBL** have traded for anywhere from $700 to $2,000, depending on how breathtaking the color is. A fully brilliant MS-66 FBL 1956-P is a rare bird. The few examples I have handled in the past couple years have sold at $1,500 to $2,000.

MS-67 and MS-67 FBL. Rare. Surprisingly, most 1956-P Franklin halves in either MS-67 or MS-67 FBL are no more attractive than the average MS-66. A 1956-P in MS-67 or MS-67 FBL with exceptional color toning is extremely rare—I have handled but two or three examples that would merit the description, back in the 1980s when PCGS and NGC first opened their doors. This date is unknown in MS-67 with fully brilliant surfaces.

Valuation —$500 to $1,000 for average color coins in **MS-67**. The typical Mint set–toned **MS-67 FBL** generally trades for between $3,000 and $8,000. Superb color specimens are extremely rare, and will understandably sell for more than these levels.

1956 DOUBLED-DIE OBVERSE VARIETY (FS-002)

A fairly common variety available in gem condition with or without FBL, this is the only business-strike doubled die known for this year. Doubling shows as extra thickness on LIBERTY, IN GOD WE TRUST, and the date. Die chips in the E of LIBERTY make this one easy to identify. Die markers include a circular die scratch from back of head; circular die scratch under Y of LIBERTY; various die scratches on reverse; and die chips above and in the upper and lower E of LIBERTY.

⊷⇒ 1957-P, Mint State ⇐⊶

MS-66 FBL

A tougher roll to locate than the 1956-P, the 1957-P is also usually of lower quality. While bagmarks are moderate and similar to the 1956-P, the strike of the 1957-P is below average for the Philadelphia Mint. Most examples are not FBL.

NGC CERTIFIED POPULATION *(from a total mintage of 5,114,000)* (WCG™)

MS-64	MS-65	MS-66	MS-67	MS-68
972	1,602	479	24	1
MS-64 FBL	**MS-65 FBL**	**MS-66 FBL**	**MS-67 FBL**	**MS-68 FBL**
87	93	46	3	0

MS-60–MS-63 and MS-60 FBL–MS-63 FBL. The most common grade for this issue. It is unusual to find a 1957-P in the lowest MS-60–MS-61 grades.

Valuation—Roll bid, unless it has color.

MS-64 and MS-64 FBL. Like the 1956-P, the 1957-P is easily obtainable in MS-64, though the 1957-P is even more elusive in MS-64 FBL than the former date. *The 1957-P is especially scarce in MS-64 FBL with fully brilliant surfaces.* When found in toned condition, most examples are comparable in eye appeal to the 1956-P.

Valuation—**MS-64s** are not really in demand. **MS-64 FBL** 1957-Ps are in high demand, and there is little supply. The average color coin sells for $50 to $100. Brilliant specimens will be $125 to $150.

MS-65 and MS-65 FBL. Semi-scarce in MS-65, the 1957-P is scarce in MS-65 FBL. Most gems are Mint set toned. A 1957-P with exceptional color toning is *extremely* scarce. While the 1957-P is semi-scarce in brilliant MS-65, it is extremely scarce in brilliant MS-65 FBL—I may handle only two to three such examples a year.

This is a great date in FBL at current price levels with either exceptional color toning or fully brilliant, haze-free surfaces.

Valuation—A $35–$75 coin in **MS-65,** whether brilliant or with average color. **MS-65 FBL** coins with average color are $110 to $200. Attractive color coins can be triple that range, or more. *Fully brilliant MS-65 FBL coins are steadily rising in value, as these coins are very few and far between, and there are many collectors seeking them out.* A recent example I handled sold for $450.

MS-66 and MS-66 FBL. This issue is about as rare as the 1956-P in both MS-66 and MS-66 FBL with Mint set–toned surfaces. Examples with exceptional color toning are approximately as rare as well. The 1957-P sets itself apart from the 1956-P in its rarity in MS-66 FBL with fully brilliant surfaces. As elusive as the 1956-P is in this ultimate brilliant state (no example has ever graded higher than MS-66 FBL), the 1957-P is rarer still. I have handled perhaps four or five examples in this condition over the past 20 years.

Valuation—$50 to $125 in **MS-66** with average color. **MS-66 FBL** coins with pleasing Mint set color are selling for $250 to $500. Exceptional color coins have gone as high as $1,500 to $2,500 of late. I recently handled a fully brilliant MS-66 FBL. That coin sold for more than $4,000.

MS-67 and MS-67 FBL. Very rare—again, similar in rarity to the 1956-P. All known examples are toned, most if not all from Mint sets. The toning ranges from average in eye appeal to breathtaking. The latter are extremely rare—only a few such pieces are known to exist. The prettier examples are typically found in deep shades of purple, blue, and golden amber.

Valuation—Almost a twin to the 1956-P. Prices range from $500 to $1,000 for average color coins in **MS-67.** The typical Mint set–toned **MS-67 FBL** generally trades for between $3,000 and $6,000. Superb color specimens are extremely rare, and will understandably sell for more than these levels. *The 1957-P is unknown in brilliant MS-67 or MS-67 FBL.*

→ ✑ 1957-D, Mint State ✑ ←

MS-67 FBL

More common than the 1957-P, the 1957-D is typical of the Denver Mint issues—great strikes and baggy surfaces. However, this particular Denver issue is a bit above average in quality compared to Denver Mint issues from the early 1950s. If a truly original roll is acquired, there is a reasonable chance there may be a gem or two—and they will likely be FBL.

NGC CERTIFIED POPULATION *(from a total mintage of 19,966,850)*   (WCG™)

MS-64	MS-65	MS-66	MS-67	MS-68
690	929	223	3	0
MS-64 FBL	MS-65 FBL	MS-66 FBL	MS-67 FBL	MS-68 FBL
650	468	98	6	0

MS-60–MS-63 and MS-60 FBL–MS-63 FBL. Deep gouges and scrapes are common on this Denver Mint coin. MS-62 to MS-63 with bell lines is the most common grade range.

Valuation—This issue is not in demand in these lower grades, unless the coin has exceptional color toning.

MS-64 and MS-64 FBL. Among the more common dates in the series in MS-64, the 1957-D is usually FBL as well. While the majority of MS-64 FBL coins are from brilliant Uncirculated rolls, most of these coins also have the water-spot problem so common on brilliant Uncirculated Franklin halves of the 1952–1963 period. Mint set–toned examples can be among the least attractive in the series—drab, dull gray toned 1957-D Franklin halves are typical. At the same time, spectacular iridescent toned examples exist. Some of the more breathtaking pieces display bright hues of crimson, apple green, and golden orange. Unfortunately, while one side of the coin may display this beautiful color, all too often the other side will offer the very disappointing gray-brown surfaces.

A 1957-D in *any* grade with exceptional color on both obverse and reverse is a rare coin—and obviously very desirable.

Valuation—An **MS-64** will command a premium if it has color. **MS-64 FBL** coins are elusive in brilliant condition, or with attractive color. The former are now in the $60 to $90 range; the latter may sell for upward of $300.

MS-65 and MS-65 FBL. This is among the most common dates in the series in MS-65 and MS-65 FBL. If you are building a brilliant set, hold out for a spot-free example. They do surface from time to time, though these coins are definitely more elusive than a decade ago. Considering their growing scarcity, the prices are still very reasonable.

While most Mint set–toned 1957-D Franklin halves are unappealing, monster color coins do pop up from time to time, though not with the frequency they did back in the 1990s and earlier. If you do come across a superb color piece in MS-65 or MS-65 FBL, be prepared to pay a strong premium. *This is a great date: the finest color coins will rank among the most spectacular in a top set—if you can find one.*

Valuation—Given that most gems feature unattractive Mint set toning, **MS-65s** in this condition will sell for as little as $40 to $60, and **MS-65 FBLs** for double that range. Fully brilliant blazers will sell for considerably more, and are now usually trading for between $250 and $350. The finest color coins have sold for more than $1,000.

MS-66 and MS-66 FBL. This is a very scarce issue. Most MS-66 and MS-66 FBL 1957-D Franklin halves display average or below average toning. The finest color-toned examples are extremely rare, and highly recommended—but be prepared to pay for them. This date is extremely rare in MS-66 and MS-66 FBL with fully brilliant surfaces as well. The last example I handled (in 2006) sold for approximately $2,000.

Valuation—Given that most examples feature very dull Mint set toning, these **MS-66** examples generally sell in the $50–$100 range. Similarly toned **MS-66 FBL** specimens are currently $150 to $300. Beautiful color toners may sell for more than $500 in MS-66 and more than $2,500 in MS-66 FBL. A fully brilliant 1957-D in MS-66 FBL is currently about a $2,000 coin!

MS-67 and MS-67 FBL. Extremely rare—even tougher than the 1957-P in this top grade. *All known examples are Mint set toned.* Of the couple I have handled in the past several years, both displayed beautiful iridescent color toning in shades of bright green, crimson, and golden amber—on both the obverse and reverse surfaces.

Valuation—With average toning, expect prices of $800 to $1,500 in **MS-67 FBL**. On the other hand, beautiful rainbow-toned coins, which are extremely rare, continue to appreciate, with a couple selling for more than $8,000.

⊷⊷ 1958-P, Mint State ⊷⊷

MS-66 FBL

The 1958-P is similar in quality and rarity to the 1957-P, except in strike—*the 1958-P is the weakest-struck Philadelphia issue of the 1948–1960 era.*

1958 Type 1 and 2 Varieties. The 1958 and 1959 business strikes are also known with two different reverse types. The Type 1's are the standard reverse used on all business strikes. The Type 2's are actually retired Proof dies. The same diagnostics can be used to differentiate these as on the 1956 Proofs. For 1958, the Type 2 is the scarcer variety, and it is estimated that 20% of the total mintage is made up of these. Gems are tough to find because the Mint sets for this year all contained Type 1's. Examples with FBLs are very rare, possibly as rare as the 1953-S, but until grading services recognize these varieties there is no way to know for sure.

NGC CERTIFIED POPULATION *(from a total mintage of 4,042,000)* (WCG™)

MS-64	MS-65	MS-66	MS-67	MS-68
1,406	1,923	801	28	0
MS-64 FBL	**MS-65 FBL**	**MS-66 FBL**	**MS-67 FBL**	**MS-68 FBL**
117	116	88	3	0

MS-60–MS-63 and MS-60 FBL–MS-63 FBL. Light scuffing and scrapes are common on this Philadelphia issue. MS-62 to MS-63 without bell lines is the most common grade range.

Valuation—No premium exists in these lower grades, unless the coin features attractive color toning.

MS-64 and MS-64 FBL. This issue is extremely common in MS-64, but surprisingly scarce in MS-64 with full bell lines. *Strike is a major problem for this date.* When found in MS-64 FBL, the 1958-P is likely to be a Mint set–toned coin. Occasionally the color will be quite attractive, with deep blues and burgundys dominating. The 1958-P is *very* scarce in MS-64 FBL with fully brilliant surfaces—it is not a common date in this condition by any means.

Valuation—A premium exists in **MS-64** if it has color. **MS-64 FBL** coins get a strong premium—brilliant coins are now at least $150 to $200. Average color-toned MS-64 FBL 1958-Ps generally trade for around $75.

MS-65 and MS-65 FBL. A more common date in MS-65. Most examples will be Mint set toned. The 1958-P is scarce in MS-65 with fully brilliant surfaces. MS-65 FBL examples of this date are considerably more elusive, which is understandable given the strike issues of this date. Again, Mint set–toned specimens constitute the majority of MS-65 FBL coins. The 1958-P is extremely scarce in MS-65 FBL with exceptional color. The finest of this type can be quite spectacular, with some offering lovely deep blue and purple hues.

Fully brilliant 1958-P MS-65 FBL Franklin halves border on rare. *Perhaps 1% of certified MS-65 FBLs are brilliant!* Original rolls, the source for such coins, are few in number. When a roll does surface, few coins will merit an FBL, and those that do generally grade MS-63 or MS-64. It has been many years since I pulled a gem FBL 1958-P from a brilliant Uncirculated roll.

There is extreme softness of detail on even the most boldly struck examples of this date, due to the worn nature of the master die.

Valuation—A $50 to $100 coin in either brilliant or toned **MS-65.** The premium explodes if the coin is an **MS-65 FBL**—*especially if it is brilliant.* Examples with average Mint-set toning go for around $150+, *but a fully brilliant example will easily sell for more than $500, and in my opinion is a bargain at $1,000. This date is almost impossible to find in this condition.* Most color-toned 1958-P Franklin halves in MS-65 FBL sell for between $150 and $350.

MS-66 and MS-66 FBL. The 1958-P ranks among the most common dates in the series in MS-66 condition. Virtually all are Mint set toned. While the majority of these Mint set–toned coins offer only average eye appeal, exceptional color-toned specimens do surface from time to time, and these merit a premium.

The 1958-P is *considerably* more elusive in MS-66 with full bell lines.. Mint set–toned examples dominate this population—a 1958-P MS-66 FBL in fully brilliant condition is *extremely rare.* I have handled only four examples since the inception of PCGS and NGC.

Valuation—$50 to $350 in **MS-66,** depending on the color. **MS-66 FBL** with relatively attractive color are easily selling for $300 to $800 or more—much more, if the color is really exceptional. This issue is so rare in brilliant MS-66 FBL that I have handled only four in the past 15 years. The last example sold for over $7,000.

MS-67 and MS-67 FBL. Rare in MS-67, the 1958-P is extremely rare in MS-67 with full bell lines. *All known examples are Mint set toned.* Most have attractive though not spectacular eye appeal. I have handled only one or two 1958-P Franklin halves in MS-67 FBL that could be described as outstanding color coins. This is a great date to tuck away in the highest MS-67 FBL with *superb* color.

Valuation—**MS-67** coins sell for $500 to $1,000. **MS-67 FBL** coins with attractive color easily sell for $6,000 to $12,000.

1958-D, MINT STATE

MS-67★ FBL

The 1958-D is very similar to the 1957-D in quality: most examples exhibit a great strike, though bagmarks are a significant problem. Water spots are a problem, though a typical brilliant Uncirculated roll will contain a large percentage of coins that will be spot free.

NGC CERTIFIED POPULATION *(from a total mintage of 23,962,412)* (WCG™)

MS-64	MS-65	MS-66	MS-67	MS-68
1,102	1,357	386	31	0
MS-64 FBL	**MS-65 FBL**	**MS-66 FBL**	**MS-67 FBL**	**MS-68 FBL**
511	448	200	9	0

MS-60–MS-63 and MS-60 FBL–MS-63 FBL. Another Denver Mint issue where deep gouges and scrapes are the rule rather than the exception. MS-62 to MS-63 with bell lines is the most common grade range.

Valuation—There is no premium in this grade unless the coin has attractive color.

MS-64 and MS-64 FBL. Most examples of the 1958-D that grade MS-64 are also FBL. Strike is almost never an issue. The population in this grade is about evenly split between Mint set–toned and brilliant coins. While many Mint State issues can be dull and unappealing, the finest examples rank among the most spectacular color-toned coins in the series. Legendary artist Peter Max couldn't have done a finer job: bright iridescent crimsons, greens, purples, golden-oranges—on occasion all those colors can be found on one coin. Of course, one can expect to pay a premium for such eye appeal.

Valuation—Color rules on MS-64 coins. **MS-64 FBL** brilliant coins that are relatively free of water spots are in strong demand, and easily sell for $50 to $100. Color coins can sell for five to ten times those amounts, as the finest color-toned 1958-D Franklins are among the prettiest coins in the series.

MS-65 and MS-65 FBL. As with the MS-64 grade, most examples of the 1958-D that grade MS-65 are also FBL, the ratio being about 70:30 FBL to non-FBL. Brilliant examples can be quite beautiful, compromised only by the lack of high-point definition on the devices—a reflection of the worn state of the original master die still in use since 1948.

If one is building a toned set, hold out for a multicolored wonder. Every Franklin collector should own a spectacular color 1958-D—such a coin will be the pride of many a collection, regardless of the grade on the holder.

Valuation—Brilliant **MS-65s** bring $50 to $100. **MS-65 FBL** coins with brilliant, relatively spot-free surfaces are now selling for $250 to $350, and are in great demand at these still very low price levels. Monster color coins in MS-65 FBL have sold for more than $1,000!

MS-66 and MS-66 FBL. A common date in MS-66, the 1958-D is the most common date in the series in MS-66 FBL. *Virtually all examples in this high Mint State grade are toned—brilliant MS-66 and MS-66 FBL 1958-D Franklin halves are very rare.* If one is building a color-toned set, a lovely 1958-D should rank among the prettiest coins in the set. Do not settle for a coin with average eye appeal: *pay the premium* for a knockout color coin. You will be glad you did.

Valuation—**MS-66s** with average color sell for as little as $60 to $100. Similarly toned **MS-66 FBL** examples are usually between $120 and $200. Multicolored rainbow examples may sell for $400 or more in MS-66, while a few MS-66 FBL coins with monster toning on the obverse and reverse have sold for more than $3,000, and continue to rise in value. Brilliant examples are also quite valuable and in demand, commanding $1,500 to $3,000.

MS-67 and MS-67 FBL. The 1958-D is the most common date in the series in MS-67 or MS-67 FBL, though still a rare coin. *There are no common-date Franklin halves in MS-67.* There are no MS-68 1958-D Franklins.

All known examples are Mint set–toned pieces. The eye appeal for most of the MS-67s ranges from attractive to simply breathtaking. Feel very fortunate if you own one of the latter—an ultimate Franklin—an MS-67 or MS-67 FBL grade, with color that few coins in numismatics, in any series, can equal in beauty.

Valuation—A few stunning color coins in NGC **MS-67★** have sold for more than $3,000. The last exceptional color **MS-67 FBL** coins I have handled sold for more than $12,000. I sold one of the most beautiful examples to a client a few years ago for more than $10,000. What seemed like a high price then looks more like a bargain today!

1959-P, MINT STATE

MS-66★

Brilliant Uncirculated rolls of the 1959-P are available. Bagmarks, poor striking characteristics, and water spots are typical for this date.

NGC CERTIFIED POPULATION *(from a total mintage of 6,200,000)* (WCG™)

MS-64	MS-65	MS-66	MS-67	MS-68
1,154 (a)	1,433 (b)	39	4	1
MS-64 FBL	**MS-65 FBL**	**MS-66 FBL**	**MS-67 FBL**	**MS-68 FBL**
277	180	12	1	0

a. Includes two coins graded MS-64 PL. b. Includes one coin graded MS-65 PL.

MS-60–MS-63 and MS-60 FBL–MS-63 FBL. MS-62 to MS-64 is the most common grade range for this date. Most 1959-Ps are not well struck enough to be FBL.

Valuation—There is no significant premium in this grade, unless the coin has attractive color.

MS-64 and MS-64 FBL. While easy to find in MS-64, the 1959-P is considerably more elusive in MS-64 FBL. Most examples are brilliant.

The government-issue cardboard Mint set holders responsible for the majority of toned Franklin halves from the 1948–1958 era were discontinued for 1959 and later. Instead, Mint sets were issued in cellophane envelopes similar to those used for Proof coins of that era. This new inert packaging allowed Mint State and Proof coins to maintain much of their original luster and brilliance. As a result, superb toned examples are rare in any grade.

Valuation—A small 50% premium over roll bid exists for **MS-64** coins, while fully brilliant **MS-64 FBL** specimens, in very short supply, are $75 to $125.

MS-65 and MS-65 FBL. The 1959-P is a scarce coin in MS-65, and very scarce in MS-65 with full bell lines. When found in brilliant condition, most examples evince some degree of haze, water spotting, or both. A fully brilliant 1959-P in MS-65 FBL is extremely scarce. Rarer still is the 1959-P in MS-65 or MS-65 FBL with exceptional color toning. About the only source for such a coin would be a cardboard collector album or paper coin envelope, where the sulfur from the paper would react with the silver Franklin. The chances of a gem MS-65 or MS-65 FBL caliber coin being stored in such a manner are slim—especially for an FBL coin.

Valuation—$50 to $75 in **MS-65** with brilliant surfaces. Fully brilliant 1959-Ps in **MS-65 FBL** typically sell for between $300 and $475. Attractive color coins can sell for far more. So few ever surface in the marketplace that a price range is difficult to establish!

MS-66 and MS-66 FBL. *Rare* in either MS-66 or MS-66 FBL. The 1959-P is especially elusive in MS-66 FBL, and ranks among the rarest Franklin dates in this high grade from the 1948–1959 era, surpassed in rarity only by the 1949-D and 1953-S. The population of MS-66 and MS-66 FBL coins is split about evenly between brilliant and toned examples.

Valuation- -A brilliant NGC **MS-66** sold in a 2010 Heritage auction for $748. Extremely rare in **MS-66 FBL**, fully brilliant 1959-Ps have traded for anywhere from $2,500 to $6,000. Color coins generally sell in the same range—a bit less if the toning is below average.

MS-67 and MS-67 FBL. *Extremely* rare. Only five exist in MS-67, one in MS-67 FBL. All are toned. A single MS-68 has also been certified since the first edition.

Valuation—$2,000 and up for an **MS-67.** The value of the unique **MS-67 FBL** is whatever the buyer and seller can agree on.

1959 Type 1 and 2 Varieties

As has been noted, the 1958 and 1959 business strikes are known with two different reverse types. The Type 1's have the standard reverse used on all business strikes, while the Type 2's are retired Proof dies. The 1959 halves are common in both types: both can be found in rolls or Mint sets. There is also a Type 2/Type 1 class III "design hub doubling" doubled-die reverse, meaning that a die was hubbed with a Type 1 design and then hubbed with a Type 2. What resulted was an eagle that has characteristics of both types. As on the Type 2, the eagle has three wing tips left of the perch, but the look of the wings more resembles the Type 1 design.

1959-D, MINT STATE

MS-67 FBL

Brilliant Uncirculated rolls of the 1959-D are about as readily available as for the 1959-P. Excessive bagmarks—the plague of Denver Mint coins in the Franklin series—are the general rule for this date. Most examples are very well struck, and merit an FBL—once again typical of Denver-minted Franklin half dollars of the 1948–1959 era.

NGC CERTIFIED POPULATION *(from a total mintage of 13,053,750)*   (WCG™)

MS-64	MS-65	MS-66	MS-67	MS-68
957	834	13	1	0
MS-64 FBL	MS-65 FBL	MS-66 FBL	MS-67 FBL	MS-68 FBL
607	427	17	1	0

MS-60–MS-63 and MS-60 FBL–MS-63 FBL. MS-62 to MS-64 is the most common grade range for this date. Most 1959-Ds in this grade range will also be FBL.

Valuation—Roll bid in these lower grades.

MS-64 and MS-64 FBL. When a 1959-D is found in MS-64, it will also likely be FBL. This date ranks among the easiest to acquire in the series in MS-64 FBL. Most example are brilliant, with minor water spotting to be expected. Exceptional color-toned examples are very rare, and worth a significant premium.

Valuation—MS-64s are not in demand in, though a problem-free MS-64 1959-D should be worth at least a 50% premium over roll bid, much more if it exhibits attractive color toning. **MS-64 FBL** coins with minimal water spotting are in great demand: these typically sell for $75 to $125 in brilliant condition, and much more if they have nice color.

MS-65 and MS-65 FBL. Easier to find in MS-65 FBL than MS-65, the 1959-D ranks among the easier dates to locate in brilliant gem FBL. Most examples will have light haze or spotting. The 1959-D becomes considerably more challenging to locate in gem FBL if one is seeking out a superb color-toned specimen. These are rare. Again, the fact that the Mint switched to inert cellophane packaging instead of cardboard packaging, as was used in Mint sets of 1958 and earlier, accounts for the dearth of superb color-toned Franklin halves of this vintage.

Valuation—**MS-65** coins are typically brilliant and can be acquired for under $100. Spot-free blazers in **MS-65 FBL** have appreciated of late, and are usually between $200 and $350 when located.

MS-66 and MS-66 FBL. This issue is *rare* in MS-66 or MS-66 FBL, though not quite as challenging to find as the 1959-P. While most 1959-D Franklin halves evidence the usual cuts and dings commonly seen on Denver-minted Franklin half dollars, once in a while a 1959-D will surface with unusually clean, minimally marked surfaces. This is still a very rare coin in MS-66 FBL, but most examples will also be FBL. A beautifully toned 1959-D Franklin in MS-66 FBL is an extremely rare coin. Few pieces have been certified by either PCGS or NGC.

Valuation—**MS-66** coins sell for $400 to $700. **MS-66 FBL** coins with reasonably attractive color toning sell for $2,500 to $4,500. Exceptional color coins will sell for more. A brilliant MS-66 FBL 1959-D is $1,500 to $3,000.

MS-67 and MS-67 FBL. *Extremely* rare. I have handled only two examples. Both exhibited exceptional color toning. I also handled an amazing brilliant example in MS-67, with nearly full bell lines!

Valuation—The last **MS-67 FBL** I handled (around 2005) sold for $15,000.

A VIEW OF THE DECADE: THE 1960S

The 1960s were lively times in the numismatic hobby. In 1960, *Coin World*—the first weekly numismatic publication—made its debut. The year 1962 saw a surge of interest in coin collecting as the Philadelphia Mint released into circulation hundreds of thousands of silver dollars; extending from November of that year to March of 1964, the great Treasury release put hundreds of millions of Morgan and Peace dollars into the hands of the public.

The assassination in 1963 of President John F. Kennedy inspired a change in the design of the half dollar to honor the slain president; as a consequence, Congress made a special provision to discontinue the Benjamin Franklin design after only 16 years in circulation.

The San Francisco Mint, temporarily reinvented as the San Francisco Assay Office, resumed operation and began striking cents in 1965. The mid-decade spike in the value of silver, and the hoarding of silver coins that occurred, created the worst coin shortage since the Civil War. Mint Director Eva Adams blamed coin collectors for the shortage, although she would later come to recognize that the general public, more than numismatists, was responsible. In response to the crisis, President Lyndon Johnson signed into law the Coinage Act of 1965, which introduced clad coinage: this eliminated the silver content in the dime and quarter, and greatly reduced it in the half dollar. Proof sets were discontinued, and Special Mint Sets were released from 1965 through 1967 as a replacement; the following year, Proof sets were reintroduced.

⚜ 1960-P, MINT STATE ⚜

MS-65★ FBL

The year 1960 witnessed the introduction of the newly reworked master die for the Franklin series. Comparing a 1960-P or Denver Franklin to a 1959-P or Denver issue, the soft, mushy detail of the late 1950s Franklin half dollar offers a stark contrast to the sharp lines in Franklin's hair on the 1960 half. The Liberty Bell is also more detailed. Unfortunately, the bell lines on the reworked Franklin master die were not as deeply cut as on the original. *As a result, while most 1960-P Franklin half dollars are well struck, a significant percentage are not quite FBL.*

Brilliant Uncirculated rolls of the 1960-P are elusive. Expect the coins to have exceptional luster, and many have full bell lines. Light ticks and scrapes can be expected on all the coins.

MS-64	MS-65	MS-66	MS-67	MS-68
1,397	1,098	21	1	0
MS-64 FBL	**MS-65 FBL**	**MS-66 FBL**	**MS-67 FBL**	**MS-68 FBL**
228	77	0	0	0

MS-60–MS-63 and MS-60 FBL–MS-63 FBL. The 1960-P is an above-average-quality date in the series. Most brilliant Uncirculated examples do not grade as low as MS-60 to MS-61. MS-63 and MS-63 FBL are probably the average grades for this date.

Valuation—Of little interest to collectors in this grade, these are basically roll bid coins, unless attractively toned.

MS-64 and MS-64 FBL. The MS-64 and MS-64 FBL population for this date is about evenly split. The strike is a common problem, and the 1960-P is increasingly difficult to acquire in MS-64 FBL. Most will be brilliant, though many examples will exhibit light grease stains. Fortunately these are usually removable with gentle cleaning. As with all Mint State Franklin halves struck after 1958, this is a very difficult date to find in attractively toned condition in any grade. Be willing to pay a premium if a lovely color-toned MS-64 1960-P does present itself.

Valuation—A small 50% premium over roll bid exists for **MS-64** non-FBL coins. Spot-free brilliant **MS-64 FBL** specimens are now bringing $75 to $125. Given the tremendous rarity of exceptional color coins, these coins may trade at huge premiums.

MS-65 and MS-65 FBL. The 1960-P is extremely elusive at current price levels in either MS-65 or MS-65 FBL. While many examples from Mint sets or original rolls may initially give the appearance of being gem quality, careful scrutiny usually reveals just enough light ticks to drop the grade into MS-64. Minimally marked fully brilliant gems offer tremendous value at current levels. *Superb color coins are almost never encountered*, and are certainly worth a hefty premium to the color aficionado who understands such a coin's rarity and appreciates its eye appeal.

Valuation—**MS-65** gems are now bringing $100 to $200, and considerably more if they are attractively toned. This date has really dried up in fully brilliant **MS-65 FBL**. Exceptional examples have been selling for $350 to $600 of late. One magnificent color-toned example, an NGC MS-65★ FBL, sold for over $4,000.

MS-66 and MS-66 FBL. *Very* rare in either MS-66 or MS-66 FBL. There are simply very few 1960-P halves that exist with the near-mark-free surfaces required for an MS-66 Mint State Franklin. On the positive side, close to half the existing pieces are of the brilliant variety. Combined with the exceptional luster typical for this date, and the sharp design detail from the newly reworked master die, a 1960-P in MS-66 grade can rank among the loveliest coins in one's high-grade collection.

Valuation—$500 to $1,000 in **MS-66,** though a beautiful color coin can sell for more. Average color-toned **MS-66 FBL** specimens have been selling in the $3,000–$4,000 price range. Exceptional brilliant coins and color coins have sold for as high as $5,000 to $6,000.

MS-67 and MS-67 FBL. Only one is known in MS-67—a testimony to the aforementioned bagmark problem for this date.

1960-D, Mint State

MS-66 FBL

As noted earlier, the year 1960 witnessed the introduction of the reworked master die for the Franklin series. Compared to a Franklin half dollar of the late 1950s, halves made from the new master die offer a stark contrast, with sharp lines in Franklin's hair and a more detailed Liberty Bell.

While brilliant Uncirculated rolls of the 1960-D are among the easiest to acquire in the series, the general quality of these rolls is extremely low. Bagmarks are a major problem for this date. Luster is average, lacking the life and almost semi-prooflike brilliance of the 1960-P, and strike is among the weakest of the Denver Mint coins. A significant percentage of 1960-D Franklin halves are not FBL. Many examples will also display an annoying luster disturbance in the area of Franklin's jowl, the result of poor metal flow during striking.

NGC CERTIFIED POPULATION *(from a total mintage of 18,215,812)*   (WCG™)

MS-64	MS-65	MS-66	MS-67	MS-68
1,399	504	9	0	0
MS-64 FBL	MS-65 FBL	MS-66 FBL	MS-67 FBL	MS-68 FBL
374	75	0	0	0

MS-60–MS-63 and MS-60 FBL–MS-63 FBL. The most common grade. The majority of brilliant Uncirculated 1960-D Franklin halves fall into the lower MS-61–MS-63 grade range. The population is about evenly split between non-FBL and FBL.

Valuation—A modest 50% premium exists over roll bid for **MS-63 FBL** coins, but any with great color is worth a look. *Exceptional color coins are rare for this date.*

MS-64 and MS-64 FBL. The 1960-D is not a difficult date to locate in MS-64, but is becoming more elusive in MS-64 FBL. Most examples will be brilliant, but many will exhibit the disappointing water spotting so typical for the series. When toned coins do appear, they are usually below average in eye appeal, with rather dull coloration. An exceptional color-toned 1960-D is a very rare coin.

Valuation—There is a modest 50% premium over roll bid for an **MS-64.** Superb brilliant **MS-64 FBL** examples are in very short supply, and have appreciated into the $80–$125 range and climbing. Superb color coins can go for huge premiums. I was the under bidder in a 2008 Goldberg auction where an exceptional color-toned MS-64 FBL 1960-D realized *more than $2,000.*

MS-65 and MS-65 FBL. The 1960-D ranks among the most difficult Denver-minted coins to find in gem condition, with or without bell lines. Spot-free, fully brilliant examples are especially rare; most gems have some light water spotting or haze. Toned examples are average in eye appeal. Beautifully toned gems are extremely rare.

Perhaps the best known, most spectacularly toned 1960-D MS-65 FBL Franklin halves reportedly originated in a small mining town with a sulfur pit. There were five or six 1960-D Franklin halves stored in a small coin collection in this town that developed the most amazing bullseye rainbow toning on their obverse and reverse. One of those coins is pictured in appendix A.

Valuation—**MS-65** coins generally trade for between $100 and $300, depending on the eye appeal. Most **MS-65 FBL** coins have some haze and water spots, which drops their selling price into the $375–$600 range. A fully brilliant, problem-free gem may command $1,000 or more. The spectacular color coin shown in appendix A sold for over $7,000.

MS-66 and MS-66 FBL. Even rarer in MS-66 and MS-66 FBL than the 1960-P, few 1960-D Franklin halves have survived with the necessary bold strikes and minimally marked surfaces to earn the MS-66 grade. The majority of examples grading MS-66 are toned. The 1960-D is extremely rare in fully brilliant MS-66 or MS-66 FBL. I have handled but one such example since the inception of PCGS and NGC.

Valuation—**MS-66** examples are very rare and have sold for between $500 and $1,500. This date is in great demand in **MS-66 FBL.** The last couple of exceptional brilliant examples to appear on the market have sold in the $6,000–$12,000 range.

MS-67 and MS-67 FBL. A few years ago I handled the first-ever 1960-D Franklin in MS-67 FBL, a beautiful multi-colored rainbow coin. It now resides in the #1 Franklin collection on the PCGS Set Registry.

1961-P, MINT STATE

MS-66 FBL

Original brilliant Uncirculated rolls of the 1961-P are occasionally available. When a roll does surface, most if not all of the coins will have average to weak strikes and will lack bell lines. On the other hand, bagmarks are usually fewer than average for the series.

NGC CERTIFIED POPULATION *(from a total mintage of 8,290,000)*   (WCG™)

MS-64	MS-65	MS-66	MS-67	MS-68
1,275	1,472	31	4	0
MS-64 FBL	MS-65 FBL	MS-66 FBL	MS-67 FBL	MS-68 FBL
48	24	3	0	0

MS-60–MS-63 and MS-60 FBL–MS-63 FBL. The most common grade range. The majority of brilliant Uncirculated 1961-P Franklin halves fall into the lower MS-62–MS-63 grade range. Nearly all examples are not FBL.

Valuation—Because of the scarcity of these coins in FBL, **MS-63 FBL** coins are worth a premium, $30 to $50 at the current time.

MS-64 and MS-64 FBL. Easy to locate in MS-64, the 1961-P is considerably more elusive in MS-64 with full bell lines. Nearly all these coins are brilliant or with minimal toning. Occasionally a 1961 Mint set may yield an FBL coin. Along with the 1953-P, the Franklins of the 1961 to 1963 era are the poorest struck in the series' Philadelphia Mint coinage.

Valuation—**MS-64** coins are worth about a 100% premium over roll bid. **MS-64 FBL** coins are in great demand, currently selling for between $150 and $250, and are headed up! Superb color coins can sell for considerably more.

MS-65 and MS-65 FBL. The 1961-P is scarce in MS-65, and *among the rarest dates in the series* in MS-65 with full bell lines, ranking behind only the 1953-S, 1962-P, and 1963-P in rarity.

Most examples are brilliant, or nearly so. Beautifully toned examples are very rare.

Valuation—$100 to $200 in brilliant **MS-65**. Brilliant **FBL** coins usually sell for between $1,500 and $2,500. There are very few exceptional color coins in this grade.

MS-66 and MS-66 FBL. A rare coin in MS-66, and extremely rare in MS-66 FBL. I have handled only a few examples in the latter MS-66 FBL classification. Incredibly, two of these coins were fully brilliant, with an almost semi-prooflike finish, and bold strike throughout—almost a specimen in appearance.

Every other known MS-66 FBL 1961-P is toned, with average to slightly above-average coloration.

Valuation—Attractive **MS-66** examples bring $500 to $1,000. **MS-66 FBL** coins are in great demand, and always sell for premiums above price guide ranges. The last two 1961-Ps I have handled in this grade sold for between $10,000 and $16,000.

MS-67 and MS-67 FBL. Unknown.

1961-D, MINT STATE

MS-66

Original brilliant Uncirculated rolls of the 1961-P are among the more common rolls in the series. The typical 1961-D roll is of poor quality. Heavily bagmarked coins are the rule, although many may have full bell lines. Most examples will have water spots as well.

NGC CERTIFIED POPULATION *(from a total mintage of 20,276,442)* (WCG™)

MS-64	MS-65	MS-66	MS-67	MS-68
1,051	743	9	0	0
MS-64 FBL	MS-65 FBL	MS-66 FBL	MS-67 FBL	MS-68 FBL
199	70	2	0	0

MS-60–MS-63 and MS-60 FBL–MS-63 FBL. This is the most common grade range for the 1961-D. A typical 1961-D roll may have 19 coins in MS-60 to MS-63, some with bell lines, with perhaps a single MS-64.

Valuation—As with most of the higher-mintage Franklin dates in the series, the value of this date in the lower Mint State grades is highly dependent on bullion values. The 1961-D can be acquired in these lower grades for a modest premium over bullion.

MS-64 and MS-64 FBL. The MS-64 population of the 1961-D is about evenly split between non-FBL and FBL. Water spots are a problem. A fully brilliant MS-64 FBL 1961-D is scarce. A 1961-D in MS-64 FBL with attractive color toning is extremely scarce.

Valuation—Under $30 for **MS-64** non-FBL examples. 1961-D Franklin halves in **MS-64 FBL** are considerably more elusive. Most examples with the typical water spots currently trade in the $60–$100 range. Fully brilliant, spot-free blazers are worth a 50% premium above these levels—$100 to $200. Superb color coins may sell for many multiples of this value range, depending on the color.

MS-65 and MS-65 FBL. The 1961-D is almost as rare as the 1961-P in both MS-65 and MS-65 FBL. While a higher percentage of Mint State 1961-Ds exhibit full bell lines, the typical 1961-D is also quite a bit baggier than the average 1961-P. When a gem does surface, it is typically nearly brilliant with light spotting or fully brilliant. Attractively toned examples are extremely rare, and worth a significant premium.

Valuation—The 1961-D is a very tough coin to locate in MS-65, and even more challenging in MS-65 FBL. Current values are quite reasonable considering the difficulty factor. Fully brilliant, spot-free **MS-65** blazers can be acquired for under $150 to $300—a tremendous value. Try finding a couple at any major coin show. The 1961-D in **MS-65 FBL** is even more elusive than the 1960-D, and has recently passed that date in value. Finer, fully brilliant, spot-free specimens have been selling in the area of $800+. The typical hazy, spotted gems in FBL have been selling for about half that price. Superb color-toned gems can sell for multiples of those levels. In my opinion, the 1961-D is the most undervalued of the 1961 to 1963 Franklins at current prices.

MS-66 and MS-66 FBL. This is another very rare Franklin date in MS-66—with or without bell lines. The population is about evenly split between brilliant examples and toned ones. This is a great date to tuck away if one is fortunate enough to stumble across an MS-66 specimen, providing the surfaces are attractive, exhibiting either exceptional brilliance or beautiful color toning.

Valuation—$1,000+ for **MS-66** coins in non-FBL. **MS-66 FBL**s typically trade in the $5,000–$10,000+ range, depending on the eye appeal. Expect these values to rise. This is a very, very rare coin in either MS-66 or MS-66 FBL, and demand greatly exceeds the miniscule supply of these coins.

MS-67 and MS-67 FBL. Unknown.

1961-D Repunched Mintmark Variety (FS-001)

The secondary D is southeast of the primary D. This repunched mintmark variety can be located in Mint sets. Die markers include a long horizontal die scratch through mintmark and a diagonal die scratch to the right of the mintmark.

⇌ 1962-P, MINT STATE ⇌

MS-66

This is an increasingly elusive date to locate in almost any brilliant Uncirculated condition. Truly original rolls—not the put-together rolls one typically sees marketed as original—are extremely scarce. When such a roll does surface, the coins are usually of poor quality. Full bell line coins are the exception. Mint sets are a good source for brilliant Uncirculateds, but interestingly almost all the 1962-P Franklin halves one finds in original government Mint sets are weakly struck and of low grade.

NGC CERTIFIED POPULATION *(from a total mintage of 9,714,000)*   (WCG™)

MS-64	MS-65	MS-66	MS-67	MS-68
1,051	849	17	1	0
MS-64 FBL	**MS-65 FBL**	**MS-66 FBL**	**MS-67 FBL**	**MS-68 FBL**
61	12	1	0	0

MS-60–MS-63 and MS-60 FBL–MS-63 FBL. This is the most common grade range. Most examples are not FBL; FBLs comprise less than 5% of this population.

Valuation—The value of this date in the lower Mint State grades is highly dependent on bullion values. The 1962-P can be acquired in these lower grades for a modest premium over bullion. 1962 Mint sets are the best source for 1962-P Franklins in these lower Mint State grades.

MS-64 and MS-64 FBL. When located in MS-64 grade, the 1962-P is almost always softly struck. This is an extremely scarce coin in MS-64 with full bell lines. Most examples in this grade are brilliant or nearly so. Water spots are a major problem. Attractive color-toned examples are rare, and worth a strong premium.

Valuation—These are a great buy in **MS-64** at under $30. The coin is tougher than that. **MS-64 FBL** examples have doubled in value in the past few years due to the almost nonexistent supply, and are currently selling for $350 to $450 in bright, problem-free condition.

MS-65 and MS-65 FBL. An elusive coin in MS-65, the 1962-P is a rare coin in MS-65 FBL. The 1962-P and 1963-P are among the rarest Franklin dates in full bell line condition, ranking behind only the ultra-rare 1953-S.

Coin-counting machine rub is a major problem for this date. I have handled many a 1962-P featuring excellent, relatively mark-free, gem surfaces, with full bell lines, that unfortunately also possessed light hairlining on the cheek of Franklin, or on the Liberty Bell, from a counting machine.

The typical gems are brilliant. Many exhibit a lovely semi-prooflike luster. Water spots can be a problem. Attractively toned examples are extremely rare in either MS-65 or MS-65 FBL.

Valuation—This issue is among the big movers in the series in **MS-65 FBL,** with this date now firmly established as the second-rarest in the series. MS-65 FBL specimens are now selling for upward of $2,500 and climbing. This was a $1,500 coin only a few years ago. The 1962-P is also very scarce in **MS-65** without full bell lines, and offers outstanding potential at the current price of under $300.

Good luck in your hunt for a superb color-toned coin. If the color is really spectacular, the owner can just about name his price. It has been more than a decade since I handled an MS-65 FBL 1962-P with great color.

MS-66 and MS-66 FBL. A rare coin in MS-66, and *extremely* rare in MS-66 FBL. I may handle a single non-FBL MS-66 1962-P in a year. The last 1962-P to surface in this grade was an attractive, fully brilliant specimen.

Valuation—This is a $15,000+ coin in **MS-66 FBL** and excessively rare. I have handled only three MS-66 FBL 1962-P's in the past ten years. When another such coin surfaces, the price will have to be negotiated between the owner and the prospective buyer. Fortunately this date is available in MS-66 without the FBL designation, though the 1962-P is quite rare in this condition as well. Non-FBL **MS-66** coins can usually be acquired for under $1,000—a very good price considering the rarity.

MS-67 and MS-67 FBL. Unknown.

1962-D, Mint State

MS-66 FBL

Almost a twin to the 1961-D in strike, luster, and surface characteristics, the 1962-D ranks among the more readily available dates in roll form. Unfortunately, original rolls are not a good source for gem-quality coins. Bagmarks are plentiful, water spots are prominent, and strike is inconsistent. Original Mint sets offer a similar scenario.

NGC CERTIFIED POPULATION *(from a total mintage of 35,473,281)* (WCG™)

MS-64	MS-65	MS-66	MS-67	MS-68
1,370	956	8	0	0
MS-64 FBL	MS-65 FBL	MS-66 FBL	MS-67 FBL	MS-68 FBL
229	99	1	0	0

MS-60–MS-63 and MS-60 FBL–MS-63 FBL. Once again, this is the most common grade range. Roll quality is typical for the date.

Valuation—As with most of the higher-mintage Franklin dates in the series, the value of this date in the lower Mint State grades is highly dependent on bullion values. The 1962-D can be acquired in these lower grades for a modest premium over the bullion price.

MS-64 and MS-64 FBL. Readily available in MS-64, the 1962-D is more elusive in MS-64 with full bell lines. Most examples are brilliant, with prominent water spots. Fully brilliant examples, or coins with minimal spotting, should be the focus when acquiring this date. Exceptional color-toned examples of the 1962-D in this grade are extremely scarce.

Valuation—Under $30 for **MS-64** non-FBL examples. 1962-D Franklin halves in **MS-64 FBL** are considerably more elusive. Most examples with the typical water spots currently trade in the $60–$100 range. Fully brilliant, spot-free blazers are worth a 50% premium above these levels. Superb color coins may sell for many multiples of this value range, depending on the color.

MS-65 and MS-65 FBL. Very scarce in MS-65, and extremely scarce in MS-65 FBL. Once again, most examples in this grade will be relatively brilliant, with spotting and haze prevalent. A fully brilliant, gem 1962-D in FBL is a rare coin. More elusive still is the gem 1962-D with exceptional color toning, with or without bell lines. Be prepared to pay a very significant premium for an exceptional color coin in this grade.

Valuation—This is the grade where the date is really a challenge—with or without bell lines—and current values are quite reasonable considering the difficulty factor. Fully brilliant, spot-free **MS-65** blazers can be acquired for around $175—a tremendous value. Try finding a couple at any major coin show. Gem **MS-65 FBL** coins are tougher still. Finer known, fully brilliant spot-free specimens have been selling in the area of $600 to $900. The typical hazy, spotted gems in FBL have been selling for about half that price. A superb color-toned gem? The last example I handled that fit that description sold for more than $2,500. These are rare.

MS-66 and MS-66 FBL. Another very rare, key date in MS-66 or MS-66 FBL. Most examples in this grade are toned, with a couple of known examples featuring very attractive rainbow hues.

While there are many extremely scarce and rare Mint State Franklin dates in MS-66 FBL, the 1960-D, 1961-P, 1961-D, 1962-P, 1962-D, and 1963-P will prove to be extremely challenging coins to locate in this grade. Good luck—you'll need it!

Valuation—$1,000+ for **MS-66** coins in non-FBL. **MS-66 FBLs** typically trade in the $5,000–$10,000+ range, depending on the eye appeal. Expect these values to rise. This is a very, very rare coin in either MS-66 or MS-66 FBL, and demand greatly exceeds the miniscule supply of these coins.

MS-67 and MS-67 FBL. Unknown.

⋘ 1963-P, MINT STATE ⋙

MS-65 FBL

Next to the 1963-D, the 1963-P is the easiest date to locate in roll quantity. The quality of original roll 1963-Ps can on occasion be relatively good, with the occasional MS-65 (not FBL) that can be cherrypicked. FBL coins in these rolls are the exception. Mint sets reflect the general quality of this date. Most 1963-P Franklin halves in Mint sets are weakly struck and well bagmarked. On occasion, however, one can pluck an FBL from a set. Unfortunately, the coin will usually be lower than MS-64 in grade.

Water spots are less of a problem for the 1963-P, though they are still very common. Many 1963-P Franklin halves exhibit heavy die polishing.

NGC CERTIFIED POPULATION *(from a total mintage of 22,164,000)*   (WCG™)

MS-64	MS-65	MS-66	MS-67	MS-68
2,690	4,654	57	5	0
MS-64 FBL	**MS-65 FBL**	**MS-66 FBL**	**MS-67 FBL**	**MS-68 FBL**
62	21	1	0	0

MS-60–MS-63 and MS-60 FBL–MS-63 FBL. Once again, this is the most common grade range. Few examples in this grade range will be FBL.

Valuation—Sensitive to silver bullion values, the 1963-P in these grades can be acquired for a minimal premium over bullion.

MS-64 and MS-64 FBL. A very common coin in MS-64. A good-quality original roll may have 5 to 10 1963-P Franklin halves in this grade. Unfortunately, it is highly unlikely that any will exhibit full bell lines.

Looking for an attractively toned 1963-P in MS-64? Again, some patience will be required, as these coins are extremely scarce.

Valuation—**MS-64** examples can be acquired for as little as $20. Fully brilliant, spot-free **MS-64 FBL** coins are *considerably* more elusive, having appreciated considerably over the past few years, and in brilliant condition are now trading between $400 and $700, up from only $200 to $400 when the second edition of this book was published!

MS-65 and MS-65 FBL. Among the most common dates in the series in MS-65 condition, the 1963-P is still an elusive, scarce coin in this grade—it is just not as rare as other dates in the series.

Much more challenging to locate will be the very well-struck 1963-P in MS-65 grade with full bell lines. Many 1963-Ps exist with bell lines that are nearly complete, with the smallest fade area on the lower set midway between the crack in the bell and the left edge. Any weakness or fade on any portion of this lower set is enough to disqualify a coin from FBL status.

If one is intent on building a superb color-toned set of Franklin half dollars in MS-65, the 1963-P will be a challenge, though these coins do pop up from time to time. If one is intent on building such a set in MS-65 FBL, this date will be more than a challenge. Over the last 20 years, I have probably handled no more than five or six 1963-P Franklin halves in MS-65 FBL that offered attractive color toning.

Valuation—Attractive **MS-65s** can be acquired for $40–$75. On the other hand, the 1963-P is a $1,500+ coin in **MS-65 FBL** with average eye appeal. Exceptional blazers have been known to sell for upward of $2,500 of late, as quality-conscious collectors gain more appreciation for the rarity of this semi-key date. Exceptional color coins are virtually nonexistent. Such a coin would be worth a huge premium if it were to surface.

MS-66 and MS-66 FBL. This is an extremely scarce coin in MS-66. On the positive side, most examples are brilliant.

On the other hand, the 1963-P is virtually impossible to locate in MS-66 FBL. To date, PCGS has certified 5 examples.

Valuation—**MS-66** coins with brilliant surfaces usually trade for between $300 and $600. Beautiful color coins will sell for more, if you can find them.

MS-67 and MS-67 FBL. Only a few 1963-Ps are known in MS-67. All featured relatively attractive color toning. This date is unknown in MS-67 FBL.

Valuation—The last 1963-P in **MS-67**, a color coin graded by NGC, sold for more than $3,000.

↞ 1963-D, MINT STATE ↠

MS-66 FBL

With a mintage of more than 67 million struck, the 1963-D is easily the most available date on the market in roll quantity. At the same time, the general quality of these rolls ranks as the poorest in the series. Bagmarks are usually severe. Strike is usually too weak for an FBL. Water spots are prevalent. Did I miss anything? Oh yes—counting-machine rub and grease stains are also quite common. Mint sets offer more of the same. Frankly, this date is a mess.

My favorite story regarding the problems associated with the 1963-D dates back to the early 1990s, when an original bag of 2,000 coins was offered. The coins were all bank-wrapped. As the rolls were opened, the quality seemed relatively good. Many coins were minimally bagmarked, though the strikes of most were somewhat weak. The finest 150 coins from this bag were subsequently submitted for grading. The highest grade was MS-64. There were no MS-64 FBLs. Needless to say, this deal was a write-off.

NGC CERTIFIED POPULATION *(from a total mintage of 67,069,292)* (WCG™)

MS-64	MS-65	MS-66	MS-67	MS-68
1,807	2,614	68	0	0
MS-64 FBL	**MS-65 FBL**	**MS-66 FBL**	**MS-67 FBL**	**MS-68 FBL**
559	320	18	0	0

MS-60–MS-63 and MS-60 FBL–MS-63 FBL. Crack open an original roll, and most of the coins will be in the MS-62 vicinity. Most will not be FBL.

Valuation—Slightly above bullion. Not recommended in this grade except as a bullion investment.

MS-64 and MS-64 FBL. A very common coin in MS-64, the 1963-D is much more challenging in MS-64 FBL—*especially without water spots.* If one really seeks a challenge, find a 1963-D in this grade with attractive color.

Valuation—**MS-64s** can be acquired for a very modest premium—under $20 a coin. **FBLs** will be at least double that price, if they are fully brilliant and without water spots. The latter offer exceptional value in the $50–$75 range, as they are far more elusive than the modest price might suggest. Attractive color coins are extremely scarce, with occasional examples selling for upward of $300.

MS-65 and MS-65 FBL. This issue is much more elusive in MS-65 than the 1963-P, even though the total mintage of the 1963-D is significantly greater. Bagmarks and water spots are the prime culprits, though all the aforementioned demons play their role as well.

This is a very tough coin to find in MS-65 FBL in superb gem, spot-free condition, and highly recommended. Expect some die polishing on these coins; it's just the way the Denver Mint did things in 1963.

The 1963-D will prove to be an extremely challenging coin to locate in either MS-65 or MS-65 FBL with attractive color toning. These coins are *rare*.

Valuation—**MS-65s** with minimal spots are $40 or so. These coins are scarce. **FBLs** with good eye appeal and no spotting typically sell in the $150–$300 range. Color coins will command three to four times that range.

MS-66 and MS-66 FBL. The 1963-D is an extremely scarce coin in MS-66 or MS-66 FBL, though either grade can be acquired with some patience. Fully brilliant examples do exist in this grade, though they represent a minority of the MS-66 and MS-66 FBL population.

A handful of beautiful color coins exist for this date in this highest Mint State grade, though these coins are obviously quite rare.

Valuation—**MS-66** non-FBL coins sell in the $300–$600 range in brilliant condition—a steal at this level, given the difficulty of finding them. Color coins may sell for up to three to four times more, depending on the rainbow. Examples of the 1963-D in **MS-66 FBL** typically sell for anywhere from $1,600 to $6,000, depending on the subjective eye-appeal factor and whether the coin is fully brilliant and spot free. I recently handled a fabulous color coin that sold for more than $7,000.

MS-67 and MS-67 FBL. Such is the generally poor quality of the 1963-D Franklin that although more than 60 million examples were struck, only three examples have ever been certified in MS-67 by either NGC or PCGS. One of these extraordinary rarities is pictured above.

For perspective, compare the rarity of the 1963-D Franklin in these MS-66 and MS-67 grades to that of any of the short-set Mint State Liberty Walking half dollars from the mid-1930s on.

Guess which coin is the rarer? And by a significant margin.

When it comes to the Mint State Franklin half series, the numbers do not lie. This is a great series to collect for the collector seeking long-term satisfaction.

Valuation—Until recently none had been professionally certified in MS-67, so establishing a price was impossible. However, the beautifully toned coin pictured on the previous page, an MS-67 FBL, sold for more than $20,000.

PROOF FRANKLIN HALF DOLLARS
⊶ 1950, PROOF ⊷

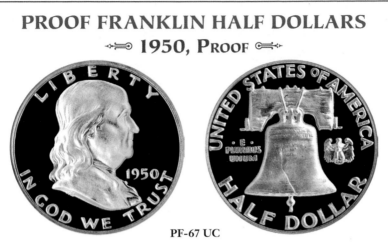

PF-67 UC

1950 marked the resumption of Proof coin production at the Philadelphia Mint after an eight-year hiatus. The last Proof half dollars had been minted in 1942, when 21,120 were struck. 51,386 Proof sets were struck in 1950.

The overall quality of the 1950 Proof Franklin is very poor. Most examples are heavily hairlined, and many are struck from Proof dies that obviously were being used beyond the point of their useful life. These latter coins exhibit shallow Proof mirrors, and may also have some pitting on the high points of Franklin's cheek and jawline on the obverse and on the center portions of the Liberty Bell on the reverse.

Another problem plaguing the 1950 Proof Franklin is glue stains acquired from the method of packaging. From 1950 through mid-1954, the Philadelphia Mint encased each Proof coin in its own small cellophane envelope, about 1 × 2 inches in dimension. Packets were then laid one on top of the other and stapled together, and the entire five-coin group was then wrapped in tissue paper and placed in a small cardboard box approximately 2 × 2 × 1 inches in size. The glue used to seal one end of the envelope would frequently leave residue on 1950 Proof coins encased in these original government-issue pouches for more than a few years.

While this original packaging would at least initially keep the delicate Proof coins from contact with one another, this packaging was also not well suited to long-term storage. Over time these brittle envelopes would often crack open, especially for the heaviest half dollar coin. No longer in its semi-protective cocoon, the coin(s) would be exposed to further abrasion.

NGC CERTIFIED POPULATION *(from a total mintage of 51,386)*   (WCG™)

PF-64	PF-65	PF-66	PF-67	PF-68	PF-69
552	577	446	118	3	0
PF-64 Cam	PF-65 Cam	PF-66 Cam	PF-67 Cam	PF-68 Cam	PF-69 Cam
180	160	50	12	1	0
PF-64 UC	PF-65 UC	PF-66 UC	PF-67 UC	PF-68 UC	PF-69 UC
2	10	0	1	0	0

Brilliant Proof. The 1950 Proof Franklin is very scarce in brilliant PF-65–66 grade. If you are seeking a gem deep-mirrored example that matches up well with the other Proof Franklins in your set, the current PCGS/NGC population numbers are very misleading. Most of the gems graded are either heavily toned or very shallow mirrored. These latter coins more closely resemble Mint State Franklins than Proofs, and they look out of place in a set containing deeply mirrored Proofs from 1951 through 1963.

Deeply mirrored gem 1950 Proof Franklins are rare, and appear to be very undervalued at current price levels. Current prices are primarily a reflection of the values of the usual unappealing shallow-mirrored variety. If a collector can acquire a beautiful deep mirror near these levels, he or she will have a tremendous buy.

The 1950 is rare in PF-67, and very rare in deep-mirrored PF-67. Of the handful of PF-67 coins graded, most have some toning, and most are, once again, of the shallow-mirrored die variety.

Valuation—Any nicely mirrored haze-free gem 1950 is very scarce, and offers tremendous value at current prices, having appreciated in recent years to the $750 to $1,100 range. **PF-66** coins sell for about 50% more. Problem-free 1950 **PF-67s** now trade between $4,000 and $6,000, about double the values listed in the second edition of this book! These coins are very rare. Exceptional deeply mirrored examples in PF-67 are most highly prized of all, and worth an additional premium. The few known **PF-68** coins have sold for more than $30,000.

Cameo Proof. This date is on fire! While the 1950 cameo Proof Franklin is the key date in the cameo Proof Franklin series, it is "only" a rarity in gem cameo, with heavy cameo contrast. Many gem lightly frosted examples exist, and many examples also exist with heavier contrast but with heavily hairlined or heavily glue-stained surfaces. A problem-free, minimally hairlined PF-65 1950 Franklin with significant cameo contrast is rare.

The 1950 Franklin in PF-65 Cam grade has become progressively rarer over the years, as Proof collectors are quick to tuck this key date away for the long term when there is opportunity to do so. Examples grading PF-65 Cam or higher are seldom encountered, while Cameo PF-67s have always been excessively rare. Finding a very early cameo strike with virtually no hairlines, toning spots, or glue spots has proven to be almost an impossibility. Note that I only handle Exceptional Cameo Contrast (ECC-designated; see the appendix for more information) cameo Franklins. The 1950 in particular is a date you can often find certified as "cameo," even when the cameo contrast is very weak, at the lowest end of the cameo spectrum.

Valuation—**PF-64** examples of the 1950 Proof generally trade for between $800 and $2,500, depending on the contrast and on whether there are glue spots. **PF-65 Cam** examples with minimal cameo contrast are selling for $1,250 to $2,500, while exceptional gems bordering on ultra or deep cameo have sold for $6,000 to $8,000. **PF-66** coins generally trade at about double those levels.

The finest 1950 **PF-67 Cam** I have handled sold for $25,000. A **PF-68** Cam recently sold for around $40,000.

Note that these prices are for Exceptional Cameo Contrast (ECC) coins only; see the appendix for more information on this designation.

Deep or Ultra Cameo Proof. The 1950 Proof Franklin in gem PCGS deep cameo or NGC ultra cameo is a great 20th-century rarity, and in my opinion among the most desirable numismatic coins of that century that one could hope to own. When one considers its large denomination, great rarity, breathtaking beauty, and the fact that it is the key cameo Franklin date in the series, it becomes quite understandable how Proof Franklin collectors could prize this coin so highly.

While many 1950 Proof dies exhibited significant cameo contrast, few 1950 cameo Proof dies exhibited the heavily frosted cameo devices and ultra-deep-mirrored fields necessary to earn the deep cameo or ultra superlative. Of the few dies that were of the spectacular cameo variety, the delicate nature of these specially prepared cameo dies meant that only the very earliest strikes could possibly exhibit the level of frost and depth of mirror necessary for this highest designation. Since 1981, of the many thousands of Proof 1950 Franklins I have seen or handled, out of a total mintage of only 51,386 perhaps 10 could have been considered deep or ultra cameo. Of those few coins, fewer than half were PF-65, the other coins being quite heavily hairlined.

It is important to understand that the total known population of only 30 ultra cameo Proof Franklins, in all grades and by NGC and PCGS combined, covers the combined experiences of many other cameo dealers, specialists, and collectors. *Certainly, most of the total Proof population of 1950 Franklin halves has been discovered and submitted for encapsulation.* Again, as with the "cameo" designation, I am only interested in ECC-designated ultra cameo Franklins. There are many 1950 Franklins certified as UC/DCAM that in my opinion are too weak to deserve that superlative.

Hoards? It depends what one's definition of a hoard is. In other coin series, a hoard of gem coins could include thousands of coins, as in the great Wells-Fargo hoard of 1908, discovered in the late 1990s, in which several thousand MS-65 and MS-66 double eagles of this date were uncovered. Given the nature of the cameo Proof-making process during the early 1950s, in which only the very earliest strikes off a new Proof die could possibly exhibit the necessary level of contrast, and further given that the rather poor government packaging of the time meant that most of those coins would be significantly hairlined, I would consider a massive hoard to be two or three gem ultra 1950 Franklin halves.

Finally, while I have handled, bought, and sold most of the ultra cameo 1950 Proof Franklins graded, I have never personally found a gem ultra cameo Franklin in a Proof set; instead, I have acquired them from other collectors or from dealers who happened to have a client who owned one.

Valuation—The king of the cameo Franklin series, any 1950 with ultra or deep cameo contrast is highly desirable. Even **PF-63** coins command $2,000 to $4,000. **PF-64 DC/UC** coins trade in the $6,000–$12,000 range. Only four **PF-65 DC** 1950 Franklin halves have been certified by PCGS, and only 13 by NGC. The last example I handled, a **PF-65★ UC**, sold for $25,000.

A fabulous 1950 Franklin in NGC **PF-66+ Ultra Cameo** recently sold for *more than $50,000.* And, in a new record for a 1950 PCGS **PF-65 DC**, one of the four known examples *recently realized $44,650 at auction!*

⊷⊷ 1951, PROOF ⊷⊷

PF-66 DC

There was a small uptick in Proof production for 1951, with 57,500 sets minted. Proof sets continued to be issued in the same packaging used the previous year, with each coin housed in its own small cellophane envelope, and all five envelopes then stapled together. The Mint obviously did not intend for these coins to remain in this packaging for very long, as it was ill suited for presentation and viewing of the contents. The brittle, crinkled cellophane was also quite abrasive, and not a very good cocoon for the delicate contents. On the plus side, while glue stains were a major problem for 1950 Proof coins housed in their original government-issue packaging for any length of time, 1951 and newer Proofs were not similarly afflicted.

NGC CERTIFIED POPULATION *(from a total mintage of 57,500)*   (WCG™)

PF-64	PF-65	PF-66	PF-67	PF-68	PF-69
435	572	475	178	8	0
PF-64 Cam	**PF-65 Cam**	**PF-66 Cam**	**PF-67 Cam**	**PF-68 Cam**	**PF-69 Cam**
154	129	83	20	0	0
PF-64 UC	**PF-65 UC**	**PF-66 UC**	**PF-67 UC**	**PF-68 UC**	**PF-69 UC**
20	18	10	4	0	0

Brilliant Proof. With a relatively small mintage of 57,500 sets issued in packaging similar to that of the previous year, the 1951 Franklin is also scarce in gem PF-65 to PF-66 condition. Like the 1950 Proof Franklin, the majority of gem 1951 Franklin halves are also of the shallow-mirrored variety. Deep-mirrored gems are considerably more rare.

The 1951 Proof Franklin is quite rare in PF-67 grade, and only a few examples have graded any higher. Virtually all PF-67 and higher-grade coins are of the shallow-mirror variety.

Valuation—The brilliant Proof is highly desirable at current levels. **PF-65s** have risen in recent years, now trading between $500 and $800, with **PF-66** coins at $900 to $1,500. Problem-free brilliant **PF-67s** have almost doubled since the second edition of this book, trading between $2,000 and $3,000. A bargain! I paid more than $9,000 for the last **PF-68** I handled.

Cameo Proof. These are almost as rare as the 1950 Proof Franklin in cameo and gem cameo. Glue spots are not a problem with this date as with the 1950. Gems are marginally easier to locate, but still quite scarce. This date is especially rare in high-grade cameo.

An interesting phenomenon appeared beginning with the 1951, continuing through 1954—the cameo struck from repolished dies. Rather than discarding worn Proof dies, the Mint chose to recycle them by repolishing to restore their Proof qualities.

Valuation—**PF-65 Cams** are a bargain at the current $800–$1,500 level; **PF-66s** sell for $1,200 to $2,500, and **PF-67 Cams** for $4,000 to $10,000. The higher prices are for especially deep-mirrored examples with strong cameo contrast.

Deep Cameo Proof. These Proofs are extremely rare in deep cameo: To date only a handful have been graded by either NGC or PCGS. All known examples have been struck from the aforementioned repolished dies. The finest of these are truly striking in their cameo contrast and eye appeal. See below for the story of one of these coins.

Valuation—A favorite among cameo collectors when struck from the "top die," **PF-64 DC/UC** coins have sold for as much as $2,000. Similar cameo specimens in **PF-65** have typically traded in the $3,500–$6,500 range. The finest **PF-66 DC/UC** coins have sold for more than $16,000. I sold a **PF-67 DC** for almost $40,000 in 2017. *In a recent new record*, a 1951 PCGS **PF-67+ DCAM** sold at auction for $82,250. This is the highest price on record for a Proof Franklin!

THE INCREDIBLE 1951 FRANKLIN

The year was about 1984. I had at that point been aggressively on the hunt for exceptional cameo Proofs of the 1950–1970 era for a few years. I was attending on average two shows a month, travelling the country, and making it a point to at least get a look at every available cameo for this era. I believed that I had gained some familiarity with these coins, and that I knew what kind of cameo quality to expect of a given date.

I knew the 1950 was the key date in "ultra heavy" cameo, the term we used at that time to describe a cameo with the heaviest possible frost on both obverse and reverse. The 1951 was a very tough coin to locate as well, and seemed almost as difficult as the 1950 to acquire in gem cameo condition. I had handled a few gem cameo 1951 Franklin halves, and they had all traded in the $300–$500 range. They were attractive coins, but could not in any way be favorably compared to the later Proof Franklin halves in exceptional cameo condition. The 1951 simply was not as deep, nor as cameo, as a nice 1956, 1962, or 1963.

Once again, it was a Long Beach coin show that was responsible for one of those lightbulb moments. I was roaming the aisles at "The Beach." I believe it was a Thursday. It was late in the day, and while I had acquired many cameo coins that day—as they were more available then than they are now—nothing really stood out. Until I walked by a table with a Proof Franklin in a small white Capital holder. I did a double take, as it was a stunning cameo, with exceptional snow-white frost and very deep fields. I looked closer, and was dumbfounded when I noticed the date. It wasn't a 1956, a 1963, or even a rarer 1954. It was a 1951, the most amazing cameo 1951 I had ever seen. I looked close to make sure the coin was real and not an artificial or enhanced cameo. It definitely looked real.

I noticed myriad die-polishing lines on the device, very similar to a spectacular 1953 cameo repolished die I was familiar with. The fields were quite clean, with but a few light scattered hairlines. The coin was definitely gem. The question I had was, where was the owner? No one was attending the booth. So I did my best helicopter imitation for 30 minutes or so, hovering around the table, waiting for the dealer to return. I did not want to miss out on this coin and have someone buy it from under me when I happened to not be around.

Finally, just before closing time, about a quarter to 7:00, the dealer appeared at the booth to close up for the day. I asked to see the 1951 in the white Capital holder. It was a breathtaking coin to behold, with a cameo contrast and depth of mirror, on both obverse and reverse, unlike any 1951 I had ever seen. It was the Everest of 1951 Proof Franklin halves, towering above the other 99.9% of the 50,000+ examples struck in eye appeal.

Well, I asked the price, expecting a quote of $300 or $400—the going rate for gem cameo 1951s at that time. Without hesitation, the dealer replied, "One thousand dollars."

My heart sank. $1,000? The most I had ever sold a gem cameo 1951 Franklin for was about $450. He was asking more than double that price. So after another minute or so of careful inspection, I made a counteroffer. He politely explained that the price was $1,000, and there was zero chance he would go lower.

It was late. I gave him the coin back. He put the coin back in the case, put the cover over his cases, and closed for the day. I had dinner in my room and spent the evening there, sipping on an adult beverage, obsessed by that 1951. $1,000 was a lot to pay in those days. I had a limited budget, and I had to be a little concerned about placing the coin with a client.

What the heck. Superb cameo Proofs were my passion. I wanted only the best for my clients, and this coin was definitely the best. And it quite possibly was irreplaceable. While that $1,000 price might be more than the market would bear at the time, I believed the coin would certainly be worth well beyond that sum in the years to come.

So I went back to the show early the next morning. I got there before the dealer with the 1951 had opened his booth—I did not want someone buying the coin out from under me. I paid his price. And I did sell the coin to a client a month later for $1,200.

But even if I hadn't sold it, that 1951 was a coin I would have been thrilled to hold in my inventory as a showpiece. And I believed that the longer I owned the coin, the more valuable it would become.

The client who purchased the coin was as impressed with the 1951 as I. And today, that 1951 is in a PF-66 DC holder and is worth well over $10,000.

In the years since that discovery 1951 Franklin, I have found other examples struck from that die. Designated die number 6 in my book *Cameo and Brilliant Proof Coinage of the 1950 to 1970 Era*, and also pictured on the jacket of that book, it continues to be the finest known cameo die for that year—in its earliest die state.

Most of the examples that surface are of course later strikes, with lighter cameo contrast and less depth of mirror, a characteristic of a cameo die exhibiting signs of wear. There have, however, been a few examples offering cameo contrast and quality similar to that first monster 1951. And I am as thrilled when I get one today as I was in those early days back in the 1980s.

⤳⟾ 1952, Proof ⟾⤶

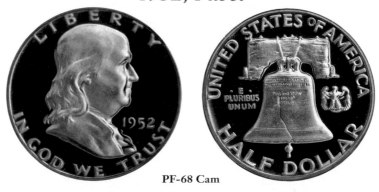

PF-68 Cam

Proof mintage took another population jump in 1952, with a total mintage of 81,980 sets. Of course, by modern standards, in terms of absolute rarity, this is an extremely low number. The same box packaging was used as in the previous year, with cellophane envelopes used to house each individual coin. The Mint was apparently aware of the quality shortcomings of the previous two years' mintage, as there continued to be modest improvements in this area. The glue stains are gone, and while many 1950 Proof coins were very shallow mirrored, the result of having been struck from overused dies, this was not an issue in 1952. Hairlines and heavy toning continue to be the major problems they were in 1950 and 1951.

NGC CERTIFIED POPULATION *(from a total mintage of 81,980)*   (WCG™)

PF-64	PF-65	PF-66	PF-67	PF-68	PF-69
374	572	654	289	17	0
PF-64 Cam	PF-65 Cam	PF-66 Cam	PF-67 Cam	PF-68 Cam	PF-69 Cam
140	184	162	82	2	0
PF-64 UC	PF-65 UC	PF-66 UC	PF-67 UC	PF-68 UC	PF-69 UC
4	10	3	1	0	0

Brilliant Proof. The 1952 Proof Franklin is almost as rare as the 1951 in high-grade gem condition. Hairlines are once again a major problem. Minimally hairlined PF-65 examples are scarce, PF-66 coins are extremely scarce, and PF-67 coins are rare. Fewer than fifty 1952 Franklins have been graded higher than PF-67. This is a relatively small number when compared to Liberty Walking Proofs of 1936 to 1942. The Liberty Walking Proofs of that era had far smaller mintages, but a *higher percentage* managed to survive in essentially hairline-free PF-68.

Many high-grade PF-67 and PF-68 1952 Franklins are toned, as they came from box sets, with a hazy golden-brown cast. *Fully brilliant PF-68 1952 Franklins are very rare.*

Valuation—This is another great date in **PF-65** at current levels—only $300 to $500. **PF-66s** are only about $100 to $200 more. **PF-67** specimens, fully brilliant, are only $800 to $1,400. If you can find a **PF-68**, superb examples have sold for $5,000 to $8,000.

Cameo Proof. Almost as rare as the 1951 Proof Franklin in Cameo, this date is quickly approaching rare status, as collectors salt away gem cameo examples for the long term. While the Proof mintage was approximately 50% greater for the 1952 Franklin than for the 1951, a large percentage of cameo Franklin 1952 dies were mismatched in their contrast, with the obverse die often exhibiting near-deep or deep cameo contrast but the reverse being at best a weak cameo. Only the earliest strikes off these dies had reverses with enough contrast for the cameo designation. While later strikes would still offer significant obverse contrast, the reverses would be too weak for the designation. These later strikes were essentially one-sided cameo Proofs.

Valuation—Only $500 to $800 in **PF-65 Cam**, $800 to $2,000 in **PF-66 Cam**, and $1,500 to $4,000 in **PF-67 Cam**!

Deep Cameo Proof. *Extremely rare* in deep cameo, to date only a handful of these Proofs have been graded by either NGC or PCGS. All known examples have been struck from the aforementioned repolished dies. The finest of these are truly striking in their cameo contrast and eye appeal.

In the first cameo book, I listed the estimated population of PF-65 and higher-grade 1952 Franklins in deep cameo at 95 to 190 coins. This estimate was based on the accepted cameo grading standards of the time. There are several cameo 1952 die varieties in which the earliest strikes exhibit spectacular snow-white ultra obverses but have more moderately contrasted reverses. Cameo dealers and collectors accepted these coins as "ultra heavy," reasoning that the spectacular cameo obverse compensated for the reverse that was not quite matching in contrast. When PCGS and NGC developed their deep cameo standards in the months following the publication of that book, both services adopted the view that the obverse and reverse count more or less equally in determining whether a coin is cameo or deep cameo. As a result, the majority of 1952 Proof Franklins included in my first estimate would not grade deep cameo using today's PCGS and NGC standards.

To date, PCGS and NGC combined have graded only a few dozen Proof 1952 Franklins in deep or ultra cameo. While there are a few more out there, there is no question that the 1952 Proof Franklin is an extremely rare coin with this level of contrast, using the standards adopted by PCGS and NGC. Consider these facts. One: There were only three or four known cameo dies that struck coins with snow-white frost on both the obverse and reverse of the coin. Two: Only the first 10 to 25 strikes off these few dies exhibited that level of contrast. Three: Only a small percentage of those 10 to 25 coins from each die survived in PF-65 or higher grade.

Valuation—This key date is almost impossible to find in deep or ultra cameo. The last couple of examples I have handled sold for between $4,000 and $8,000 in **PF-65**. But that must be considered a very low price range, given this date's rarity. **PF-66 DC/ UC** coins have generally traded for between $8,000 and $15,000. Regarding the lone PCGS **PF-67 DC** and NGC **PF-67 UC**, it is needless to say that the owners of these two ultra rarities are not interested in selling. *In a recent new record*, a 1952 PCGS **PF-67 DCAM** sold for more than $50,000!

1953, PROOF

PF-69

Proof production increased again in 1953, to 128,800 sets. Very modest improvements in quality were again evident. While hairlines and unattractive toning pose the major quality drawbacks for this date, the 1953 does not suffer the hairline malady to quite the same degree as the 1952 issues. On the other hand, whereas virtually all 1952 Proof Franklins were deeply mirrored, the mirror quality of the 1953 Proof Franklin run was inconsistent, with many examples being struck from very worn dies. Like the 1950 Franklin struck from similarly worn dies, these coins could almost pass for brilliant Uncirculated commercial strikes, with satiny fields exhibiting little if any mirror quality, though they are differentiated by their very full strikes and surfaces that are essentially devoid of any bagmarks.

NGC CERTIFIED POPULATION *(from a total mintage of 128,800)*   (WCG™)

PF-64	PF-65	PF-66	PF-67	PF-68	PF-69
356	503	655	450	48	1
PF-64 Cam	PF-65 Cam	PF-66 Cam	PF-67 Cam	PF-68 Cam	PF-69 Cam
127	302	353	185	23	0
PF-64 UC	PF-65 UC	PF-66 UC	PF-67 UC	PF-68 UC	PF-69 UC
7	9	15	4	1	0

Brilliant Proof. With the continued improvements in quality coupled with the higher mintage, the 1953 Proof Franklin is slightly easier to locate in the higher PF-66 to PF-68 grades than the previous two years. The 1953 is still a rare coin in PF-67, particularly in fully brilliant condition, as the majority of high-grade examples possess the original toning acquired from the decade's storage in the government-issue cellophane envelope. This date is very rare in PF-68—but not as rare as the 1952. A couple of 1953 Proof Franklins have even been graded in PF-69, one by PCGS and one by NGC.

The 1953 has seen quite a bit of appreciation in the lower grades during the past few years, as the demand for these earlier Proof issues continues to grow in the face of a shrinking supply. The future for these early Proof Franklin halves is indeed a bright one!

Valuation—While not quite as elusive in **PF-65** as the preceding issues, the 1953 is nevertheless a very scarce coin in PF-65, and an excellent value in the current $200 to $300 range. **PF-66s** are a little more. Certainly the 1953 in **PF-67** is a tremendous value at current levels when it appears, as these usually sell for only $800 to $1,200. **PF-68s** are in tremendous demand, and are now commanding $2,500 and more in fully brilliant condition. The last **PF-69** I handled sold for almost $20,000.

Cameo Proof. The 1953 approaches the rarity of the 1952 in gem PF-65 Cam, though the 1952 is considerably more elusive in the higher PF-66 to PF-68 grades. The differential is greatest in PF-68 Cam, for while the 1953 is rare in this condition, examples have surfaced from time to time, as the population numbers attest. The 1952, on the other hand, is extraordinarily rare in this grade.

A strong recommendation for gem cameo examples. Proof set values for the Franklin series have exploded over the past several years, and the premium for a superb cameo 1953 is quite modest at current levels, despite these coins' being more elusive now than ever.

Valuation—$300 to $500 in **PF-65 Cam,** $400 to $800 in **PF-66 Cam,** and $800 to $2,000 in **PF-67 Cam.** Given the tremendous rarity of the **PF-68 Cam,** this is a solid $3,000+ coin. At a FUN Show auction several years ago, a PCGS PF-67 Cam realized $6,900. This was a superb specimen with cameo contrast bordering on deep cameo.

Deep Cameo Proof. While the 1953 Proof Franklin is not quite as rare in gem cameo as the earlier dates, it is *extremely rare in ultra or deep cameo,* as are the 1950, 1951, and 1952 Proof Franklins. There are only a few known cameo dies that struck any examples possessing the intense obverse and reverse cameo contrast needed for a deep cameo designation, though only the very earliest strikes off these dies possessed the level of cameo and depth of mirror required for a deep or ultra cameo designation. Additionally, the few that were struck are typically heavily hairlined, which is not surprising since the same packaging was used for 1953 as for the earlier years.

A handful of examples have been graded in PF-67 UC/DC. Only one or two new examples have been certified in recent years, attesting to the distinct possibility that most of the finest cameo Franklins from this early era have now been certified. If one has the opportunity to acquire one of these spectacular 1953 Franklins, they are highly recommended. You may never have the opportunity to acquire another.

Valuation—**PF-65 DC/UC** coins have sold for as little as $1,000 and as much as $2,500. Generally, the lower-valued coins exhibit obvious spotting. Values for **PF-66 DC/UC** examples are approximately double those numbers. In **PF-67 DC/UC,** this is a $10,000–$20,000 coin. However, expect this value to increase in the years ahead. These coins are simply not being graded anymore.

There is a lone NGC **PF-68 UC,** which realized $63,250 in a Heritage auction in August 2006, and a lone PCGS **PF-68 DCAM** (pictured) which I handled in 2017.

⋆⟹ 1954, Proof ⟸⋆

PF-68 UC

Two major occurrences in 1954 benefited collectors of high quality gem U.S. Proof coins: first, mintages increased once again, with 233,300 Proof sets being released; and second, in the middle of the year the Mint switched from the brittle cellophane envelopes used to house the Proofs to softer polyvinyl envelopes. On the plus side, the softer polyvinyl material did not hairline the delicate Proof surfaces. These envelopes also did not dry and crack open over time, as did the earlier cellophane envelopes. On the minus side, the new polyvinyl was not inert. Because it was a new creation, the Mint may not have been aware of the reactive properties of this material when it came into contact with silver. As a result of many years' storage in these envelopes, most 1954 silver Proof coins are very heavily toned in a dark purplish tone on at least one side. Trying to remove this toning has proved fruitless. Coin-dipping solutions, which may work quite well on silver coins that have toned while in cardboard holders or paper envelopes, are not recommended for silver Proof coins housed in these soft polyvinyl envelopes for any length of time. While the dipping will remove the dark purple toning, which many collectors may even find attractive, it will leave a dull brown haze in its place—which no collector finds particularly appealing.

NGC CERTIFIED POPULATION *(from a total mintage of 233,300)*   (WCG™)

PF-64	PF-65	PF-66	PF-67	PF-68	PF-69
211	432	738	992	335	6
PF-64 Cam	PF-65 Cam	PF-66 Cam	PF-67 Cam	PF-68 Cam	PF-69 Cam
88	182	424	498	137	3
PF-64 UC	PF-65 UC	PF-66 UC	PF-67 UC	PF-68 UC	PF-69 UC
5	10	19	22	10	0

Brilliant Proof. Quality took a leap forward midyear with the switch to the new soft envelopes, reducing the number of hairlines. However, unsightly toning from these envelopes can sometimes present a new problem.

Valuation—The 1954 is the first year of Franklin Proofs that is fairly easy to locate in PF-65 and even in PF-66 in brilliant condition. Examples can be found for around $150. These values have been on the upswing with the growing difficulty of finding finer specimens. The 1954 has become very elusive in brilliant **PF-67**; coins in that condition are a bargain at the current $300 to $450 level.

Virtually flawless, hairline-free 1954 Franklins in **PF-68** are much rarer, but are occasionally attainable. These examples now usually trade for between $800 and $1,500. Some have attractive cameo contrast.

Cameo Proof. At one time this date was relatively easy to find in gem cameo condition. Each new year brings more new cameo collectors, however, and the supply of gem cameo 1954 halves has now dwindled to a trickle. Very high-grade specimens in PF-67 or PF-68 are now extremely scarce, and will probably be rarities in the not-too-distant future.

Valuation—A bargain at current levels, with **PF-65** and **PF-66 Cams** usually selling for under $200, and **PF-67 Cams** now trading in the $500–$900 range, depending on the cameo contrast. This issue is a rare coin in **PF-68 Cam,** yet still inexpensively priced, usually trading for between $1,000 and $2,500, with the higher-priced examples generally having cameo contrast approaching deep or ultra cameo.

Deep Cameo Proof. The 1954 Proof Franklin has always been rare in ultra or deep cameo. While nicely contrasted examples were abundant at one time, exceptional snow-white cameo coins with deep, black-mirrored fields have always been rare. These latter coins can be quite spectacular in their cameo contrast and eye appeal.

How rare is the 1954 in ultra or deep cameo? I have personally found only two to three 1954 Proof Franklins in exceptional deep cameo condition in an original set, going back to 1981, when I first started scouring original Proof sets for cameos.

To date, PCGS and NGC have graded a only relatively small handful in deep or ultra cameo, with most of these falling between PF-65 and PF-67.

Valuation—**PF-65** and **PF-66 DC/UC** coins are bargains priced in the current $700–$1,500 range. Highly desirable **PF-67 DC/UCs** have been selling in the $1,800–$5,000 range. The ultimate and very rare **PF-68 DC/UC** 1954 Franklin is a $12,000–$25,000 coin.

⊶⊷ 1955, Proof ⊶⊷

PF-69 UC

Another small leap forward in quality occurred in 1955. Much of this improvement was due to the Mint's abandonment midway through the 1955 Proof run of the soft polyvinyl envelopes it had been using to house the Proof coins, as the Mint switched to the familiar flat-pack design, which was used through 1964. The new flat-pack design comprised a single cellophane envelope divided into six compartments. Each of the five Proof coins was encased in one of the compartments, with the sixth compartment remaining empty. In subsequent years, the Mint would enclose a small silver label in the sixth compartment, with "U.S. Mint Philadelphia" inscribed in blue on the label. Unlike the earlier cellophane envelopes used through mid-1954, this newer cellophane retained its durability over the years. To this day, one can acquire original Proof sets from the late 1950s and early 1960s in these envelopes that appear in quite good condition. While many Proof coins develop some toning in these flat packs, many are surprisingly brilliant and free of any toning or haze.

NGC CERTIFIED POPULATION *(from a total mintage of 378,200)* (WCG™)

PF-64	PF-65	PF-66	PF-67	PF-68	PF-69
140	335	788	1,689	1,065	45
PF-64 Cam	PF-65 Cam	PF-66 Cam	PF-67 Cam	PF-68 Cam	PF-69 Cam
45	120	414	635	327	5
PF-64 UC	PF-65 UC	PF-66 UC	PF-67 UC	PF-68 UC	PF-69 UC
3	7	23	32	35	2

Brilliant Proof. While the new flat-pack design did a wonderful job of protecting its delicate contents, the envelopes are flexible. As a result, many Proof coins have developed some hairlines due to abrading against the cellophane envelope. However, these new inert envelopes did a much better job of preserving the original luster of the delicate Proof coins, and heavily toned coins are not as big a problem as they were in 1954.

Valuation—A large percentage of surviving 1955 Proof Franklin half dollars are gem-quality **PF-65s** and now sell for $100 or more. **PF-67s** are in great demand, and may trade anywhere from $150 to $300, depending on eye appeal. This is a much tougher coin to locate in **PF-68,** but a bargain when found, as these are still priced under $400. The 1955 is possible to locate in **PF-69,** though it is quite rare in this highest Proof grade. PF-69 specimens generally sell for between $1,000 and $2,000.

Cameo Proof. Despite its higher mintage (approximately 50% higher than that of the 1954) and superior packaging, the 1955 Proof Franklin is almost as rare as the 1954 in gem cameo condition. Moderately contrasted NGC-graded coins are most frequently encountered. Examples with heavy cameo contrast bordering on ultra or deep cameo are far more elusive.

The 1955 is a bit easier to locate in the high PF-68 Cam grade than the 1954, though it is extremely scarce in this grade, and far more elusive than the 1956 Type 2 Franklin that follows.

Valuation—Only $100 to $200 in **PF-65** to **PF-66 Cam,** $250 to $400 in **PF-67 Cam,** and $600 to $1,500 in **PF-68 Cam.** A few **PF-69 Cam** examples have surfaced; they sell for at least $2,000, and a recent coin I handled sold for more than $4,000.

Deep Cameo Proof. While the 1955 Proof Franklin is about as rare as the 1954 in gem cameo, the 1955 is not quite as rare as the 1954 in gem deep cameo or ultra cameo. Again, this is relative, as the 1955 is still *rare* with this degree of cameo contrast. As a point of reference, in more than 30 years of hunting for cameo Franklin halves, I have personally located perhaps two or three examples from original Proof sets that were subsequently graded ultra or deep cameo by NGC or PCGS.

Fortunately, with most 1955 Proof Franklin halves having fewer hairlines than the 1954 issue that preceded it, there have been a few more 1955 Proof Franklins graded in PF-68 UC/DC. There have even been a couple of examples graded in PF-69 UC by NGC.

Valuation—Almost as rare as the 1954, this date can usually be acquired for $400 to $1,000 in **PF-65** to **PF-66 DC/UC.** Considerably rare in **PF-67 DC/UC,** most specimens sell in a wide range between $1,500 and $3,500 for the finest, deepest specimens. **PF-68 DC** is the highest deep cameo grade PCGS has given this date. Ordinary specimens trade at a slight premium over the best PF-67 DC/UC coins, but the truly superb, spot-free examples usually can sell for between $7,000 and $12,000. Coins on the lower end of the DCAM spectrum may sell for as little as $4,000 to $5,000. Superb ECC-quality DCAMs typically sell between $9,000 and $12,000. *New record:* A spectacular 1955 NGC **PF-69 UC** sold for more than $30,000 in a private transaction.

❦ 1956, Proof, Type 1 ❦

PF-69 Cam

The eagle on the Type 1 Proof

1956 marked the first year that the entire run of Proof sets was issued in the flat pack. The 1956 Proof year was, coin for coin, among the highest-quality years at the Mint. While mirror quality of many 1956 Proof Franklins was not always the best, with many coins being not as deeply mirrored as some of the earlier-strike specimens, this issue had few of the flaws found on the earlier Franklins. The typical 1956 Proof Franklin exhibits very few hairlines and little or no toning. In addition, a comparatively high percentage of examples exhibits cameo contrast compared to the earlier years. This last bit of comparative data must be kept in context, however: cameos were by no means the rule, but were still the exception. I estimate that only 2% to 3% of the examples struck exhibit significant cameo contrast that might earn them a cameo designation.

The Type 1 Franklin uses the same reverse as the 1950–1955 Proof Franklins. While there are many minor detail changes in the reverse design from the Type 1 to the Type 2, the most notable difference can be found in the articulation of the eagle's neck, wing, and leg feathers. On the Type 1, these feathers appear more as a solid mass, while on the Type 2 the individual feathers of the neck, wing, and legs are sharply defined.

The Type 1 Franklin ranks among the most popular varieties in the series, along with the very rare Doubled-Die Reverse of 1961. The popularity of these two varieties is due to the fact that both varieties are very obvious and visible to the naked eye.

While exact mintage figures for the 1956 Type 1 cannot be known, based on my experience over the decades looking through 1956 Proof sets, a good estimate would be about 3% of the total mintage, or only approximately 20,000 coins struck.

However, some of these coins were likely melted during the silver boom of the late 1970s and early 1980s, when silver bullion briefly touched $50 an ounce. *So it is possible that no more than 10,000 to 15,000 examples have survived in all grades.*

NGC CERTIFIED POPULATION *(from a total mintage of 669,384)* (WCG™)

PF-64	PF-65	PF-66	PF-67	PF-68	PF-69
13	42	126	355	274	72
PF-64 Cam	PF-65 Cam	PF-66 Cam	PF-67 Cam	PF-68 Cam	PF-69 Cam
1	5	8	46	43	6
PF-64 UC	PF-65 UC	PF-66 UC	PF-67 UC	PF-68 UC	PF-69 UC
0	0	0	1	1	0

Brilliant Proof. Most examples of the 1956 Type 1 are gem quality and typically grade PF-65 to PF-66. The mirror quality of the Type 1 is typically superior to the average Type 2, the Type 1 normally being very deeply mirrored.

Valuation—This date has been skyrocketing in value of late, as more and more collectors discover how hard it is to find one of these specimens. **PF-65** and **PF-66** coins now command $150 to $300, while **PF-67s** are at least double that range. A few Type 1's in **PF-68** have recently sold for close to $1,500. This rare and popular variety has nowhere to go but up from these still very low levels. A few **PF-69s** have appeared on the market, with asking prices close to $3,000.

Cameo Proof. The 1956 Type 1 is extremely scarce in gem cameo—even rarer than the low mintage figures would suggest. When located, most examples grade PF-66 to PF-67, with the occasional PF-68. Curiously, most cameo Type 1 Franklin halves are mismatched, with much heavier cameo contrast on the reverse than on the obverse. Some of the finer examples in cameo exhibit snow-white deep or ultra cameo reverse contrast, with a moderate to heavy obverse cameo.

Valuation—This is a $300–$600 coin in **PF-65** to **PF-66 Cam,** and double that range in **PF-67 Cam.** Highest grade PCGS **PF-68 Cams** are currently trading for between $3,000 and $7,000 for problem-free (spot-free) specimens. NGC has graded a handful in **PF-69 Cam.** The last example I handled sold for more than $10,000.

Deep Cameo Proof. While the 1956 Type 1 Proof Franklin is extremely scarce in cameo, it is *extremely* rare in ultra or deep cameo. In fact, aside from the 1961 Doubled-Die Reverse Franklin, the 1956 Type 1 is currently the *rarest* Franklin issue in the series, in DCAM/Ultra. NGC and PCGS have certified only a handful in ultra cameo and deep cameo.

Valuation—The first PCGS **PF-68 DC** to come on to the market, sometime around the year 2000, was acquired by me for more than $30,000. That was admittedly a very high price. Still, a superb **PF-68 UC/DC** example should be *at least* a $20,000 coin. *A new auction record for the 1956 Type 1* was established when a PCGS **PF-68 DCAM** sold for $25,850.

1956 PROOF DOUBLED-DIE OBVERSE VARIETY (FS-003)
A moderate spread is seen on the date, TRUST, and LIBERTY. This is a scarce variety. Die markers for this variety are a chip on the 9 and a chip on the upper tail of the 6.

1956 PROOF DOUBLED-DIE REVERSE VARIETY (FS-001)
Doubling shows as extra thickness on UNITED STATES OF AMERICA, HALF DOLLAR, and E PLURIBUS UNUM. Doubling can also be seen on the eagle and bell hanger. This variety can be found with nice cameo devices.

⟶ 1956, Proof, Type 2 ⟵

PF-69 UC

The eagle on the Type 2 Proof

With a mintage of almost 670,000, well above the Proof mintages of the earlier Franklins but well below the mintages of the Franklins to follow, one would guess that this issue might still be scarce in high-grade brilliant condition. This assumption would not fully account for the generally very high quality of this issue.

A major reason for the improvement was that this year the entire Proof set run was issued in the flat pack. But while the flat-pack packaging offered better protection, later Proof Franklin issues, also issued in the flat pack, did not survive in high grade in the same high percentages as the 1956 Type 2 Franklin.

NGC CERTIFIED POPULATION *(from a total mintage of 669,384)* (WCG™)

PF-64	PF-65	PF-66	PF-67	PF-68	PF-69
31	136	464	1,177	807	177
PF-64 Cam	PF-65 Cam	PF-66 Cam	PF-67 Cam	PF-68 Cam	PF-69 Cam
9	30	90	327	312	106
PF-64 UC	PF-65 UC	PF-66 UC	PF-67 UC	PF-68 UC	PF-69 UC
3	1	21	71	155	50

Brilliant Proof. For reasons known only to the Mint at that time, production quality was simply at a very high level. Milk spots, a major problem on many silver Proof issues of the 1958–1964 era, are not found on 1956 silver Proof coins. Hairlines, the biggest problem encountered with all Proof coins, are minimal on a surprisingly high percentage of 1956 Type 2 Proof Franklins. As a result, when located in the original flat pack, the typical 1956 Franklin will grade at least PF-66, with a very high percentage, perhaps as much as 20%, grading PF-67 or higher.

The only real negative that can be attached to this date is the general design detail of 1956 Proof Franklin halves. If one compares the design detail of a 1950 or 1951 Proof

Franklin to the detail on the 1956 Type 2, one will notice a distinct softness of the latter's design elements, which are found in sharper relief on the earlier issues.

This difference has nothing to do with the techniques used at the Mint, and everything to do with the working dies the Mint was given to prepare for Proof dies. The original master die from 1948 was still being used to create all subsequent working dies, and by the mid-1950s was beginning to exhibit serious signs of wear, which are most noticeable in the finer details of the coin's design.

Valuation—This high-quality date can generally still be acquired for $75 to $110 in **PF-67**, $125 to $175 in **PF-68,** and $350 to $500 in **PF-69.**

Cameo Proof. As a percentage of the total Proof mintage for that year, the cameo Franklin production of 1956 is the most prolific of the entire 1950–1963 series. While the total number of cameos in existence for this year may not be as high as for the most common years, 1962 and 1963, the 1956 has a total Proof mintage barely 20% of those years.

Yet *common* is a relative term. Once easy to locate in PF-65 to PF-68 Cam, the 1956 Type 2 has in recent years become quite scarce as astute collectors salt these finest Proof coins away for their own collection. The continued rise in Proof set values for these earlier issues, coupled with the growing scarcity, is driving values up.

Valuation—A **PF-65 Cam** 1956 that I would have sold for $25 in the late 1990s would likely sell for at least $60 to $70 today. **PF-68 Cam** examples that used to trade for $60 to $80 now trade for $250 and up, and **PF-69 Cams** for $500 to $1,000. Expect this trend to continue.

Deep Cameo Proof. The finest 1956 Type 2 ultra or deep cameo Franklins rank among the most stunning cameos in the entire series. Again, for reasons known only to the Mint, there were several exceptional cameo dies in 1956 that struck a surprisingly high number of exceptional cameo Franklins before the dies began to show wear. For a few of the finest cameo dies, as many as 200 ultra or deep cameo Franklin halves may have been struck per die. This is a very high number compared to other years in the series, and much higher than the 1957, 1958, and 1959 to follow.

Coupled with the generally very high quality of these coins—the majority of ultra or deep cameo coins grade at least PF-67—the 1956 Type 2 is also the issue with the most examples graded in PF-69 UC/DC.

It is important to note that most of the finest, heaviest cameo 1956 Franklin halves have now been graded and certified by the major services. Compared to the peak years of submission during the 1990s, if one reviews the evolving population figures from NGC and PCGS, it is apparent that these services are being offered fewer of these coins for grading. The well is evidently running dry on exceptional cameo Franklin halves. Even the prolific 1956, once a common coin on the market in ultra or deep cameo (again, "common" only in the context of the general great rarity of most issues in the series), is now more elusive than ever. As a result, values have been creeping up of late, with future long-term gains almost guaranteed.

Valuation—Only $100 to $350 in **PF-65** to **PF-66 DC,** depending on the contrast. Prices range from $300 to $600 in **PF-67 DC/UC**, and from $700 to $1,800 in **PF-68 DC/UC**.

This is a great type coin in **PF-69 DC/UC**; specimens on the low end of the deep or ultra cameo spectrum have risen considerably in value in recent years, now trading in the $2,500 to $3,500 range. The heavier, finer ECC-designated cameo specimens generally trade for $5,000 to $9,000.

⇥⇒ 1957, Proof ⇐⇤

PF-69 UC

For the first time in the history of the Mint, over one million Proof sets were issued. This figure represented about a twentyfold increase from 1950 and 1951.

The deterioration of the master die still in use was even more obvious on the 1957 half dollar. Design detail on Franklin's bust and on the Liberty Bell is mushy and soft, even though these coins were 100% fully struck.

Aside from this problem, production quality of the Mint Proof product continued at a very high level in 1957.

NGC CERTIFIED POPULATION *(from a total mintage of 1,247,952)*   (WCG™)

PF-64	PF-65	PF-66	PF-67	PF-68	PF-69
123	425	1,196	2,979	1,471	113
PF-64 Cam	PF-65 Cam	PF-66 Cam	PF-67 Cam	PF-68 Cam	PF-69 Cam
29	61	238	575	326	15
PF-64 UC	PF-65 UC	PF-66 UC	PF-67 UC	PF-68 UC	PF-69 UC
2	2	20	44	39	2

Brilliant Proof. While PF-65 to PF-67 gem Proof Franklins of 1957 are understandably easier to locate than any previous year, the 1957 is marginally more elusive in the highest PF-68 to PF-69 grades than the 1956 Type 2. Hairlines are the primary culprit. While rare, the 1957 is not as rare in the highest PF-68 and 69 grades as the 1958 and 1959. Even so, it must still be considered a very scarce coin in the higher PF-68 grade.

Valuation—A great buy in **PF-67** in the current $60–$100 range. **PF-68s** are likewise a tremendous value at $125 to $200. Rare in **PF-69,** the 1957 is still comparatively inexpensive at only $600 to $1,000.

Cameo Proof. Despite having a mintage approximately 50% higher than the 1956, the 1957 is far more elusive in cameo. **Mintage figures are not a reliable indicator of an issue's rarity.**

This phenomenon would continue through the balance of the decade of the 1950s. While the 1958 and 1959 Proof Franklins had mintages very close to the 1957, the 1958 is far more elusive in cameo than the already elusive 1957, and the 1959 is far more elusive than the extremely scarce cameo 1958.

Due to apparent changes at the Mint in the die and planchet preparation, the 1957 cameo dies struck far fewer cameo coins before die wear set in than in the previous year. Additionally, many 1957s are one-sided cameo Proofs. It was the practice of the Mint during the 1950s and 1960s to replace dies only when they were worn. Since the obverse and reverse dies wore at different rates, the Mint would replace either the obverse or reverse, rather than both at the same time.

Valuation—Under $100 for the average **PF-65** to **PF-66 Cam** coin. **PF-67s** sell for $150 to $300, **PF-68** for $400 to $1,000, though a few examples with monster cameo obverses have sold for more.

Deep Cameo Proof. The 1957, despite its much higher mintage than the 1956, is approximately five times rarer in deep or ultra cameo than the 1956 Type 2. It is also virtually nonexistent in PF-69 DC/UC, with only four examples graded to date, while the 1956 Type 2 population in this grade approaches 50.

Most of the 1957 Proof Franklins graded in DC/UC do not exhibit the extraordinary matching snow-white frosted cameo devices of the finer 1956 Type 2 Franklins. There were three, possibly four, 1957 Franklin Proof dies that struck a handful of exceptional cameos each, but *only the very earliest strikes* off these dies exhibited cameo contrast that approaches the finest 1956 Type 2 Franklins. These finer 1957 deep or ultra cameo Franklin halves understandably sell for premiums over the more typical examples. In recognition of the superior cameo contrast of these finer specimens, NGC has ascribed their star designation to a few examples. This designation is given by NGC only to those coins that exhibit unusually superior eye appeal for their grade. One of these coins, a PF-68★ UC, sold for over $6,000, where the typical PF-68 UC will normally sell for between $1,500 and $3,000.

Valuation—This most desirable deep or ultra cameo issue generally commands $300 to $600 in **PF-65** to **PF-66 DC/UC**, and $1,000 to $2,000 in **PF-67.** This date trades in a very wide range in **PF-68 DC/UC**. Spotted examples with mismatched cameo contrast featuring a deep cameo obverse and a reverse that just sneaks into deep cameo have sold for as little as $1,150. However, the finest specimens, with very heavy cameo contrast (ECC quality) on both obverse and reverse, have usually sold for between $4,000 and $10,000.

The few **PF-69 DC/UC** specimens have sold in the past for between $18,000 and $27,000. However, *the most recent example to appear in auction realized $37,600!* This is currently the record.

⋯⇒ 1958, Proof ⇐⋯

PF-69 UC

While not quite as many Proof sets were produced in 1958 as 1957, the overall quality, while very high, was not quite on a par with the earlier 1956 and 1957 Proof Franklin issues. The great majority of 1958 Proof Franklins are very deeply mirrored. The heavy and abusive die polishing so prevalent on Proof Franklins from the early 1950s is no longer in evidence by 1958.

Nevertheless, a new phenomenon reared its head in 1958—milk spots. Many silver Proof coins struck between 1958 and 1964 have these spots, white splotches that may be as small and round as a pinhead, or large enough to cover half the surface of the coin and as irregularly shaped and numerous as the Aleutian Islands. The composition of these spots has never been determined, although the random nature of their appearance (no two Proofs have conclusively been shown to have identical milk spots in identical locations) and recent evidence suggest that the spots are a cleaning-agent residue left on the planchets as they went to the die press. If the spots had been the result of die imperfection, all Proof coins struck consecutively off that die would exhibit spotting in the same location. They do not.

Additionally, the very deeply mirrored surfaces of the typical 1958 Proof Franklin were typically not as free from hairlines as the 1956 and 1957 Proof Franklins.

NGC CERTIFIED POPULATION *(from a total mintage of 875,652)* (WCG™)

PF-64	PF-65	PF-66	PF-67	PF-68	PF-69
133	471	1,027	2,121	839	40
PF-64 Cam	**PF-65 Cam**	**PF-66 Cam**	**PF-67 Cam**	**PF-68 Cam**	**PF-69 Cam**
25	98	286	448	177	13
PF-64 UC	**PF-65 UC**	**PF-66 UC**	**PF-67 UC**	**PF-68 UC**	**PF-69 UC**
0	3	6	15	12	1

Brilliant Proof. As a result of the production problems outlined, superb high-grade PF-67 Franklins are more elusive than the 1957 and 1956 Type 2, and much more elusive in the highest PF-68 and PF-69 grades. At current levels, the 1958 offers tremendous value in PF-68 and PF-69. These examples are now more elusive than ever, and the premium over typical PF-65 and PF-66 examples is currently quite small.

Valuation—This date is a bargain in **PF-67** at the current $75–$125 price range, and at $250 to $500 for **PF-68s**. Given all the aforementioned problems, the 1958 is a tough, tough coin to find in these higher grades. The few **PF-69s** to appear on the market recently sold for $1,100 to $1,500—really quite a value, considering the tremendous rarity of the 1958 in this highest grade. On the rare occasions they surface, PF-69s have been trading at $1,100 to $1,500.

Cameo Proof. Gem minimally spotted 1958 cameo Proof Franklins exhibiting enough obverse and reverse contrast to earn a cameo designation are scarce, and far more elusive now than even six or seven years ago. Many cameo Franklins are mismatched, with heavier obverse contrast than reverse.

The 1958 is particularly elusive in very high-grade PF-68 Cam. Very few 1958 Proof Franklin halves were struck that exhibit the cameo contrast required for a PCGS or NGC cameo in virtually flawless, hairline-free, spot-free condition.

My recommendation is to focus on acquiring the especially superb examples that fall on the higher end of the cameo spectrum of NGC and PCGS, with ECC contrast.

Valuation—Only $100 to $200 for the average **PF-65** to **PF-66 Cam,** $300 to $500 for a **PF-67 Cam,** and $700 to $2,000 for a **PF-68 Cam.**

Deep Cameo Proof. As discussed in the chapter on Proof production, the increasing rarity of cameo Proof Franklins through the late 1950s could possibly be related to the wearing of the master die. The detail on the master die noticeably softened as the decade of the 1950s progressed, to the point where the Mint felt it necessary to rework the master die for the 1960 production year. Recognizing this deterioration in 1957, Mint personnel may have consciously shortened the pickling time for the Franklin Proof dies during preparation in an effort to retain as much of whatever detail was left on these dies. This theory would appear to be supported by the fact that Franklin Proof dies once again began to strike more cameos per die in 1960, when the new reworked master die was introduced. And unlike the Franklins, the cameo Proof dies striking the minors (quarters, dimes, nickels, and cents) did not experience the same phenomena as the cameo Franklin dies during the late 1950s, as their master dies did not suffer from the same wear problems as the larger Franklin master die. (The larger half dollar die required more die pressure for striking than the smaller denominations, accelerating the rate of wear.)

Ultra or deep cameo 1958 Franklin halves are extremely rare. In my 1991 book on cameos, I wrote that "Only 20 to 40 high-level, ultra heavy cameo Franklins may have been struck from Franklin Proof dies in 1958 before these dies would experience substantial frost fade on their devices." That statement was written before PCGS and NGC adopted new deep and ultra cameo standards for their services in 1992—as those standards came about as a result of my book. The deep and ultra cameo standards that were subsequently adopted by these services were slightly stricter than the ultra heavy standard used in my book and by cameo dealers and collectors at the time. In other words, there were some cameos we may have termed ultra heavy that PCGS or NGC might only grade cameo.

The net result is that the 1958, given the PCGS/NGC standard for deep or ultra cameo, is even rarer in this highest-level cameo condition than my 1991 book estimated, with its softer ultra heavy standard. In 1991 I estimated that as many as 440 1958 Proof Franklin halves might exist in DC or UC in PF-65 and higher. That number must now be revised downward; *probably only 200 to 300 examples survive in deep or ultra cameo.*

Most of these 1958s grade between PF-65 and PF-67, the aforementioned hairline and milk-spotting issues being the primary causes. Few 1958 Proof Franklins grade as high as PF-68 DC/UC, and only one example has been graded in PF-69 DC/UC.

Valuation—Under $1,000 in **PF-65** to **PF-66 DC/UC,** $2,000 to $4,000 in **PF-67 DC/UC.** Problem-free examples in **PF-68 DC/UC** have sold for as little as $6,000 but as much as $15,000+ for a couple of examples struck from the most phenomenal Franklin cameo die known. In a recent auction, a PCGS **PF-68+ DC** *sold for $32,900!*

There is a lone **PF-69 UC,** which sold for over $30,000.

⚬═ 1959, PROOF ═⚬

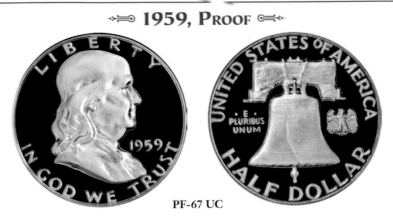

PF-67 UC

More than one million Proof sets were minted for the second time in Mint history. The quality of the 1959 Proof Franklins was very similar to that of the 1958s. 1959 was the final year the original master die would be in use. Much of the original detail found on the master die from its first years in use was by now almost gone. The Mint would rework the master die for 1960, restoring the lost detail, but in the meantime, it had to make do with the die at hand. Possibly due to the fact that it was working with worn dies, the pickling of the 1959 Proof Franklin dies was apparently used for a far shorter period for the 1959 Franklin than any year previously. 1959 Proof Franklins with deep acid-etched cameo surfaces similar to the finest 1956, 1957, and even 1958 Proof Franklins are virtually nonexistent.

NGC CERTIFIED POPULATION *(from a total mintage of 1,149,291)* (WCG™)

PF-64	PF-65	PF-66	PF-67	PF-68	PF-69
130	492	1,179	2,415	979	39
PF-64 Cam	PF-65 Cam	PF-66 Cam	PF-67 Cam	PF-68 Cam	PF-69 Cam
20	72	180	249	91	2
PF-64 UC	PF-65 UC	PF-66 UC	PF-67 UC	PF-68 UC	PF-69 UC
1	2	2	5	0	0

Brilliant Proof. The 1959 Proof Franklins are typically gem-quality coins with attractive, deep mirrors and minimal hairlines. However, like 1958 Proof Franklins they are often found with milk spots. Most 1959 Proof Franklins grade between PF-64 and PF-66. PF-67 examples are very scarce. The 1959 is quite challenging to locate in essentially flawless PF-68, and it is *very rare* in flawless PF-69.

Valuation—This issue has approximately the same rarity as the 1958 and the same approximate price range in brilliant condition, with **PF-67s** selling in the $75–$120 price range, and **PF-68s** in the $200–$400 range. Examples in **PF-69** are very rare, and have recently appreciated into the $1,100 to $1,500 range.

Cameo Proof. This is the toughest of the 1954–1963 Franklin issues to find in gem cameo. A significant percentage of 1959 Proof Franklins, perhaps 2% to 3%, was struck with at least mild cameo contrast, but a far smaller percentage, far less than 1% of the total mintage, exhibits enough cameo contrast on both obverse and reverse to warrant a cameo designation from either PCGS or NGC.

When found in cameo, most 1959 Franklin halves grade between PF-64 and PF-67. NGC-graded PF-68 cameo examples are rare. PCGS-graded PF-68 cameo examples are very rare.

Valuation—Even tougher than the 1958 in cameo, despite its million-plus mintage, the 1959 ranks among the key dates in the series. As such, it is a true bargain at current levels, with **PF-65** and **PF-66** specimens generally trading for as little as $250 to $500, and **PF-67 Cam** coins for $700 to $1,500. **PF-68 Cam** examples sell for $2,000 to $8,000, depending on the cameo contrast, with ECC-designated coins being fast sellers up to $10,000.

Deep Cameo Proof. *Extremely* rare! Despite having a mintage of over one million sets, the 1959 Proof Franklin ranks among the key dates in the series in ultra or deep cameo condition. Check the population numbers: they are an accurate reflection of this date's true rarity. As further evidence, I have been treasure hunting for superb cameo Proof coins since 1981. In that time, I have had the opportunity to look through well over one hundred thousand 1959 Proof sets, a significant percentage of which were still sealed from the day they left the Mint. After all this effort, while I have handled some ultra or deep cameo 1959 Lincoln cents, a Jefferson nickel or two, a few Roosevelt dimes, and a few Washington quarters, I have *never* had the good fortune of finding a 1959 Franklin in ultra or deep cameo.

The most likely explanation for the tremendous rarity of this issue in ultra or deep cameo is linked to the decline in the quality of the master die. In use since 1948, the master die by 1959 was quite worn, with almost all the original fine detail of Franklin's bust and the Liberty Bell having deteriorated to a soft mush. The Mint was obviously very aware of this decline in quality, as it reworked the master die prior to the 1960 Proof Franklin run.

Obviously, an extensive acid bath to create the desired cameo effect would further erode whatever detail was left on the 1959 working dies. The most likely scenario is that Mint personnel, in an effort to conserve design detail, cut short the pickling time of the Proof Franklin dies. As a result, only the very, very earliest strikes off these dies exhibited enough contrast to earn an ultra or deep cameo designation. The lightly acid-etched frost of the die would rapidly wear thereafter.

Compounding the problem in finding superb 1959 cameo Franklin halves are two other factors. The first is the great "silver melt" of 1979 and 1980, when silver exploded in value, briefly touching $50 per ounce, with the result that many 1957–1963 Proof

Franklins were melted for their bullion. The second factor is that many cameo 1959 Proof Franklin halves were ruined through incorrect dipping.

This latter phenomenon is most prevalent in the 1958 and 1959 Proof silver issues. Before the advent of conservation services like Numismatic Conservation Services (NCS), collectors would often attempt to remove toning or spots on their Proof coins with one of the many available acid-based coin dips on the market. Most silver Proof coins react surprisingly well to this process. Not so with 1958 and 1959 silver Proof coins. 1958 or 1959 Proof silver Franklin half dollars, Washington quarters, and Roosevelt dimes typically come out of a dip exhibiting myriad light green spots. If dipped a second time, these coins will have even more spots.

Why the silver Proof issues of these two years react in this manner likely has something to do with the surface film left on the planchet after striking—perhaps a lubricant used on the dies that was not used previous to those years or after them.

Good luck in your hunt for the elusive deep or ultra cameo 1959. It ranks in the big three in the series in rarity in this condition, alongside the 1950 and 1952 Proof Franklins. Again, for the record, I have never personally found an example of any of these three dates in gem ultra or deep condition.

The likelihood that any new "discovery coins" from these three years will surface grows slimmer with each passing year, as by this time, it is estimated that well over 95% of the total mintage of 1950–1964 Proof coins has been picked through many times over for the elusive cameo.

Valuation—Along with the 1950 and 1952, the 1959 is the rarest nonvariety Franklin in deep or ultra cameo. **PF-65** and **PF-66** coins are $3,000 to $6,000 and climbing. **PF-67 DC/UC** coins, which do not often surface, have traded across an enormous range from $8,900 to $18,000 in recent years. In fact, this coin is a chance to illustrate why the buyer needs to study the market carefully before trusting the grade on the holder. As a dealer, I have seen this coin (and others) slabbed as PF-67 DC, only to develop myriad white spots after encapsulation. Such a coin, if cracked out, professionally restored, and resubmitted, might grade at only PF-66 DC or even lower. The collector buying a PF-67 DC–graded coin with spots for about $9,000 may be getting a PF-66 DC for which he could have paid $5,500. Among 1959 Franklins, truly beautiful PF-67 DC coins have traded at around $12,000 to $15,000, and I believe this date is likely headed for the $30,000 plateau, given its importance as a key-date issue within the series.

1960, PROOF

PF-68 DC

Almost 1.7 million Proof sets were minted in 1960, surpassing the previous high that was set in 1957 of 1.25 million sets. The year 1960 is also notable for the reworked master die used for the Franklin half. The design detail that had eroded on the original master die from many years of use was restored on the master die. The definition of Franklin's hair is much sharper, as is the detail on the Liberty Bell.

NGC CERTIFIED POPULATION *(from a total mintage of 1,691,602)*   (WCG™)

PF-64	PF-65	PF-66	PF-67	PF-68	PF-69
194	589	1,210	2,616	1,000	34
PF-64 Cam	PF-65 Cam	PF-66 Cam	PF-67 Cam	PF-68 Cam	PF-69 Cam
29	146	452	757	321	5
PF-64 UC	PF-65 UC	PF-66 UC	PF-67 UC	PF-68 UC	PF-69 UC
0	14	51	91	63	1

Brilliant Proof. Because of the high mintage, the 1960 Proof Franklin was one of the issues melted in quantity during the bullion boom of the late 1970s. Additionally, this date is plagued by the highest incidence of milk spotting of any issue in the Proof Franklin series. Milk spots, which mysteriously first appeared on silver Proof coins in 1958, occur on a very high percentage of 1960 Proof Franklin halves, with about one in four Proof 1960 Franklins, or 25%, exhibiting some degree of spotting. Milk spots would continue to be a problem, although to a somewhat lesser degree, on silver Proof issues from 1961 through 1964.

Virtually all 1960 Proof Franklin halves are very deeply mirrored. Many examples have very hazy toned surfaces from the many years' storage in the original government-issue flat pack. Mysteriously, most of the 1960 Proof Franklin halves found in flat packs with the rare Small Date Lincoln cent variety are very heavily toned.

Hairlines are also a major problem for this date. Most 1960 Proof Franklin halves exhibit some degree of hairlining. When these are combined with the milk spots often found, most examples grade between PF-64 and PF-66. Near-perfect PF-68 examples are extremely scarce, and PF-69 examples are very rare.

Valuation—The higher-grade PF-68 and PF-69 1960 Franklins offer exceptional value at current levels. With average **PF-65** certified examples selling for $15 to $20, and **PF-67s** at $60 to $100, the date is a real bargain in **PF-68,** given its rarity, offering excellent upside at the current $150–$250 trade levels. **PF-69** examples are extremely rare, and will bring between $1,000 and $1,800.

Cameo Proof. As further evidence that the deteriorated condition of the master die in 1959 may have been responsible for changes in working die preparation that resulted in fewer cameos being struck, with a reworked master die in use in 1960 there was a major increase in the percentage of cameos struck. The finest cameo examples are quite spectacular, ranking among the most visually appealing cameo Franklins in the series, exhibiting obverse cameo frost and depth of mirror that few other Franklin issues can match. The only small negative is the fact that the reverses of these coins generally do not match the obverse in cameo contrast.

Additionally, many 1960 cameo Franklins are marred by milk spots, hairlines, or both. This date is approaching rarity status in the higher PF-68 Cam grade. Flawless PF-69 Cam examples have always been very rare.

Valuation—This issue is a very uncommon "common date" in cameo, a bargain in the current $50–$100 range for coins in **PF-65** and **PF-66 Cam** coins, and $175 to $325 for **PF-67 Cams. PF-68 Cams** rarely surface anymore, and are still quite inexpensive when they do, usually selling for $400 to $600 for nice solid cameos. This date is due for some appreciation.

Deep Cameo Proof. Two kinds of ultra or deep cameo 1960 Franklins are typically encountered. Most examples feature very attractive matching obverse and reverse cameo contrast. When devoid of milk spots, these coins are very attractive. If one is seeking out the most stunning cameo example possible of this date, it will likely be an example with mismatched cameo contrast. Mismatched 1960 ultra and deep cameo Franklin halves feature truly stunning obverse cameo contrast, with thick white frost and jet-black mirrored fields that few other Franklin issues can match. Think of these obverses as UC+ or DC+. The reverses of these examples do not exhibit the same degree of contrast. They offer exceptional contrast, but not of the thickly frosted snow-white variety, and might best be described as UC– or DC–.

While problem-free PF-68 DC/UC Franklins typically trade for between $1,000 and $2,000, the more spectacular examples have traded for $3,000 or more on the rare occasions they have surfaced.

A handful of 1960 Franklins have been certified in ultimate PF-69 UC/DC: one by NGC and five by PCGS at the time of this writing. It should be noted that PCGS has not graded an example in many years, with the NGC example having been graded in 2002.

This is a highly recommended date if you can find one in exceptional cameo.

Valuation—$100 to $300 in **PF-65** and **PF-66 DC/UC**, $350 to $700 in **PF-67 DC/ UC**, and $2,000 to $4,500 in **PF-68 DC/UC**. Examples selling in the lower price ranges generally have noticeable milk spots. *A new record was established* when a spectacular NGC **PF-69 UC** off a top cameo die sold for *more than $30,000*.

1960 PROOF DOUBLED-DIE OBVERSE VARIETY

This doubled die is the second strongest in this series. Doubling is seen on LIBERTY, IN GOD WE TRUST, and the date, with quadrupling on the Y of LIBERTY. Some of the early strikes from this die have nice cameo devices. This is a nice variety to find.

⇜ 1961, Proof ⇝

PF-68 DC

The Mint took another quantum leap forward in Proof production in 1961. Over *three million* Proof sets were issued that year—a plateau that, with few exceptions, they have remained at ever since, generally producing three to four million Proof sets every year. The one glaring exception to this monumental output was the 1965–1967 period, when no Proof sets were issued at all, the Mint producing the short-lived Special Mint Set series instead.

The tremendous growth in Proof set production was obviously a response to the tremendous growth in numismatics in the United States from the early 1950s to the early 1960s. It was, after all, the time of the "baby boom" generation, and middle-class Americans were experiencing a level of affluence no generation before had ever experienced in such numbers.

The 1961 Franklin was one of the issues *melted in large quantity* for its bullion content during the silver boom of the late 1970s, by virtue of its high mintage and common-date status.

NGC CERTIFIED POPULATION *(from a total mintage of 3,028,244)*   (WCG™)

PF-64	PF-65	PF-66	PF-67	PF-68	PF-69
251	841	1,718	4,179	1,565	51
PF-64 Cam	PF-65 Cam	PF-66 Cam	PF-67 Cam	PF-68 Cam	PF-69 Cam
28	104	477	983	531	14
PF-64 UC	PF-65 UC	PF-66 UC	PF-67 UC	PF-68 UC	PF-69 UC
9	13	35	119	67	4

Brilliant Proof. Despite the much higher mintage, the Proof coins struck were generally of gem quality. 1961 Franklin halves in PF-65 are not terribly difficult to acquire. This date becomes much more challenging to locate in PF-67, with perhaps one of every ten original sets grading that high.

The 1961 Franklin is rare in the higher PF-68 grade. Again, hairlines and minor milk spotting generally knock at least a point or two off the grade of an otherwise flawless, deeply mirrored, attractive coin.

The 1961 is *very rare* in the highest PF-69 grade. Close inspection under a strong halogen light almost always reveals tiny imperfections, small hairlines, that keep even the loveliest examples from this highest grade.

Valuation—Given their scarcity, **PF-67s** are a great value at the current $100–$200 price level. **PF-68** 1961 Franklins are double those numbers, making this another date that offers great "upside" in these higher grades. Good luck looking for a PF-69—a couple of those have sold for $1,500.

Cameo Proof. Proof mintage is *not* an accurate indicator of an issue's relative rarity in cameo condition. No better example exists to illustrate this fact than the 1961 Proof Franklin. Despite having a mintage of over three million sets, a total virtually identical to the 1962 and 1963 Proof Franklins that follow, the 1961 is many times more elusive in cameo than either of those years.

The 1961 Franklin is elusive in all grades of Proof cameo, but especially PF-68 Cam. It is extremely rare in PF-69 Cam, with only a few examples having been certified by either PCGS or NGC.

Valuation—**PF-65** and **PF-66 Cam** coins with minor spotting usually sell for between $40 and $60. Superb **PF-67 Cam** 1961 Franklin halves are a great buy at the current $125–$225 level, though examples with exceptional deep or ultra cameo obverses will command considerably more. **PF-68 Cam** specimens are rarely encountered anymore, but when they do surface, they are in the $275–$475 range. Again, specimens with superior cameo contrast for the grade will command more.

Deep Cameo Proof. The 1961 is extremely scarce in ultra or deep cameo, easily as rare as the 1960, despite the fact the 1961 has a total Proof mintage almost double the 1960. I noted this fact back in 1991 in my book on cameos and brilliant proofs. Though PCGS and NGC had not yet adopted ultra and deep cameo standards for this coinage, knowledgeable dealers and collectors knew that the 1961 was far more elusive in exceptional cameo condition than the high mintage figures might initially lead one to believe.

The greatest obstacle in locating fully ultra or deep cameo examples is finding coins that exhibit this level of cameo contrast on both obverse and reverse. On occasion a 1961 will surface with extraordinary obverse cameo contrast, but with reverse contrast considerably lighter. As with the 1960, the finest ultra or deep cameo 1961 Proof Franklin halves are mismatched cameos, with superb, intensely frosted cameo obverses, and reverses that, while very well contrasted, fall into the lower range of the ultra or deep cameo standard. A couple of the finest of these examples have been certified as PF-68★ UC by NGC and have traded for more than $4,000.

Attesting to the challenge in locating superb ultra or deep cameo 1961 Proof Franklins, a large percentage of the population graded in PF-68 UC/DC often exhibits a small milk spot or two. Until recently, the 1961 was the only issue of the 1960–1963 era not to have a single example graded in PF-69 UC/DC. A magnificent specimen eventually surfaced in mid-2004, handled by yours truly. The coin ranked among the earliest strikes off one of the most arresting cameo dies known for that year. It was of the mismatched cameo variety, with a lovely snow-white ultra reverse, but an even more sensational, thickly frosted UC+ obverse.

Having dealt in superb cameo Proofs since 1981, I was beginning to wonder if I would ever have the opportunity of handling a 1961 in this grade—PF-69 UC/DC—particularly when the reality was that superb cameo coinage of the 1950–1967 era was more difficult to locate with each passing year. Having the great pleasure of placing this magnificent 1961 with a client ranked among the highlights of 2004 for me.

Valuation—Spotted **PF-65** and **PF-66 DC/UC** coins are generally priced between $100 and $300. The 1961 in **PF-67 UC** is a solid $400–$900 coin. **PF-68 DC/UC** coins trade in a very wide range. Examples on the low end of the deep or ultra cameo spectrum have sometimes been sold for under $1,000 (usually if they are spotted). At the other end of the spectrum, a couple of specimens with truly superior (ECC) cameo contrast compared to what one typically finds for this date have sold for between $4,000 and $5,000. *A new price record was recently set* when a PCGS **PF-69 DCAM** sold $40,800.

1961 Proof Doubled-Die Reverse Variety

This is the king of 20th-century Proof half dollar error varieties! When they think of major doubled-die varieties in U.S. coinage, the coin that first comes into many collectors' and dealers' mind is the 1955-P Mint State Doubled-Die Obverse Lincoln cent. And rightly so. An important criterion for determining the potential collector interest in a die variety is its visibility. The 1955 Doubled-Die Obverse Lincoln cent exhibits doubling that is very dramatic, and clearly visible to the naked eye.

The 1961 Doubled-Die Reverse Proof Franklin is just such a variety. There are several Doubled-Die Reverse 1961 varieties, but only one exhibits dramatic doubling that is clearly visible

Doubling evident in legend

under even the most casual inspection. The doubling on this variety can be seen very clearly in the phrase E PLURIBUS UNUM and the word UNITED.

Brilliant Proof. The 1961 Doubled-Die Reverse is extremely rare in any condition. To date, PCGS and NGC combined have certified a total of only 128 examples in all grades. Comparing this number to the totals of the 1955 Doubled-Die Lincoln cent (of which more than 5,000 have been graded), there is no question that the 1961 Franklin is by far the rarer of the two varieties.

Most examples that surface exhibit no cameo contrast, and often are severely hairlined with some milk spotting. The 1961 is very rare in PF-65 and PF-66, and extremely rare in PF-67.

When one compares the far smaller current population totals of the 1961 Doubled-Die Reverse Proof Franklin to the far higher population numbers of the 1955 Doubled-Die Obverse Lincoln, with both doubled-die varieties being of major status, and sees the Franklin currently selling for a fraction of the price of the Lincoln, it would seem there is tremendous potential for future long-term appreciation for the Franklin—particularly for those examples without milk spots.

Valuation—This is a $2,000–$4,000 coin in **PF-64**—usually with milk spots. Exceptional spot-free **PF-65** and **PF-66** gems currently command little more ($3,000 to $5,000). **PF-67** specimens are a tremendous value at current levels of $6,000 to $10,000!

Cameo Proof. Although *extremely* rare, it does exist. To date a few examples have surfaced. There is a good chance a few more may appear in the years ahead, as many of the non-cameo-designated examples currently certified display some cameo contrast, with the obverse usually exhibiting slightly more contrast than the reverse.

The finest example known in cameo was a specimen I handled around the year 2000. It was a magnificent PCGS PF-67 Cam, with a borderline deep cameo obverse and heavily contrasted reverse.

Certainly at current levels the 1961 Doubled-Die Reverse Franklin offers exceptional value in cameo.

Valuation—I have handled only a single coin in cameo, a coin graded **PF-67** by PCGS. That coin sold for well over $20,000—but that was around the year 2000. The coin should be worth considerably more today.

Deep Cameo Proof. It *does* exist, with one example certified many years ago. Handled by me, the coin is an exceptional example graded by NGC in PF-67 UC. The obverse and reverse cameo contrast of this coin is outstanding, and fully deserving of the ultra classification. The coin has a couple of light, faint milk spots in the obverse field that would be consistent with a PF-67 grade, considering that the coin is essentially hairline free.

Of course, the existence of this single example raises a question: If this example was struck in ultra, there must have been others, as even the most delicate cameo Franklin dies of that era still possessed the durability to strike at least 5 to 10 high-quality ultra or deep cameo coins before frost-fade would set in. What of the other possible half dozen or more examples? It is quite possible that they were all melted down during the silver melt of the late 1970s. It is also possible that they still exist and are waiting to be discovered.

Valuation—Only one is known, a **PF-67 UC** currently owned by a client of mine. The selling price is confidential, though it was over $25,000.

⋙ 1962, PROOF ⋘

PF-69 DC

In 1962, once again, more than three million Proof sets were struck. Mintage has consistently been around this level or higher ever since, with the occasional lapses in years when no Proof coins were struck. As with other higher-mintage Proof Franklins in the series, many examples were melted down decades ago for their bullion value when silver was up near $50 an ounce.

NGC CERTIFIED POPULATION *(from a total mintage of 3,218,019)* (WCG™)

PF-64	PF-65	PF-66	PF-67	PF-68	PF-69
335	979	2,047	3,942	1,664	67
PF-64 Cam	PF-65 Cam	PF-66 Cam	PF-67 Cam	PF-68 Cam	PF-69 Cam
96	374	1,315	2,637	1,289	53
PF-64 UC	PF-65 UC	PF-66 UC	PF-67 UC	PF-68 UC	PF-69 UC
21	99	230	518	224	21

Brilliant Proof. The quality of the 1962 non-cameo Proof Franklin is roughly equivalent to the quality of the 1961. Milk spots are still a problem. The very high comparable mintages of the 1961 and 1962 result in these two issues' being approximately equal in rarity in PF-65–PF-68 condition. This date has also had several dozen examples graded in non-cameo PF-69, while the 1961 has had relatively fewer of such coins certified.

Valuation—This is a good coin in **PF-67,** now selling for between $40 and $80. Since publication of the second edition of this book, the 1962 in **PF-68** has become considerably more difficult to locate. I am often out of stock. This is a solid $100 to $200 value. Meanwhile, **PF-69**s generally trade in the $500 to $1,000 range.

Cameo Proof. When beginning a cameo Franklin set, the date a novice collector is most likely to first acquire would be the 1962, for two reasons. First, it is a very attractive high-quality issue, with most cameo examples displaying very even, matching cameo contrast on obverse and reverse. Second, it is the easiest date to acquire.

To call the 1962 a common date might be misleading, as it might give the uninitiated collector the impression that the 1962 is easy to acquire. While that may have been true many years ago, back in the 1990s, this is no longer the case.

Indeed, prior to the 21st century, I could always count on having at least a few dozen cameo-designated 1962 Franklins halves in stock. In fact, they were easy enough to acquire that I never bothered handling any cameo-designated examples in grades lower than PF-67.

Since the early 2000s, even PF-65 Cam examples have become elusive, and I have been raising my buy prices in an effort to lure more examples into inventory.

Valuation—The rise in value of late of this issue in cameo is a good reflection of the increasing scarcity of this issue. NGC examples in **PF-65** and **PF-66** have increased from $20 to $25 to the $30–$50 range.

The increase in value in PF-67 and PF-68 has been even more dramatic. NGC and PCGS **PF-68 Cam** examples could be acquired for as little as $60 to $70 in the 1990s. They have more than doubled in price since then, usually trading for $120 to $200 for **PF-67 Cams,** and for about double that for PF-68s.

Deep Cameo Proof. The so-called common date in the series in deep or ultra cameo, this issue is by no means common. *All Franklin dates have become difficult to acquire with this degree of cameo contrast in the past few years*, but it is all relative, and some issues are far more rare than others.

The 1962 deep or ultra cameo Franklin most closely resembles the 1880-S deep mirror prooflike Morgan dollar, in terms of its rarity and quality within the series. Morgan collectors are aware that, when found in exceptional deep mirror prooflike (DMPL) condition, the 1880-S ranks among the most visually appealing issues in the series, exhibiting lovely heavily frosted cameo devices contrasted against deeply mirrored fields. There was also a time, going back to the 1980s, when the 1880-S was the common date of the series in gem DMPL and was readily available in this condition. Those days are gone, as knowledgeable DMPL Morgan collectors have salted these most attractive coins away.

So it is with the 1962 deep cameo Proof Franklin.

Valuation—Once available in at least small quantities in deep or ultra cameo, the 1962 is approaching rarity status. **PF-65** and **PF-66 DC/UC** examples generally trade for between $100 and $200. This date is in high demand in spot-free **PF-67 DC/UC,** now commanding $300 to $500.

The finest **PF-68** examples have crept up in value recently from their lows of $250 to $500, for NGC and PCGS examples with slightly less cameo contrast, to $1,000 to $2,000 for the occasional monster black-and-white.

The 1962 is available in **PF-69 DC/UC**, but it is very rare in this ultimate condition. The last PCGS-graded example I handled was sold for $15,000. A similar NGC example in **PF-69** UC commanded more than $9,000.

There would appear to be plenty more upside for these ultimate-grade Proof Franklin halves. Fresh reserves of deep or ultra cameo 1962s are few and far between, with at least 90% of existing Proof sets of this year having now been picked through. The chances of finding a 1962 with ultimate matching snow-white frost *and* flawless, spot-free, hairline-free surfaces is very small.

Indeed, in some 30 years of searching through original Proof sets, over which time I have probably handled 200,000 to 300,000 sets, there has been only one 1962 that received a PF-69 DC/UC grade.

⊷⊳ 1963, Proof ⊲⊶

PF-69 DC

The Franklin series came to a premature end with the assassination of President John F. Kennedy in November 1963. The Mint once again cranked out just over three million sets. As was the case with the Proof sets of 1957 to 1962, a large number of these sets forever disappeared from the marketplace in late 1979 and early 1980 during the silver boom, when these common-date silver Proof coins were melted for their silver content.

NGC CERTIFIED POPULATION *(from a total mintage of 3,075,645)*   (WCG™)

PF-64	PF-65	PF-66	PF-67	PF-68	PF-69
283	824	1,755	5,044	2,463	118
PF-64 Cam	PF-65 Cam	PF-66 Cam	PF-67 Cam	PF-68 Cam	PF-69 Cam
54	249	1,059	2,252	1,077	56
PF-64 UC	PF-65 UC	PF-66 UC	PF-67 UC	PF-68 UC	PF-69 UC
13	47	130	292	157	5

Brilliant Proof. The quality of the 1963 is only slightly better than that of the 1961 and 1962. Milk spots continue to be a problem. Hairlines can still be found on virtually all 1963 Proof Franklin halves, though usually in smaller numbers than on the earlier issues.

Valuation—This is a good coin in **PF-67,** generally selling for between $40 and $75. In PF-68 the price range is now $80 to $175.

Cameo Proof. The 1963 is approximately as rare as the 1962 in cameo, and is also found in one-sided cameo condition almost as frequently as in full cameo obverse and reverse. These coins are all very elusive. At current values, these later-date cameo Franklin half dollars offer tremendous value and upside potential.

But the well is pretty dry, folks. Virtually all the Proof sets from the 1950–1964 era have now been drilled, plundered, for their precious cameo coins. Specimens that surface today are more typically from already-established collections where they have been residing for many years.

Valuation—This issue is a $30–$60 coin in **PF-65** and **PF-66 Cam.** It is a strong $120–$200 coin in **PF-67 Cam,** and a $250–$400 coin in **PF-68 Cam. PF-69 Cam** specimens have sold for over $1,000.

Deep Cameo Proof. Some of the most beautiful deep or ultra cameo coins are of 1963 vintage. While all deep or ultra cameos in spot-free condition are stunning and beautiful, some are more stunning and beautiful than others. Indeed, when PCGS needed a Franklin in DC+ grade for their grading set, the only coin I could find that offered DC+ cameo contrast on both obverse *and* reverse was a 1963, one of only three I had from a spectacular hoard that had surfaced in the late 1980s.

While I don't like to engage in crystal-ball price predictions, I do feel comfortable with this final statement on the Proof Franklin half dollar series: superb non-cameo Proof specimens are rarer with each passing year. At current price levels, these coins will only increase in value over time.

The same can be said for the Franklin cameo. There will always be collectors who seek the best and who have the financial resources to pay for it. For those individuals, the increasingly elusive, rare, and beautiful Franklin cameo coin will attract their interest. There is no other Proof half dollar in U.S. numismatics that offers so much in terms of eye appeal, quality, and rarity, for the numismatic dollar.

Valuation—All Franklin half dollars, whether cameo or deep or ultra cameo, are approaching rarity status. **PF-65** and **PF-66 DC/UC** examples generally trade for between $100 and $200. This date is in high demand in spot-free **PF-67 DC/UC**, which is now commanding $300 to $500.

The finest **PF-68** examples currently trade in a range between $600 and $2,000, depending on the cameo contrast.

The finest **PF-69 DC/UC** examples have increased in value over the past three years. The few coins that have surfaced have sold for $10,000 to $17,000!

KENNEDY HALF DOLLAR
ANALYSIS BY DATE,
MINTMARK, AND VARIETY

INTRODUCTION

BIOGRAPHY OF JOHN F. KENNEDY

John Fitzgerald Kennedy was born on May 29, 1917, in Massachusetts, the second son of Joseph and Rose Kennedy. His father was a wealthy businessman with powerful political connections and great ambitions for his family. John went to several schools in his youth, graduating from Choate in June 1935, with the yearbook (of which he was the business manager) noting that he was "the most likely to succeed." In October 1935 he enrolled late for the term at Princeton University where he spent six weeks, but was beset with health problems. After recuperation in 1936 he enrolled as a freshman at Harvard College, from which he graduated. In June 1938 he went with his father and his brother Joe on the SS *Normandie* to spend July working with his father, who had been appointed United States ambassador to the Court of St. James by President Franklin Roosevelt. For much of 1939 he toured through Europe including the Soviet Union, the Middle East, and the Balkan countries, concluding in late August with a visit to Czechoslovakia and Germany before returning to London on September 1, 1939, the day that Germany invaded Poland.

In 1940, Kennedy finished a thesis for Harvard, "Appeasement in Munich," about the part the British held in the Munich agreement. In June 1940 he graduated cum laude from Harvard with a degree in international affairs. His thesis was published in July 1940, somewhat revised, titled *While England Slept*, and became a best seller. From September to December 1940, Kennedy attended the Stanford Graduate School of Business in Palo Alto. In May and June 1941 he traveled in South America.

In the spring of 1941 Kennedy volunteered for the Army but was rejected because of chronic lower-back problems that would plague him for the rest of his life. However, in September the Navy accepted him because of influence brought by his father. He attended training, then was assigned duty in Panama, then eventually in the Pacific. On August 2, 1943, the *PT-109*, with Kennedy in command, and the *PT-162* and *PT-169* were sent on nighttime patrol near New Georgia in the Solomon Islands. Kennedy's ship was rammed by a Japanese destroyer. He was thrown across the deck, but rallied his men and swam for safety to an island, towing a badly burned crew member with a jacket strap clenched in his teeth. The survivors went to another island where they were eventually rescued. After other service, Kennedy was honorably discharged early in 1945. He received multiple decorations for his service. His exploits with *PT-109* became the subject of several articles, books, and even a song.

After the war Kennedy represented the 11th Congressional District in the U.S. House of Representatives from 1947 to 1953 on the Democratic ticket,. Then he served in the United States Senate from 1953 until 1960. In the presidential election of 1960 he defeated Republican candidate Richard Milhous Nixon in a close contest. He was the first president born in the 20th century and, after Theodore Roosevelt, at age 43 was the youngest to take the office. He was the first Catholic to serve as president, which caused some unfavorable comment during his campaign, as news media wondered whether anyone claiming responsibility to the Pope could put the interests of America first. He was also the first Irish-American to become president and the only president who was awarded the Pulitzer Prize.

Before the presidency, though, came a variety of political experiences. In 1946 when Representative James Michael Curley vacated his seat in the House of Representatives to become mayor of Boston, Kennedy ran for the position, easily overcoming his Republican opponent. He served in Congress for six years, with a mixed record, often dissenting from President Harry S Truman and other Democrats. In 1952 he upset incumbent Republican Henry Cabot Lodge Jr., in the race for the United States Senate. On September 12, 1953, he married Jacqueline Lee Bouvier. His health continued to be a great problem, and he underwent several spinal operations and was often absent from Washington. During one convalescent period in 1956 his *Profiles in Courage* book was published, exploring eight instances in which senators put their personal beliefs in front of their political careers. This gained a Pulitzer Prize for biography in 1957. Later it was revealed that a close advisor, Ted Sorensen, had been the co-author.

In the 1956 presidential election, Democratic nominee Adlai Stevenson considered Kennedy as his running mate, but the party chose Senator Estes Kefauver instead. Kennedy received much favorable attention. Probably his appearance on the ticket would not have made much difference, as Eisenhower was extremely popular and won overwhelmingly in the election. In 1958 Kennedy was elected to a second term in the Senate.

On January 2, 1960, Kennedy declared his intention to run for president of the United States. In the Democratic primary he was challenged by Senator Hubert Humphrey of Minnesota and Senator Wayne Morse of Oregon. At the nominating convention in Los Angeles he faced Senator Lyndon B. Johnson of Texas, who had great support among the delegates, as did Senator Stuart Symington of Missouri. On July 13, 1960, the convention nominated Kennedy as its candidate, and Kennedy chose Johnson as vice president, despite objections from others, including his brother, Robert Kennedy. He felt Johnson provided the strength to win in the South. Election issues and challenges included problems with the economy, Kennedy's Catholic religion, and Soviet accomplishments in space and in missiles which seemed to be outpacing those of the United States. His challenger was Richard M. Nixon, of California. The two engaged in the first-ever televised debates between two presidential candidates. Kennedy came across as confident and outgoing, while Nixon appeared uncomfortable and awkward. In November, Kennedy carried the day, with many saying that the debates were a pivotal point. He was inaugurated on January 30, 1961, as the thirty-fifth president. At his address he adapted a saying from Winston Churchill, now given as "Ask not what your country can do for you, ask what you can do for your country."

Before Kennedy was elected, the Eisenhower administration devised a plan to invade Cuba to instigate citizens to rise up against dictator Fidel Castro. On April 17, 1961, Kennedy ordered this to proceed. A brigade of Cuban exiles, about 1,500 in number, came to the island, but Kennedy was reluctant to supply air support. Within two days the Cubans had captured or killed many people, and Kennedy was humiliated to negotiate for the release of 1,189 survivors. Twenty months later Cuba released the exiles in exchange for $53 million worth of food and medicine. From that point onward, the United States and Cuba were at odds, and Cuba, which never did anything to actually harm the American government, was treated as an enemy.

On the other hand his handling of the Cuban Missile crisis was considered to be masterful. The confrontation started on October 14, 1962, when U-2 spy planes took pictures of a ballistic missile site being constructed by the Soviets in Cuba. Kennedy saw the pictures on October 16, and realized that soon there would be a threat to America. If the United States attacked the sites it might precipitate war, but if it did nothing, then these missiles would be put in place, ready to go. Certain Cabinet members and advisors wanted an air assault, but Kennedy elected to negotiate with the Soviets and order them to remove all material being built in Cuba. A week later, Soviet Premier Nikita Khrushchev and Kennedy reached a cordial agreement, which lasted. In the meantime, American citizens were on the edge of their seats thinking that a confrontation might happen at any time. This was probably the highlight accomplishment of the young president's political career.

In Vietnam, in early 1961 Kennedy used limited military action to fight Communist forces led by Ho Chi Minh. He viewed this as necessary to fight Communism, and authorized military support for the South Vietnamese government, an unstable group put in place by the French who had earlier controlled the area. Some 16,000 military advisors and special forces were sent there, beginning an escalation which led to the Vietnam War, which became one of the most divisive actions in American history when it was vastly expanded by his successor in office, President Lyndon B. Johnson. The Berlin Wall was built during his administration, separating East Berlin from West Berlin. The Peace Corps was found, and advances were made in civil rights.

The Kennedy family—the president, wife Jackie, and children John and Caroline—became a favorite news subject, in a favorable manner. Young children in the Oval Office were a novelty to magazine readers and television viewers. The Kennedys were considered to be an ideal American family, and his administration to be ideal in many ways.

At the height of his popularity, JFK, as he often referred to himself, went to Dallas with his wife and various officials. While in a ceremonial motorcade he was fired upon by Lee Harvey Oswald, who had hidden in room high in a nearby building. The president was gravely injured and was rushed to a hospital, but died soon afterward. The nation mourned his loss. On November 25, 1963, Kennedy's body was buried in the Arlington National Cemetery. He was survived by his widow Jacqueline and his children. His brothers, Robert Kennedy and Edward Kennedy, each went on to notable political careers.

HISTORY OF THE KENNEDY HALF DOLLAR

Shortly after President John F. Kennedy's death on November 23, 1963, plans for a memorial coin began. In fact, Mint Director Eva Adams authorized work on the coin as early as November 27, and the first dies were completed by January 2, 1964. Chief Engraver Gilroy Roberts accomplished this feat by adapting the design of Kennedy's inaugural medal of 1961.

While Roberts was busy making modifications for the obverse, Assistant Engraver Frank Gasparro designed the reverse to incorporate the presidential seal. IN GOD WE TRUST appears in a straight line below the left-facing bust, and the motto LIBERTY along with the year arcs around the periphery. On the obverse, the value HALF DOLLAR, Gasparro's initials, and UNITED STATES OF AMERICA are the only elements besides the seal. The Presidential seal incorporates the basic elements of the Great Seal of the United States and features a heraldic eagle within a circle of 50 stars. The Kennedy half dollar has a reeded edge.

In a manifestation of Red Scare rumors, Roberts's stylized initials were once interpreted to have been the Soviet hammer and sickle.

In 1964 only, the Kennedy half dollar was produced in 90 percent silver for both circulation strikes and Proofs. The silver percentage was reduced to 40 in 1965, and was eliminated entirely in 1971.

An instant collectible, the Kennedy half dollar was sought after worldwide. In fact, the silver coins were hoarded to the extent that they never saw significant circulation. However, they were a mainstay of gambling casinos for many years. Casinos have since phased out acceptance of the half dollars in favor of their own tokens.

UNCIRCULATED KENNEDY HALF DOLLARS
⊷ 1964-P, MINT STATE ⊷

MS-67

With the assassination of President John F. Kennedy on November 22, 1963, Congress voted to prematurely end the Franklin half dollar series and replace it with a new Kennedy half dollar. The response from the public was overwhelmingly favorable, and the new Kennedy half dollar was struck in record numbers for a half dollar. In 1964 alone, the Philadelphia Mint struck more than 273 million coins, while the Denver Mint struck over 156 million. The total for this year alone was close to the entire circulation-strike production of the Franklin half series, spanning from 1948 through 1963. This is the only circulation-strike Kennedy half dollar that is 90% silver.

The 1964 Kennedy half dollar was hoarded in record numbers. This is an extremely common coin in Mint State condition.

NGC CERTIFIED POPULATION *(from a total mintage of 273,304,004)* (WCG™)

MS-64	MS-65	MS-66	MS-67	MS-68	MS-69	MS-70
1,451	1,844	1,161	78	0	0	0
MS-64 PL	MS-65 PL	MS-66 PL	MS-67 PL	MS-68 PL	MS-69 PL	MS-70 PL
0	0	0	0	0	0	0

MS-60–MS-64. The 1964-P Kennedy is generally a very baggy coin. Most examples in Mint State grade between MS-60 and MS-64. Most examples are well struck with good luster. Attractive color-toned coins are more elusive and worth a premium depending on the color.

Valuation—Barely above bullion for the lowest Mint State grades. **MS-64** examples sell for $16 to $20.

MS-65–MS-66. Although relatively plentiful in MS-65, the 1964-P is not as easy to acquire in that grade as it was just a few years ago! And MS-66 examples are very scarce. While this date has been hoarded by the bagful, minimally marked MS-66 coins are scarce.

Valuation—$45 to $75 for **MS-65** coins, though attractively toned color coins may sell for *many* times that level. **MS-66** 1964-P Kennedy halves generally trade for between $100 and $200 in brilliant condition.

MS-67–MS-68. This is where the 1964-P Kennedy becomes a true rarity. Most examples exist in brilliant condition, and locating a brilliant 1964-P with the near-flawless, pristine surfaces required for an MS-67 grade is extremely difficult.

Valuation—**MS-67** coins generally trade for anything from $1,200 to $2,500. The higher end of the range is for exceptional color coins, of which there are very few in MS-67. The best place to find this date is in U.S. Mint sets.

↔ 1964, SPECIAL MINT SET ↔

About 10 are known of this extremely rare Proof pattern.

NGC CERTIFIED POPULATION *(from a total mintage of about 10)* (WCG™)

SP-64	SP-65	SP-66	SP-67	SP-68	SP-69	SP-70
0	0	1	3	1	1	0

·✦⇒ 1964-D, MINT STATE ⇐✦·

MS-67

While the mintage of 156 million was a little more than half that of the 1964-P Kennedy, both were still record totals in comparison to any other half dollar previously struck.

As with the 1964-P Kennedy, the 1964-D was hoarded in record numbers, and is also an extremely common coin in Mint State condition.

The 1964-D is twice as rare to find as the Philadelphia Mint in MS-65 or better grade.

NGC CERTIFIED POPULATION *(from a total mintage of 156,205,446)* (WCG™)

MS-64	MS-65	MS-66	MS-67	MS-68	MS-69	MS-70
808	807	544	41	1	0	0
MS-64 PL	MS-65 PL	MS-66 PL	MS-67 PL	MS-68 PL	MS-69 PL	MS-70 PL
0	1	0	0	0	0	0

MS-60–MS-64. As noted, the 1964-D Kennedy is a very baggy coin, and most examples in Mint State grade between MS-60 and MS-64. Most are well struck with good luster, but attractive color-toned coins are more elusive and worth a premium depending on the color.

Valuation—These sell for barely above bullion value in the lowest Mint State grades. **MS-64** examples sell for $20 to $30.

MS-65–MS-66. The 1964-D is more elusive than the 1964-P in these higher Mint State grades. They were hoarded by the bagful, but minimally marked MS-65 and MS-66 coins are scarce.

Valuation—$45 to $70 for **MS-65** coins, though attractively toned color coins may sell for many times that range. **MS-66** 1964-D Kennedy halves generally now trade for between $150 and $300 in brilliant condition.

MS-67–MS-68. The 1964-D Kennedy is truly rare at this level. Locating a brilliant 1964-D with the near-flawless, pristine surfaces required for an MS-67 grade is extremely difficult.

Valuation—**MS-67** coins generally trade for anything from $1,650 to $4,000. The higher end of the range is for exceptional color coins, of which there are very few in MS-67. A beautifully toned **MS-68** sold for more than $20,000 at auction.

⇒ 1965-P, Mint State ⇐

MS-67

In this, the first year of the silver clad half dollar, the total silver content of the 1965 Kennedy half dollars was reduced from 90% to 40%. The silver appearance was nearly identical to that of the previous year, as the 1965–1970 half dollars attained the 40% content using an inner core composed of .209 silver and .791 copper, but with outer layers of .800 silver and .200 copper. The majority have been melted over the last 50 years. High grades are rare above MS-65.

The 1965 Kennedy was hoarded in much smaller numbers than the previous year's issue.

NGC CERTIFIED POPULATION *(from a total mintage of 65,879,366)* (WCG™)

MS-64	MS-65	MS-66	MS-67	MS-68	MS-69	MS-70
220	324	125	16	0	0	0

MS-60–MS-64. The 1965-P Kennedy is another very baggy coin, though strike is generally acceptable. More elusive in Mint State than the 1964-P or 1964-D, this date is actually collectible in MS-64 grade, and is a surprisingly elusive coin in this grade.

Valuation—Barely above bullion for the lowest Mint State grades; **MS-64** examples are valued in the $20–$30 range.

MS-65–MS-66. *Scarce.* This grade range is much tougher to find than the current low value indicates. The value of this issue has risen over the past few years as more collectors become aware of the difficulty in locating this date in gem condition. Attractive color-toned coins in gem are rare.

Valuation—$75 to $150 for **MS-65** coins. Attractively toned color coins will sell for much more. **MS-66** 1965-P Kennedy halves now generally trade for $200 to $400 in brilliant condition and are a bargain at these still undervalued levels.

MS-67–MS-68. The 1965-P Kennedy is very rare in MS-67. Few examples have survived with the near-perfect surfaces required for the MS-67 grade. Superb color coins in this grade are extremely rare as well.

Valuation—MS-67 coins generally trade for $3,500 to $6,500. The higher end of the range is for exceptional color coins, of which there are very few in MS-67.

The only way to find this date is in original rolls. Good luck in finding any, and I would advise paying a premium to get one.

⊶ 1966-P, Mint State ⊷

MS-66

Although the 1966-P was struck in greater numbers than the 1965 Kennedy, nevertheless only a small percentage of the total mintage has survived in Mint State condition. Most were melted, making it difficult to find in grades above MS-65.

NGC CERTIFIED POPULATION *(from a total mintage of 108,984,932)*   (WCG™)

MS-64	MS-65	MS-66	MS-67	MS-68	MS-69	MS-70
232	263	78	6	1	0	0

MS-60–MS-64. The 1966-P Kennedy is another very baggy coin. Original rolls are not common, and when a roll does surface, most coins will be very low grade, the primary problem being the marks. The strike and luster of the typical 1966-P are usually good. This is a scarce coin in MS-64.

Valuation—Barely above bullion for the lowest Mint State grades, but **MS-63** examples are valued in the $8–$10 range; **MS-64** coins sell for $15 to $20.

MS-65–MS-66. Another scarce date in MS-65, and especially elusive in MS-66. As with the 1965-P Kennedy, the value of this issue has been rising as more collectors become aware of the difficultly in locating this date in gem condition. Attractive color-toned coins in gem are very rare!

Valuation—$80 to $175 for **MS-65** coins. Attractively toned color coins will sell for much more. **MS-66** 1966-P Kennedy halves generally trade for between $350 and $800 in brilliant condition.

MS-67–MS-68. The 1966-P Kennedy is extremely rare in MS-67, with only a few examples having been certified to date. A lone MS-68 has been certified, this one by PCGS.

Superb color coins in this grade are obviously extremely rare as well. There is plenty of upside to this date in superb MS-67 condition. It is a key date in the series, and will prove to be quite challenging to acquire.

Valuation—When one does surface, an **MS-67** coin generally trades for $4,000 to $7,000. his is one of the hardest-to-find coins in original rolls.

⤜⟶ 1967-P, MINT STATE ⟵⤛

MS-66

With a mintage of nearly 300 million coins, the 1967 Kennedy ranks among the most common issues in Mint State condition. Most of this date has been melted. Finding a coin that grades better than MS-65 is difficult.

NGC CERTIFIED POPULATION *(from a total mintage of 295,046,978)* (WCG™)

MS-64	MS-65	MS-66	MS-67	MS-68	MS-69	MS-70
278	308	166	14	0	0	0

MS-60–MS-64. Bagmarks and inconsistent strike relegate virtually all Mint State 1967-P Kennedy half dollars to the lowest Mint State grades. Despite the very high mintage, original rolls of the 1967-P Kennedy are surprisingly elusive. And once again, when a roll does surface, most coins will be very low grade. This is another scarce coin in MS-64.

Valuation—Barely above bullion for the lowest Mint State grades, but **MS-63** examples are valued in the $10–$12 range; **MS-64s** sell for $15 to $20.

MS-65–MS-66. As with the 1965 and 1966 Philadelphia Mint coins, none of which were available in Mint sets, these are scarce in MS-65 and especially scarce in MS-66. Attractive color-toned coins in gem are very rare.

Valuation—$75 to $150 for **MS-65** coins. Attractively toned color coins will sell for much more. **MS-66** 1967-P Kennedy halves generally trade for between $350 and $800. This is another date rapidly increasing in value.

MS-67–MS-68. The 1967-P Kennedy is very nearly as rare as the 1966-P in MS-67, with only a handful of examples having been certified to date. Superb color coins in this grade are obviously extremely rare as well. Another date with plenty of upside, even though MS-67 coins already trade in the mid-four figures. It is rare to find this date in original rolls.

Valuation—The few **MS-67** coins now sell for $3,500 to $7,000!

1968-D, MINT STATE

MS-66

Another high-mintage issue, the 1968-D Kennedy is common in Mint State. From 1968 to the present, most of this date has been melted. It's easier to find the 1965–1967 issues. A primary reason for this is the 1968-D's availability in Mint sets.

NGC CERTIFIED POPULATION *(from a total mintage of 246,951,930)* (WCG™)

MS-64	MS-65	MS-66	MS-67	MS-68	MS-69	MS-70
442	891	418	23	0	0	0

MS-60–MS-64. This issue is usually well struck, but excessive bagmarks relegate most Mint State 1968-D Kennedy half dollars to the lower MS-61–MS-63 grades, even in Mint sets. This date ranks among the easiest to locate in MS-64.

Valuation—Barely above bullion for the lowest Mint State grades, **MS-63s** sell for $8 to $10; **MS-64** examples are valued in the $10–$12 range.

MS-65–MS-66. Among the most common dates of the 1964–1970 era in MS-65— but "common" relative only to other dates in the series. MS-66 examples are scarce, but again, this ranks among the most common dates of the 1964–1970 period. Attractive color-toned coins in gem are *rare*.

Valuation—$30 to $60 for **MS-65** coins. Attractively toned color coins will sell for much more. **MS-66** 1968-D Kennedy halves generally trade for between $80 and $175.

MS-67–MS-68. While relatively common in the lower Mint State grades, the 1968-D jumps in rarity in the higher MS-67 grade, and is comparable in rarity in this condition to other dates in the series.

Valuation—**MS-67** coins generally trade for $2,000 to $4,000.

⊷⟹ 1969-D, MINT STATE ⟸⊷

MS-67★

The 1969-D saw a drop in production from the previous year to about half the previous year's levels. The 1969-D is noteworthy for being the last Mint State Kennedy intended for commercial use that was struck with any silver content. While the 1970-D was also struck with silver content, it was issued only in Mint sets.

NGC CERTIFIED POPULATION *(from a total mintage of 129,881,800)*   (WCG™)

MS-64	MS-65	MS-66	MS-67	MS-68	MS-69	MS-70
394	527	177	10	0	0	0
MS-64 PL	**MS-65 PL**	**MS-66 PL**	**MS-67 PL**	**MS-68 PL**	**MS-69 PL**	**MS-70 PL**
2	0	0	0	0	0	0

MS-60–MS-64. This issue is generally of very low quality. The 1969-D is usually well struck, but excessive bagmarks relegate most Mint State 1969-D Kennedy half dollars to the lower MS-61–MS-63 grades.

Valuation—Barely above bullion for the lowest Mint State grades. **MS-63s** trade for $9 to $11, but this date is elusive in **MS-64,** currently valued in the $12–$15 range. Attractive color-toned coins will sell for more.

MS-65–MS-66. *Scarce* in MS-65, the 1969-D is extremely scarce in MS-66. Attractive color-toned coins in gem are very rare.

Valuation—$75 to $150 for **MS-65** coins. Attractively toned color coins will sell for much more. **MS-66** 1969-D Kennedy halves are now trading in the area of $350 to $800.

MS-67–MS-68. Among the rarest dates in the series in MS-67 grade. I have only handled two or three examples in MS-67! Good luck finding your coin. A Mint set is your best bet to find this date 80% of the time; lower quality can be found in rolls approximately 20% of the time.

Valuation—If you can find one, for an attractive **MS-67** in either brilliant or color toned condition, expect to pay upward of $4,000.

A View of the Decade: The 1970s

The 1970s saw some changes to familiar coin denominations. In 1971 the Eisenhower dollar, designed by Chief Engraver Frank Gasparro, was released. During 1975 and 1976 the quarter, half dollar, and dollar coins were given special Bicentennial reverse designs. In 1979 the ill-fated Susan B. Anthony dollar made its debut; it was so unpopular that in 1981 production of this design would cease for almost two decades.

Other landmarks in the numismatic world included the founding in 1973 of the American Numismatic Association Certification Service (ANACS). In 1974 President Gerald Ford lifted the 40-year ban on gold ownership by U.S. citizens, permitting the public once again to collect and save gold coins. In 1976 the ANA set an attendance record of 21,900 attendees at its New York convention—a record that would stand until the 1990s. Also in 1976, *Numismatic Scrapbook* ceased publication after more than 40 years. Late in the decade, the prices of bullion gold and silver began to rise, a trend that would have strong repercussions for coin collectors.

⤙ 1970-D, Mint State ⤚

MS-66

The 1970-D was produced in *extremely small* numbers for a Mint State coin—only 2.2 million 1970-D Kennedy half dollars were struck. A key date in the series, all were Uncirculated, as the date could be acquired only if a collector purchased a 1970 Mint set. I would estimate about one third of this date was melted, leaving 1.5 million available today.

NGC CERTIFIED POPULATION *(from a total mintage of 2,150,000)* (WCG™)

MS-64	MS-65	MS-66	MS-67	MS-68	MS-69	MS-70
1,511	1,627	324	7	0	0	0
MS-64 PL	MS-65 PL	MS-66 PL	MS-67 PL	MS-68 PL	MS-69 PL	MS-70 PL
8	3	1	0	0	0	0
MS-64 DPL	MS-65 DPL	MS-66 DPL	MS-67 DPL	MS-68 DPL	MS-69 DPL	MS-70 DPL
1	0	0	0	0	0	0

MS-60–MS-64. While it is found only in Mint sets, the typical quality of the 1970-D is quite low—most Mint set specimens are in the lowest MS-61–MS-63 grades. MS-64 coins can be located with some patience. While the strikes are normally good on these coins, bagmarks knock the grade down. Given that this coin was issued only in U.S. Mint sets with inert cellophane packaging, this date is extremely rare in attractively toned condition.

Valuation—There is a premium for this date in any condition, given its low mintage. In the lowest Mint State grades, at bullion values of about $20 per ounce the 1970-D is priced in the $18–$23 range for **MS-63. MS-64** coins are around $30 to $35.

MS-65–MS-66. The 1970-D is somewhat scarce in MS-66, and attractive color-toned coins in gem are *extremely* rare. For all intents and purposes, MS-66 is the highest grade a collector can hope to acquire this date in, given its extreme rarity in MS-67.

Valuation—$75 to $115 for **MS-65** coins. Attractively toned color coins? Good luck finding one. **MS-66** 1970-D Kennedy halves generally sell for $200–$300.

MS-67–MS-68. Along with the 1969-D, this is among the rarest dates in the series in MS-67 grade. I have yet to handle a 1970-D in MS-67. Good luck finding your coin.

Valuation—If you can find one, for an attractive **MS-67** in either brilliant or color toned condition, expect to pay $5,000 or more.

⊷⊜ 1971-P, MINT STATE ⊜⊶

MS-65

Struck in high numbers, the 1971-P is readily available in Mint State condition. These coins were poorly struck. The best place to find this date 90% of the time is in original U.S. Mint sets, with 10% in rolls.

NGC CERTIFIED POPULATION *(from a total mintage of 155,164,000)*   (WCG™)

MS-64	MS-65	MS-66	MS-67	MS-68	MS-69	MS-70
117	218	117	11	0	0	0

MS-60–MS-64. Abundant in the lowest Mint State grades, the 1971-P is scarce in MS-64. Attractively color-toned coins are rare in any Mint State grade.

Valuation—**MS-63s** are valued at $9; **MS-64** 1971-P Kennedy halves generally trade for between $12 and $18.

MS-65–MS-66. The 1971-P is very elusive in MS-65, and extremely scarce in MS-66. Bagmarks in the form of light abrasions and hairline scratches are the primary culprit, though inconsistent strike is also a contributing factor.

Valuation—$35 to $65 for **MS-65** coins. **MS-66** 1971-P Kennedy halves have sold for anything from $225 to $550.

MS-67–MS-68. Among the elite key dates in the series in MS-67 condition. Only a handful of examples have been certified by PCGS and NGC.

Valuation—Another rare date. If you can find one, an attractive **MS-67** in either brilliant or color-toned condition, a tremendous value at current levels, is valued at $800 or more.

1971-D, Mint State

MS-67

With more than 300 million coins struck, the 1971-D is the highest-mintage issue in the Kennedy half dollar series to date.

NGC CERTIFIED POPULATION *(from a total mintage of 302,097,424)*   (WCG™)

MS-64	MS-65	MS-66	MS-67	MS-68	MS-69	MS-70
191	447	1,056	266	6	0	0
MS-64 PL	MS-65 PL	MS-66 PL	MS-67 PL	MS-68 PL	MS-69 PL	MS-70 PL
0	1	0	0	0	0	0

MS-60–MS-64. Abundant in the lowest Mint State grades, the 1971-D is easy to acquire in choice and gem condition. Bagmarks are few, and strike is generally good, with excellent luster and eye appeal.

Valuation—**MS-63s** sell for $7 to $9. **MS-64** 1971-D Kennedy halves generally trade for between $11 and $14.

MS-65–MS-66. The 1971-D ranks among the most common dates of the pre-2000 era in MS-65 and MS-66 condition. However, as with all Mint State Kennedy halves, this date is rare with exceptional color toning.

Valuation—$15 to $25 for **MS-65** coins. **MS-66** 1971-D Kennedy halves sell for about double those levels, at $35 to $50.

MS-67–MS-68. Although this is a relatively easy date to find compared to other dates in the series in MS-67 condition, it is still a scarce coin.

Valuation—$100 to $175 for **MS-67** coins; $2,000 to $4,000 for **MS-68s.**

⊷ 1972-P, Mint State ⊶

MS-65

Struck in the same approximate numbers as the 1971-P Kennedy, the 1972-P is slightly higher quality, but poorly struck and abraded. Your best bet for this date is in U.S. Mint sets.

NGC CERTIFIED POPULATION *(from a total mintage of 153,180,000)*   (WCG™)

MS-64	MS-65	MS-66	MS-67	MS-68	MS-69	MS-70
130	415	101	15	0	0	0

MS-60–MS-64. Abundant in the lowest Mint State grades, the 1972-P is scarce in MS-64. Attractively color-toned coins are rare in any Mint State grade.

Valuation—**MS-63s** sell for $9; **MS-64** 1972-P Kennedy halves generally trade for between $13 and $23.

MS-65–MS-66. The 1972-P is elusive in MS-65, and scarce in MS-66.

Valuation—$20 to $30 for **MS-65** coins. **MS-66** 1972-P Kennedy halves sell in a wide range between $50 and $120.

MS-67–MS-68. Another very rare date in MS-67. Fewer than 20 examples have been certified by the major grading services to date (NGC and PCGS) combined.

Valuation—**MS-67s** can still be acquired for $1,000–$2,000.

☞ 1972-D, MINT STATE ☜

MS-67

Struck in the same approximate numbers as the 1972-P Kennedy, the 1972-D is a generally much higher-quality issue when found in Mint State condition. This coin offers a better strike than the 1972-P.

NGC CERTIFIED POPULATION *(from a total mintage of 141,890,000)*   (WCG™)

MS-64	MS-65	MS-66	MS-67	MS-68	MS-69	MS-70
135	269	412	99	0	0	0
MS-64 PL	MS-65 PL	MS-66 PL	MS-67 PL	MS-68 PL	MS-69 PL	MS-70 PL
0	0	1	0	0	0	0

MS-60–MS-64. The 1972-D is a high-quality issue very similar to the 1971-D. Given the lower mintage of the 1971-D, brilliant Uncirculated rolls are not as readily available as they are for the 1971-D. Most 1972-D Kennedy halves are boldly struck, with exceptional luster and minimal bagmarks.

Valuation—**MS-63s** sell for $9 to $11; **MS-64** 1972-D Kennedy halves generally trade for between $13 and $18.

MS-65–MS-66. The 1972-D is almost as common as the 1971-D in MS-65 and scarcer in MS-66 condition. As with all Mint State Kennedy halves, this date is rare with exceptional color toning.

Valuation—$15 to $25 for **MS-65** coins. **MS-66** 1972-D Kennedy halves sell for about double those levels, at $30 to $60.

MS-67–MS-68. More elusive than the 1971-D in MS-67, the 1972-D is a very scarce coin in this higher Mint State grade.

Valuation—$180 to $350 for **MS-67** coins.

↠ 1973-P, MINT STATE ↞

MS-67

Struck in smaller numbers than the 1972-P, the 1973-P is elusive in the higher Mint State grades.

NGC CERTIFIED POPULATION *(from a total mintage of 64,964,000)*   (WCG™)

MS-64	MS-65	MS-66	MS-67	MS-68	MS-69	MS-70
105	130	133	36	0	0	0

MS-60–MS-64. Abundant in the lowest Mint State grades, the 1973-P is surprisingly scarce in MS-64. Attractively color-toned coins are rare in any Mint State grade.

Valuation—**MS-63s** sell for $9 to $11; **MS-64** 1973-P Kennedy halves generally trade for between $13 and $18.

MS-65–MS-66. The 1973-P is another elusive date in MS-65 and MS-66, and is tougher to locate in this condition than the 1972-P. Bagmarks in the form of light abrasions and hairline scratches are once again the primary culprits, though inconsistent strike is also a contributing factor.

Valuation—$20 to $30 for **MS-65** coins. **MS-66** 1973-P Kennedy halves sell in a wide range between $65 and $120.

MS-67–MS-68. This is another rare date in MS-67, though currently the combined PCGS and NGC population for this date in MS-67 is higher than for the 1972-P.

Valuation—**MS-67s** can be acquired for $300 to $800.

⋘ 1973-D, MINT STATE ⋙

MS-67

Struck in the same approximate numbers as the 1973-P Kennedy, the 1973-D is similar in quality to its sibling issue.

NGC CERTIFIED POPULATION *(from a total mintage of 83,171,400)*   (WCG™)

MS-64	MS-65	MS-66	MS-67	MS-68	MS-69	MS-70
112	228	322	69	0	0	0

MS-60–MS-64. The 1973-D is a slightly higher-quality issue than the 1973-P. While bagmarks are the major problem, the strike of the 1973-D tends to be sharper than its Philadelphia Mint counterpart.

Valuation—**MS-63** $9 to $11; **MS-64** 1973-D Kennedy halves generally trade for between $13 and $18.

MS-65–MS-66. The 1973-D is a bit easier to locate than the 1973-P in MS-65 and MS-66 condition. Exceptional color-toned examples are rare.

Valuation—$15 to $25 for **MS-65** coins. **MS-66** 1973-D Kennedy halves sell for about double those levels: $45 to $50.

MS-67–MS-68. This is an extremely scarce coin in MS-67, though slightly easier to locate than the 1972-D.

Valuation—$200 to $500 for **MS-67** coins.

⟿ 1974-P, MINT STATE ⟸

MS-65

Among the highest-mintage issues in the series, the 1974-P is nevertheless difficult to locate in the higher states of preservation. The best place to find this date is in U.S. Mint sets.

NGC CERTIFIED POPULATION *(from a total mintage of 201,596,000)*   (WCG™)

MS-64	MS-65	MS-66	MS-67	MS-68	MS-69	MS-70
107	142	146	13	0	0	0

MS-60–MS-64. Abundant in the lowest Mint State grades, the 1974-P is a bit tougher to locate in MS-64. Attractively color-toned coins are rare in any Mint State grade.

Valuation—**MS-63** coins sell for $5 to $10. **MS-64** 1974-P Kennedy halves generally trade for between $6 and $12.

MS-65–MS-66. The 1974-P is a bit tougher to find in MS-65, though it is still relatively easy to locate. Strike is often a problem with this date, as it is with many Philadelphia half dollars. Bagmarks are the primarily culprit when it comes to grade.

Valuation—$20 to $30 for **MS-65** coins. **MS-66** 1972-P Kennedy halves sell in a wide range between $60 and $100.

MS-67–MS-68. This is another tough date in MS-67, despite the astronomical mintage, with only a handful graded by PCGS and NGC.

Valuation—In **MS-67**, $1,500 to $4,000.

⟿ 1974-D, MINT STATE ⟿

MS-67

Normal 1974-D

Doubled-Die Obverse variety

Struck in smaller numbers than the 1974-P Kennedy, the 1974-D is a higher-quality issue, generally with a bolder strike.

NGC CERTIFIED POPULATION *(from a total mintage of 79,066,300)* (WCG™)

MS-64	MS-65	MS-66	MS-67	MS-68	MS-69	MS-70
638	304	260	32	0	0	0

MS-60–MS-64. The 1974-D is a generally well-struck coin with excellent luster. Bagmarks in the form of myriad ticks and scratches drop most examples into the lower Mint State grades.
   Valuation—**MS-64** 1974-D Kennedy halves generally trade for between $8 and $17.

MS-65–MS-66. The 1974-D is not a difficult date to locate in either MS-65 or MS-66 condition. Once again, exceptional color-toned examples are rare.
   Valuation—$20 to $35 for **MS-65** coins. **MS-66** 1974-D Kennedy halves sell for $45 to $75.

MS-67–MS-68. Extremely scarce, though not as rare as the 1974-P in MS-67.
   Valuation—**MS-67** coins generally sell for $350 to $600.

1974-D DOUBLED-DIE OBVERSE VARIETY
On this rare variety, doubling is evident in WE TRUST.

⋙ 1976-P BICENTENNIAL, MINT STATE ⋘

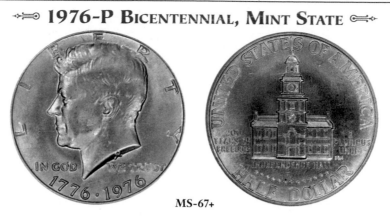

MS-67+

A one-year type coin, the 1976-P Bicentennial Kennedy half dollar was actually struck during 1975 and 1976. This is a very high-mintage issue of generally poor quality: overall a nice coin, but with too many bagmarks.

NGC CERTIFIED POPULATION *(from a total mintage of 234,308,000)* (WCG™)

MS-64	MS-65	MS-66	MS-67	MS-68	MS-69	MS-70
182	225	127	16	0	0	0

MS-60–MS-64. Most brilliant Uncirculated examples are baggy and softly struck. Because of the large numbers hoarded in brilliant Uncirculated condition, there is very little premium for this date in the lowest Mint State grades—unless the coin has exceptional color toning.

Valuation—**MS-63** coins sell for $9 to $11. Certified **MS-64** 1976-P Kennedy halves generally trade for between $12 and $18.

MS-65–MS-66. The 1976-P is not a difficult date to locate in MS-65 but is surprisingly elusive in the higher MS-66 grade. Bagmarks and poor strike are the biggest hurdle to overcome for this date. Exceptional color-toned examples in gem are rare.

Valuation—$30 for **MS-65** coins. **MS-66** 1976-P Kennedy halves may sell for $125 to $250.

MS-67–MS-68. This is where the 1976-P Kennedy is truly rare. Near-flawless, boldly struck 1976-P Kennedy halves of MS-67 quality are seldom encountered. This is a bit surprising considering the mintage of over 200,000,000 coins. But the fact is that virtually all examples of this date exhibit a mediocre strike, plentiful light abrasions, or both.

Valuation—On the rare occasion when an **MS-67** coin appears on the market, it may command anywhere from $1,000 to $2,000.

⊷⊶ 1976-D BICENTENNIAL, MINT STATE ⊶⊷

MS-67

Another very high-mintage issue, the 1976-D is plagued by similar problems as the Philadelphia Mint issue. It is readily available in Mint State.

NGC CERTIFIED POPULATION *(from a total mintage of 287,565,248)* (WCG™)

MS-64	MS-65	MS-66	MS-67	MS-68	MS-69	MS-70
214	482	403	48	0	0	0

MS-60–MS-64. Most brilliant Uncirculated examples of the 1976-D are quite baggy. As is the case with the Philadelphia issue, because of the large numbers hoarded in brilliant Uncirculated condition, there is very little premium for this date in the lowest Mint State grades unless the coin has exceptional color toning.

Valuation—**MS-63** coins sell for $8. Certified **MS-64** 1976-D Kennedy halves generally trade at $13.

MS-65–MS-66. The 1976-D is not a difficult date to locate in MS-65, though it is understandably slightly more elusive in MS-66 grade. Bagmarks are the biggest hurdle to overcome for this date. However, the date does come with a generally better strike, and is somewhat easier to locate in gem than the 1976-P. Exceptional color-toned examples in gem are rare.

Valuation—$25 for **MS-65** coins. **MS-66** 1976-D Kennedy halves may sell for $50 to $75.

MS-67–MS-68. Extremely scarce in MS-67 condition, though three times as many 1976-D Kennedy halves have been certified in this top grade than for the 1976-P.

Valuation—A $600–$1,000 coin in **MS-67**.

⊷⊸ 1976-S SILVER BICENTENNIAL, MINT STATE ⊶⊷

MS-68

The 1976-S was composed of 40% silver and distributed only through government-issue Mint sets. While it is a low-mintage issue, virtually all 1976-S Silver Bicentennial Kennedy half dollars have survived in uncirculated condition.

There are three types of envelopes. The first, issued in December 1975, is a white envelope with a Christmas motif; the second, issued in January 1976, is a red envelope, and there is a white line on the top of the cellophane. These first two are generally where the high grades are. In July 1976, the last group of one million sets was issued in a blurry red envelope with no white line on the cellophane. These are usually ground-up bagmarked coins.

NGC CERTIFIED POPULATION *(from a total mintage of 11,000,000)* (WCG™)

MS-64	MS-65	MS-66	MS-67	MS-68	MS-69	MS-70
181	341	757	1,920	230	1	0

MS-60–MS-64. It would be unusual to find a 1976-S Silver Kennedy in the lowest Mint State grades. Most examples fall in the MS-63–MS-65 range. Strike and luster are generally excellent.

Valuation—There is no significant premium in this grade range above the bullion value. **MS-63s** sell for $10; **MS-64s**, for $12 to $15.

MS-65–MS-66. This issue is common in the MS-65 and MS-66 grades as well. There is a small premium for the 1976-S in MS-65 and MS-66.

Valuation—$20 to $25 for **MS-65** coins. **MS-66** 1976-S Kennedy halves may sell for $25 to $45.

MS-67–MS-68. A bit more elusive in MS-67, the 1976-S becomes truly scarce in MS-68, and is the only Mint State Kennedy from this early era in the series that a collector has a chance of acquiring in this lofty grade.

Valuation—A $40–$80 coin in **MS-67,** the 1976-S trades in the $200–$400 range in MS-68. Only one **MS-69** has been graded by PCGS, and it is valued at over $5,000.

⊷⊜ 1977-P, MINT STATE ⊜⊶

MS-67

Total mintage took a major drop for the 1977-P Kennedy to just under 44 million coins, the second lowest of the series to date (with the exception of the Mint set–only 1970-D). It was surpassed only by the 1977-D, which had a mintage of just 31 million.

NGC CERTIFIED POPULATION *(from a total mintage of 43,598,000)* (WCG™)

MS-64	MS-65	MS-66	MS-67	MS-68	MS-69	MS-70
49	147	256	58	1	0	0

MS-60–MS-64. Most 1977-P Mint State Kennedy half dollars fall in the MS-62–MS-64 range. Strike and luster are generally good.

Valuation—There is no significant premium above roll bid in this grade range. **MS-63** coins sell for $6 to $8; **MS-64s,** for $10 to $15.

MS-65–MS-66. Still common in MS-65, the 1977-P is a bit more elusive in the minimally bagmarked MS-66 grade.

Valuation—$25 to $40 for **MS-65** coins. **MS-66** 1977-P Kennedy halves may trade in the area of $50–$60. Examples with color may command significant premiums.

MS-67–MS-68. Extremely scarce in this higher grade. Well-struck coins with near-flawless surfaces are seldom encountered.

Valuation—**MS-67** coins sell for $300 to $600.

ᴅ 1977-D, MINT STATE ᴄ

MS-67

Total mintage for the 1977-D Kennedy was just 31 million coins, the lowest of the series to date (with the exception of the Mint set–only 1970-D).

NGC CERTIFIED POPULATION *(from a total mintage of 31,449,106)* (WCG™)

MS-64	MS-65	MS-66	MS-67	MS-68	MS-69	MS-70
69	73	116	53	1	0	0

MS-60–MS-64. Most 1977-D Mint State Kennedy half dollars fall in the MS-62–MS-64 range. Strike and luster are generally good.

Valuation—There is no significant premium above roll bid in this grade range. **MS-63s** sell for $3 to $5. **MS-64s** bring $6 to $10.

MS-65–MS-66. Like the 1977-P, the 1977-D is still common in MS-65, though a bit more elusive in minimally bagmarked MS-66 grade.

Valuation—$25 to $40 for **MS-65** coins. **MS-66** 1977-D Kennedy halves usually trade in the $70–$100 range. Examples with color will command significant premiums.

MS-67–MS-68. In this higher grade the 1977-D is extremely scarce. Well-struck coins with near-flawless surfaces are seldom encountered.

Valuation—This is a $200–$400 coin in **MS-67. MS-68s** may sell for $2,500 or more.

❧ 1978-P, MINT STATE ☙

MS-67

The 1978-P Kennedy saw total mintage take another major drop, with just over 14 million coins being struck. A significant percentage of this mintage is Uncirculated, as over two million Mint sets were issued that year.

NGC CERTIFIED POPULATION *(from a total mintage of 14,350,000)*   (WCG™)

MS-64	MS-65	MS-66	MS-67	MS-68	MS-69	MS-70
64	141	209	36	0	0	0

MS-60–MS-64. Most 1978-P Mint State Kennedy half dollars fall in the MS-62–MS-64 range. Strike and luster are generally good.

Valuation—**MS-63s** sell for $3. Because of the lower mintage, the 1978-P may be worth a small premium in the higher **MS-64** grade, with examples currently trading for $6 to $10.

MS-65–MS-66. The 1978-P is semi-scarce in MS-65 and scarce in MS-66. Attractive color coins are rare in any grade.

Valuation—$15 to $30 for **MS-65** coins. **MS-66** coins trade in the $30–$60 range.

MS-67–MS-68. Once again, this issue is extremely scarce in this higher grade. Well-struck Kennedy halves from this era with near-flawless surfaces are seldom encountered.

Valuation—This is a $500–$1,000 coin in **MS-67**.

➤➤ 1978-D, MINT STATE ➤➤

MS-67

Under 14 million of the 1978-D were struck, though the government issued over two million Mint sets in 1978, making this coin readily available in average brilliant Uncirculated condition.

NGC CERTIFIED POPULATION *(from a total mintage of 13,765,799)* (WCG™)

MS-64	MS-65	MS-66	MS-67	MS-68	MS-69	MS-70
54	102	181	36	0	0	0

MS-60–MS-64. Most Mint State 1978-D Kennedy half dollars grade between MS-62 and MS-64. Strike and luster are generally good.

Valuation—**MS-63s** sell for $3 to $5. Because of the lower mintage, the 1978-D may be worth a small premium in the higher **MS-64** grade, with examples currently trading for $6 to $10.

MS-65–MS-66. The 1978-D is semi-scarce in MS-65, and scarce in MS-66. Attractive color coins are rare in any grade.

Valuation—$10 to $20 for **MS-65** coins. **MS-66** coins trade in the $50–$70 range.

MS-67–MS-68. Once again, this issue is extremely scarce in this higher grade. Well-struck Kennedy halves with near-flawless surfaces from this era are seldom encountered.

Valuation—This is a $575–$800 coin in **MS-67.**

1979-P, MINT STATE

MS-67

Production increased to 68 million, with more than 2.5 million 1979-P Kennedy halves issued in Mint sets.

NGC CERTIFIED POPULATION *(from a total mintage of 68,312,000)* (WCG™)

MS-64	MS-65	MS-66	MS-67	MS-68	MS-69	MS-70
50	112	255	62	2	0	0

MS-60–MS-64. Most 1979-P Mint State Kennedy half dollars grade MS-62 to MS-64. Strike and luster are generally good.

Valuation—**MS-63** coins sell for $3 to $5, with a small premium for **MS-64** coins, which sell for $5 to $10. Attractive color coins trade at a premium in any grade.

MS-65–MS-66. The 1979-P is easy to acquire in MS-65, a bit more elusive in MS-66.

Valuation—$15 to $25 for **MS-65** coins. **MS-66** coins trade in the $25 to $50 range.

MS-67–MS-68. While not as rare as the 1978-P, this is a scarce coin in the higher MS-67 grade. Well-struck Kennedy halves with near-flawless surfaces from this era are seldom seen.

Valuation—The 1979-P is a $250–$450 coin in **MS-67. MS-68** examples sell for $2,500 to $4000!

1979-D, MINT STATE

MS-66

Only 16 million examples were struck. A significant percentage of brilliant Uncirculated coins are to be found in Mint sets, with more than 2.5 million issued in 1979.

NGC CERTIFIED POPULATION *(from a total mintage of 15,815,422)* (WCG™)

MS-64	MS-65	MS-66	MS-67	MS-68	MS-69	MS-70
42	128	225	39	0	0	0

MS-60–MS-64. The most common grade range for the 1979-D Mint State Kennedy half dollar is MS-62 to MS-64. Strike and luster are generally good.

Valuation—**MS-63** coins sell for $3 to $5. A small premium exists for **MS-64** coins, which bring $5 to $10. Attractive color coins trade at a premium in any grade.

MS-65–MS-66. The 1979-D is easy to acquire in MS-65 if one goes through a few dozen Mint sets, a bit more difficult in MS-66.

Valuation—$10 to $20 for **MS-65** coins. **MS-66** coins trade in the $35 to $75 range.

MS-67–MS-68. Rarer than the 1979-P. This is another scarce Kennedy in the higher MS-67 grade.

Valuation—The 1979-D is a $500 to $1,000 coin in **MS-67**.

A VIEW OF THE DECADE: THE 1980s

The decade began memorably for numismatics when, in 1980, the prices of gold and silver hit all-time highs of, respectively, $873 and $49.45 per ounce. New buyers, including coin investment corporations, began snapping up coins as investments, while collectors waited out the high prices until the inevitable crash came. "Investment-grade" coins—silver and gold Proof or Mint State examples—became increasingly popular among the new buyers of coins.

The Numismatic Bibliomania Society was founded in 1980 by George F. Kolbe and Jack Collins; this nonprofit organization promoted the use and collecting of numismatic literature. In 1981 Elizabeth Jones became the first woman to be appointed chief sculptor and engraver. Commemorative-coin releases resumed in 1982 with the George Washington 250th anniversary half dollar (the first U.S. commemorative coin released since 1954). In 1984 the Mint struck its first gold coin in 50 years as the Olympic commemorative $10 gold coin debuted. In 1986, the Professional Coin Grading Service (PCGS) was formed; next year, the Numismatic Guaranty Corporation of America (NGC) followed. The encapsulation and grading provided by these services permitted coins to be bought as investments sight unseen, leading to a more corporate and less personal tendency in coin grading and collecting.

⋯⊙ 1980-P, MINT STATE ⊙⋯

MS-67

For the 1980-P, production dropped to 44 million. This year was among the peak years for Mint sets, with over 2.8 million issued.

NGC CERTIFIED POPULATION *(from a total mintage of 44,134,000)*   (WCG™)

MS-64	MS-65	MS-66	MS-67	MS-68	MS-69	MS-70
34	123	317	182	0	0	0

MS-60–MS-64. Once again, most 1980-P Mint State Kennedy half dollars range between MS-62 and MS-64. Strike and luster are generally good.

Valuation—**MS-63** coins sell for $3 to $5. There is a small premium for **MS-64** coins, which bring $8 to $15. Attractive color coins trade at a premium in any grade.

MS-65–MS-66. The 1980-P is easy to acquire in MS-65, a bit more elusive in MS-66.
Valuation—$15 to $30 for **MS-65** coins. **MS-66** coins trade in the $80–$125 range.

MS-67–MS-68. This is an interesting date in MS-67. Its PCGS certified population in MS-67 and finer ranks it among the highest totals, with the obvious exception of the 1976-S silver, for Kennedy half dollars struck prior to 1995. On the other hand, the NGC population for this date in MS-67 is extremely low—a couple dozen coins—making it approximately as rare as other dates from this era.

What are we to make of this? It has been my experience that the 1980-P suffers from all the same problems as other Mint State Kennedy half dollars of this era: strike is inconsistent, and bagmarks are generally plentiful. Not having seen most of the examples graded by PCGS in MS-67, I find it difficult to explain the very high population for this coin, as it seems to be as rare as other Philadelphia examples from this era.

Valuation—This is a $90–$400 coin in **MS-67.**

⋖══ 1980-D, MINT STATE ══⋗

MS-67

Just over 33 million 1980-D Kennedy half dollars were struck. A significant percentage of brilliant Uncirculated coins are to be found in Mint sets, with over 2.8 million issued in 1980.

NGC CERTIFIED POPULATION *(from a total mintage of 33,456,449)* (WCG™)

MS-64	MS-65	MS-66	MS-67	MS-68	MS-69	MS-70
45	57	95	42	1	0	0

MS-60–MS-64. The most common grade range for the 1980-D Mint State Kennedy half dollar is MS-62 to MS-64. Strike and luster are generally good.

Valuation—**MS-63s** sell for $3 to $5. A small premium exists for **MS-64** coins, which bring $8 to $15. Attractive color coins trade at a premium in any grade.

MS-65–MS-66. The 1980-D is much more difficult to locate in gem than the 1980-P. Bagmarks are the major problem.

Valuation—$15 to $30 for **MS-65** coins. **MS-66** coins trade in the $100 to $150 range.

MS-67–MS-68. This is a very tough coin to locate in MS-67, and even harder in MS-68.

Valuation—In **MS-67** this coin brings $400 to $700. **MS-68** coins bring $3,000 or more.

⊶⇒ 1981-P, MINT STATE ⇐⊷

MS-66

Production dropped once again to 29.5 million. Production of Mint sets continued to increase, with over 2.9 million issued.

NGC CERTIFIED POPULATION *(from a total mintage of 29,544,000)*   (WCG™)

MS-64	MS-65	MS-66	MS-67	MS-68	MS-69	MS-70
115	181	206	37	1	0	0

MS-60–MS-64. Most 1981-P Mint State Kennedy half dollars fall in the MS-62–MS-64 range. Strike and luster are generally good, though most examples suffer from light hairline abrasions.

Valuation—**MS-63** coins bring $5 to $10. There is a small premium for **MS-64** coins, which sell for $12 to $18. Attractive color coins trade at a premium in any grade.

MS-65–MS-66. The 1981-P is somewhat challenging to acquire in MS-65, and is surprisingly scarce in MS-66. Bagmarks and hairline abrasions are the obstacles to locating examples in these higher grades.

Valuation—$35 to $40 for **MS-65** coins. **MS-66** coins trade in the $100–$120 range.

MS-67–MS-68. A very challenging coin to locate in MS-67. Well-struck examples nearly devoid of the aforementioned abrasions and scratches are rarely encountered.

Up until the second edition of this book, there were none known in MS-68. Only one has been graded since then.

Valuation—**MS-67s** bring $750 to $1,200.

1981-D, MINT STATE

MS-67

Just under 28 million 1981-D Kennedy half dollars were struck. A significant percentage of brilliant Uncirculated coins are to be found in Mint sets, with more than 2.9 million issued in 1981.

NGC CERTIFIED POPULATION *(from a total mintage of 27,839,533)* (WCG™)

MS-64	MS-65	MS-66	MS-67	MS-68	MS-69	MS-70
87	48	87	30	0	0	0

MS-60–MS-64. The most common grade range for the 1981-D Mint State Kennedy half dollar is MS-62 to MS-64. Strike and luster are generally good. This is a surprisingly challenging coin to locate in MS-64.

Valuation—**MS-63** coins bring $3 to $5. There is a small premium for **MS-64** coins, which sell for $6 to $10. Attractive color coins trade at a premium in any grade.

MS-65–MS-66. The 1981-D is difficult to locate in gem condition. Bagmarks, in the form of light scratches and abrasions, are the major obstacle to locating gems.

Valuation—$20 to $40 for **MS-65** coins. **MS-66** coins trade in the $75 to $150 range.

MS-67–MS-68. Another very, very tough coin to locate in MS-67. No example has graded higher to date.

Valuation—This is an $800 to $2,000 coin in **MS-67**.

❧ 1982-P, Mint State ❧

MS-66

A relatively small number, 10.8 million, of Kennedy half dollars were struck at the Philadelphia Mint in 1982. Adding to the scarcity of this date in Mint State, no Mint sets were issued in 1982.

NGC CERTIFIED POPULATION *(from a total mintage of 10,819,000)* (WCG™)

MS-64	MS-65	MS-66	MS-67	MS-68	MS-69	MS-70
110	409	223	14	0	0	0

MS-60–MS-64. Most 1982-P Mint State Kennedy half dollars fall in the MS-62–MS-64 range. Strike and luster are generally good, though most examples suffer from light hairline abrasions.

Valuation—**MS-63** coins bring $3 to $5. There is a small premium for **MS-64** coins, which sell for $6 to $15. Attractive color coins trade at a premium in any grade.

MS-65–MS-66. The 1982-P is somewhat challenging to acquire in MS-65, and is scarce in MS-66. Bagmarks and hairline abrasions make it difficult to locate examples in these higher grades, though soft strikes are also a common problem. With no Mint sets available, only a few rolls are to be found. The rare No FG variety (see below) brings three to four times the price of MS-65 or better.

Valuation—$20 to $75 for **MS-65** coins. **MS-66** coins offer good value in their current $75 to $200 trading range.

MS-67–MS-68. *Very* rare in MS-67. The fact that there were no Mint sets issued in 1982, coupled with the extremely low mintage, makes the 1982-P among the key dates in this highest Mint State grade. No examples have been certified in MS-68 at the time of this writing.

Valuation—In **MS-67** this is a $2,000–$3,000 coin.

1982-P, "No FG" Variety

One of the few major varieties or Mint errors in the Franklin/Kennedy series, the No FG variety is easily detected with the naked eye. The initials of Frank Gasparro, the artist who rendered the original design of the Kennedy half dollar, are normally tucked between the eagle's left leg and its tail feathers.

1982-P, No FG

1982-P, With FG

1982-D, MINT STATE

MS-66

Only 13.1 million 1982-D Kennedy half dollars were struck—almost as low a mintage as the 1982-P. Adding to the scarcity of this date in Mint State, no Mint sets were issued in 1982.

NGC CERTIFIED POPULATION *(from a total mintage of 13,140,102)* (WCG™)

MS-64	MS-65	MS-66	MS-67	MS-68	MS-69	MS-70
40	142	225	25	0	0	0

MS-60–MS-64. The most common grade range for the 1982-D Mint State Kennedy half dollar is MS-62 to MS-64. Strike and luster are generally good. This is a surprisingly challenging coin to locate in MS-64.

Valuation—**MS-63** coins sell for $3 to $5. **MS-64** coins bring a small premium, selling for $6 to $15. Attractive color coins trade at a premium in any grade.

MS-65–MS-66. The low mintage and the fact that no Mint sets were issued, coupled with the fact that most surviving Mint State specimens are low quality with numerous ticks and abrasions, conspire to make the 1982-D a scarce coin in gem condition. Only a few rolls exist, appearing infrequently.

Valuation—This issue falls in about the same range as the 1982-P: $20 to $75 for **MS-65** coins. **MS-66** coins generally trade for between $75 to $200.

MS-67–MS-68. The 1982-D is a rare coin in MS-67, though not quite as rare as the 1982-P. No example has graded higher than MS-67 to date.

Valuation—$1,200 to $2,500 in **MS-67**.

1983-P, Mint State

The mintage of the 1983-P Kennedy jumped to 34 million. However, once again no Mint sets were issued, making the 1983-P a challenging coin to locate in high grade Mint State condition.

NGC CERTIFIED POPULATION *(from a total mintage of 34,139,000)*   (WCG™)

MS-64	MS-65	MS-66	MS-67	MS-68	MS-69	MS-70
71	72	128	19	1	0	0

MS-60–MS-64. Most 1983-P Mint State Kennedy half dollars grade between MS-62 and 64. Strike and luster are generally good, though most examples suffer from light hairline abrasions.

Valuation—**MS-63** coins bring $3 to $5. A small premium exists for **MS-64** coins, which sell for $6 to $15. Attractive color coins trade at a premium in any grade.

MS-65–MS-66. The 1983-P is a scarce coin in MS-65, and is very scarce in MS-66. This date is noted for its bagmarks and poor strike. Well-struck, minimally marked coins are a real challenge to locate.

Valuation—$25 to $75 for **MS-65** coins. **MS-66** coins offer good value in their current $100–$200 trading range.

MS-67–MS-68. A rare coin in MS-67. Once again, the fact there were no Mint sets issued in 1983, along with the generally poor quality of this issue, makes the 1983-P a real challenge to find in this highest grade. There has been a single coin graded in MS-68 to date.

Well-struck examples nearly devoid of the aforementioned abrasions and scratches are rare.

Valuation—The **MS-67** is a $500–$1,250 coin; **MS-68** examples bring $3,000 or more!

1983-D, MINT STATE

MS-67

Some 32 million 1983-D Kennedy half dollars were struck. Adding to the scarcity of this date in Mint State is the fact that no Mint sets were issued in 1983.

NGC CERTIFIED POPULATION *(from a total mintage of 32,472,244)* (WCG™)

MS-64	MS-65	MS-66	MS-67	MS-68	MS-69	MS-70
44	60	147	30	0	0	0

MS-60–MS-64. The most common grade range for the 1983-D Mint State Kennedy half dollar is MS-62 to MS-64. Strike and luster are generally good. This date is rarely seen in the few rolls that appear in the market.

Valuation—**MS-63s** sell for $3 to $5. A small premium exists for **MS-64** coins, which bring $8 to $20. Attractive color coins trade at a premium in any grade.

MS-65–MS-66. The lack of Mint sets and the generally poor quality make this another scarce coin in gem. While strike is generally better than the 1983-P, bagmarks are a problem.

Valuation—**MS-65** coins bring $25 to $75; **MS-66** coins, $100 to $200.

MS-67–MS-68. This is a rare coin in MS-67. No example has graded higher to date.

Valuation—In **MS-67** this is a $800–$1,250 coin.

1984-P, MINT STATE

MS-67

The mintage of the 1984-P Kennedy stands at 26 million. Mint set production resumed in 1984, with more than 1.8 million issued.

NGC CERTIFIED POPULATION *(from a total mintage of 26,029,000)* (WCG™)

MS-64	MS-65	MS-66	MS-67	MS-68	MS-69	MS-70
57	127	176	50	0	0	0

MS-60–MS-64. Most 1984-P Mint State Kennedy half dollars are in the MS-62–MS-64 range. Luster is generally good, though most examples suffer from light hairline abrasions and are somewhat softly struck.

Valuation—**MS-63** examples of the 1984-P sell for $3 to $5. **MS-64** coins bring $8 to $15. Attractive color coins trade at a premium in any grade.

MS-65–MS-66. Although more than 1.8 million Mint sets were issued in 1984, the 1984-P is almost as scarce as the 1983-P in MS-65 and MS-66 grades. Once again, most examples are noted for their numerous bagmarks and weak strike.

Valuation—$15 to $45 for **MS-65** coins. **MS-66** coins offer good value in their current $60 to $125 trading range.

MS-67–MS-68. This issue is *rare* in MS-67, though not quite as rare as the 1982-P and 1983-P. No examples have been certified higher than MS-67 to date by NGC or PCGS.

Valuation—This is a $500–$1,000 coin in **MS-67**.

◄═══ 1984-D, Mint State ═══►

MS-67

The mintage of the 1984-D Kennedy half dollar is virtually identical to that of the 1984-P: just over 26 million coins were struck. This was a poorly struck date with rough surfaces, making this date costly in high grades.

NGC CERTIFIED POPULATION *(from a total mintage of 26,262,158)*   (WCG™)

MS-64	MS-65	MS-66	MS-67	MS-68	MS-69	MS-70
57	117	131	21	0	0	0
MS-64 PL	MS-65 PL	MS-66 PL	MS-67 PL	MS-68 PL	MS-69 PL	MS-70 PL
4	2	1	1	0	0	0

MS-60–MS-64. The most common grade range for the 1984-D Mint State Kennedy half dollar is MS-62 to MS-64. Strike and luster are generally good.

Valuation—1984-Ds in **MS-63** sell for $3 to $5; in **MS-64,** $8 to $15. Attractive color coins trade at a premium in any grade.

MS-65–MS-66. Despite the fact that this date is available in the 1.8 million Mint sets issued in 1984, it is still very elusive in gem condition, as the great majority of uncirculated specimens are abraded to an appreciable degree.

Valuation—$20 to $40 for **MS-65** coins, $100 to $200 for **MS-66** examples.

MS-67–MS-68. The 1984-D is a very rare coin in MS-67—tougher to find than the 1984-P. Very few Mint State 1984-D Kennedy halves have survived in the nearly mark-free condition required for an MS-67 grade.

No example has graded higher to date.

Valuation—A $2,000–$4,000 coin in **MS-67.** Several prooflike coins have been graded by NGC; they can cost four times more than these prices.

1985-P, Mint State

MS-67

Just under 19 million half dollars were struck at the Philadelphia Mint in 1985. 1.7 million of these coins found their way into Mint sets that year.

NGC CERTIFIED POPULATION *(from a total mintage of 18,706,962)* (WCG™)

MS-64	MS-65	MS-66	MS-67	MS-68	MS-69	MS-70
34	87	244	95	1	0	0

MS-60–MS-64. Most 1985-P Mint State Kennedy half dollars range from MS-62 to MS-64. Luster is generally good, though most examples suffer from light hairline abrasions and bagmarks.

Valuation—**MS-63** coins sell for $3 to $5, while **MS-64s** go for $8 to $20. Attractive color coins trade at a premium in any grade.

MS-65–MS-66. The 1985-P is slightly higher quality than the 1984-P and 1984-D. MS-65 coins can be located with a minimum of difficulty. MS-66 coins are more challenging, but can still be acquired with just a little patience.

Valuation—$20 to $40 for **MS-65** coins. **MS-66** coins generally fall in the $40–$60 range.

MS-67–MS-68. This issue is extremely scarce in MS-67. The 1985-P is slightly more available in near-flawless MS-67 condition than the 1981-P to 1984-P issues. Still, only one example has been certified higher to date—an MS-68.

Valuation—This is a $250 to $400 coin in **MS-67.**

ᐧ⇒ 1985-D, MINT STATE ⇐ᐧ

MS-67

Just under 20 million 1985-D Kennedy half dollars were struck. Of these, 1.7 million found their way into Mint sets.

NGC CERTIFIED POPULATION *(from a total mintage of 19,814,034)* (WCG™)

MS-64	MS-65	MS-66	MS-67	MS-68	MS-69	MS-70
17	96	364	145	2	0	0

MS-60–MS-64. The most common grade range for the 1985-D Mint State Kennedy half dollars is MS-62 to MS-64. Strike and luster are generally good.

Valuation—**MS-63** examples sell for $3 to $5. There is a small premium for **MS-64** coins, which sell for $8 to $15. Attractive color coins trade at a premium in any grade.

MS-65–MS-66. The 1985-D ranks among the easier-to-locate dates in MS 65 and MS-66 grade from the 1980s and earlier Mint State Kennedy series. This Denver Mint issue offers slightly better quality, with generally fewer bagmarks, than Denver issues of previous years.

Valuation—$20 to $30 for **MS-65** coins, $30 to $60 for **MS-66** examples.

MS-67–MS-68. This issue is scarce in MS-67. This date has been graded in MS-68, though these coins are extremely rare. To date, only a few examples have been certified in MS-68.

Valuation—This date generally sells in the $150–$300 range in **MS-67. MS-68** examples are valued at $2,500 or higher.

⋙ 1986-P, MINT STATE ⋘

MS-67

Only 13.1 million half dollars were struck at the Philadelphia Mint in 1986—among the lowest mintages in the series for clad nonsilver issues in the Mint State Kennedy series. Fortunately, 1.15 million of these coins found their way into Mint sets that year. This is one of the nicest Kennedys in the series.

NGC CERTIFIED POPULATION *(from a total mintage of 13,107,633)*   (WCG™)

MS-64	MS-65	MS-66	MS-67	MS-68	MS-69	MS-70
38	90	296	102	1	0	0
MS-64 PL	MS-65 PL	MS-66 PL	MS-67 PL	MS-68 PL	MS-69 PL	MS-70 PL
0	0	1	0	0	0	0

MS-60–MS-64. Most 1986-P Mint State Kennedy half dollars range from MS-62 to MS-64. Luster is generally good, though most examples suffer from light hairline abrasions and bagmarks.

Valuation—**MS-63** examples sell for $3 to $5, **MS-64** coins for $8 to $15. Attractive color coins trade at a premium in any grade.

MS-65–MS-66. Despite the extremely low total mintage, the 1986-P is about equal in rarity to the 1985-P. It is a slightly higher-quality issue than the 1981-P to 1984-P Kennedy half dollars. MS-65 coins can be located with a minimum of difficulty. MS-66 coins are more challenging, but still be acquired with just a little patience.

Valuation—$20 to $40 for **MS-65** coins. **MS-66** coins generally fall in the $35–$80 range.

MS-67–MS-68. Extremely scarce in MS-67. Again, the 1986-P is slightly more available in near-flawless MS-67 condition than the 1981-P to 1985-P issues. Very few have been certified at MS-68.

Valuation—This issue is a $200–$400 coin in **MS-67.** The **MS-68** is valued at $3,000 or more.

◆➤ 1986-D, MINT STATE ◆➤

MS-68

A mere 15.3 million Kennedy half dollars were struck in 1985. 1.15 million were issued in Mint sets, so this date is not scarce in Mint State condition. With new recut dies, this is a perfect strike with frosty surfaces.

NGC CERTIFIED POPULATION *(from a total mintage of 15,336,145)*   (WCG™)

MS-64	MS-65	MS-66	MS-67	MS-68	MS-69	MS-70
26	118	350	180	5	3	0

MS-60–MS-64. The 1986-D ranks among the highest-quality dates of the decade. While most examples range in grade between MS-62 and MS-64, MS-64 coins are very easy to locate. Strike and luster are generally excellent, with fewer bagmarks than average for the series.

Valuation—**MS-63** coins sell for $3 to $5; **MS-64** coins, $8 to $15. Attractive color coins trade at a premium in any grade.

MS-65–MS-66. The 1986-D is relatively easy to locate in MS-65 and even in MS-66. This is a very high-quality Denver Mint issue with generally fewer bagmarks than Denver issues of previous years.

Valuation—$20 to $30 for **MS-65** coins, $35 to $50 for **MS-66** coins.

MS-67–MS-68. While the 1986-D is a high-quality date, it is still a scarce coin in MS-67. However, this is one Mint State Kennedy issue that the collector stands a chance of acquiring in a grade higher than MS-67. To date, NGC and PCGS combined have graded fewer than a dozen examples higher than MS-67.

Valuation—This date generally sells in the $75–$150 range in **MS-67. MS-68** coins may command $2,000 to $2,500.

⊶⊜ 1987-P, Mint State ⊜⊷

MS-67

A mere 2.9 million half dollars were struck at the Philadelphia Mint in 1986. This date was issued in Mint sets only, with no examples being struck for circulation.

NGC CERTIFIED POPULATION *(from a total mintage of 2,890,758)* (WCG™)

MS-64	MS-65	MS-66	MS-67	MS-68	MS-69	MS-70
85	142	301	120	1	0	0
MS-64 PL	MS-65 PL	MS-66 PL	MS-67 PL	MS-68 PL	MS-69 PL	MS-70 PL
0	0	1	0	0	0	0

MS-60–MS-64. The 1987-P is among the higher-quality issues from this period. Abrasions and bagmarks are minimal.

Valuation—**MS-63** coins sell for $3 to $5; **MS-64** coins, $8 to $15. Attractive color coins trade at a premium in any grade.

MS-65–MS-66. Despite the record low total mintage, the 1987-P ranks among the easier dates to locate in MS-65 and MS-66 condition.

Valuation—$25 to $35 for **MS-65** coins. **MS-66** coins generally sell for between $40 and $60.

MS-67–MS-68. The 1987-P is extremely scarce in MS-67, but among the least rare issues of the decade. Gems are very well struck, with excellent luster and nearly mark-free surfaces. One example has been certified higher to date, graded MS-68.

Valuation—This is a $250 to $400 coin in **MS-67.**

⋙ 1987-D, MINT STATE ⋘

MS-68

A mere 2.9 million half dollars were struck at the Denver Mint in 1986. This date was issued in Mint sets only, with no examples being struck for circulation. It boasts a gorgeous strike and frosty surfaces. Due to the low mintage, finding a high grade is difficult.

NGC CERTIFIED POPULATION (*from a total mintage of 2,890,758*)   (WCG™)

MS-64	MS-65	MS-66	MS-67	MS-68	MS-69	MS-70
52	144	515	218	7	0	0
MS-64 PL	MS-65 PL	MS-66 PL	MS-67 PL	MS-68 PL	MS-69 PL	MS-70 PL
0	1	1	0	0	0	0

MS-60–MS-64. The 1987-D ranks among the highest-quality dates of the decade. While most examples range in grade between MS-62 and MS-64, MS-64 coins are very easy to locate. Strike and luster are generally excellent, and this issue features fewer bagmarks than average for the series.

Valuation—In **MS-63** the 1987-D sells for $3 to $5. A small premium exists for **MS-64** coins, which sell for $8 to $15. Attractive color coins trade at a premium in any grade.

MS-65–MS-66. Like the 1987-P, The 1987-D ranks among the easier dates to locate in MS-65 and MS-66. This is another very high-quality Denver Mint issue with generally fewer bagmarks than Denver issues of previous years.

Valuation—$20 to $30 for **MS-65** coins, $30 to $45 for **MS-66** coins.

MS-67–MS-68. The 1987-D is a generally high-quality date that can be located in MS-67 with a little patience. This date is also available in MS-68 condition, but is quite rare in this highest Mint State grade.

Valuation—This date generally sells in the $100–$200 range in **MS-67. MS-68** coins can command between $1,750 and $3,000.

⊶ 1988-P, Mint State ⊷

MS-67

The 1988-P is another low-mintage year, with only 13.6 million half dollars struck at the Philadelphia mint. 1.65 million coins were issued in Mint sets. This issue features a super-nice strike and almost prooflike surfaces.

NGC CERTIFIED POPULATION *(from a total mintage of 13,626,000)*   (WCG™)

MS-64	MS-65	MS-66	MS-67	MS-68	MS-69	MS-70
46	78	411	87	1	0	0
MS-64 PL	MS-65 PL	MS-66 PL	MS-67 PL	MS-68 PL	MS-69 PL	MS-70 PL
0	0	1	0	0	0	0

MS-60–MS-64. The 1988-P is a relatively high-quality issue, though not quite on a level with the 1987-P, primarily due to the light bagmarks that are typically found.

Valuation—In **MS-63** the 1988-P sells for $3 to $5. There is a small premium for **MS-64** coins, which sell for $8 to $15. Attractive color coins trade at a premium in any grade.

MS-65–MS-66. The 1988-P can located in MS-65 with minimal difficulty, though MS-66 coins are more challenging.

Valuation—$25 to $35 for **MS-65** coins. **MS-66** coins generally sell for between $50 and $80.

MS-67–MS-68. This issue is rare in MS-67, with only one example graded higher to date—an MS-68 graded by NGC.

Valuation—This is a $250–$450 coin in **MS-67**—a tremendous value considering the difficulty of locating it.

1988-D, MINT STATE

MS-68

Only 12 million half dollars were struck at the Denver Mint in 1988, with 1.65 issued in Mint sets.

NGC CERTIFIED POPULATION *(from a total mintage of 12,000,096)*   (WCG™)

MS-64	MS-65	MS-66	MS-67	MS-68	MS-69	MS-70
28	80	378	234	3	0	0

MS-60–MS-64. The 1988-D is a much higher-quality date, similar to the 1987-D. Bagmarks are fewer than average with generally excellent strikes.

Valuation—In **MS-63** the 1988-D sells for $3 to $5. A small premium exists for **MS-64** coins, which sell for $8 to $15. Attractive color coins trade at a premium in any grade.

MS-65–MS-66. The 1988-D is among the easiest dates in the Kennedy series to locate in MS-65 and MS-66. This is a very high-quality Denver Mint issue with generally fewer bagmarks than Denver issues of the mid-1980s and earlier.

Valuation—$20 to $35 for **MS-65** coins, $40 to $60 for **MS-66** coins.

MS-67–MS-68. Like the 1987-D, the 1988-D is a generally high-quality date that can be located in MS-67 with a little patience. This date is also available in MS-68 condition, but is quite rare in this highest Mint State grade.

Valuation—The 1988-D generally sells in the $125–$200 range in **MS-67,** but **MS-68** coins sell for between $2,000 and $2,500. The 1988-D offers especially good value in MS-67, as the coin is far more difficult to locate than the current value might suggest.

⋙ 1989-P, MINT STATE ⋘

MS-67

Mintage increased at the Philadelphia Mint in 1989 for the Kennedy half dollar, though at 24.5 million coins struck the 1989-P Kennedy must still be considered a low-mintage date—especially when one compares the mintage of this coin to the 1989-P Washington quarter, with 512.8 million coins struck.

Almost two million of the Kennedy halves could be found in government-issue Mint sets for that year.

NGC CERTIFIED POPULATION *(from a total mintage of 24,542,000)* (WCG™)

MS-64	MS-65	MS-66	MS-67	MS-68	MS-69	MS-70
71	109	254	88	0	0	0
MS-64 PL	MS-65 PL	MS-66 PL	MS-67 PL	MS-68 PL	MS-69 PL	MS-70 PL
2	4	12	2	0	0	0
MS-64 DPL	MS-65 DPL	MS-66 DPL	MS-67 DPL	MS-68 DPL	MS-69 DPL	MS-70 DPL
0	1	0	0	0	0	0

MS-60–MS-64. The 1988-P is a relatively high-quality issue, though not quite on a par with the 1987-P, primarily due to light bagmarks typically being found.

Valuation—There is a small premium for **MS-64** coins, which sell for $6 to $15. Attractive color coins trade at a premium in any grade.

MS-65–MS-66. The 1988-P can be located in MS-65 with minimal difficulty, though MS-66 coins are more challenging.

Valuation—$25 to $40 for **MS-65** coins. **MS-66** coins generally sell for between $40 and $65.

MS-67–MS-68. This issue is rare in MS-67.

Valuation—This is a $300 to $500 coin in **MS-67**—a tremendous value considering the difficulty factor. None have been graded in **MS-68** to date.

⊸⟳ 1989-D, MINT STATE ⟳⊷

MS-67

896 million 1989-D Washington quarters were struck at the Denver Mint in 1989, but only 23 million Kennedy half dollars were struck at that mint—about 2.5% of the total of the Washington quarters. Almost two million of the Kennedy halves could be found in government-issue Mint sets for that year.

NGC CERTIFIED POPULATION *(from a total mintage of 23,000,216)*   (WCG™)

MS-64	MS-65	MS-66	MS-67	MS-68	MS-69	MS-70
48	99	397	120	2	0	0
MS-64 PL	MS-65 PL	MS-66 PL	MS-67 PL	MS-68 PL	MS-69 PL	MS-70 PL
1	0	2	0	0	0	0

MS-60–MS-64. The 1989-D is a high-quality date a notch down from the 1988-D. Most examples grade MS-63 and MS-64.

Valuation—In **MS-63** this coin sells for $3 to $5. A small premium for **MS-64** coins exists; these sell for $6 to $12. Attractive color coins trade at a premium in any grade.

MS-65–MS-66. The 1989-D is slightly rarer in MS-65 and MS-66 condition than the previous 1987-D and 1988-D Kennedy half dollars. Bagmarks are the culprit.

Valuation—$20 to $40 for **MS-65** coins, $40 to $75 for **MS-66** examples.

MS-67–MS-68. The 1989-D is extremely scarce in MS-67 condition. The last Denver-minted Kennedy of the decade, it is a mid-range rarity issue—more elusive than the 1985–1989 Denver Mint Kennedy halves, but not as rare as the 1981–1984 ones. Only two certifications to date have been higher: an MS-68 by each of the major grading services, NGC and PCGS.

Valuation—The 1989-D generally trades in the $225–$400 range in **MS-67** grade. Exceptional color coins will of course be considerably higher.

A View of the Decade: The 1990s

As the 1990s began, the boom in "investment-grade" coins ended, and collectors once again came to the fore as investors receded. This decade would be distinguished by the introduction of new coin types. The first U.S. platinum coins were struck in 1997 as part of the American Eagle bullion series. In 1999 the U.S. Mint 50 State Quarters® program was launched. This 10-year program produced quarters with designs commemorating each of the 50 states in the order in which they attained statehood. Due in part to the popularity of these coins, the Mint estimated that 130 million people were now coin collectors. Paper money also saw innovations, with the introduction in 1995 of a redesigned $100 bill that included more security features.

In the late 1990s legislation was passed to create the Sacagawea "golden" dollar coins (first struck for circulation in 2000). In hobby news, in 1996, a coin broke the $1 million barrier for the first time, when the Eliasberg 1913 Liberty Head nickel sold for $1,485,000. The Internet began to have a tremendous impact on the sale and collecting of coins.

⊷ 1990-P, Mint State ⊶

MS-67

The 1990-P Kennedy half dollar is another relatively low-mintage issue, with only 22.3 million examples struck. By comparison, almost 614 million Washington quarters were struck at the Philadelphia Mint that year. 1.8 million Mint sets were issued in 1990. This date is heavily bagmarked, with poor surfaces.

NGC CERTIFIED POPULATION *(from a total mintage of 22,278,000)* (WCG™)

MS-64	MS-65	MS-66	MS-67	MS-68	MS-69	MS-70
51	64	151	63	2	0	0
MS-64 PL	MS-65 PL	MS-66 PL	MS-67 PL	MS-68 PL	MS-69 PL	MS-70 PL
0	3	1	1	0	0	0

MS-60–MS-64. The 1990-P is not among the higher-quality issues in the series. This is a date plagued by minor bagmarks.

Valuation—There is a small premium for **MS-64** coins, which sell for $6 to $12. Attractive color coins trade at a premium in any grade.

MS-65–MS-66. The 1990-P is elusive in MS-65 and quite scarce in MS-66.

Valuation—$20 to $30 for **MS-65** coins. **MS-66** coins sell for between $40 and $60.

MS-67–MS-68. This issue is extremely scarce in MS-67, with only two examples graded higher—both MS-68 specimens that were certified by NGC.

Valuation—The 1990-P generally trades for a substantial premium in **MS-67** grade—$500 to $1,000. The two coins that have been graded **MS-68** are valued at $3,000+.

·→⇒ 1990-D, MINT STATE ⇐←·

MS-67

Only 20.1 million Kennedy half dollars were struck at the Denver Mint in 1990. Fortunately, 1.8 million of these coins were issued in government Mint sets, so the 1990-D is easy to find in brilliant Uncirculated condition, if not gem condition.

NGC CERTIFIED POPULATION *(from a total mintage of 20,096,242)*   (WCG™)

MS-64	MS-65	MS-66	MS-67	MS-68	MS-69	MS-70
54	92	197	29	0	0	0

MS-60–MS-64. The 1990-D is below average in quality compared to previous Denver products. MS-62–MS-64 is the most common grade range for brilliant Uncirculated coins.

Valuation—A small premium exists for **MS-64** coins, which sell for $10 to $25. Attractive color coins trade at a premium in any grade.

MS-65–MS-66. The 1990-D is scarce in MS-65 and very scarce in MS-66. This is a very difficult date to locate in minimally marked condition.

Valuation—$20 to $30 for **MS-65** coins. **MS-66** 1990-D Kennedy halves trade in the $40–$60 range.

MS-67–MS-68. The 1990-D is rare in MS-67 condition. Bagmarks are a huge problem for this date, as strike and luster are generally exceptional. This date ranks among the rarest in the series in MS-67 of the Kennedy half dollars from 1972 to the present. No 1990-D has been graded higher to date by PCGS or NGC.

Valuation—The 1990-D Kennedy in PCGS/NGC **MS-67** usually trades for between $1,000 and $2,000.

ᵕ⁼ 1991-P, MINT STATE ᵕ⁼

MS-68

The design of the Kennedy half dollar was recut for 1991, featuring sharpening the detail in the president's portrait. The Mint had apparently concluded that as a tool for commerce the half dollar was becoming something of a relic, as in 1991 production of the Kennedy half dollar once again took a precipitous drop, with the Philadelphia Mint striking only 14.9 million coins. On the other hand, 571 million Washington quarters were struck that year at the Philadelphia Mint.

Fortunately, 1.35 million Mint sets were issued in 1991, so this date is not difficult to locate in uncirculated, if not gem, condition.

NGC CERTIFIED POPULATION *(from a total mintage of 14,874,000)* (WCG™)

MS-64	MS-65	MS-66	MS-67	MS-68	MS-69	MS-70
49	93	160	86	2	0	0
MS-64 PL	MS-65 PL	MS-66 PL	MS-67 PL	MS-68 PL	MS-69 PL	MS-70 PL
1	0	9	2	0	0	0

MS-60–MS-64. The 1991-P is a much higher-quality date than the 1990-P, though the majority of examples found in Mint sets or rolls will still be below gem quality. Nevertheless, most coins in Mint sets and rolls grade in the MS-63–MS-64 range.

Valuation—There is a small premium for **MS-64** coins: $10 to $20. Attractive color coins trade at a premium in any grade.

MS-65–MS-66. The 1991-P is easier to find in MS-65 and MS-66 condition than the 1990-P. MS-65 1991-P coins can be located with a minimum of difficulty in Mint sets, while examples in MS-66 are more challenging.

Valuation—$20 to $40 for **MS-65** coins. **MS-66** coins generally sell for between $50 and $80.

MS-67–MS-68. The 1991-P is much more challenging to acquire in the higher MS-67 and MS-68 grades. The Kennedy half dollar is a large coin, and to merit a grade of MS-67 a half dollar must approach perfection to the unaided eye, with few observable bagmarks, an excellent strike, and good luster or attractive toning. Few 1991-P Kennedy half dollars found in Mint sets offer that level of quality.

To date, only a handful of coins have been certified in MS-68.

Valuation—The 1991-P **MS-67** generally sells in the $175–$275 range. An **MS-68**? The owner can almost name his or her price, though $2,500 would probably be a good place to start.

⊷⇒ 1991-D, MINT STATE ⇐⊷

MS-68

Only 15.1 million Kennedy half dollars were struck at the Denver Mint in 1991. Most gems come from Mint sets, as 1.35 million sets were issued by the Mint in 1991. This low-mintage issue has a poor strike and surfaces. Grades of MS-60 to MS-63 are common.

NGC CERTIFIED POPULATION *(from a total mintage of 15,054,678)*   (WCG™)

MS-64	MS-65	MS-66	MS-67	MS-68	MS-69	MS-70
39	114	191	70	3	1	0
MS-64 PL	MS-65 PL	MS-66 PL	MS-67 PL	MS-68 PL	MS-69 PL	MS-70 PL
0	1	1	1	0	0	0

MS-60–MS-64. The 1991-D is of generally lower quality than the 1991-P, with the Denver issue usually exhibiting more bagmarks than its Philadelphia counterpart.

Valuation—A small premium exists for **MS-64** coins, which sell for between $8 and $15. Attractive color coins trade at a premium in any grade.

MS-65–MS-66. The 1991-D is fairly easy to locate in MS-65 but is scarce in MS-66.

Valuation—$15 to $30 for **MS-65** coins. **MS-66** examples sell for between $50 and $100.

MS-67–MS-68. The 1991-D is very difficult to locate in near mark-free MS-67 condition, and will prove to be quite a challenge for the collector attempting to build a really top-quality set. Still, with patience, MS-67 coins do surface on occasion. Only three examples have even been certified in MS-68.

Valuation—The 1991-D Kennedy in PCGS/NGC **MS-67** usually trades for between $500 and $1,500.

1992-P, MINT STATE

MS-68

17.6 million Kennedy half dollars were struck at the Philadelphia Mint in 1992. 1.5 million of these found their way into Mint sets. This total mintage figure is still very small by modern standards, especially when compared to Washington quarter production figures. While almost 200 million fewer 1992 Washington quarters were struck at the Philadelphia Mint in 1992 than 1991, 385 million quarters were still being produced.

NGC CERTIFIED POPULATION *(from a total mintage of 17,628,000)* (WCG™)

MS-64	MS-65	MS-66	MS-67	MS-68	MS-69	MS-70
32	91	347	194	7	0	0
MS-64 PL	MS-65 PL	MS-66 PL	MS-67 PL	MS-68 PL	MS-69 PL	MS-70 PL
0	0	3	0	0	0	0

MS-60–MS-64. Quality continued to improve in 1992 for Philadelphia-minted Kennedy half dollars. While the majority of examples found in Mint sets or rolls will fall below gem quality, most coins will grade in the MS-63–MS-64 range.

Valuation—A small premium exists for **MS-64** coins, which sell for between $6 and $12. Attractive color coins trade at a premium in any grade.

MS-65–MS-66. The 1991-P is more available in MS-65 and MS-66 than the 1990-P, and the 1992-P is easier to locate in this grade than the 1991-P. MS-66 should be the minimum collectible grade for this date, as it is still quite inexpensive, though more elusive than the MS-65 grade.

Valuation—$20 to $30 for **MS-65** coins. **MS-66** coins can generally be acquired for between $25 and $45.

MS-67–MS-68. The 1992-P ranks among the higher-population dates in the series in MS-67 struck before 1996, though it is still a scarce coin in this grade. A handful of examples have also been certified in MS-68.

Valuation—The 1992-P is currently a $65–$125 coin in **MS-67**. The premium jumps considerably for the rare **MS-68** examples, which are valued at $1,000+.

·◦⇒ 1992-D, MINT STATE ⇐◦·

MS-68

17 million Kennedy half dollars were struck at the Denver Mint in 1992. Most gems come from Mint sets, as 1.5 million sets were issued by the Mint in 1992.

NGC CERTIFIED POPULATION *(from a total mintage of 17,000,106)*   (WCG™)

MS-64	MS-65	MS-66	MS-67	MS-68	MS-69	MS-70
26	53	370	168	3	1	0

MS-60–MS-64. The 1992-D is of the same approximate quality as the 1992-P. It is a comparatively high-quality issue, among the highest of the pre-1996 Mint State Kennedy half dollars.

Valuation—There is a small premium for **MS-64** coins—between $8 and $16. Attractive color coins trade at a premium in any grade.

MS-65–MS-66. The 1992-D is easy to locate in MS-65 and MS-66. Given the higher quality of this date, MS-66 should be the minimum grade to go after if one is assembling a gem set.

Valuation—A small premium exists for **MS-65** coins; they sell for between $20 and $30. **MS-66** coins bring between $25 and $50.

MS-67–MS-68. The 1992-D is approximately as available as the 1992-P in MS-67 grade. While scarce, this date is not as rare as many Denver-minted issues struck in 1991 and earlier.

A few examples have been certified in MS-68 to date, and, surprisingly, four examples have been certified in MS-69 by NGC.

Valuation—The 1992-D trades for between $65 and $100 in **MS-67. MS-68** coins have sold for upward of $1,500.

⇌ 1993-P, MINT STATE ⇋

MS-67

The Mint continued its trend of deemphasizing the half dollar for commerce, striking only 15.5 million Kennedy half dollars at the Philadelphia Mint in 1993. Of these, 1.3 million found their way into Mint sets, meaning only 14.2 million coins went directly for commercial use.

NGC CERTIFIED POPULATION *(from a total mintage of 15,510,000)* (WCG™)

MS-64	MS-65	MS-66	MS-67	MS-68	MS-69	MS-70
26	55	292	242	2	1	0
MS-64 PL	MS-65 PL	MS-66 PL	MS-67 PL	MS-68 PL	MS-69 PL	MS-70 PL
0	0	1	1	0	0	0

MS-60–MS-64. The 1993-P is a fairly high-quality issue. Strikes are generally excellent, as is luster. Bagmarks are average for the series.

Valuation—There is a small premium for **MS-64** coins—between $6 and $12. Attractive color coins trade at a premium in any grade.

MS-65–MS-66. The 1993-P is more available in MS-65 and MS-66 than the 1990-P, and the 1992-P is easier to locate in this grade than the 1991-P. MS-66 should be the minimum collectible grade for this date, as it is still quite inexpensive, though more elusive than the MS-65 grade.

Valuation—$20 to $35 for **MS-65** coins. **MS-66** coins can generally be acquired for between $30 and $60.

MS-67–MS-68. The 1993-P is slightly tougher to locate in MS-67 than its 1992-P predecessor. To date, only a handful of examples have been certified in MS-68 and MS-69.

Valuation—The 1993-P generally trades in a wide range, between $85 and $150 in **MS-67**. In **MS-68** it is valued at $2,000. One **MS-69** was graded by NGC and valued at $10,000.

⊷⇒ 1993-D, MINT STATE ⇐⊶

MS-68

15 million Kennedy half dollars were struck at the Denver Mint in 1993. Most gems come from Mint sets, as 1.3 million sets were issued by the Mint in 1993.

NGC CERTIFIED POPULATION *(from a total mintage of 15,000,006)* (WCG™)

MS-64	MS-65	MS-66	MS-67	MS-68	MS-69	MS-70
19	94	540	186	5	0	0
MS-64 PL	MS-65 PL	MS-66 PL	MS-67 PL	MS-68 PL	MS-69 PL	MS-70 PL
0	1	1	0	0	0	0

MS-60–MS-64. The 1993-D is similar to the 1993-P in quality. It is a comparatively high-quality issue, with most examples found in Mint sets grading in the MS-63–MS-64 range.

Valuation—There is a small premium for **MS-64** coins, which are valued at $8. Attractive color coins trade at a premium in any grade.

MS-65–MS-66. The 1993-D is a bit tougher to locate in the higher gem grades than the 1992-D. This date is generally found with slightly fewer bagmarks than the 1992-D.

Valuation—**MS-65** coins are valued at $15 to $25; **MS-66** coins, between $20 and $40.

MS-67–MS-68. The 1993-D is scarce in the higher MS-67 grade, and is about as elusive as the 1993-P. A handful of examples (about a dozen at the time of this writing) have been certified in MS-68.

Valuation—The 1993-D usually trades at $100 to $200 in **MS-67**. A couple of PCGS-graded **MS-68** examples have sold for more than $2,500.

1994-P, Mint State

MS-67

A surprising increase in production to levels not seen since 1989 took place at the Philadelphia Mint in 1994, with the striking of 23.7 million Kennedy half dollars. On the other hand, only 1.2 million of these coins found their way into Mint sets, the lowest Mint set total since 1986.

NGC CERTIFIED POPULATION *(from a total mintage of 23,718,000)*   (WCG™)

MS-64	MS-65	MS-66	MS-67	MS-68	MS-69	MS-70
48	103	432	195	9	0	0
MS-64 PL	MS-65 PL	MS-66 PL	MS-67 PL	MS-68 PL	MS-69 PL	MS-70 PL
0	0	1	0	0	0	0

MS-60–MS-64. The 1994-P is a high-quality issue, comparable to the 1992-P. Strikes are generally excellent, as is luster. Bagmarks are fewer than average for the series.

Valuation—A small premium exists for **MS-64** coins, which are valued at $8. Attractive color coins trade at a premium in any grade.

MS-65–MS-66. The 1994-P is common in MS-65 and MS-66 grades. MS-66 would be the minimum recommended grade for this high-quality date.

Valuation—$15 to $25 for **MS-65** coins. **MS-66** coins can generally be acquired for between $25 and $50.

MS-67–MS-68. The 1994-P can be located in MS-67 with a minimum of difficulty, though it still must be considered a scarce coin in this grade. If one's budget allows, this is also a date the collector can hope to locate in MS-68, as about a dozen examples have been certified at the time of this writing.

Valuation—The 1994-P generally trades for between $75 and $150 in **MS-67. MS-68** coins are valued at $1,500 and up.

1994-D, MINT STATE

MS-67

23.8 million Kennedy half dollars were struck at the Denver Mint in 1994, an almost identical total to the 1994-P. Only 1.2 million of these coins were issued in Mint sets, a low total by modern standards. This date has a better strike and surface but a lot of bagmarking.

NGC CERTIFIED POPULATION *(from a total mintage of 23,828,110)* (WCG™)

MS-64	MS-65	MS-66	MS-67	MS-68	MS-69	MS-70
18	69	211	75	4	0	1
MS-64 PL	MS-65 PL	MS-66 PL	MS-67 PL	MS-68 PL	MS-69 PL	MS-70 PL
0	3	3	1	0	0	0

MS-60–MS-64. While the mintage of the 1994-D is almost identical to the 1994-P, the quality is not. The Denver Mint releases generally suffer from more marks than the Philadelphia issues—a common trait going all the way back to the Franklin half dollar series.

Valuation— A small premium exists for **MS-64** coins—between $8 and $15. Attractive color coins trade at a premium in any grade.

MS-65–MS-66. The 1994-D is more difficult to locate in the higher gem grades than the 1994-P due to the aforementioned bagmark problems.

*Valuation—***MS-65** coins sell at about $15 to $25. **MS-66** coins sell for between $30 and $60.

MS-67–MS-68. A healthy premium exists for this date in MS-67. It is considerably more scarce than the Philadelphia Mint counterpart for 1994.

This date is extremely rare in MS-68, with about half as many examples certified as for the 1994-P.

*Valuation—*The 1994-D usually trades for $200 to $400 in **MS-67.** In **MS-68** it is valued upward of $2,500.

⋘⇒ 1995-P, Mint State ⇐⋙

MS-68

Mintage totals remained steady for the 1995-P Kennedy, with approximately 26.5 million coins struck. Just over one million Mint sets were issued in 1995, the lowest total since 1964.

NGC CERTIFIED POPULATION *(from a total mintage of 26,496,000)* (WCG™)

MS-64	MS-65	MS-66	MS-67	MS-68	MS-69	MS-70
41	50	260	158	10	0	0
MS-64 PL	MS-65 PL	MS-66 PL	MS-67 PL	MS-68 PL	MS-69 PL	MS-70 PL
0	0	0	1	0	0	0

MS-60–MS-64. The 1995-P Kennedy is in the mid-range of difficulty for the later Kennedy half dollars. This coin is abundant in the MS-63–MS-64 grade range. Attractive color-toned coins are more elusive and worth a premium depending on the color.
Valuation—**MS-64** examples sell for around $10.

MS-65–MS-66. The 1995-P is fairly easy to acquire in either MS-65 or MS-66. MS-66 would be the minimum recommended grade for this date.
Valuation—$15 to $25 for **MS-65** coins, $30 to $60 for **MS-66** coins.

MS-67–MS-68. MS-67 is the grade to shoot for if one wants a rare 1995-P Kennedy. The coin is extremely elusive in this higher Mint State grade, and is much tougher than the 1996-P that follows a year later. This date is also available in MS-68, though it is extremely rare.
Valuation—**MS-67** coins generally trade for between $100 and $250. **MS-68** coins have sold for upward of $1,500.

✦ 1995-D, Mint State ✦

MS-68

Mintage totals for the 1995-D are almost identical to the 1995-P, with 26.3 million coins struck. Just over one million Mint sets were issued in 1995, the lowest total since 1964.

NGC CERTIFIED POPULATION *(from a total mintage of 26,288,000)* (WCG™)

MS-64	MS-65	MS-66	MS-67	MS-68	MS-69	MS-70
15	69	232	163	10	0	0

MS-60–MS-64. The 1995-D Kennedy is generally a bit baggier than the 1995-P, though it is still abundant in the MS-63–MS-64 grade range. Attractive color-toned coins are more elusive and worth a premium depending on the color. With this date you can start to upgrade to MS-68.

Valuation—**MS-64** examples sell for around $10 to $15.

MS-65–MS-66. The 1995-D is approximately as scarce as the 1995-P in MS-65–66. It must still be considered fairly common in these higher Mint State grades.

Valuation—$15 to $25 for **MS-65** coins, $30 to $60 for **MS-66** coins.

MS-67–MS-68. Very scarce in MS-67, this grade has a similar rarity to the 1995-P. And as with the 1995-P, MS-68 coins are available, though are once again very rare.

Valuation—**MS-67** coins generally trade for between $100 and $250. **MS-68** coins are valued upward of $1,000.

⊶ 1996-P, MINT STATE ⊷

MS-68

Mintage totals dropped slightly from the previous year, with 24.4 million coins struck. Of these, almost 1.5 million were issued in Mint sets.

NGC CERTIFIED POPULATION *(from a total mintage of 24,442,000)* (WCG™)

MS-64	MS-65	MS-66	MS-67	MS-68	MS-69	MS-70
32	77	298	429	59	0	0

MS-60–MS-64. The 1996-P Kennedy ranks among the highest-quality dates of the modern Kennedy era. This date is common in gem condition. Attractive color-toned coins are extremely scarce and worth a premium depending on the color.

Valuation—**MS-64** examples sell for around $8.

MS-65–MS-66. This issue is easy to acquire in either MS-65 or MS-66.

Valuation—$12 to $20 for **MS-65** coins, $15 to $30 for **MS-66** coins.

MS-67–MS-68. While not a common coin in MS-67, the 1996-P is much easier to locate in this lofty Mint State grade than any previous Mint State Kennedy date struck. This date can also be located in MS-68 with just a little patience.

Valuation—**MS-67** coins generally trade for between $40 and $80. **MS-68** coins generally sell in the $150–$300 range.

⤖ 1996-D, Mint State ⤔

MS-68

In a total almost identical to the mintage of the 1996-P, 24.7 million 1996-D Kennedy half dollars were struck.

NGC CERTIFIED POPULATION *(from a total mintage of 24,744,000)*   (WCG™)

MS-64	MS-65	MS-66	MS-67	MS-68	MS-69	MS-70
44	92	312	422	18	0	0
MS-64 PL	MS-65 PL	MS-66 PL	MS-67 PL	MS-68 PL	MS-69 PL	MS-70 PL
0	1	3	0	0	0	0

MS-60–MS-64. Despite the modest mintage, the 1996-D is as common as the 1996-P Kennedy in MS-63 and MS-64. Attractive color-toned coins are more elusive and worth a premium depending on the color.

Valuation—**MS-64** examples sell for around $8.

MS-65–MS-66. This issue is common in MS-65 and MS-66.

Valuation—$12 to $15 for **MS-65** coins, $15 to $25 for **MS-66** coins.

MS-67–MS-68. The 1996-D is still relatively common in the higher MS-67 grade, and similar in rarity to the 1996-P. However, it is rarer than the 1996-P in the higher MS-68 grade.

Valuation—**MS-67** coins generally trade for between $40 and $80. **MS-68** coins usually sell for between $500 and $1,000, on the rare occasion that an example comes onto the market.

1997-P, Mint State

MS-68

Mintage totals dropped once again from the previous year, with only 20.9 million coins struck. For the first time since 1963, Mint set production dropped below one million, with .95 million sets issued. This was the second year of the new redesigned higher-relief design, but this issue has many abrasions. It is available 50% in Mint sets and 50% in rolls, with better quality being found in rolls.

NGC CERTIFIED POPULATION *(from a total mintage of 20,882,000)* (WCG™)

MS-64	MS-65	MS-66	MS-67	MS-68	MS-69	MS-70
41	68	135	124	14	0	0

MS-60–MS-64. While a higher-quality issue compared to most pre-1995 Philadelphia Mint Kennedy half dollars, by the previous year's (1996-P) standard the 1997-P is a tougher date to locate in high-grade Mint State. However, in the lowest Mint State grades (MS-63 and MS-64) it is a common coin. Attractive color-toned coins are extremely scarce and worth a premium depending on the color.

Valuation—**MS-64** examples sell for around $8 to $10.

MS-65–MS-66. The 1997-P is relatively easy to acquire in the MS-65 and MS-66 grades.

Valuation—$10 to $15 for **MS-65** coins, $30 to $60 for **MS-66** coins.

MS-67–MS-68. The 1997-P is scarce in MS-67 and extremely scarce in the highest MS-68 grade.

Valuation—**MS-67** coins generally trade for between $100 and $200. **MS-68** coins generally sell in the $800–$1,500 range.

⤛⊷ 1997-D, MINT STATE ⊷⤜

MS-68

Only 19.9 million Kennedy half dollars were struck at the Denver Mint in 1997 as the Kennedy half dollar continued its decline in importance as a denomination commonly utilized for commercial use. Adding to the scarcity of this date in high-grade brilliant Uncirculated condition, the Mint only released approximately 950,000 Mint sets that year, the lowest total since 1963.

NGC CERTIFIED POPULATION *(from a total mintage of 19,876,000)*   (WCG™)

MS-64	MS-65	MS-66	MS-67	MS-68	MS-69	MS-70
30	98	207	93	7	0	0
MS-64 PL	MS-65 PL	MS-66 PL	MS-67 PL	MS-68 PL	MS-69 PL	MS-70 PL
0	4	1	1	0	0	0

MS-60–MS-64. The 1997-D is similar in quality to the 1997-P. This date is easy to locate in MS-63 and MS-64.

Valuation—**MS-64** coins sell for $8 to $10. Exceptional color coins are rare in any grade.

MS-65–MS-66. More elusive than the 1996-D in MS-65 to MS-66 condition.

Valuation—$15 to $25 for **MS-65** coins, $40 to $60 for **MS-66** coins.

MS-67–MS-68. This issue is very scarce in MS-67 and rare in MS-68. To date, about a dozen coins have been certified in the higher MS-68 grade.

Valuation—**MS-67** coins generally trade for between $150 and $300. **MS-68** coins are valued at $1,000 to $2,000.

↔ 1998-P, MINT STATE ↔

MS-67

Mintage totals dropped significantly once again at Philadelphia for the Kennedy half dollar, with only 15.6 million half dollars struck. Compare that to the mintage total for the 1998-P Washington quarter—896 million. Fortunately, 1.2 million Mint sets were issued in 1998—so almost 10% of the total production for that year found its way into these collector sets.

NGC CERTIFIED POPULATION *(from a total mintage of 15,646,000)*   (WCG™)

MS-64	MS-65	MS-66	MS-67	MS-68	MS-69	MS-70
32	65	174	172	14	0	0

MS-60–MS-64. A higher-quality issue midway in rarity between the most common 1996-P and rarer 1997-P in the higher Mint State grades. In the lower MS-63–MS-64 grades this is a common coin.

Valuation—**MS-64** examples sell for around $7 to $9, though exceptional color coins could command significantly more.

MS-65–MS-66. The 1998-P is still common in MS-65, though more of a challenge in MS-66.

Valuation—$15 to $25 for **MS-65** coins, $25 to $50 for **MS-66** coins.

MS-67–MS-68. The 1998-P is semi-scarce in MS-67 and extremely scarce in the highest MS-68 grade.

Valuation—**MS-67** coins generally trade for between $85 and $175. On the other hand, **MS-68** coins may sell for $700 or more.

This is a perfect date for a type set. You can buy a near perfect MS-67 for under $100.

⤖ 1998-D, MINT STATE ⤖

MS-67

Low . . . lower . . . and lower—just over 15 million Kennedy half dollars were struck at the Denver Mint in 1998. This was the lowest total to come from the Denver Mint since 1993. Try to buy rolls, as they occasionally offer better quality than Mint set coins.

NGC CERTIFIED POPULATION *(from a total mintage of 15,064,000)*   (WCG™)

MS-64	MS-65	MS-66	MS-67	MS-68	MS-69	MS-70
46	77	192	93	3	0	0
MS-64 PL	MS-65 PL	MS-66 PL	MS-67 PL	MS-68 PL	MS-69 PL	MS-70 PL
3	3	11	2	0	0	0

MS-60–MS-64. The 1998-D is as readily available as the 1998-P in the lower Mint State grades. As with virtually all Mint State Kennedy half dollars, the 1998-D is common in the lower MS-63–64 grades.

Valuation—**MS-64** coins sell for $8. Exceptional color coins are rare.

MS-65–MS-66. This coin is more elusive than the 1998-P in MS-65 to MS-66 condition.

Valuation—$15 to $25 for **MS-65** coins, $40 to $75 for **MS-66** coins.

MS-67–MS-68. The 1998-D is very scarce in minimally marked MS-67 grade, and is very rare in MS-68, with a mere *three* examples certified to date.

Valuation—**MS-67** coins generally trade for between $125 and $300. **MS-68** coins have sold for between $2,000 and $3,500.

1998-S, SPECIAL MINT SET

MS-70

The 1998-S Special Mint Set (SMS) Kennedy features a matte finish, is fully struck, and is generally free of bagmarks. The coin has the appearance of a Matte Proof. These coins were meticulously handled at the Mint. They are usually very high grade, averaging MS-68 to MS-69.

PCGS considers the 1998-S Kennedy part of the Mint State Kennedy set in the PCGS registry, while NGC includes this issue as part of the Proof Kennedy set in its registry.

NGC CERTIFIED POPULATION   (WCG™)

SP-64	SP-65	SP-66	SP-67	SP-68	SP-69	SP-70
1	7	10	36	241	2,844	509

MS-67. This grade is actually below-average quality for this issue.
Valuation—$125 to $250 in **MS-67.**

MS-68. This grade is the typical 1998-S SMS Kennedy.
Valuation—$125 to $175 in **MS-68.**

MS-69. This grade is common, but represents premium quality for the issue.
Valuation—$150 to $200 in **MS-69.**

MS-70. Flawless MS-70s are semi-scarce.
Valuation—$500 to $1,000 in **MS-70.**

⊷⇛ 1999-P, MINT STATE ⇚⊶

MS-68

Wow. Only 8.9 million Kennedy half dollars were struck in Philadelphia in 1999. This was the lowest total ever for any Kennedy half dollar. One has to go all the way back to 1987, when the Kennedy half dollar was released only in Mint sets, to find a lower mintage.

Fortunately, over 1.2 million Mint sets were issued in 1999, so for a relatively small premium the 1999-P Kennedy is available to the average collector in Mint State condition. The quality is nicer than most dates, with fewer abrasions. Better grades can be found in rolls.

NGC CERTIFIED POPULATION *(from a total mintage of 8,900,000)*   (WCG™)

MS-64	MS-65	MS-66	MS-67	MS-68	MS-69	MS-70
59	64	298	529	41	1	0
MS-64 PL	MS-65 PL	MS-66 PL	MS-67 PL	MS-68 PL	MS-69 PL	MS-70 PL
0	2	7	5	0	0	0

MS-60–MS-64. While the 1999-P is an extremely low-mintage date, the quality is very high. MS-63 and MS-64 actually represent the lowest Mint State grades one is likely to find for this date. A grade of MS-61 to MS-62 is unusual for a Mint State 1999-P.

Valuation—Very little premium for the lowest Mint State grades. This is not a recommended date in these lower grades, unless the coin offers exceptional color toning. In these lower grades, the coin is valued at $8 to $10.

MS-65–MS-66. The 1999-P is a minimally marked high-quality date, and is very common in MS-65 and MS-66 condition.

Valuation—$10 to $20 for **MS-65** coins, $15 to $25 for **MS-66** examples.

MS-67–MS-69. The 1999-P is still relatively common in MS-67 and only becomes a challenge to locate in MS-68 grade. A single example has been graded in MS-69.

Valuation—**MS-67** coins generally trade at between $50 and $100. **MS-68** examples generally trade at between $450 and $650. Only one **MS-69** has been graded by NGC, and is valued at $7,000+.

1999-D, MINT STATE

MS-68

In 1999 at the Denver Mint, 10.7 million Kennedy half dollars were struck, the lowest total in the entire series from Denver, with the exception of the 1987-D—a date that was issued only in Mint set form.

NGC CERTIFIED POPULATION *(from a total mintage of 10,682,000)* (WCG™)

MS-64	MS-65	MS-66	MS-67	MS-68	MS-69	MS-70
41	86	281	392	12	0	0
MS-64 PL	MS-65 PL	MS-66 PL	MS-67 PL	MS-68 PL	MS-69 PL	MS-70 PL
0	2	7	5	0	0	0

MS-60–MS-64. The 1999-D offers similar very high quality to the 1999-P. Most examples in Mint sets grade at least MS-63.

Valuation—$8 to $12 for **MS-63** and **MS-64** coins. Exceptional color coins can sell for much more.

MS-65–MS-66. This issue is still very common in these grades, approximately as available as the 1999-P.

Valuation—$10 to $20 for **MS-65** coins, $15 to $25 for **MS-66** examples.

MS-67–MS-68. The 1999-D is about as available as the 1999-P in MS-67 condition. It is in the highest MS-68 grade that the 1999-D is rarer than its sister from the Philadelphia Mint. Most examples display minor ticks that keep them out of MS-68 territory.

Valuation—**MS-67** coins generally trade at between $60 and $125. **MS-68** examples may sell for $1,500 and up.

A VIEW OF THE DECADE: THE 2000S

The year 2000 created an exciting start to the new decade, as the sale of g
ingots began from the wreck of the SS *Central America*, which had sunk in
the previous decade, the U.S. Mint brought new designs to circulating coins
release of new series. From 2004 to 2006, the Westward Journey Nickel Series
tured new designs on the nickel to commemorate the bicentennial of the Louis
Purchase and the Lewis and Clark expedition. Also bearing new designs was the cen
which in 2009 appeared with four different new reverses to commemorate four major
stages in Abraham Lincoln's life. The presidential dollar series was launched in 2007 to
depict former presidents on the dollar coin; it was accompanied by the First Lady gold
bullion series. Starting in 2009, the Sacagawea dollar gave way to the similar Native
American dollar, which featured an annual change to the reverse design.

Paper money also saw changes, as colorization and new security features were added
to the $50, $20, $10, and $5 bills. Meanwhile, popular Internet bidding sites like eBay
made it easier for unwary buyers to be fooled by counterfeit coins, but among established
sellers, more coins broke the $1 million mark at auction. In 2007 the remaining collec-
tion of John J. Ford Jr. was auctioned, the sale of the entire collection reaching a stagger-
ing sum of more than $50 million, making it the most valuable collection ever sold.

⤜⊷ 2000-P, MINT STATE ⊶⤛

MS-68

In Philadelphia in 2000, 22.6 million Kennedy half dollars were struck, the highest
total since 1996. Compared to Mint State Washington quarter totals (over 900 million
were struck of the 2000-P Virginia quarter), these were still very small numbers. Strike
is above average, but rough surfaces around the rim can be a problem. Better-grade
coins are found in Mint sets.

Almost 1.5 million Mint sets were issued in 2000.

NGC CERTIFIED POPULATION *(from a total mintage of 22,600,000)*   (WCG™)

MS-64	MS-65	MS-66	MS-67	MS-68	MS-69	MS-70
44	48	140	272	26	0	0
MS-64 PL	MS-65 PL	MS-66 PL	MS-67 PL	MS-68 PL	MS-69 PL	MS-70 PL
0	0	2	2	0	0	0

MS-60–MS-64. Quality continues at a very high level for the Kennedy series as
we begin the new millennium. The 2000-P Kennedy is almost always boldly struck,
with relatively few bagmarks. It is unusual to find a Mint State 2000-P grading
below MS-63.

...e is very little premium for the lowest Mint State grades. This is not
...date in these lower grades, unless the coin offers exceptional color ton-
...$8 to $10 in lower Mint State grades.

...S-66. The 2000-P is a minimally marked high-quality date, and is very
...in MS-65 and MS-66 condition.

...ation—$10 to $15 for **MS-65** coins, $15 to $25 for **MS-66** examples.

...-67–MS-68. The 2000-P is still relatively easy to locate in MS-67 and, like the
...999-P, only really becomes a challenge to locate in MS-68 grade.

Valuation—**MS-67** coins generally trade at between $40 and $100. On the other
hand, the **MS-68** is valued at $600 to $1,200.

⌖ 2000-D, MINT STATE ⌖

MS-67

In this year, 19.5 million Kennedy half dollars were struck in Denver, the highest total
since 1997. These were still comparatively very small numbers compared to Mint State
quarter, dime, nickel, and cent production totals. The strike is better than most dates,
but the surface can be abraded or have bagmarks.

NGC CERTIFIED POPULATION *(from a total mintage of 19,466,000)* (WCG™)

MS-64	MS-65	MS-66	MS-67	MS-68	MS-69	MS-70
49	108	259	102	0	0	0
MS-64 PL	**MS-65 PL**	**MS-66 PL**	**MS-67 PL**	**MS-68 PL**	**MS-69 PL**	**MS-70 PL**
0	0	1	0	0	0	0

MS-60–MS-64. The 2000-D strays a bit from the playbook regarding the quality of
later-date Mint State Kennedy half dollars, as this D-Mint issue generally does not
compare favorably in quality to the 2000-P or 1999-D.

Valuation—$6 to $10 for **MS-63** and **MS-64** coins. Exceptional color coins can sell
for much more.

MS-65–MS-66. This issue is still very common in MS-65, though a bit tougher to
locate in MS-66 than one might expect for a late-date Mint State Kennedy half.

Valuation—$15 to $20 for **MS-65** coins, $30 to $50 for **MS-66** examples.

MS-67–MS-68. The 2000-D is very scarce in MS-67, and no example has graded
higher to date. This date owes its scarcity to the light bagmarks and ticks that plague
virtually all specimens.

Valuation—**MS-67** coins generally trade at between $200 and $300.

⇌ 2001-P, MINT STATE ⇌

MS-68

In 2001 in Philadelphia, 21.2 million Kennedy half dollars were struck. Of these, 1.1 million were issued in Mint sets.

NGC CERTIFIED POPULATION *(from a total mintage of 21,200,000)* (WCG™)

MS-64	MS-65	MS-66	MS-67	MS-68	MS-69	MS-70
59	94	257	608	194	2	0
MS-64 PL	MS-65 PL	MS-66 PL	MS-67 PL	MS-68 PL	MS-69 PL	MS-70 PL
0	0	4	1	0	0	0

MS-60–MS-64. Production quality took a quantum leap forward in 2001. The typical Mint State 2001-P Kennedy found in a Mint set is gem quality. Strike and luster are excellent.

Valuation—There is very little premium for the lowest Mint State grades. This is not a recommended date in these lower grades, unless the coin offers exceptional color toning. Valued at $6 to $8 in lower Mint State grades.

MS-65–MS-66. The 2001-P is a minimally marked, very high-quality date, and is very common in MS-65 and MS-66 condition.

Valuation—$10 for **MS-65** coins, $15 for **MS-66** examples.

MS-67–MS-68. The 2001-P is still easy to locate in MS-67. While more challenging to locate in MS-68 grade, this date ranks among the most common dates in the series in this higher Mint State grade.

Valuation—**MS-67** coins generally trade at between $35 and $75. **MS-68s** generally trade at between $100 and $300. This date is great for a type set, as you can buy an MS-68 for a modest sum.

⟨⟩ 2001-D, MINT STATE ⟨⟩

MS-68

In Denver, 19.5 million Kennedy half dollars were struck in 2001. Mint sets will offer better quality than rolls.

NGC CERTIFIED POPULATION *(from a total mintage of 19,504,000)*   (WCG™)

MS-64	MS-65	MS-66	MS-67	MS-68	MS-69	MS-70
53	179	407	529	50	0	0
MS-64 PL	MS-65 PL	MS-66 PL	MS-67 PL	MS-68 PL	MS-69 PL	MS-70 PL
0	1	1	0	0	0	0

MS-60–MS-64. This issue is not quite as high quality as the 2001-P, due primarily to the tendency of this D-Mint issue to have more bagmarks than its P-Mint counterpart.

Valuation—There is very little premium for the lowest Mint State grades. This is not a recommended date in these lower grades, unless the coin offers exceptional color toning. Valued at $6 to $8 in lower Mint State grades.

MS-65–MS-66. The 2001-D is almost equal to the 2001-P in quality. This date is usually minimally marked and is very common in MS-65 and MS-66 condition.

Valuation—$10 to $15 for **MS-65** coins, $15 to $20 for **MS-66** examples.

MS-67–MS-68. The 2001-D is almost as easy to locate in MS-67 as the 2001-P. The 2001-D is considerably more elusive in MS-68 condition, but can be located with a bit of patience.

Valuation—**MS-67** coins generally trade at between $35 and $125. **MS-68s** generally trade at between $225 and $500.

⊶⇒ 2002-P, Mint State ⇐⊷

MS-68

The 2002-P was available only by ordering from the Mint, and a mere 3.1 million Kennedy half dollars were struck in Philadelphia in 2002. This was the first year of Mint-only half dollars. No coins were issued for circulation.

In this year, 1.1 million Mint sets were issued.

NGC CERTIFIED POPULATION *(from a total mintage of 3,100,000)* (WCG™)

MS-64	MS-65	MS-66	MS-67	MS-68	MS-69	MS-70
35	101	188	429	111	0	0
MS-64 PL	MS-65 PL	MS-66 PL	MS-67 PL	MS-68 PL	MS-69 PL	MS-70 PL
0	2	3	1	1	0	0

MS-60–MS-64. Production quality remains at a very high level for the 2002-P Kennedy half dollar. Most examples found in Mint sets are gem quality. Strike and luster are excellent.

Valuation—There is very little premium for the lowest Mint State grades. This is not a recommended date in these lower grades, unless the coin offers exceptional color toning. In lower Mint State grades it is valued at $10.

MS-65–MS-66. Again, there is very little premium for these grades.

Valuation—$12 to $15 for **MS-65** coins, $10 to $20 for **MS-66** examples.

MS-67–MS-68. The 2002-P can be located in MS-67 with little difficulty. This date becomes challenging in the higher MS-68 condition.

Valuation—**MS-67** coins generally trade at between $35 and $60. **MS-68s** generally trade between $125 and $500.

⋙ 2002-D, MINT STATE ⋘

MS-68

Only 2.5 million Kennedy half dollars were struck in Denver in 2002. These were a Mint-only production, with none issued for circulation.

NGC CERTIFIED POPULATION *(from a total mintage of 2,500,000)* (WCG™)

MS-64	MS-65	MS-66	MS-67	MS-68	MS-69	MS-70
61	121	249	317	15	1	0
MS-64 PL	**MS-65 PL**	**MS-66 PL**	**MS-67 PL**	**MS-68 PL**	**MS-69 PL**	**MS-70 PL**
0	0	2	0	0	0	0

MS-60–MS-64. As with other D-Mint issues, compared to its Philadelphia Mint counterpart the 2002-D is a notch lower in quality. This is all relative, given the exceptional quality of the 2002-P.

Valuation—There is very little premium for the lowest Mint State grades. This is not a recommended date in these lower grades, unless the coin offers exceptional color toning. In lower Mint State grades it is valued at $9 to $10.

MS-65–MS-66. The 2002-D is very common in MS-65 and MS-66 condition.

Valuation—$12 to $15 for **MS-65** coins, $15 to $30 for **MS-66** examples.

MS-67–MS-68. The 2002-D is another late-date Mint State Kennedy that is relatively easy to locate in MS-67. The 2002-D is very challenging to locate in near-flawless MS-68, with MS-67s outnumbering MS-68s by about 20 to 1.

Valuation—**MS-67** coins generally trade at between $40 and $100. This is a pricey date in **MS-68**, valued upward of $1,000.

2003-P, MINT STATE

MS-68

The 2003-P was available only through the Mint, with 2.5 million Kennedy half dollars struck in Philadelphia in 2003.

NGC CERTIFIED POPULATION *(from a total mintage of 2,500,000)*   (WCG™)

MS-64	MS-65	MS-66	MS-67	MS-68	MS-69	MS-70
52	121	304	199	11	0	0
MS-64 PL	MS-65 PL	MS-66 PL	MS-67 PL	MS-68 PL	MS-69 PL	MS-70 PL
1	1	1	0	0	0	0

MS-60–MS-64. Production quality took a dive for the 2003-P. In the lower Mint State grades this is a common coin. Strike and luster are generally good for this date.

Valuation—There is very little premium for the lowest Mint State grades. This is not a recommended date in these lower grades, unless the coin offers exceptional color toning. In lower Mint State grades this coin sells for $8 to $10.

MS-65–MS-66. Only a small premium exists for these grades.

Valuation—$15 to $25 for **MS-65** coins, $25 to $50 for **MS-66** examples.

MS-67–MS-68. The 2003-P is scarce in MS-67, and extremely difficult to locate in MS-68.

Valuation—**MS-67** coins generally trade at $75 to $200. The few **MS-68s** that have been graded are currently valued at more than $1,500.

2003-D, MINT STATE

MS-68

The 2003-D halves were available from the U.S. Mint in rolls or bags. None were issued for circulation. Better-quality coins are available in rolls; those in bags are abraded.

NGC CERTIFIED POPULATION *(from a total mintage of 2,500,000)*   (WCG™)

MS-64	MS-65	MS-66	MS-67	MS-68	MS-69	MS-70
37	184	249	186	5	0	0

MS-60–MS-64. Continuing the trend of previous years, compared to its Philadelphia mint counterpart the 2002-D is a notch lower in quality than the 2003-P.

Valuation—There is very little premium for the lowest Mint State grades. This is not a recommended date in these lower grades, unless the coin offers exceptional color toning. This issue in lower Mint State grades sells for $10 to $12.

MS-65–MS-66. The 2003-D is very common in MS-65 and MS-66 condition.

Valuation—$15 to $30 for **MS-65** coins, $30 to $50 for **MS-66** examples.

MS-67–MS-68. The 2003-D is more elusive than the previous year, 2002-D, in the higher MS-67 grade. This date is very rare in the highest MS-68 grade, with but a handful of examples certified to date by NGC and PCGS combined.

Valuation—**MS-67** coins generally trade for between $80 and $200. This is another pricey date in **MS-68**—some examples have sold for more than $2,000.

⁕═⊃ 2004-P, MINT STATE ⊂═⁕

MS-67

The 2004-P is available only through the U.S. Mint, with only 2.9 million Kennedy half dollars struck. Of these, 842,507 were issued in Mint sets.

NGC CERTIFIED POPULATION *(from a total mintage of 2,900,000)*   (WCG™)

MS-64	MS-65	MS-66	MS-67	MS-68	MS-69	MS-70
27	75	219	138	9	0	0

MS-60–MS-64. Strike and luster are generally good for this date. The U.S. Mint sealed rolls will offer the best chance for higher grades.

Valuation—There is very little premium for the lowest Mint State grades. This is not a recommended date in these lower grades, unless the coin offers exceptional color toning. In lower Mint State grades this sells for $8 to $10.

MS-65–MS-66. A greater premium exists for this issue, given its greater scarcity.

Valuation—$15 to $30 for **MS-65** coins, $30 to $60 for **MS-66** examples.

MS-67–MS-68. The 2004-P is extremely scarce in MS-67, and rare in MS-68.

Valuation—**MS-67** coins generally trade at $100 to $200. A couple of the **MS-68s** that have been graded are valued at $1,500+.

2004-D, MINT STATE

MS-68

The 2004-D is available only through the U.S. Mint, with only 2.9 million Kennedy half dollars struck. None were issued for circulation, but 842,507 were issued in Mint sets.

NGC CERTIFIED POPULATION *(from a total mintage of 2,900,000)* (WCG™)

MS-64	MS-65	MS-66	MS-67	MS-68	MS-69	MS-70
18	50	281	510	38	0	0
MS-64 PL	MS-65 PL	MS-66 PL	MS-67 PL	MS-68 PL	MS-69 PL	MS-70 PL
0	1	3	0	0	0	0

MS-60–MS-64. The 2004-D is a much higher-quality date. Gems are easy to locate.

Valuation—There is very little premium for the lowest Mint State grades. This is not a recommended date in these lower grades, unless the coin offers exceptional color toning. These sell for $8 to $10 in lower Mint State grades.

MS-65–MS-66. The 2004-D is very common in MS-65 and MS-66 condition.

Valuation—$12 to $20 for **MS-65** coins, $20 to $30 for **MS-66** examples.

MS-67–MS-68. The 2004-D ranks among the easiest dates to locate in the series in MS-67. MS-68s are far more elusive but can be located with a bit of patience.

Valuation—**MS-67** coins generally trade for between $35 and $50. **MS-68s** have sold for between $600 and $900.

⤜⧉ 2005-P, MINT STATE, BRILLIANT ⧉⤛

MS-65

Only 3.8 million of the 2005-P Kennedy half dollars with brilliant finish were struck. Beginning in 2005, Kennedy half dollars issued in Mint sets offer a satin finish, quite distinct in texture and appearance from their brilliant Uncirculated counterpart.

NGC CERTIFIED POPULATION *(from a total mintage of 3,800,000)* (WCG™)

MS-64	MS-65	MS-66	MS-67	MS-68	MS-69	MS-70
41	86	281	392	12	0	0

MS-60–MS-64. The 2005-P brilliant Kennedy is a relatively low-quality issue. Strike and luster are generally good for this date. Bagmarks are prevalent.

Valuation—There is very little premium for the lowest Mint State grades. This is not a recommended date in these lower grades, unless the coin offers exceptional color toning. This is a $10 coin in lower Mint State grades.

MS-65–MS-66. There is a greater premium for this Philadelphia issue, given its greater scarcity.

Valuation—$30 for **MS-65** coins, $75 for **MS-66** examples.

MS-67–MS-68. The 2005-P brilliant is extremely scarce in MS-67, and rare in MS-68.

Valuation—**MS-67** coins trade for between $300 and $600. **MS-68s** are valued at $500 to more than $1,000.

⊶⊜ 2005-P, Mint State, Satin ⊜⊷

MS-70

The 2005-P Kennedy satin finish was issued only in Mint sets, and 1,160,000 Mint sets were issued in 2005. These look like our early 1909–1916 Matte Proofs. This issue is gorgeous looking and quite easy to find in MS-69.

NGC CERTIFIED POPULATION *(from a total mintage of 1,160,000)*   (WCG™)

MS-64	MS-65	MS-66	MS-67	MS-68	MS-69	MS-70
2	18	815	1,419	1,428	725	7

MS-60–MS-64. The 2005-P satin finish Kennedy half dollar is a very high-quality issue—among the highest in the series. This is actually a scarce coin in the lower MS-60–MS-64 grades, as most satin finish Kennedy half dollars grade MS-67 and higher.

Strikes are very bold, with exceptional satin finish surfaces. Bagmarks are very few.

Valuation—There is no premium for the lowest Mint State grades. This is not a recommended date in these lower grades, unless the coin offers exceptional color toning. This is a $5 coin in lower Mint State grades.

MS-65–MS-66. A minimal premium exists.

Valuation—$7 for **MS-65** coins, $10 for **MS-66** examples.

MS-67–MS-70. The 2005-P is relatively easy to locate in both MS-67 and MS-68. This is a semi-scarce coin in MS-69 grade, and is only rare in the highest, ultimate MS-70 grade.

Valuation—**MS-67** coins generally trade at around $15, **MS-68s** at $20. **MS-69s** bring $30 to $60. A small number of **MS-70s** were graded by PCGS and are valued at $2,000+.

⟿ 2005-D, MINT STATE, BRILLIANT ⟾

MS-67

Only 3.5 million 2005-D Kennedy half dollars were struck with the normal brilliant finish. They were not issued for circulation.

NGC CERTIFIED POPULATION *(from a total mintage of 3,500,000)* (WCG™)

MS-64	MS-65	MS-66	MS-67	MS-68	MS-69	MS-70
40	62	188	105	21	0	0
MS-64 PL	**MS-65 PL**	**MS-66 PL**	**MS-67 PL**	**MS-68 PL**	**MS-69 PL**	**MS-70 PL**
0	4	0	0	0	0	0

MS-60–MS-64. The 2005-D is a much higher-quality date. Gems are easy to locate.

Valuation—There is very little premium for the lowest Mint State grades. This is not a recommended date in these lower grades, unless the coin offers exceptional color toning. In these grades this issue sells for $8 to $10.

MS-65–MS-66. The 2005-D is easy to acquire in MS-65, and is slightly more difficult in MS-66 condition.

Valuation—$25 for **MS-65** coins, $50 for **MS-66** examples.

MS-67–MS-68. The 2005-D is scarce in MS-67, and is conditionally rare in MS-68. To date, no example has graded higher than MS-68.

Valuation—**MS-67** coins generally trade for between $100 and $200, while near-flawless **MS-68** examples have been know to sell for between $850 and $1,500.

⋙ 2005-D, MINT STATE, SATIN ⋘

MS-68

The 2005-D satin finish Kennedy was a Mint set–only issue. 1,160,000 Mint sets were issued in 2005. The look of this issue is similar to the 1909–1916 Matte Proofs or a sandblast finish.

NGC CERTIFIED POPULATION *(from a total mintage of 1,160,000)* (WCG™)

MS-64	MS-65	MS-66	MS-67	MS-68	MS-69	MS-70
5	15	955	1,312	491	290	0

MS-60–MS-64. While not as high-quality a date as the 2005-P satin finish, the 2005-D satin finish is a much higher-quality issue than its brilliant counterpart. Most examples are fully struck, with lovely satin finishes, as the name suggests. Bagmarks are few.

Valuation—There is very little premium for the lowest Mint State grades. This is not a recommended date in these lower grades, unless the coin offers exceptional color toning.

MS-65–MS-66. The 2005-D satin finish Kennedy is very common in MS-65 and MS-66 condition.

Valuation—$12 for **MS-65** coins, $15 for **MS-66** examples.

MS-67–MS-70. The 2005-D is still relatively easy to locate in both MS-67 and MS-68, though somewhat more difficult in MS-69.

Valuation—**MS-67** coins generally trade for around $18, **MS-68s** for $70 to $90. A couple of **MS-69s** graded by NGC are valued at $500 and more. The D-Mint issue is much rarer than the P-Mint.

⋙ 2006-P, Mint State, Brilliant ⋘

MS-68

The 2006-P brilliant-finish Kennedy half dollars were not issued for circulation.

NGC CERTIFIED POPULATION *(from a total mintage of 2,400,000)* (WCG™)

MS-64	MS-65	MS-66	MS-67	MS-68	MS-69	MS-70
4	40	167	221	43	0	0

MS-60–MS-64. The 2006-P is a higher-quality issue. Strike and luster are generally good, with fewer than average bagmarks.

Valuation—There is very little premium for the lowest Mint State grades. This is not a recommended date in these lower grades, unless the coin offers exceptional color toning. In these grades the value is $10.

MS-65–MS-66. MS-65 represents a below-average grade for this date. This date is more elusive in MS-66, which is the minimum recommended grade for investment.

Valuation—$12 to $15 for **MS-65** coins, $15 to $20 for **MS-66** examples.

MS-67–MS-68. The 2006-P is scarce in MS-67. MS-68 examples are extremely scarce.

Valuation—**MS-67** coins are generally valued at $75 to $150. The **MS-68s** that have been graded are valued at between $400 and $650.

⊶⊷ 2006-P, MINT STATE, SATIN ⊶⊷

MS-69

This is another Mint set–only issue. 847,361 Mint sets were issued in 2006.

NGC CERTIFIED POPULATION *(from a total mintage of 847,361)* (WCG™)

MS-64	MS-65	MS-66	MS-67	MS-68	MS-69	MS-70
2	11	459	882	815	104	0

MS-60–MS-64. Consistent with satin finish Mint State Kennedy half dollars, the 2006-P is a very high-quality issue, though not quite on a par with the previous year's 2005-P. Strike and luster are generally exceptional, and bagmarks are few. This date is not recommended in the lowest Mint State grades.

Valuation—There is very little premium for the lowest Mint State grades. This is not a recommended date in these lower grades, unless the coin offers exceptional color toning.

MS-65–MS-66. Again, gems in this grade range represent below-average quality for the date.

Valuation—$10 for **MS-65** coins, $12 for **MS-66** examples.

MS-67–MS-69. The 2006-P is relatively easy to locate in MS-67 and MS-68. This date has been graded in MS-69, though it is quite rare in that condition.

Valuation—**MS-67** coins generally trade for between $16 and $30. **MS-68** examples bring $35 to $60, and **MS-69s** $200 to $400.

2006-D, Mint State, Brilliant

MS-67

The 2006-D Kennedy half with brilliant finish is another date available only through the U.S. Mint, with only two million struck. Of these, 847,361 were issued in Mint sets. Although these have a superb strike, they also display porous surfaces, and rusted rim surfaces. Higher grades are harder to find. These are available only in Mint sealed rolls or bags. None were issued for circulation.

NGC CERTIFIED POPULATION *(from a total mintage of 2,000,000)* (WCG™)

MS-64	MS-65	MS-66	MS-67	MS-68	MS-69	MS-70
12	74	164	119	7	0	0
MS-64 PL	MS-65 PL	MS-66 PL	MS-67 PL	MS-68 PL	MS-69 PL	MS-70 PL
0	1	0	0	0	0	0

MS-60–MS-64. The 2006-D is elusive in the highest Mint State grades, though gems in the MS-65 range are easy to locate.

Valuation—There is very little premium for the lowest Mint State grades. This is not a recommended date in these lower grades, unless the coin offers exceptional color toning. In lower Mint State grades this coin sells for $10.

MS-65–MS-66. The 2006-D is common in MS-65. This date can be challenging to locate in MS-66.

Valuation—$12 to $15 for **MS-65** coins, $35 to $50 for **MS-66** examples.

MS-67–MS-68. The 2006-D is scarce in MS-67, and extremely scarce in MS-68. To date, no example has been graded higher than MS-68 by either PCGS or NGC.

Valuation—**MS-67** coins generally trade at $125 to $250. **MS-68s** bring $750+.

2006-D, MINT STATE, SATIN

MS-69

This is another Mint set–only issue. Some 847,361 Mint sets were issued in 2006.

NGC CERTIFIED POPULATION *(from a total mintage of 847,361)*   (WCG™)

MS-64	MS-65	MS-66	MS-67	MS-68	MS-69	MS-70
0	12	452	1,036	644	36	0

MS-60–MS-64. This is below average quality for an issue that is easy to find in gem condition.

Valuation—There is very little premium for the lowest Mint State grades. This is not a recommended date in these lower grades, unless the coin offers exceptional color toning. In lower Mint State grades this is a $6 coin.

MS-65–MS-66. The 2006-D is very common in MS-65 and MS-66 condition.

Valuation—$7 to $9 in **MS-65;** $10 in **MS-66.**

MS-67–MS-69. A high-quality date, readily available in MS-67–68, but rare in MS-69.

Valuation—**MS-67** coins sell for $15 to $20; **MS-68s,** for $30 to $60; **MS-69s,** for $500 to $1,000.

2007-P, MINT STATE, BRILLIANT

MS-68

This issue is found only in U.S. Mint sealed rolls or bags. None were struck for circulation.

NGC CERTIFIED POPULATION *(from a total mintage of 2,400,000)*   (WCG™)

MS-64	MS-65	MS-66	MS-67	MS-68	MS-69	MS-70
1	44	183	317	40	0	0

MS-60–MS-64. Despite the low mintage, the 2007-P is most common in the lower Mint State grades, given the high number of Mint sets issued for the year. Strike and luster are generally good for this date.

Valuation—There is very little premium for the lowest Mint State grades. This is not a recommended date in these lower grades, unless the coin offers exceptional color toning.

MS-65–MS-66. Still common in these gem grades.

Valuation—$10 to $12 for **MS-65** coins, $15 to $20 for **MS-66** examples.

MS-67–MS-68. The 2007-P is very scarce in MS-67, and extremely scarce in MS-68.

Valuation—**MS-67** coins generally trade for between $50 and $100. **MS-68s** are valued at $200 to $500.

⊶⊷ 2007-P, MINT STATE, SATIN ⊶⊷

MS-69

This is another Mint set–only issue, with 895,628 Mint sets issued in 2007. Buying one of these is like buying a matte Proof; you are getting a near perfect coin.

NGC CERTIFIED POPULATION *(from a total mintage of 895,628)* (WCG™)

MS-64	MS-65	MS-66	MS-67	MS-68	MS-69	MS-70
1	6	181	133	763	200	0

MS-60–MS-64. Below average quality in this condition.

Valuation—There is very little premium for the lowest Mint State grades. This is not a recommended date in these lower grades, unless the coin offers exceptional color toning.

MS-65–MS-66. There is a greater premium for this P-Mint issue, given its greater scarcity.

Valuation—$6 for **MS-65** coins, $8 for **MS-66** examples.

MS-67–MS-68. MS-67–68 is typical quality for this very high-quality date.

Valuation—**MS-67** coins generally trade for $10. **MS-68s** are valued at $18 to $40; **MS-69s,** at $100 to $250.

⭑⭑ 2007-D, Mint State, Brilliant ⭑⭑

MS-68

The 2007-D is only found in U.S. Mint–issued sealed rolls and bags. None were issued for circulation.

NGC CERTIFIED POPULATION *(from a total mintage of 2,400,000)*   (WCG™)

MS-64	MS-65	MS-66	MS-67	MS-68	MS-69	MS-70
4	61	130	85	6	0	0
MS-64 PL	MS-65 PL	MS-66 PL	MS-67 PL	MS-68 PL	MS-69 PL	MS-70 PL
0	1	0	0	0	0	0

MS-60–MS-64. The 2007-D is generally lower quality than its "P" Mint counterpart.

Valuation—There is very little premium for the lowest Mint State grades. This is not a recommended date in these lower grades, unless the coin offers exceptional color toning.

MS-65–MS-66. The 2007-D is available in MS-65 and MS-66 condition.

Valuation—$10 to $12 in **MS-65**; $35 in **MS-66.**

MS-67–MS-68. This issue is elusive in the higher Mint State grades, and rare in MS-68.

Valuation—**MS-67** examples are valued at $100 to $200; **MS-68s,** at $2,000+.

2007-D, Mint State, Satin

MS-69

Available only in Mint sets. 895,628 Mint sets were issued in 2007. A perfect strike and a near-perfect coin, the 2007-D has the lowest mintage in the Kennedy series and is only found in U.S. Special Mint Sets. I would recommend that you try to buy a few of these.

NGC CERTIFIED POPULATION *(from a total mintage of 895,628)*   (WCG™)

MS-64	MS-65	MS-66	MS-67	MS-68	MS-69	MS-70
0	3	167	102	887	274	1

MS-60–MS-64. The 2007-D is a much higher-quality date. Gems are easy to locate.
Valuation—There is very little premium for the lowest Mint State grades. This is not a recommended date in these lower grades, unless the coin offers exceptional color toning.

MS-65–MS-66. The 2007-D is very common in MS-65 and MS-66 condition.
Valuation—In **MS-65,** this issue sells for $6. **MS-66** examples sell for $7.

MS-67 to 69. Again, MS-68 is the average for this date!
Valuation—**MS-67** examples sell for $8; **MS-68s,** for $30 to $65; **MS-69s,** for $100 to $250. One **MS-70** was graded by PCGS and valued at $5,000+.

2008-P, Mint State, Brilliant

MS-67

The 2008-P is a slightly lower-quality issue compared to the previous 2007-P Philadelphia issue. Despite the low mintage, it is most common in the lower Mint State grades, given the number of Mint sets issued for the year. Strike and luster are generally good for this date. This issue is found only in U.S. Mint–issued sealed rolls and bags; none were issued for circulation.

NGC CERTIFIED POPULATION *(from a total mintage of 1,700,000)* (WCG™)

MS-64	MS-65	MS-66	MS-67	MS-68	MS-69	MS-70
4	33	227	245	8	0	0

MS-60–MS-64. Very low quality for this date.

Valuation—There is very little premium for the lowest Mint State grades. This is not a recommended date in these lower grades, unless the coin offers exceptional color toning.

MS-65–MS-66. A greater premium exists for this P-Mint issue, due to its greater scarcity.

Valuation—$12 for **MS-65** coins, $30 to $40 for **MS-66** examples.

MS-67–MS-68. The 2008-P is scarce in MS-67, and rare in MS-68.

Valuation—**MS-67** coins generally trade for between $70 and $100. **MS-68s** sell for $1,000+.

⊶≋ 2008-P, MINT STATE, SATIN ≋⊷

MS-68

745,464 Mint sets were issued in 2008. Half dollars feature a full strike, near mark-free surfaces, and a low price. This date is only found in government-issued Special Mint Sets.

NGC CERTIFIED POPULATION *(from a total mintage of 735,683)* (WCG™)

MS-64	MS-65	MS-66	MS-67	MS-68	MS-69	MS-70
0	10	15	109	642	55	0

MS-60–MS-64. This is below average quality.

Valuation—There is very little premium for the lowest Mint State grades. This is not a recommended date in these lower grades, unless the coin offers exceptional color toning.

MS-65–MS-66. Still below average. The typical 2008-P satin is about MS-67.

Valuation—$10 to $15 for **MS-65** coins, $12 to $20 for **MS-66** examples.

MS-67–MS-68. The grade to seek out for this date.

Valuation—**MS-67** coins generally trade for between $15 and $30. **MS-68s** sell for $20 to $60; **MS-69** examples, for $400 to $1,500.

⊷⧟ 2008-D, Mint State, Brilliant ⧟⊷

MS-67

NGC CERTIFIED POPULATION *(from a total mintage of 1,700,000)* (WCG™)

MS-64	MS-65	MS-66	MS-67	MS-68	MS-69	MS-70
10	31	184	201	8	0	0

MS-60–MS-64. Once available only from the Mint. Coins are generally baggy. While gems are easy to locate, this date is more difficult in the highest grades.

Valuation—There is very little premium for the lowest Mint State grades. This is not a recommended date in these lower grades, unless the coin offers exceptional color toning.

MS-65–MS-66. The 2008-D is common in MS-65 and MS-66 condition.

Valuation—**MS-65s** sell for $15; **MS-66** examples bring $40 to $50.

MS-67–MS-68. This issue is very elusive in the higher MS-67 grade. Only eight have been graded MS-68.

Valuation—Value in **MS-67** ranges from $400 to $700.

2008-D, MINT STATE, SATIN

MS-67

The 2008-D Satin Finish is a bit tougher than other 2005 to 2010 Mint set issues. Highest-grade examples are elusive.

NGC CERTIFIED POPULATION *(from a total mintage of 735,683)*   (WCG™)

MS-64	MS-65	MS-66	MS-67	MS-68	MS-69	MS-70
1	5	12	56	390	6	0

MS-60–MS-64. The 2008-D is a much higher-quality date. Gems are easy to locate.
Valuation—There is very little premium for the lowest Mint State grades. This is not a recommended date in these lower grades, unless the coin offers exceptional color toning.

MS-65–MS-66. The 2008-D is very common in MS-65 and MS-66 condition.
Valuation—Value for this coin in **MS-66** is $10.

MS-67–MS-69. MS-67–68 is the most common grade for this date. MS-69s are very rare.
Valuation—**MS-67s** bring $15 to $20; **MS-68** examples sell for $30 to $60.

⋙ 2009-P, MINT STATE, BRILLIANT ⋘

MS-67

The quality of the 2009-P coinage was on par with that of the preceding year, with strike and luster generally good. These coins were available only through the Mint, in rolls and bags sold for a premium over face value; none were issued for circulation.

NGC CERTIFIED POPULATION *(from a total mintage of 1,900,000)* (WCG™)

MS-64	MS-65	MS-66	MS-67	MS-68	MS-69	MS-70
9	29	217	113	7	0	0

MS-65–MS-66. The 2009-P brilliant is semi-scarce in MS-66.
   Valuation—Coins in **MS-65** sell for $12 to $15; in **MS-66,** for $30 to $40.

MS-67–MS-68. This date will be a bit tougher to find in the higher Mint State grades. Only a handful have been graded in MS-68.
   Valuation—**MS-67** examples trade for $125 to $250; **MS-68,** $1,000 to $1,500.

⇢⇒ 2009-P, Mint State, Satin ⇐⇠

MS-67

In 2009 the U.S. Mint issued 784,614 Mint sets. As with the preceding Mint-set issues of 2005 through 2008, their coins featured a Satin Finish somewhat different from the finish on these years' Uncirculated coins. (This format would continue through 2010 before returning to a normal brilliant finish.)

NGC CERTIFIED POPULATION *(from a total estimated mintage of 643,897)*   (WCG™)

MS-64	MS-65	MS-66	MS-67	MS-68	MS-69	MS-70
0	9	18	135	432	28	0

MS-65–MS-66. This is a very high-quality date. Coins grading MS-65 and MS-66 actually represent below-average quality for the 2009-P Satin Finish Kennedy half dollar.
Valuation—In **MS-66,** this coin sells for $12.

MS-67–MS-68. A high-quality coin, available in MS-68.
Valuation—Examples graded **MS-67** sell for $20 to $25; **MS-68** coins bring $30 to $100.

2009-D, MINT STATE, BRILLIANT

MS-67

Only 1.9 million 2009-D halves were minted. Most are on the baggy side. As with other Kennedy half dollars minted in and since 2002, regular 2009 coins were made not for general circulation but for distribution directly from the Mint to collectors, in rolls of 20 and bags of 200 coins, at a premium of 1.5 to 2 times their face value, plus shipping.

NGC CERTIFIED POPULATION *(from a total mintage of 1,900,000)* (WCG™)

MS-64	MS-65	MS-66	MS-67	MS-68	MS-69	MS-70
14	29	144	58	4	0	0

MS-65–MS-66. These are surprisingly low quality for a modern issue.
Valuation—In **MS-65,** this issue brings $15 to $20; **MS-66** examples sell for $40.

MS-67–MS-68. This issue is scarce in MS-67!
Valuation— **MS-67** examples sell for $200 to $400.

⊷⇒ 2009-D, Mint State, Satin ⇐⊷

MS-67

The U.S. Mint issued 784,614 Mint sets in 2009, each containing 36 coins in total (including two Kennedy half dollars: one from Philadelphia and the other from Denver). The year's Mint-set coins were produced with a Satin Finish.

NGC CERTIFIED POPULATION *(from a total estimated mintage of 643,897)*   (WCG™)

MS-64	MS-65	MS-66	MS-67	MS-68	MS-69	MS-70
0	2	15	116	489	27	0

MS-65–MS-66. The 2009-D Satin Finish is another very high-quality issue in the Kennedy half dollar series. Grades of MS-65 and MS-66 indicate below-average quality for this coin.

Valuation—In **MS-66,** this coin sells for $8.

MS-67–MS-68. A higher-quality satin finish characterizes these grades, with a few graded in MS-69.

Valuation—Value in **MS-67** is $20 to $25; in **MS-68,** $35 to $75; and in **MS-69,** $500 to $1,500.

⟫⟫ 2010-P, MINT STATE, BRILLIANT ⟪⟪

MS-68

Mintage for this issue was 1.8 million. This date is easier to find than the D-Mint issues, but still tough in high grades. With nice strike and above-average surfaces, the 2010-P was available only from the U.S. Mint in sealed rolls and bags. None were issued for circulation.

NGC CERTIFIED POPULATION *(from a total estimated mintage of 1,800,000)* (WCG™)

MS-64	MS-65	MS-66	MS-67	MS-68	MS-69	MS-70
4	26	342	213	31	0	0

MS-65–MS-66. Gems are collectible. I would recommend at least MS-66.
 Valuation—**MS-65** coins sell for $10 to $13; **MS-66** examples bring $20.

MS-67–MS-68. Scarce in MS-67, rare in MS-68!
 Valuation—In **MS-67,** this coin brings $90.

2010-P, Mint State, Satin

MS-69

Production of the 2010 Mint set was 583,897 units. As with the other Satin Finish Kennedy half dollars of 2005 through 2010, the 2010-P was struck exclusively for distribution in Uncirculated Mint sets. The 2010 set consisted of 14 coins from each mint, for a total of 28 pieces. In addition to the half dollars, the sets included all of the year's Presidential dollars (Andrew Johnson, Ulysses S. Grant, Rutherford B. Hayes, Chester Arthur, and Benjamin Harrison); the 2010 Native American dollar (representing the Great Law of Peace); the first five quarters of the America the Beautiful series (Hot Springs, Yellowstone, Yosemite, the Grand Canyon, and Mount Hood); and the well-known Roosevelt dime, Jefferson nickel, and Lincoln cent.

NGC CERTIFIED POPULATION *(from a total mintage of 583,897)* (WCG™)

MS-64	MS-65	MS-66	MS-67	MS-68	MS-69	MS-70
0	4	126	130	31	0	0

MS-65–MS-66 Valuation—**MS-65** coins sell for $10; **MS-66,** $15.

MS-67–MS-68 Valuation—In **MS-67,** this is a $20 to $25 coin. **MS-68s** go for $30 to $50.

2010-D, Mint State, Brilliant

MS-67

Mintage for this issue was 1.7 million. I would call this date one of the poorest-looking coins in the series. Strong strike, abrasions, and bagmarks abound. This is going to be a tough coin to find in high grade; it was available only in sealed U.S. Mint rolls or bags, with none made for circulation.

NGC CERTIFIED POPULATION *(from a total mintage of 1,700,000)* (WCG™)

MS-64	MS-65	MS-66	MS-67	MS-68	MS-69	MS-70
1	38	250	106	1	0	0

MS-65–MS-66. MS-65 gems represent good quality for this date. Try to get at least a "66."
   Valuation—The 2010-D in **MS-65** sells for $20; in **MS-66,** it trades for $100.

MS-67–MS-68. Very scarce in these highest grades!
   Valuation—**MS-67** examples bring $300+.

⟿ 2010-D, Mint State, Satin ⟾

MS-69

Mintage for this issue was just under 584,000 coins. As with the other satin-finish Kennedy half dollars of 2005 through 2010, these were struck exclusively for distribution in Uncirculated Mint sets. The 2010 set consisted of 14 coins from each Mint, for a total of 28 pieces; in addition to the half dollars, the sets included all four of the year's Presidential dollars, the Native American dollar, the five America the Beautiful quarter dollars, and the dime, nickel, and cent.

NGC CERTIFIED POPULATION *(from a total mintage of 583,897)* (WCG™)

MS-64	MS-65	MS-66	MS-67	MS-68	MS-69	MS-70
41	20	15	101	511	32	0

MS-65–MS-66 Valuation—**MS-65** coins sell for $6; **MS-66s** go for $10 to $15.

MS-67–MS-68 Valuation—For an **MS-67**, expect to pay $20 to $25. In **MS-68**, this is a $30 to $50 coin.

⤜⊐ 2011-P, Mint State ⊏⤛

MS-68

The Kennedy half dollar series saw continued improvement in general quality in 2011. This date is not difficult to find fully struck and minimally bagmarked.

CERTIFIED POPULATION *(from a total mintage of 1,750,000)* (WCG™)

MS-64	MS-65	MS-66	MS-67	MS-68	MS-69	MS-70
0	0	285	320	27	1	0

MS-65–MS-66. These grades represent good quality for the issue.

Valuation—The 2011-P is a $10 to $15 coin in **MS-65**. Prices in **MS-66** are $20 to $30.

MS-67–MS-68. A large percentage of certified examples of 2011-P grade MS-67, although the issue is considerably more elusive in MS-68.

Valuation—Prices range from $35 to $75 in **MS-67**, and reach $250 to $500 in **MS-68**.

⇒ 2011-D, MINT STATE ⇐

MS-68

Collectors can anticipate exceptional overall quality with the year's Denver Mint issue, as with the 2011-P. This date is easy to find fully struck and with minimal bagmarks.

NGC CERTIFIED POPULATION *(from a total mintage of 1,700,000)* (WCG™)

MS-64	MS-65	MS-66	MS-67	MS-68	MS-69	MS-70
0	2	313	219	32	0	0

MS-65–MS-66. These mid-range Mint State levels offer good quality for the 2011-D Kennedy half dollar.

Valuation—This is a $10 to $15 coin in **MS-65**. In **MS-66** prices range from $20 to $40.

MS-67–MS-68. This is a scarce coin in MS-67, and rare in MS-68.

Valuation—The market commands $50 to $150 for a 2011-D in **MS-67**, with the considerably rarer **MS-68** examples bringing $1,000 or more!

⊷⊜ 2012-P, MINT STATE ⊜⊶

MS-68

This is a high-quality P-Mint Kennedy, though up to now it has been more elusive than the 2011-P in the highest grades.

NGC CERTIFIED POPULATION *(from a total mintage of 1,800,000)*   (WCG™)

MS-64	MS-65	MS-66	MS-67	MS-68	MS-69	MS-70
0	1	69	159	23	0	0

MS-65–MS-66. These grades are good quality for the issue.
   Valuation—A $10 to $15 coin in **MS-65**, the value doubles in **MS-66** to $20 to $40.

MS-67–MS-68. The 2012-P is scarce in MS-67, and rare in MS-68.
   Valuation—Prices range from $50 to $150 in **MS-67**, and up to $600 (or more) in **MS-68**.

⌐⇒ 2012-D, MINT STATE ⇐⌐

MS-68

The Denver Mint's high standards for quality continued with its 2012 Kennedy half dollar.

NGC CERTIFIED POPULATION *(from a total mintage of 1,700,000)* (WCG™)

MS-64	MS-65	MS-66	MS-67	MS-68	MS-69	MS-70
1	16	74	183	17	0	0

MS-65–MS-66. These mid-level Mint State grades offer a good combination of affordable price and attractive quality.

Valuation—An example in **MS-65** can be added to your collection for $10 to $15. For an **MS-66** example, expect to pay $20 to $40.

MS-67–MS-68. The 2012-D is a scarce coin at the MS-67 level—and considerably more elusive in MS-68.

Valuation—For an **MS-67** example you will pay $50 to $150. Those certified as **MS-68** sell for $650 or more.

⊷☞ 2013-P, MINT STATE ☜⊶

MS-68

The Philadelphia Mint's coinage of Kennedy half dollars in 2013 closely mirrored the past couple Philadelphia issues in quality.

NGC CERTIFIED POPULATION *(from a total mintage of 5,000,000)*   (WCG™)

MS-64	MS-65	MS-66	MS-67	MS-68	MS-69	MS-70
1	5	66	201	26	0	0

MS-65–MS-66. These grades are good quality for the issue.

Valuation—The 2013-P is a $10 to $15 coin in **MS-65**, and a $20 to $40 coin in **MS-66**.

MS-67–MS-68. The 2013-P Kennedy half dollar is scarce in MS-67, and considerably more elusive in MS-68.

Valuation—Values in **MS-67** range widely from $50 to $150. In **MS-68** this is $600+ coin!

2013-D

MS-68

This higher-mintage production is of superb quality. Though it's a very recent issue, a fair number of examples have already graded MS-68, and there are a few MS-69s, as well!

NGC CERTIFIED POPULATION *(from a total mintage of 4,600,000)* (WCG™)

MS-64	MS-65	MS-66	MS-67	MS-68	MS-69	MS-70
0	3	75	144	57	3	0

MS-65–MS-66. This represents good quality for the issue.

Valuation—The 2013-D is an $8 to $12 coin in **MS-65**. An **MS-66** example can be added to your collection for $12 to $20.

MS-67–MS-68. A large percentage of the 2013-D's professionally certified coins are graded MS-67. A good number (although considerably fewer) have graded higher.

Valuation—$20 to $40 in **MS-67**, and $100 to $200 in **MS-68**.

⤖ 2014-P, Mint State ⤖

MS-68

Philadelphia's regular production of 2014 Kennedy half dollars is very similar in quality to recent previous issues of that mint—although a notch below the quality of the Denver Mint's coins for that year.

NGC CERTIFIED POPULATION *(from a total mintage of 2,500,000)* (WCG™)

MS-64	MS-65	MS-66	MS-67	MS-68	MS-69	MS-70
1	27	106	240	48	0	0

MS-65–MS-66. This is good quality for the issue.
Valuation—In **MS-65** the 2014-D brings $10 to $15. In **MS-66** it is a $15 to $30 coin.

MS-67–MS-68. A high percentage of certified examples are graded MS-67. As with earlier Philadelphia Mint coins, the 2014-P is considerably more elusive in MS-68.
Valuation—$30 to $75 in **MS-67**, and $150 to $300 in **MS-68**.

2014-D, MINT STATE

MS-68

The regular-production 2014-D Kennedy half dollar is among the highest-quality dates in the series in Mint State. With a little patience it can be located in MS-68 . . . and even MS-69!

NGC CERTIFIED POPULATION *(from a total mintage of 2,100,000)*   (WCG™)

MS-64	MS-65	MS-66	MS-67	MS-68	MS-69	MS-70
0	13	143	226	229	47	0

MS-65–MS-66. These mid-level Mint State grades represent *below-average* quality for this issue.

Valuation—In **MS-65** the 2014-D is a $6 to $10 coin; in **MS-66**, $10 to $15.

MS-67–MS-68. A large percentage of certified 2014-D Kennedy half dollars grade MS-67; the coin is more elusive in MS-68, although that lofty grade is not the limit for this high-quality date.

Valuation—$15 to $30 in **MS-67**; $30 to $75 in **MS-68**; and $100 to $250 in **MS-69**.

2014, 50TH ANNIVERSARY SPECIAL EDITIONS

The Kennedy half dollar was first struck in 1964, and its original design has seen some changes over the years. The first obvious change occurred in 1990, most visible in alterations in Kennedy's hair detail. The most dramatic change took place in 1997, when the relief on President Kennedy's portrait was substantially lowered. Where in earlier years his facial features were full and rounded, in this latest design there is an obvious concave curvature running through the central portion of Kennedy's cheek area. On the reverse, the eagle received design changes as well, most obviously in the edges of the shield being sharpened. From an aesthetic standpoint, the original design is considered superior to this later reduced-relief design.

The United States Mint truly provided a tremendous collector service in the Special Edition Kennedy half dollars offered in 2014. For these 50th-anniversary issues, the Mint wanted to bring the original designs back. The original plaster casting made by Chief Engraver Gilroy Roberts while the president was still alive, intended as a Presidential medal and approved by Kennedy himself, could no longer be located. But the Mint did locate a bronze galvano of the original casting, as well as one original 1964 Kennedy die! Using laser technology, Mint technicians were able to recreate this original design for the 2014 Special Edition Kennedy coins.

This recreation "High Relief" was used on seven different coins for 2014, in three different releases. The first release featured the 0.75-ounce dual-date solid gold half dollar. A two-coin set featured Uncirculated copper-nickel-clad half dollars struck at the Philadelphia and Denver mints. A third offering was an intriguing four-coin set, all struck of 90 percent silver, with each coin made at a different mint (Philadelphia, Denver, San Francisco, and West Point), and each featuring a unique finish distinctive from the other three!

1964–2014, HIGH-RELIEF GOLD

2014, High-Relief Gold

When first announced, this three-quarter–ounce .999 fine gold dual-date commemorative issue was the subject of incredible anticipation among dealers and collectors. With an original issue price $1,240, dealers and collectors were waiting in a line blocks long to be among the first to acquire one of the coins at the American Numismatic Association show in July of 2014! Within a couple days there were reported sales of Proof-70 DCAM and Ultra Cam examples selling for upward of $3,000. Some of these coins were being listed on eBay in the neighborhood of $6,000! It was also reported that the very first 2014 gold Kennedy sold by the Mint was immediately re-sold for *$100,000.*

Later in the year the Mint announced the coin's mintage would be limited to 75,000. While 75,000 would be an extremely low mintage for a silver or clad Kennedy half dollar (coins with a much broader collector base), this quantity seems to have saturated the market for the gold commemorative Kennedy, for the time being.

Valuation—Superb certified examples in **PF-69** and **PF-70** currently can be acquired at close to their original issue price ($1,240). Essentially all of these gold Kennedy commemoratives exhibit DCAM or ultra cameo contrast. Most grade at least PF-69.

✦═▷ 2014-P AND 2014-D, HIGH-RELIEF CLAD UNCIRCULATED SET ◁═✦

With an original issue price of only $9.95, and a mintage limited to just 200,000, this copper-nickel-clad Uncirculated set would seem to have tremendous long-term potential. Its two coins did not receive the special care and handling of the Mint's Proof and Special Mint Set products. Many examples exhibit nicks and/or scratches; some have slight planchet flaws. To date, the highest grade one of these Uncirculated coins has received is MS-69. The majority grade MS-66 or MS-67. Some have graded as low as MS-63. The Philadelphia Mint specimens on average grade a little bit higher than those of the Denver Mint.

2014 High-Relief Uncirculated Set

As a collector this set is one of my favorites, because the mintage is extremely low and the quality is not uniform from one coin to the next.

MS-66. This is one of the most common grades for these clad issues. The coins of the Denver Mint are found in MS-66 more often than those of the Philadelphia Mint.

Valuation—In **MS-66**, given the limited total mintage, these would appear to be a very good value at the current $20 to $50 price range.

MS-67. In the lower prices levels this very low-mintage high-relief Kennedy half dollar seems to offer the collector tremendous long-term potential.

Valuation—Certified examples in **MS-67** currently can be acquired in a range from about $40 to $100 per coin.

MS-68. These coins are very scarce in this condition, with only about 3% to 5% of the mintage submitted being certified at MS-68. As of press date, NGC has certified approximately 1,300 of the Philadelphia Mint coins in MS-68, and 1,100 of the Denver Mint coins.

Valuation—I have seen 2014-P and -D Kennedy half dollars in **MS-68** offered as low as $100 per coin, and as high as $500 per.

MS-69. *Very elusive!* This is the highest grade this Uncirculated issue has received. Far fewer than 1% submitted for grading are certified at MS-69.

Valuation—If you can acquire a set in MS-69, a good price would fall in the range of $700 per coin up to $1,500 per coin.

≈ 2014-P, 2014-D, 2014-S, 2014-W Silver Set ≈

This is a great set! It was originally offered as a four-coin collection, with each Kennedy half dollar struck in high-relief 90% silver. The four coins were each produced at a different mint (Philadephia, Denver, San Francisco, and West Point), and each featuring its own distinctive finish. The Mint limited the total release of these sets to only 225,000.

2014-P, High-Relief Cameo Proof

The *2014-P High-Relief Cameo Proof* is one of my favorites in the set—and in the entire Kennedy Proof series! First of all, it is a Cameo Proof, and would seem to be a "must have" addition for any Proof Kennedy collector. Its mintage of 225,000 represents the lowest in the series for a Cameo Proof coin (with the notable exception of the 1964 Accented Hair Kennedy, which does not have a published mintage, but is estimated at about 100,000 coins), and it has a P mintmark! Along with the 1964 Kennedy half dollar, these are the only two regular Proof Kennedy half dollars struck at the Philadelphia Mint.

Valuation—Currently **PF-69 DCAM / Ultra** examples can be acquired for as little as $50 to $75. **PF-70 DCAM / Ultra** coins are usually offered in the $100 to $300 range. Both grades seem to offer a *lot* of potential for the Kennedy collector. After all, the coin is priced far below the 2012-S, which has a considerably higher mintage (395,443)!

2014-D, High-Relief Uncirculated

The *2014-D High-Relief Uncirculated*, while referred to as "Uncirculated," is a superb coin more closely resembling a specimen strike. The quality is far superior to that of the regular-mintage (clad) 2014-P and -D clad Kennedy half dollars. All 2014-D silver Kennedy half dollars are fully struck, with essentially flawless surfaces.

Valuation—Most examples grade either MS-69 or MS-70. The latter currently can be acquired for around $100.

2014-S, High-Relief Enhanced Finish

The *2014-S High-Relief Enhanced Finish* is a fascinating coin, with perhaps the greatest potential if you can locate one of the finer examples. The 2014-S exhibits a laser-etched snow-white cameo finish. The surrounding fields are typically very shallow-mirrored, semi-prooflike in nature. *However*—if you do enough research and some coin hunting, you may find examples with deeper mirrors, approaching Proof quality. And if you are *really* fortunate, there is that rare example with full black mirrored fields, almost identical to Cameo Proof coins of the era in their cameo contrast and black-mirrored, Proof-quality mirrors! The only significant difference can be noted on the high portions of the eagle's shield on the reverse, which are not frosted on this issue.

Valuation—The typical grade is **MS-69** with shallow mirrors, valued around $50. Coins in **MS-70** with shallow-mirrored surfaces sell for $75. MS-69 PL and MS-70 PL coins, more deeply mirrored and approaching a Proof look, are almost as readily available as non-PL coins. **MS-69 PL** examples currently trade in the $50 to $75 range, and **MS-70 PL** for $100 to $150. Deep Prooflike (DPL) examples are also seen, and DPL the 2014-S Enhanced Finish ranks among my favorite Kennedy half dollars. Given the fact that almost all Kennedy half dollars struck since the late 1970s exhibit exceptional cameo contrast and deeply mirrored fields (though poor packaging ruined many over the years), with the 2014-S in deep prooflike condition you have the opportunity to acquire a coin that is visually far superior in eye appeal to the typical issue for that year, and they represent only a small percentage of the total original mintage. Given the fact that this release is only a few years old, I would prefer a couple more years' time to get a better handle on the true rarity of this coin in DPL. But I think it is pretty safe to say the DPL version represents about 2% to 4% of the total mintage. **MS-69 DPL** examples currently trade in the $150 to $300 range. Ultimate **MS-70 DPL** examples have sold for as high as $4,000, and recently have generally settled into a range between $800 and $2,000.

2014-W, High-Relief Reverse Proof

The *2014-W High-Relief Reverse Proof* is part of the U.S. Mint's offerings of Reverse Proofs going back to 2006. In that year the Mint began to strike Reverse Proofs in limited quantity in the American Silver Eagle program. Collector response was positive, so the Mint continued with the format, offering some issues in the Presidential dollar series as well. The "Reverse Proof" is exactly what the name suggests. Where a Cameo Proof would feature a frosted white portrait of President Kennedy surrounded by a deeply mirrored "black" field, the Reverse Proof features a shiny mirrored image of Kennedy surrounded by a frosted field. This reverse design is of course carried over on the coin's reverse.

Valuation—Most examples grade MS-69 or MS-70. With a very limited mintage, this coin appears to be a very good value at its current asking prices of about $75 in **MS-69** and $125 in **MS-70**.

⊰⊷ 2015-P, MINT STATE ⊷⊱

MS-68

The 2015-P Kennedy half dollar is a tougher late-date issue in gem condition. Compared to other recent Philadelphia Mint coinages, a larger percentage of the mintage of 2015-P grades MS-66 and lower.

NGC CERTIFIED POPULATION *(from a total mintage of 2,300,000)*   (WCG™)

MS-64	MS-65	MS-66	MS-67	MS-68	MS-69	MS-70
19	55	125	209	8	0	0

MS-65–MS-66. These grades represent good quality for this date.
Valuation—$10 to $15 in **MS-65**; $15 to $40 in **MS-66**.

MS-67–MS-68. A significant percentage of certified examples grade MS-67, though very few grade higher! Currently the 2015-P is rare in MS-68, with only about a dozen examples certified.
Valuation—$40 to $90 in **MS-67**. This is a $150 to $300 coin in **MS-68**.

⇒ 2015-D, MINT STATE ⇐

MS-68

The 2015-D Kennedy half dollar is more in line with the 2013-D and earlier Denver Mint productions in terms of quality. While it is scarce in MS-67, MS-68 examples are rare.

NGC CERTIFIED POPULATION *(from a total mintage of 2,300,000)*   (WCG™)

MS-64	MS-65	MS-66	MS-67	MS-68	MS-69	MS-70
15	72	156	179	8	0	0

MS-65–MS-66. These grades are good quality for the issue.
Valuation—An $8 to $12 coin in **MS-65**, the 2015-D sells for $12 to $20 in **MS-66**.

MS-67–MS-68. A large percentage of certified examples grade MS-67. The 2015-D is considerably harder to find in MS-68.
Valuation—$25 to $60 in **MS-67**.

PROOF KENNEDY HALF DOLLARS
⚈ 1964, PROOF, TYPE 1 ⚈
(ACCENTED HAIR)

PF-69 Cam

Type 1, "Accented Hair," is the first Kennedy half listed in the date-by-date analysis for this Proof series, as the Accented Hair was actually the first design struck by the Mint in Proof.

While just under four million 1964 Kennedy half dollars were struck in Proof, it is estimated that only about 100,000 of those were of the Accented Hair variety—just over 2% of the total Proof production for that year. As many as 30% to 50% of this total may have been melted for their bullion in 1979 and 1980.

The story behind the Accented Hair and its premature demise began when the Mint invited Jacqueline Kennedy to inspect the new half dollars struck with her deceased husband's portrait. The story goes that when Mrs. Kennedy saw these coins she did not approve some of the design elements in her husband's hair and recommended changes. The Mint of course complied, and the subsequent design that met her approval was the more common "normal" variety, or Type 2.

While there are many subtle details in the portrait of the Accented Hair Kennedy compared to the normal variety, the most obvious differences are in the design detail of Kennedy's hair just above his ear on the obverse: with two prominent strands of hair that form a V shape just above Kennedy's ear, which are not on the normal variety. Once a collector knows what to look for, this distinction is very obvious to the naked eye.

The eagle's shield on the reverse is normally slightly pitted on the Accented Hair variety, and slightly rounded at the edges. The shield of the later variety appears more crisply struck, with a squared edge, and without the pitting problem.

NGC CERTIFIED POPULATION   (WCG™)

PF-64	PF-65	PF-66	PF-67	PF-68	PF-69	PF-70
537	1,036	1,507	2,351	1,357	264	0
PF-64 Cam	PF-65 Cam	PF-66 Cam	PF-67 Cam	PF-68 Cam	PF-69 Cam	PF-70 Cam
99	185	315	488	263	41	0
PF-64 UC	PF-65 UC	PF-66 UC	PF-67 UC	PF-68 UC	PF-69 UC	PF-70 UC
14	20	28	35	18	1	0

Proof. What makes the Accented Hair Kennedy especially challenging for collectors is the fact that the general quality of this variety, when compared to the normal variety, is usually quite poor. Most Accented Hair Kennedy halves exhibit considerable hairlining in the fields. Additionally, milk spots are a major problem. Because of these flaws, the typical Accented Hair Kennedy grades between PF-62 and PF-64, assuming it's even gradeable! Many Accented Hair Kennedy halves are so heavily spotted they do not even grade when submitted to PCGS and NGC, instead being labeled with "Environmental Damage." This coin is quite challenging to locate in PF-65 and higher grade, and is rare in PF-68.

Why this variety should be plagued with these imperfections is a matter of conjecture. The planchets apparently were not prepared in the same meticulous fashion as planchets for the normal variety, hence the hairlines. And the Accented Hair planchets were obviously not as carefully washed, as many a planchet was left with an indelible imprint of the solution during striking, in the form of the infamous milk spot.

Valuation—The Accented Hair in certified **PF-65** to **PF-66** generally now brings $150 to $250—the higher for relatively milk-spot-free coins. **PF-67** coins sell in the $200 to $350 range. The Accented Hair in **PF-68** has appreciated considerably of late. About a $75 coin in 2003 and 2004, it was worth $250 when the first edition of this book was published, $550 when the second edition was published, and in today's market is a $500 to $1,000 coin. **PF-69s** have exploded in value. At one time an NGC-graded PF-69 Accented Hair could be acquired for as little as $300. This is a $2,000+ coin today.

Cameo Proof. On the positive side for this date, in terms of general quality, many Accented Hair Kennedy halves display at least mild cameo contrast. A fair number have been certified in cameo by PCGS and NGC, though most fall into the PF-64–PF-66 range. The finest known examples in PF-67 and PF-68 are very scarce. This coin is very rare in PF-69 cameo.

Valuation—Even in **PF-64** and **PF-65 Cam** the Accented Hair is a $100 to $250 coin . . . even more if the cameo contrast approaches deep or ultra cameo. **PF-66** coins are about double that level. An Accented Hair in **PF-67 Cam** will typically bring $500 to $1,000; a **PF-68**, $1,500 to $2,500; a **PF-69 Cam**, $5,500. In fact, the last PCGS PF-69 Cam I handled, a spectacular coin bordering on DC, sold for more than $8,000.

Deep / Ultra Cameo Proof. The Accented Hair Kennedy is the rarest *Proof* Kennedy in the series in deep or ultra cameo condition. I emphasize the word "Proof" to highlight the point that the 1965 and 1966 SMS Kennedy half dates are slightly rarer than the Accented Hair with deep or ultra cameo contrast.

When located with exceptional cameo contrast, the Accented Hair is usually hairlined, with minor milk spots often a problem. Most examples grade between PF-65 and PF-67. PF-68 Accented Hair Kennedy halves with deep or ultra cameo contrast are very rare. To date, only one example has graded higher, a PF-69 graded by NGC that I originally handled in the late 1990s.

Valuation—The Accented Hair is a $500–$1,000 coin even in the lower **PF-65** and **PF-66** grades. **PF-67** coins generally trade for between $1,500 and $4,000. This variety trades very rarely in **PF-68 DC/UC** condition—only one or two examples may come onto the market in any given year. The last coins to surface sold for $9,000. I sold the lone **PF-69 UC** for just under $10,000 in the 1990s. That coin might realize triple that price if it were to come on the market today.

⊷⊛ 1964, Proof, Type 2 ⊛⊷

PF-69★ UC

Over 97% of the approximately four million 1964 Proof Kennedy half dollars struck are of the normal or Type 2 variety. The overall quality of this variety is generally far superior to that of the Accented Hair Kennedy, although there are notable exceptions. While hairlines are much less a problem, the Type 2 Proof Kennedy still suffers from the milk-spot problem, a phenomenon that first appeared on silver Proof coins in 1958. 1964 would be the last year this would be a major concern of the Mint.

NGC CERTIFIED POPULATION *(from a total mintage of 3,950,762)*   (WCG™)

PF-64	PF-65	PF-66	PF-67	PF-68	PF-69	PF-70
477	1,493	2,741	4,841	6,364	3,556	29
PF-64 Cam	PF-65 Cam	PF-66 Cam	PF-67 Cam	PF-68 Cam	PF-69 Cam	PF-70 Cam
43	178	552	1,381	1,667	665	0
PF-64 UC	PF-65 UC	PF-66 UC	PF-67 UC	PF-68 UC	PF-69 UC	PF-70 UC
22	57	179	378	527	160	0

Proof. The 1964 Type 2 Kennedy is often a gem coin, grading PF-64 to PF-66 when found in sets. *Milk spots* continue to be a problem. This phenomenon occurred from 1958 through 1964 on the silver Proof issues only. *While extremely scarce in PF-69, the 1964 Type 2 Kennedy is not as rare in this grade as the Proof Franklin issues of the 1950–1963 era.* There are more 1964 Kennedy half dollars certified in PF-69 than for the entire series of Franklin half dollar Proofs!

Valuation—The 1964 Type 2 Kennedy is not worth a significant premium in grades below PF-66. **PF-67** coins in certified slabs will bring around $30 to $60. **PF-68** coins bring $60 to $150. This date brings a significant premium in **PF-69,** with examples now selling in the $125–$300 range.

The 1964 Type 2 Kennedy is the first silver half dollar issue to have been graded in **PF-70.** One PCGS-certified PF-70 that sold for about $1,000 in 2008 changed hands for almost $10,000 in 2015!

Cameo Proof. Scarce. The 1964 Kennedy Type 2 is much more elusive than the 1968-S and later Proof Kennedy halves in cameo condition. While milk spots pose an occasional problem, when found in cameo, most 1964 Type 2 Kennedy halves average PF-66 to PF-67. This date can be located in PF-69 with patience.

Valuation—$25 to $35 in **PF-65** and **PF-66.** **PF-67** coins still can be acquired for as little as $50 to $75. **PF-68 Cam** examples will usually trade for between $150 and $250. Ultimate **PF-69 Cam** 1964 Kennedy halves sell in a wide $350 to $600 range.

Deep / Ultra Cameo Proof. The 1964 Kennedy Type 2 is far more challenging to locate in deep or ultra cameo than in cameo. In this ultimate contrasted condition, the 1964 Kennedy is actually rarer than the 1962 and 1963 Proof Franklin halves, and much more elusive than the 1968-S to 1970-S Kennedy halves, though those coins have lower Proof mintages than the 1964.

When found in DC/UC, most examples grade relatively high, most frequently between PF-66 and PF-68. This date is rare in the highest PF-69 DC/UC grade.

Valuation—$75 to $125 in **PF-65** and **PF-66,** $175 to $300 in **PF-67,** and $250 to $800 in **PF-68**—depending on the contrast. There have been a couple of phenomenal examples in NGC **PF-68★ UC**—"star" because of the phenomenal UC+ contrast—which sold for over $2,500. **PF-69 DC/UC** examples have increased in value in recent years, today generally trending in the $2,000 to $4,000 range when they do surface. A couple especially deep cameo specimens have sold for $7,000!

1965, Special Mint Set

MS-67 UC

Here's where it all began for me. The 1965 SMS issues are among my favorite three dates in the cameo Kennedy series. It was an SMS Kennedy (a 1967) that originally got me enthused about 1950–1970 cameo coinage and cameo coinage in general. (See my story in the author's preface.)

The 1965 SMS Kennedy is a most fascinating date. While the 1965 half appeared similar in composition to the 90% silver half dollars of previous years, this new coin was actually only 40% silver, with outer layers composed of 80% silver and 20% copper, sandwiched around a core composed of 79% copper and 21% silver.

There were no Proof coins minted from 1965 through 1967. The Special Mint Set coins would represent the best of U.S. coin production. Special Mint Set coins differed from Proof coins in several significant ways:

> While SMS dies received more preparation and polishing than commercial dies, they were not polished to the same degree as Proof dies.
>
> SMS planchets were not burnished, as were Proof planchets.
>
> SMS dies were used for a far longer period of time before being removed and repolished or discarded, than were Proof dies.
>
> SMS planchets were struck under higher pressure than commercial planchets, as were Proof planchets, though Proof planchets were also double struck, sometimes triple struck, to bring out the boldest possible relief, while SMS planchets were only struck once.
>
> SMS dies did not receive the same cleaning and maintenance procedures as Proof dies.
>
> Most significantly, SMS coins were not individually handled once struck, as were Proof coins, but were instead dumped into bins similar to those used for commercial coinage. While bagmarks are therefore almost unheard of for Proof coins of this era, virtually *all* SMS half dollars have bagmarks to some degree.

The 1965 SMS sets were issued in a Mylar flat pack similar to those used for Proof coins of the period from mid-1955 to 1964. The Mint did change the color of the envelopes, from the brown used for the earlier Proof sets to white for the 1965 SMS sets.

NGC CERTIFIED POPULATION *(from a total mintage of 2,360,000)* (WCG™)

MS-64	MS-65	MS-66	MS-67	MS-68	MS-69	MS-70
307	663	1,985	1,976	259	3	0
MS-64 Cam	MS-65 Cam	MS-66 Cam	MS-67 Cam	MS-68 Cam	MS-69 Cam	MS-70 Cam
99	245	555	338	27	1	0
MS-64 UC	MS-65 UC	MS-66 UC	MS-67 UC	MS-68 UC	MS-69 UC	MS-70 UC
8	18	20	29	0	0	0

Mint State. The overall quality of 1965 SMS sets is fair at best. Most half dollars appear little different from commercial brilliant Uncirculateds. The typical 1965 SMS Kennedy exhibits frosty, non-prooflike surfaces, average strike, and plentiful bagmarks.

Deep-mirrored coins can be found, and some exhibit modest cameo contrast. When found minimally bagmarked, they are reasonably attractive coins. The average grade for these coins is MS-64 to MS-66. This date becomes extremely elusive in MS-68. *MS-69s are extremely rare!*

Valuation—There is a premium for this date in near mark-free **MS-67** grade. These coins generally trade in the $75–$125 range. **MS-68** coins rarely surface, but will sell for $350 to $800. The last **MS-69** I handled around 2012 sold for about $3,800. This would be a bargain in today's market!

Mint State Cameo. The 1965 SMS Kennedy is scarce with full cameo contrast, though it can be located with a bit of patience. Most examples display moderately deep fields, and grade MS-65 or MS-66. This date is very scarce in MS-67 Cam, and is rare in near mark-free MS-68 Cam condition.

Valuation—$75 to $200 in **MS-65** and **MS-66 Cam,** depending more on the cameo than on whether the coin is MS-65 or MS-66. An outstanding near DC/UC MS-65 Cam will command more than an MS-66 Cam that barely earns the designation.

MS-67 Cam coins will trade in a wide range as well, depending on the cameo contrast. The weaker cameos may sell for only $300 to $500. The finest, deepest examples may command over $1,000.

Mint State Deep / Ultra Cameo. The 1965 SMS Kennedy is rare with deep or ultra cameo contrast. Few examples were struck from dies that received the necessary preparation to struck coins that display the "black-and-white" cameo contrast necessary for the coveted deep or ultra cameo designation.

When a spectacular deep or ultra cameo 1965 SMS Kennedy does appear, it usually has a modest number of bagmarks, and will grade in the MS-64–MS-66 range. MS-67 DC/UC coins are very rare—the 1965 SMS Kennedy is the rarest date in the series in this grade.

This was, until fairly recently, the only Kennedy date in the entire series that did not have any examples certified as MS-68 DC/UC—another testament to this date's rarity in exceptional cameo condition.

Valuation—This is a $500–$2,500 coin in **MS-65** and **MS-66 DC/UC**. In the highest **MS-67** grade, NGC-certified examples are now selling in the $4,000 to $10,000 range. The last couple of PCGS-graded coins to appear on the market have sold for almost $10,000. The lone **MS-68 DCAM** I handled sold for more than $20,000.

⌁ 1966, Special Mint Set ⌁

MS-68 DC

The Mint must have received some complaints from collectors regarding the quality of the 1965 SMS coinage, as there was a noticeable improvement in quality for the year 1966. Virtually all 1966 SMS Kennedy halves are well mirrored and noticeably superior in quality to the commercially struck coins. Some 1966 SMS Kennedys have bagmarks, but these tend not to be as serious as on the 1965 SMS Kennedys.

The Mint also changed its packaging for SMS coinage, with all 1966 SMS sets issued in a snap-lock plastic holder in a cardboard box.

NGC CERTIFIED POPULATION *(from a total mintage of 2,261,583)* (WCG™)

MS-64	MS-65	MS-66	MS-67	MS-68	MS-69	MS-70
161	420	1,705	2,651	493	8	0
MS-64 Cam	**MS-65 Cam**	**MS-66 Cam**	**MS-67 Cam**	**MS-68 Cam**	**MS-69 Cam**	**MS-70 Cam**
34	198	583	546	70	3	0
MS-64 UC	**MS-65 UC**	**MS-66 UC**	**MS-67 UC**	**MS-68 UC**	**MS-69 UC**	**MS-70 UC**
3	11	42	50	11	0	0

Mint State. MS-67 grade coins are almost as difficult to locate as the 1965 SMS Kennedy. This is a very tough coin to find in the higher MS-68 grade. MS-69s are almost as rare as the 1965.

Valuation—There is a premium for **MS-67** coins, which trade in the $40 to $75 range, **MS-68** 1966 SMS Kennedy halves may command upward of $200.

Mint State Cameo. The 1966 SMS Kennedy is almost as rare in cameo condition as the 1965 SMS Kennedy. Compared to the 1968 and later Proof Kennedy halves in the series, the 1966 SMS is a much rarer coin. Most 1966 SMS Kennedy halves in cameo grade MS-66 to MS-67. MS-68 Cam coins are rare.

Valuation—$75 to $150 in **MS-65** and **MS-66 Cam,** depending more on the cameo than on whether the coin is MS-65 or MS-66. **MS-67 Cam** coins have seen considerable appreciation, now trading in the $200 to $500 range. PCGS-graded **MS-68 Cam** 1966 SMS Kennedy halves have sold for over $1,000.

Mint State Deep / Ultra Cameo. The 1966 SMS Kennedy is very nearly as rare as the 1965 in deep or ultra cameo condition. Few 1966 SMS Kennedy halves were struck exhibiting the necessary intensity of frost, coupled with the depth of mirror, to earn the coveted deep cameo designation from PCGS or the ultra cameo designation from NGC.

On the plus side, when located, the 1966 is a bit better quality, with most examples grading either MS-66 or MS-67.

There are a handful of examples certified in MS-68 DC/UC by PCGS and NGC. Significantly, the 1966 SMS Kennedy is the rarest date in the series in this top DC/UC grade, as no 1965 SMS Kennedy halves have received this grade to date.

Valuation—This is a $500–$2,000 coin in **MS-65** and **MS-66 DC/UC.** In **MS-67,** certified examples are now selling in the $1,500 to $3,000 range. A monster DC+ sold for $6,000 in MS-67 DC! **MS-68 DC/UC** coins will trade for four or five those numbers, in the rare instance when one becomes available. Expect to pay $8,000 to $15,000.

As the key date in the series in the top MS-68 DC/UC grade, the 1966 SMS Kennedy would seem to have tremendous potential over the long term. Few examples were struck exhibiting this top level of cameo contrast, and of the coins struck, virtually all are flawed in some respect, grading below MS-68.

1966, Special Mint Set, No FG

One of the few major varieties or Mint errors in the Franklin/Kennedy series, the No FG variety is easily detected with the naked eye. The initials of Frank Gasparro, the artist who rendered the original design of the Kennedy half dollar, are normally tucked between the eagle's left leg and its tail feathers.

1966 SMS, No FG   1966 SMS, With FG

There are corollaries in other series, where a Mint employee would inadvertently overpolish a die, accidentally removing a design element. The 1941 Proof Liberty Walking No AW half dollar is the nearest relative, with the initials of designer Adolf Weinman accidentally having been removed through overpolishing.

However, there are two major differences between the 1941 No AW Proof Liberty Walking half and 1966 No FG SMS Kennedy half. The first is rarity—the 1966 No AW SMS Kennedy is much rarer than the 1941 No AW Liberty Walking. The second difference is in the quality of the coins struck bearing this variety. While no 1941 No AW Proof Liberty Walking half dollars have been certified in cameo, from time to time a No AW will appear on the market exhibiting some attractive cameo contrast, nicely frosted devices, and very deep fields.

NGC CERTIFIED POPULATION   (WCG™)

MS-64	MS-65	MS-66	MS-67	MS-68	MS-69	MS-70
20	31	55	20	0	0	0

Mint State. The 1966 No FG SMS Kennedy to this day exists only in non-cameo condition. In fact, this variety can often be spotted just by looking at the obverse, without even turning the coin over to check for the initials.

Every example of this variety that I have ever seen or handled presents a distinct prooflike appearance over the surface. The coins are completely mono-colored, with no cameo contrast and not even the slightest hint of frost on the devices.

Estimating the total population of this variety is difficult. They were apparently all struck from one die, late in the life of that die, hence the overpolishing. From my own experience, going through at least 100,000 1966 SMS sets over the years, I have come across approximately 25 to 40 coins of this variety. Extrapolating that over the total mintage for the date, that would translate to something in the neighborhood of 500 coins, maybe 1,000.

So this is a tough coin to find in any grade, but it is especially elusive in very high grade. Most examples are between MS-63 and MS-66. The highest grade this variety has ever received to date is MS-67.

Valuation—A "red hot" variety, the 1966 No FG in **MS-63** and **MS-64** generally trades for between $200 and $300. **MS-65** coins are $500 to $1,000, and **MS-66s** may be priced anywhere from $700 to $2,000. The last **MS-67** I handled sold for almost $4,000, and the few other examples have traded in a wide range, from $2,500 to $5,000.

There is a tremendous upside for this variety, given its rarity and the significance of the error. This variety has really been exploding in value since PCGS included the coin in its Major Variety Kennedy Set.

1966, Special Mint Set, Doubled-Die Obverse

Also found in this date is a very rare, major doubled-die variety—major in that the doubling can be easily seen with the naked eye. It is most evident in the area of Kennedy's chin. There are a couple variations of this variety, noted in the *Cherrypickers' Guide to Rare Die Varieties of United States Coins*, fifth edition, volume 2.

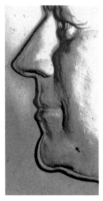

1966 SMS,
Doubled-Die
Obverse

1967, SPECIAL MINT SET

MS-67 DC

1967 was the final year of the short-lived SMS series. Total production dropped for the third straight year, to only 1.86 million sets. Quality continued to improve, as most coins are minimally bagmarked, with reasonably deep mirrored fields, though usually far from Proof quality. The packaging begun in 1966 was continued for the 1967 SMS coinage.

NGC CERTIFIED POPULATION *(from a total mintage of 1,863,344)* (WCG™)

MS-64	MS-65	MS-66	MS-67	MS-68	MS-69	MS-70
166	363	1,299	1,846	305	11	0
MS-64 Cam	MS-65 Cam	MS-66 Cam	MS-67 Cam	MS-68 Cam	MS-69 Cam	MS-70 Cam
106	399	1,049	1,048	139	2	0
MS-64 UC	MS-65 UC	MS-66 UC	MS-67 UC	MS-68 UC	MS-69 UC	MS-70 UC
13	39	130	157	15	0	0

Mint State. MS-67 grade coins are about as scarce as 1966 SMS Kennedy halves.

Valuation—A premium exists for **MS-67** coins, which trade in the $40–$60 range. **MS-68** 1967 SMS Kennedy halves may command upward of $200. *Note that this is still a scarce coin!*

Mint State Cameo. The 1967 SMS Kennedy is the least rare of the SMS Kennedy halves in cameo condition. Most examples grade MS-66 or MS-67. MS-68 Cam coins are rare.

Valuation—$50 to $75 in **MS-65** and **MS-66 Cam. MS-67 Cam** coins generally trade in the $100–$200 range. Certified **MS-68 Cam** 1967 SMS Kennedy halves have sold for more than $500.

Mint State Deep / Ultra Cameo. While not as rare as the 1965 or 1966 SMS Kennedy in deep or ultra cameo, the 1967 is still an *extremely scarce* coin with this level of cameo contrast, particularly when compared to the Proof Kennedy halves in the series (with the sole exception of the 1964 Accented Hair).

One of the most stunning SMS Kennedy cameo die varieties known is the 1967 "Birthmark" die, named for the birthmark-shaped frost-fade spot on Kennedy's temple, a characteristic of early strikes off this die. Of the handful of 1967 SMS Kennedy halves that have been certified in MS-68 DC/UC by PCGS and NGC, about half have been from this top die.

At one time it was speculated that these Birthmark coins were actually clandestine Proof strikings, given the exceptional near-Proof quality of their appearance. That is highly unlikely. For one thing, bagmarks are as prevalent on coins struck from this die as on those from other cameo dies for the year. It seems unlikely that Mint personnel would sneak these clandestine Proof strikes through and then allow them to be dumped in the same bins as the other SMS Kennedy halves.

Valuation—The 1967 SMS is a $200 to $500 coin in **MS-65** and **MS-66 DC/UC.** In **MS-67,** NGC-certified examples have increased in value to the $700–$1,500 range, depending on the cameo contrast, though exceptional examples of the Birthmark will sell for more. The finest few **MS-68 DC/UC** examples to appear in the last few years have all sold for between $7,000 and $12,000. There is a lone NGC **MS-69 UCAM** that reportedly sold for more than $20,000.

⊷⊶ 1968-S, Proof ⊷⊶

PF-70 DC

After a three-year hiatus, the Mint resumed Proof production in 1968. *For the first time*, Proof sets were no longer struck in Philadelphia, but in San Francisco. There was great anticipation in the numismatic community, and over three million Proof sets were minted in response. Even though these latest Proof sets' "silver" coins were only 40% silver in content, unlike the 1964 sets' 90% silver-content coins, the Mint bumped the price for the new sets to $5.00, compared to the old issue price of $2.10.

The Mint did change the packaging for these latest Proof sets to a hard plastic holder. While an excellent holder overall, it was not airtight. Many Proof coins stored in these holders for a period of time will show some oxidation and toning.

NGC CERTIFIED POPULATION *(from a total mintage of 3,041,506)*   (WCG™)

PF-64	PF-65	PF-66	PF-67	PF-68	PF-69	PF-70
67	115	204	447	740	403	0
PF-64 Cam	PF-65 Cam	PF-66 Cam	PF-67 Cam	PF-68 Cam	PF-69 Cam	PF-70 Cam
11	41	164	441	556	357	0
PF-64 UC	PF-65 UC	PF-66 UC	PF-67 UC	PF-68 UC	PF-69 UC	PF-70 UC
14	51	202	800	1,554	665	16

Proof. The 1968-S Kennedy is generally a high-quality coin. Most coins grade between PF-66 and PF-68.

Valuation—There is no premium for **PF-66** and lower-grade coins in non-cameo condition, and only a modest $10 to $30 value for **PF-67s** and **PF-68s**. In non-cameo **PF-69**, the 1968-S is now valued around $75 to $100.

Cameo Proof. The Mint apparently took notice of collectors' preference for the lovely frosted cameo coins over the non-cameo variety, as there is a noticeable increase in the percentage of coins struck in frosted cameo condition in 1968 compared to the earlier Proof years.

Pay special attention to the following! As a rough comparison, if one were fortunate enough to acquire 1,000 unopened 1963 Proof sets—a very unlikely event in this day and age, as probably 95% of the Proof sets from that era have been searched many times over, and most of the remaining 5% of sets have been opened—if one opened the sets and looked for cameo halves, the likelihood is that anywhere from zero to 10 half dollars might have enough cameo contrast on both obverse and reverse to earn a cameo designation. Moreover, the probability is that there would be *no* (as in *zero*) half dollars with the exceptional cameo contrast on both obverse and reverse that would earn the ultimate deep cameo or ultra cameo designation.

On the other hand, if one had a similar hoard of 1,000 unopened 1968-S Proof sets, one might find 25 to 50 half dollars with enough contrast to earn a cameo designation, and perhaps 5 to 10 coins with enough contrast to earn the deep or ultra cameo designation. *This is still a low number when compared to the modern era!*

Valuation—$20 to $40 in **PF-65** and **PF-66 Cam. PF-67 Cam** coins generally sell in the $45–$75 range, and **PF-68s** for around $75 to $150. A **PF-69 Cam** will generally bring between $150 and $300.

Deep / Ultra Cameo Proof. This is the most desirable condition for this date; the 1968-S is a scarce coin in this condition.

Most examples grade in the PF-66–PF-67 range, though PF-68s can still be located with just a little patience.

The 1968-S in PF-69 DC/UC is quite scarce, and a most desirable acquisition at current price levels.

Interestingly, the 1968-S is the first half dollar graded in PF-70 DC by PCGS. At the time of this writing, a handful more than a dozen examples have received this ultimate grade. *It is important to note*, however, that these coins were certified when PCGS first began issuing the grade in the late 1990s, and no 1968-S Kennedy halves have been certified in this grade since that time.

Valuation—The 1968-S is a $30–$60 coin in **PF-65** and **PF-66 DC/UC,** and a $75–$125 value in **PF-67.** The typical **PF-68** will sell for around $100 to $150, though exceptional frosted examples with DC+ or UC+ contrast may sell for many times that level. **PF-69s** with average deep cameo contrast generally sell for between $400 and $700. The finest known DC+/UC+ coins have sold for more than $1,500.

The last PCGS **PF-70** DC I handled, a true **PF-70 DC,** sold for $6,000 in 2009.

⋙ 1969-S, Proof ⋘

PF-69★ UC

NGC CERTIFIED POPULATION *(from a total mintage of 2,934,631)* (WCG™)

PF-64	PF-65	PF-66	PF-67	PF-68	PF-69	PF-70
57	114	245	550	423	236	0
PF-64 Cam	PF-65 Cam	PF-66 Cam	PF-67 Cam	PF-68 Cam	PF-69 Cam	PF-70 Cam
24	49	201	633	1,056	845	1
PF-64 UC	PF-65 UC	PF-66 UC	PF-67 UC	PF-68 UC	PF-69 UC	PF-70 UC
20	60	184	879	2,000	1,190	1

Proof. The quality of the 1969-S Kennedy half is similar to that of the 1968-S. Most examples grade between PF-66 and PF-68. The percentage of 1969-S Kennedy halves struck with cameo contrast is slightly greater than that of the 1968-S Kennedy.

Valuation—The 1969-S represents the end of an era in U.S. Proof production. **PF-67s** have been selling in the $10 to $30 range, **PF-68s** around $20 to $40, and **PF-69s** around $75 to $100.

Cameo Proof. The 1969-S Kennedy is the most common cameo half dollar of the 1950–1970 era, slightly more common than the 1968-S or 1970-S. Of course, it is extremely scarce in comparison to Kennedy halves minted in the mid-1970s and later.

Valuation—$20 to $40 in **PF-65** and **PF-66 Cam**. **PF-67 Cam** coins are generally in the $30–$60 range, and **PF-68s** around $50 to $80. A **PF-69 Cam** will generally bring between $100 and $200.

Deep / Ultra Cameo Proof. Like the 1968-S Kennedy, the 1969-S Kennedy should be sought out in deep or ultra cameo condition.

Most examples grade PF-66 to PF-68. PF-69 DC/UC coins are *scarce*, but are 50 to 100 times easier to find than the most common Franklin of the earlier 1950–1963 era in PF-69 DC/UC—the 1956 Type 2 Franklin.

Valuation—This is a $30–$50 coin in **PF-65** and **PF-66 DC/UC,** and a $60–$100 value in **PF-67.** The typical **PF-68** will sell for around $65 to $125, though exceptional frosted examples with DC+ or UC+ contrast may sell for many times that level. **PF-** with average DC contrast generally command between $200 and $400. The known UC+ coins, graded **PF-69★ UC** by NGC, have sold for over $2,000.

There is one example certified as **PF-70 DC** by PCGS, which I placed with a the 1990s.

⤜ 1970-S, PROOF ⤛

PF-69★ UC

1970 would be the last year that silver was used in the Proof half dollar until 1992 (with the exception of the 1976-S Bicentennial issue). This was a significant event, as the silver look that collectors had become accustomed to in their coins would be replaced by a tan cast.

NGC CERTIFIED POPULATION *(from a total mintage of 2,632,810)*   (WCG™)

PF-64	PF-65	PF-66	PF-67	PF-68	PF-69	PF-70
48	97	301	617	489	271	0
PF-64 Cam	**PF-65 Cam**	**PF-66 Cam**	**PF-67 Cam**	**PF-68 Cam**	**PF-69 Cam**	**PF-70 Cam**
25	48	233	688	994	788	0
PF-64 UC	**PF-65 UC**	**PF-66 UC**	**PF-67 UC**	**PF-68 UC**	**PF-69 UC**	**PF-70 UC**
9	28	114	464	1,115	517	0

Proof. The general quality of the 1970-S Kennedy half dollar is very similar to that of the 1968-S and 1969-S issues. A significant percentage, perhaps 3% to 5%, was struck with cameo contrast, as the Mint responded to the collector demand for the more attractive two-toned cameo coins.

Valuation—This was the last year of the Kennedy Proof struck in silver and using the old-fashioned die-preparation techniques. This is a $10 to $30 coin in **PF-67** and **PF-68**. In non-cameo **PF-69**, the 1970-S sells for around $75 to $100.

Cameo Proof. The 1970-S Kennedy is the most common cameo half dollar of the 1950–1970 era, slightly more common than the 1968-S or 1970-S.

Valuation—$25 to $35 in **PF-65** and **PF-66 Cam; PF-67 Cam** coins generally sell in the $45–$65 range, and **PF-68s** for $65 to $100. A **PF-69 Cam** will generally bring $125 to $250.

Deep / Ultra Cameo Proof. As with the 1968-S and 1969-S Kennedy halves, the 970-S is most desirable in deep or ultra cameo condition.

Most examples grade PF-66 to PF-68. PF-69 DC/UC coins are more elusive than the)-S Kennedy, and approximately as rare as the 1968-S.

uation—This is a $40–$60 coin in **PF-65** and **PF-66 DC/UC,** and a $60–$110 **PF-67.** The typical **PF-68** will command $85 to $175, though, as with the nd 1969-S exceptional frosted examples with DC+ or UC+ contrast, it may sell imes that range. **PF-69s** with average deep cameo contrast generally sell for)0 and $800.

1971–1976: ENTERING THE MODERN ERA

In 1971, the Mint was still using the tried-and-true acid-dipping technique (they referred to it as "pickling") to create its cameo Proof dies. The harder nonsilver planchet complicated this process, as the harder planchet wore these delicate cameo dies at an even faster rate than the earlier silver planchet. The half dollar was the last denomination to go clad, beginning in 1971.

The quality improved in 1972, with a far higher percentage of exceptional cameos being struck than in the previous year, but it was not until 1973 that real change occurred: the Mint began using a sandblasting technique to create a much heavier cameo effect in the die preparation. The die was then given added durability when it was chrome plated. This basic technique has been employed ever since.

However, in these early years, the technique was really not yet state of the art. Ticks and scratches were still a problem, and the Mint changed the packing contents of the packaging in 1973, to the detriment of the delicate Proof coins. The materials used were apparently not inert. Most Proof coins housed in the new packaging for a considerable length of time (several decades) have developed a heavy dull toning. Of the five denominations, cents through halves, the Lincoln cents are by far the toughest denomination to locate in PF-69 deep or ultra cameo condition.

⊷ 1971-S, PROOF ⊶

PF-69 UC

My 1991 book, *Cameo and Brilliant Proof Coinage of the 1950 to 1970 Era* could easily have been titled . . . *of the 1950 to 1971 Era*. I debated whether to include the 1971 year, as I knew that Proof coins from that year were also quite scarce in the higher grades of DC/UC condition. I decided to end my study at 1970 for two reasons. First, while I had some familiarity with the 1971 year, up to that point most of my attention had been focused on cameo coinage of 1970 and earlier. I felt I needed more information on the year 1971 before I could offer an analysis of the date. Second, 1971 was the first year the Kennedy Proof was struck without any silver content, so it seemed like a natural place to end the study of the series. A follow-up book including Proof coinage struck after 1970 could always come later.

PF-64	PF-65	PF-66	PF-67	PF-68	PF-69	PF-70
32	63	240	559	711	307	0
PF-64 Cam	PF-65 Cam	PF-66 Cam	PF-67 Cam	PF-68 Cam	PF-69 Cam	PF-70 Cam
9	19	84	300	682	369	0
PF-64 UC	PF-65 UC	PF-66 UC	PF-67 UC	PF-68 UC	PF-69 UC	PF-70 UC
4	3	7	66	321	84	0

Valuation—There is no premium for **PF-67** and lower-grade 1971-S Kennedy half dollars in non-cameo condition. There is a modest $15 to $50 premium for **PF-68** and **PF-69** coins.

Cameo Proof. The 1971-S Kennedy is elusive. Many 1971-S Kennedy halves are struck with phenomenal DC+/UC+ obverse cameo contrast but *little or no reverse cameo contrast*. This is true across the board with all the denominations for this year, but especially so with the half dollar. It is as if the Mint focused on making the coins look as attractive as possible when one first opens the box and sees the lovely cameo coins, with the reverse as a kind of afterthought: "Oh well. The reverse isn't much to look at, but the obverse sure is pretty."

Valuation—Examples in **PF-65** and **PF-66 Cam** bring $15 to $30, **PF-67 Cam** coins generally command a value in the $20–$30 range, and **PF-68s** sell for around $40. A **PF-69 Cam** will generally bring $100 to $200.

Deep / Ultra Cameo Proof. This is where the 1971-S is *really* challenging. Again, many 1971-S Kennedy halves exist with full deep or ultra cameo obverses but usually have little if any cameo contrast on the reverse. A coin must be deep or ultra cameo on both obverse and reverse to earn that top designation.

Valuation—This is a $75–$150 coin in **PF-65** and **PF-66 DC/UC,** and a $150 to $300 value in **PF-67.** This date is especially scarce in **PF-68 DC/UC** and now generally trades at around $300 to $500. Problem-free, solid **PF-69s** in **DC/UC** have appreciated since the earlier editions of this book were published, and now sell for $2,500 to $4,000.

⋙ 1972-S, Proof ⋘

PF-69 DC

I regard the 1972-S Kennedy as a transition year in the Kennedy cameo Proof series. It was the last year that the Mint apparently still utilized the traditional acid-dipping method to create cameo Proofs, but at the same time, the Mint obviously put far more effort into striking cameo coins than ever before. There is a significantly higher percentage of Kennedy halves struck in cameo, including deep or ultra cameo, than in previous years.

NGC CERTIFIED POPULATION *(from a total mintage of 3,260,996)* (WCG™)

PF-64	PF-65	PF-66	PF-67	PF-68	PF-69	PF-70
19	36	55	199	196	107	0
PF-64 Cam	PF-65 Cam	PF-66 Cam	PF-67 Cam	PF-68 Cam	PF-69 Cam	PF-70 Cam
2	5	52	206	420	287	0
PF-64 UC	PF-65 UC	PF-66 UC	PF-67 UC	PF-68 UC	PF-69 UC	PF-70 UC
1	0	15	95	674	718	0

Proof. As with the 1971-S Kennedy, many 1972-S Kennedy halves that appear with cameo contrast are one-siders with strong obverse contrast but moderate or weak reverse cameo contrast. At the same time, a significantly higher number than the previous year exhibit exceptional cameo contrast on both obverse and reverse.

Valuation—There is no premium for **PF-67** and lower-grade 1972-S Kennedy half dollars in non-cameo condition, and a modest $10 to $30 premium for coins in **PF-68** and **PF-69.**

Cameo Proof. The 1972-S Kennedy is common in cameo, with perhaps 25% or more of the total mintage being struck with appreciable cameo contrast on both obverse and reverse.

Valuation—**PF-67 Cam** coins generally sell in the $20–$30 range, and **PF-68s** for around $20 to $35. A **PF-69 Cam** will generally bring between $30 and $70.

Deep / Ultra Cameo Proof. The 1972-S is scarce in deep or ultra cameo, and is very scarce in the highest PF-69 grade, though not as rare as the 1971-S. It is far more elusive than the 1973-S that follows.

Valuation—The **PF-68 DC/UC** is now a $50 to $100 coin. Problem-free, solid **PF-69s** in **DC/UC** have appreciated to $200 to $400, though I handled a fabulous **PF-69 UC+** that sold for more than $700.

⋙ 1973-S–1976-S, Clad Proof ⋘

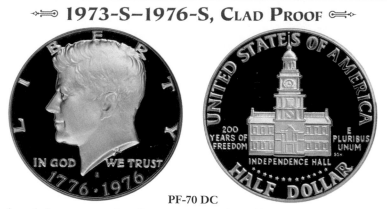

PF-70 DC

Collectors loved the cameo coins. In response to the collector demand, in 1973 the Mint began using a sandblasting technology, blasting the working dies with small glass bits, to create the cameo effect. A chrome-plating technology was then utilized to give the working dies greater durability.

As a result of this new technology, cameo Proof production took another incremental jump forward. It would take years for the Mint to perfect these new technologies, until in 1977 virtually every Proof Kennedy struck that year would have deep cameo or ultra cameo contrast on both obverse and reverse.

The 1973-S, 1974-S, and 1976-S clad Kennedy half dollars are all very similar in their quality and cameo characteristics, so they will be treated here as a group. There was no 1975-dated Kennedy. Instead, the 1976-S was struck for two years, featuring the Bicentennial reverse.

NGC CERTIFIED POPULATION *(from a total mintage of 2,760,339 / 2,612,568 / 7,059,099)*   (WCG™)

PF-64	PF-65	PF-66	PF-67	PF-68	PF-69	PF-70
58	72	90	239	237	69	0
PF-64 Cam	PF-65 Cam	PF-66 Cam	PF-67 Cam	PF-68 Cam	PF-69 Cam	PF-70 Cam
17	58	145	443	783	380	1
PF-64 UC	PF-65 UC	PF-66 UC	PF-67 UC	PF-68 UC	PF-69 UC	PF-70 UC
6	21	64	415	1,047	21,967	55

Proof. While most examples are fairly well preserved in the hard plastic government-issue holders they were originally encased in, quite a few coins have developed considerable hazy toning over the years that cannot always be removed through conservation.

Valuation—There is no premium for **PF-68** and lower-grade Kennedy half dollars in **non-cameo** condition from this era. **PF-69s** might sell for $15 to $25.

Cameo Proof. The 1973-S to 1976-S clad Kennedy is extremely common in cameo, with at least 50% or more of the total mintage being struck with appreciable cameo contrast on both obverse and reverse.

Valuation—**PF-69 Cam** coins might be valued in the $20–$40 range.

Deep / Ultra Cameo Proof. The 1973-S to 1976-S clad Kennedy is also very common in deep or ultra cameo. PF-69 DC/UC coins can be acquired with little difficulty.

Valuation—A $20 coin in **PF-68 DC/UC**. Problem-free, solid **PF-69s** in **DC/UC** have traded for between $25 and $60. A sensational DC+/UC+ coin may trade for more, however. There are a handful of 1973-S to 1976-S clad Kennedy halves certified in **PF-70 DC** by PCGS. These coins have generally traded in the $2,500–$4,500 range.

·⇒ 1976-S, SILVER PROOF ⇐·

PF-69 DC

The 1976-S silver Bicentennial Kennedy is actually a two-year type coin featuring the Bicentennial reverse designed by Seth G. Huntington. The coin is 40% silver in composition, with outside layers composed of 80% silver and 20% copper, which are sandwiched around an inner core of .209 silver and .791 copper.

NGC CERTIFIED POPULATION *(from a total mintage of 4,000,000)*   (WCG™)

PF-64	PF-65	PF-66	PF-67	PF-68	PF-69	PF-70
50	57	49	144	73	10	0
PF-64 Cam	PF-65 Cam	PF-66 Cam	PF-67 Cam	PF-68 Cam	PF-69 Cam	PF-70 Cam
12	43	71	271	395	176	0
PF-64 UC	PF-65 UC	PF-66 UC	PF-67 UC	PF-68 UC	PF-69 UC	PF-70 UC
4	16	40	303	617	11,404	19

Proof. The quality of this issue is very similar to the clad Kennedy of the same year. Most examples are high grade, though many examples have developed spotted or hazy toning from years spent in the government-issue plastic capsules, which were not airtight.

Valuation—There is no premium for **PF-68** and lower-grade 1976-S silver Kennedy half dollar in non-cameo condition from this era. **PF-69s** might sell for $15 to $20.

Cameo Proof. The 1976-S silver Kennedy is extremely common in cameo, with at least 50% or more of the total mintage being struck with appreciable cameo contrast on both obverse and reverse.

Valuation—**PF-69 Cam** coins might command a value in the $20–$30 range.

Deep / Ultra Cameo Proof. The 1976-S silver Kennedy is very common in deep cameo or ultra cameo. PF-69 DC/UC coins can be acquired with little difficulty.

Valuation—A $20–$30 coin in **PF-68 DC/UC.** Problem-free, solid **PF-69s** in **DC/ UC** have traded between $50 and $100. A sensational DC+/UC+ coin may sell for $200 or more.

There are a handful of 1976-S silver Kennedy halves certified in **PF-70 DC** by PCGS. The finest, heaviest DCAM examples sell for as much as $1,500 to $2,500.

1977–1989: The Modern Era in Its Infancy

PF-70 UC

With the yearly improvements in production techniques, by 1977 virtually all Proof coins struck and released by the Mint exhibited deep or ultra cameo contrast. I have yet to see a Proof coin from this era in fully brilliant condition.

The biggest problem is the packaging. While the Mint used a hard plastic inert case to protect and view the coins, it continued to use materials inside the holder that were not inert, and which continued to tone the coins.

The majority of Proof Kennedy halves in this era, if minimally toned, grade PF-69 DC/UC. Occasionally a coin will grade PF-70.

Valuation—Kennedy halves in **PF-69 DC/UC** will sell for a modest premium over the Proof set price for that year, including the grading fee. **PF-70** coins will sell at higher premiums, depending on the latest population total for that date in PF-70.

1990 to the Present: The Modern Era and the Perfect Cameo?

PF-70 UC, Clad

PF-70 UC, Silver

The last major hurdle, the packaging materials, seems to finally have been overcome in this modern era. One can purchase an original Proof set from this period, and generally be assured that most if not all the coins in the set will grade at least PF-69 DC/UC if submitted, with little or no toning.

Valuation—Kennedy halves in **PF-69 DC/UC** will sell for a small premium over the Proof set price for that year including the grading fee. **PF-70** coins will sell at higher premiums, depending on the latest population total for that date in PF-70.

MODERN DEEP CAMEO / ULTRA CAMEO PROOF POPULATIONS

In 1973 the Mint introduced methods of Proof-making that, over time, as the relevant technologies were gradually perfected, resulted in the perfect Proof: Kennedy halves of such quality they received the ultimate grade of PF-70 Deep Cameo or Ultra Cameo—in a word, perfection. The technological improvements have continued to this day, and as a result, the percentage of submissions of Proof Kennedy half dollars that receive this ultimate grade has increased with each passing decade.

The experts at PCGS and NGC take extra care to scrutinize the best Proofs under high magnification before awarding the ultimate grade. To the average collector, the difference between a PF-69 DC/UC and a PF-70 DC/UC are scarcely visible to the naked eye—but to those collectors who are interested in assembling a top-ranking set for the NGC and PCGS Set Registries, the difference is critical.

This chart shows the certified populations (NGC and PCGS) for the Proof half dollars not covered individually in the text. Congratulations to the Mint on a job well done!

PF-70 DEEP CAMEO / ULTRA CAMEO CERTIFIED POPULATION TOTALS

	1973-S	1974-S	1976-S	1977-S	1978-S	1979-S, T1
Clad	17	17	63	127	181	243
	1979-S, T2	1980-S	1981-S, T1	1981-S, T2	1982-S	1983-S
Clad	69	152	137	96	129	243
	1984-S	1985-S	1986-S	1987-S	1988-S	1989-S
Clad	143	196	196	284	189	271
	1990-S	1991-S	1992-S	1993-S	1994-S	1995-S
Clad	325	532	430	424	418	352
Silver	n/a	n/a	383	242	326	302
	1996-S	1997-S	1998-S	1999-S	2000-S	2001-S
Clad	307	338	355	371	526	351
Silver	208	389	503	618	1,657	945
	2002-S	2003-S	2004-S	2005-S	2006-S	2007-S
Clad	471	610	292	1,103	847	924
Silver	1,556	1,311	1,330	2,048	1,501	1,240
	2008-S	2009-S	2010-S	2011-S	2012-S	2013-S
Clad	622	1,154	494	849	594	667
Silver	1,512	1,448	2,195	1,955	1,200	1,362
	2014-S	2015-S	2016-S	2017-S		
Clad	660	1,146	453	101		
Silver	2,740	1,392	1,780	1,202		

BEAUTIFULLY TONED COINS

While toned Mint State Franklin halves are common, examples with exceptional color on the obverse or reverse are extremely elusive—almost impossible to find for some dates, in any grade. The pages that follow feature some attractive color coins I hope you will enjoy. Once again, I thank all the collectors who lent us these treasures for your enjoyment.

PCGS, MS-65 FBL

(Images 1.5x actual size.)

MS-66 FBL

PCGS, MS-65 FBL

NGC, MS-67★ FBL

NGC, MS-66 FBL

PCGS, MS-66 FBL

PCGS, MS-66 FBL

PCGS, MS-66 FBL

MS-66 FBL

NGC, MS-67 FBL

NGC, MS-67★

NGC, MS-67 FBL

PCGS, MS-65 FBL

PCGS, MS-66

PCGS, MS-65

PCGS, MS-65

PCGS, MS-66 FBL

PCGS, MS-66

PCGS, MS-65

APPENDIX

MINTAGES AND EXPANDED VALUATIONS

The values in this appendix should not be regarded as absolutes, but as the midpoints of price ranges that may vary widely (especially at upper grade levels, where contrast and other qualities within a single grade can make an enormous value difference). Value ranges are discussed at length in the text.

NOTE: Values for lower-grade silver coins may move with changes in bullion value ($17/oz. as of press time).

FRANKLIN HALF DOLLARS: CIRCULATION STRIKES

	Mintage	VF-20	EF-40	MS-60	MS-63	MS-64	MS-65	MS-66
1948	3,006,814	$9	$11	$20	$27	$35	$80	$300
1948, FBL	*					55	140	350
1948D	4,028,600	9	11	20	24	30	115	600
1948D, FBL	*					55	185	800
1949	5,614,000	12	18	40	70	75	130	375
1949, FBL	*					80	155	550
1949D	4,120,600	12	18	45	70	85	550	2,500
1949D, FBL	*					120	750	10,000
1949S	3,744,000	12	20	65	95	115	140	225
1949S, FBL	*					250	500	750
1950	7,742,123	9	11	30	40	55	110	385
1950, FBL	*					80	190	575
1950D	8,031,600	9	11	25	38	70	250	1,000
1950D, FBL	*					95	375	1,350
1951	16,802,102	9	11	16	24	35	70	225
1951, FBL	*					85	235	775
1951D	9,475,200	9	11	30	45	70	150	675
1951D, FBL	*					100	250	1,000
1951S	13,696,000	9	11	25	35	50	70	275
1951S, FBL	*					175	375	1,000
1952	21,192,093	9	11	16	23	32	70	235
1952, FBL	*					65	120	430
1952D	25,395,600	9	11	16	23	32	125	600
1952D, FBL	*					65	180	1,150
1952S	5,526,000	12	16	50	65	80	100	225
1952S, FBL	*					425	725	2,850
1953	2,668,120	9	10	16	25	40	105	475
1953, FBL	*					150	635	2,750
1953D	20,900,400	9	10	16	23	38	110	550
1953D, FBL	*					55	175	725

* Included in number above.

	Mintage	VF-20	EF-40	MS-60	MS-63	MS-64	MS-65	MS-66
1953S 4,148,000		$9	$10	$25	$35	$48	$70	$350
1953S, FBL. . . . .*						10,000	25,500	
1954 13,188,202		9	10	16	20	30	70	300
1954, FBL. . . . .*						45	120	1,100
1954D 25,445,580		9	10	16	24	28	90	375
1954D, FBL . . . .*						40	135	800
1954S 4,993,400		12	14	16	26	35	55	240
1954S, FBL. . . . .*						85	250	1,050
1955 2,498,181		18	22	25	35	40	60	150
1955, FBL. . . . .*						50	115	425
1955, "Bugs Bunny" Variety . . . .*					48	65	130	265
1955, "Bugs Bunny" Variety, FBL . . . .*						85	350	700
1956 4,032,000		9	10	16	25	28	48	80
1956, FBL. . . . .*						38	100	275
1957 5,114,000		9	10	16	19	25	50	85
1957, FBL. . . . .*						55	125	225
1957D 19,966,850		9	10	16	18	23	52	85
1957D, FBL . . . .*						38	75	375
1958 4,042,000		9	10	14	19	24	45	80
1958, FBL. . . . .*						55	125	350
1958D 23,962,412		9	10	14	18	19	45	75
1958D, FBL . . . .*						33	70	500
1959 6,200,000		9	10	14	18	20	70	800
1959, FBL. . . . .*						50	225	1,750
1959D 13,053,750		9	10	14	18	22	90	775
1959D, FBL . . . .*						32	140	1,050
1960 6,024,000		9	10	14	18	19	100	550
1960, FBL. . . . .*						40	225	2,000
1960D 18,215,812		9	10	14	18	28	200	900
1960D, FBL . . . .*						45	425	4,250
1961 8,290,000		9	10	14	18	25	75	600
1961, FBL. . . . .*						160	900	5,000
1961D 20,276,442		9	10	14	18	25	110	1,000
1961D, FBL . . . .*						60	450	3,000
1962 9,714,000		9	10	14	18	25	90	750
1962, FBL. . . . .*						225	1,750	11,000
1962D 35,473,281		9	10	14	18	25	120	1,000
1962D, FBL . . . .*						75	450	3,500
1963 22,164,000		9	10	14	18	19	40	750
1963, FBL. . . . .*						145	1,150	2,500
1963D 67,069,292		9	10	14	18	19	45	350
1963D, FBL . . . .*						40	175	1,050

* Included in number above.

FRANKLIN HALF DOLLARS: PROOF STRIKES

	Mintage	PF-64	PF-65	PF-65 Cam	PF-65 DC	PF-66
1950 51,386		$400	$475	$1,200	$10,000	$575
1951 57,500		300	375	600	2,500	425
1952 81,980		180	230	375	4,500	265
1953 128,800		125	190	225	1,400	235
1954 233,300		60	85	110	425	100
1955 378,200		50	75	90	425	85
1956 669,384		35	45	55	100	70

	Mintage	PF-64	PF-65	PF-65 Cam	PF-65 DC	PF-66
1957	1,247,952	$25	$28	$60	$250	$35
1958	875,652	32	38	75	675	52
1959	1,149,291	18	22	60	2,000	38
1960	1,691,602	18	22	45	100	30
1961	3,028,244	22	25	40	125	35
1961, DblDie Rev (a) . . . .*		2,200	2,900	4,000		3,750
1962	3,218,019	17	22	32	60	25
1963	3,075,645	17	22	30	52	25

* Included in number above. a. Other reverse doubled dies exist for this date. The variety listed (FS-50-1961-801) is by far the most dramatic. Very strong doubling is evident on the reverse lettering.

KENNEDY HALF DOLLARS: CIRCULATION STRIKES

	Mintage	MS-63	MS-64	MS-65	MS-66	MS-67	MS-68	MS-69	MS-70
1964	273,304,004	$12	$18	$20	$40	$625			
1964D	156,205,446	12	19	20	40	825	—		
1965	65,879,366	6	18	25	150	675			
1966	108,984,932	6	17	22	170	400	—		
1967	295,046,978	6	17	22	95	750			
1968D	246,951,930	6	11	20	40	235			
1969D	129,881,800	6	12	30	225	1,100			
1970D	2,150,000	20	30	42	215	775			
1971	155,164,000	2	9	15	45	200			
1971D	302,097,424	2	6	10	22	70	$2,350		
1972	153,180,000	2	9	15	50	290			
1972D	141,890,000	2	6	10	23	85			
1973	64,964,000	2	9	15	45	155			
1973D	83,171,400	2	7	11	20	160			
1974	201,596,000	2	16	22	35	145			
1974D	79,066,300	2	12	15	35	165			
1976	234,308,000	2	9	15	50	125			
1976D	287,565,248	2	7	12	25	375			
1976S, Silver Clad (a). . .	11,000,000	8	9	10	15	30	300	$5,000	
1977	43,598,000	2	9	15	28	120	—		
1977D	31,449,106	2	6	10	22	85	—		
1978	14,350,000	2	7	12	20	80			
1978D	13,765,799	3	7	10	23	145			
1979	68,312,000	2	6	10	25	150	2,500		
1979D	15,815,422	2	7	12	25	160			
1980P	44,134,000	2	6	10	17	35			
1980D	33,456,449	2	8	13	55	145	2,500		
1981P	29,544,000	2	7	12	25	260	3,000		
1981D	27,839,533	2	10	17	40	325			
1982P	10,819,000	5	13	20	70	425			
1982D	13,140,102	5	12	18	40	325			
1983P	34,139,000	6	13	20	38	165	2,500		
1983D	32,472,244	7	11	15	30	330			
1984P	26,029,000	2	10	12	38	250			
1984D	26,262,158	2	10	17	40	350			
1985P	18,706,962	5	10	15	25	80	2,500		
1985D	19,814,034	5	9	12	15	45	2,000		
1986P	13,107,633	6	10	13	28	70	2,750		
1986D	15,336,145	5	8	11	20	45	2,250	8,000	
1987P (b)	2,890,758	5	10	15	30	80	3,000		
1987D (b)	2,890,758	5	9	12	23	50	2,100		

a. Mintage figures for 1976-S silver coins are approximate. b. Not issued for circulation; included with Mint and Souvenir sets. Many were melted in 1982.

	Mintage	MS-63	MS-64	MS-65	MS-66	MS-67	MS-68	MS-69	MS-70
1988P	13,626,000	$5	$10	$15	$28	$40	$2,500		
1988D	12,000,096	4	8	12	25	40	2,250		
1989P	24,542,000	4	8	12	23	90			
1989D	23,000,216	3	7	11	18	55	—		
1990P	22,278,000	3	7	11	17	145	2,000		
1990D	20,096,242	3	10	16	32	200			
1991P	14,874,000	4	8	12	25	180	2,500		
1991D	15,054,678	4	11	15	25	250	—	—	
1992P	17,628,000	2	7	11	22	25	1,600		
1992D	17,000,106	3	7	10	18	30	2,500	$10,000	
1993P	15,510,000	3	7	11	20	40	2,000	10,000	
1993D	15,000,006	3	8	10	22	60	2,500		
1994P	23,718,000	2	8	10	20	55	1,850		
1994D	23,828,110	2	6	10	18	70	2,500	—	—
1995P	26,496,000	2	6	10	17	40	1,800		
1995D	26,288,000	2	6	10	20	50	2,100		
1996P	24,442,000	2	8	10	17	35	225		
1996D	24,744,000	2	7	10	17	35	950		
1997P	20,882,000	2	9	12	25	50	1,250		
1997D	19,876,000	2	9	13	25	60	1,750		
1998P	15,646,000	2	8	15	35	70	1,000		
1998D	15,064,000	2	8	11	20	60	2,750		
1999P	8,900,000	2	9	10	20	30	480	6,000	
1999D	10,682,000	2	7	10	16	23	1,500		
2000P	22,600,000	2	6	10	17	35	900		
2000D	19,466,000	2	6	9	20	40			
2001P	21,200,000	2	5	8	15	28	275	—	
2001D	19,504,000	2	5	8	13	28	365		
2002P (c)	3,100,000	2	5	8	15	30	300		
2002D (c)	2,500,000	2	5	8	20	40	1,750	6,500	
2003P (c)	2,500,000	2	5	8	20	30	1,650		
2003D (c)	2,500,000	2	5	8	16	25	2,000		
2004P (c)	2,900,000	2	5	8	17	30	1,500		
2004D (c)	2,900,000	2	5	8	16	25	750		
2005P, Brilliant (c)	3,800,000	3	10	18	25	38	750		
2005P, Satin (c)	1,160,000				10	12	20	62	$2,000
2005D, Brilliant (c)	3,500,000	3	9	15	23	35	1,175		
2005D, Satin (c)	1,160,000				15	18	80	500	
2006P, Brilliant (c)	2,400,000	2	6	9	22	26	525		
2006P, Satin (c)	847,000				12	22	48	300	
2006D, Brilliant (c)	2,000,000	2	5	7	15	28	750		
2006D, Satin (c)	847,000				10	18	45	525	
2007P, Brilliant (c)	2,400,000	2	4	6	11	17	350		
2007P, Satin (c)	649,000				8	10	30	175	
2007D, Brilliant (c)	2,400,000	2	4	6	15	30	2,000		
2007D, Satin (c)	649,000				7	8	48	175	5,000
2008P, Brilliant (c)	1,700,000	2	5	8	20	40	1,000		
2008P, Satin (c)	663,000				16	22	60	950	
2008D, Brilliant (c)	1,700,000	2	5	8	20	40	2,500		
2008D, Satin (c)	663,000				10	15	45	—	
2009P, Brilliant (c)	1,900,000	2	4	6	12	25	1,250		
2009P, Satin (c)	643,897				10	22	120	—	
2009D, Brilliant (c)	1,900,000	2	4	6	12	25	—		
2009D, Satin (c)	643,897				8	12	115	1,750	
2010P, Brilliant (c)	1,800,000	2	4	6	12	25	—		

. Minted for collectors only; not issued for circulation.

	Mintage	MS-63	MS-64	MS-65	MS-66	MS-67	MS-68	MS-69	MS-70
2010P, Satin (c)	 527,742				$10	$22	$30		
2010D, Brilliant (c)	1,700,000	$2	$4	$6	12	25	—		
2010D, Satin (c)	 527,742				10	22		—	
2011P (c)	1,750,000	2	4	6	12	25	—	—	
2011D (c)	1,700,000	2	4	6	12	25	—		
2012P (c)	1,800,000	2	4	6	12	25	—		
2012D (c)	1,700,000	2	4	6	12	25	—		
2013P (c)	5,000,000	2	4	6	12	25	—		
2013D (c)	4,600,000	2	4	6	12	25	—		
2014P (c)	2,500,000	2	4	6	12	25	—		
2014D (c)	2,100,000	2	4	6	12	25	—		
2015P (c)	2,300,000	2	4	6	12	25	—		
2015D (c)	2,300,000	2	4	6	12	25	—		
2016P (c)	....	2	4	6	12	25	—		
2016D (c)	....	2	4	6	12	25	—		
2017P (c)	....	2	4	6	12	25	—		
2017D (c)	....	2	4	6	12	25	—		

c. Minted for collectors only; not issued for circulation.

KENNEDY HALF DOLLARS: PROOF STRIKES

	Mintage	PF-65	PF-67Cam	PF-68DC	PF-69DC
1964, Type 2	 3,950,762	$15	$45	$200	$1,600
1964, Type 1, Accented Hair	............*	32	180	4,900	
1965, SMS (a)	 2,360,000	12	175		
1966, SMS (a)	 2,261,583	15	80		
1966, SMS, No FG (a)	................*				
1967, SMS (a)	 1,863,344	14	60		
1968S	 3,041,506	8	22	50	175
1969S	 2,934,631	8	23	45	135
1970S	 2,632,810	16	30	50	335
1971S	 3,220,733	5	20	90	1,200
1972S	 3,260,996	5	16	25	60
1973S	 2,760,339	4	16	25	50
1974S	 2,612,568	5	9	18	25
1976S	 7,059,099	5	13	20	25
1976S, Silver Clad (b)	.... *4,000,000*	10	15	25	35

* Included in number above. **a.** These coins are graded as Mint State. **b.** Mintage figures for 1976-S silver coins are approximate. Many were melted in 1982.

RECORD PRICES

The following are record prices paid for exceptional Franklin and Kennedy half dollars since publication of the second edition of *A Guide Book of Franklin and Kennedy Half Dollars* in 2012. Some of these coins were sold at auction and others in private transactions. (Several record prices dating from earlier years are also listed, with their dates in parentheses.)

FRANKLIN HALF DOLLARS

Date/Variety	Certification	Grade	Price	Transaction
1948	NGC	MS-68 STAR FBL	$50,000+	Private
1948-D	PCGS	MS-67 FBL	$19,975	Auction
1949	PCGS	MS-67 FBL	$12,925	Auction
1950	PCGS	PF-67+ CAMEO	$24,150	Auction
1950	PCGS	PF-68	$33,000	Private
1950	PCGS	PF-65 Deep Cameo	$27,000	Private
1950	PCGS	PF-66 Deep Cameo	$65,000	Private (2004)
1950	NGC	PF-66+ Ultra Cameo	$51,000	Private
1950	PCGS	MS-67 FBL	$28,000	Auction
1950-D	PCGS	MS-66+ FBL	$17,625	Auction
1951	PCGS	PF-67 Deep Cameo	$37,000	Private
1951	PCGS	MS-67 FBL	$18,800	Auction
1951-S	PCGS	MS-67 FBL	$30,550	Auction
1952	NGC	PF-68 Star Cameo	$29,000	Private
1952-S	PCGS	MS-67 FBL	$25,850	Auction
1953	NGC	PF-68 Ultra Cameo	$63,250	Auction (2006)
1953	PCGS	PF-68 Deep Cameo	$52,000	Private
1953	PCGS	MS-66+ FBL	$16,000	Private
1953-D	PCGS	MS-67 FBL	$33,000	Auction
1953-S	PCGS	MS-65+ FBL	$52,000	Private
1953-S	PCGS	MS-66 FBL	$69,000	Auction (2002)
1954-S	PCGS	MS-67 FBL	$21,000	Private
1955	PCGS	MS-67 FBL	$14,100	Auction
1955	PCGS	PF-68 Deep Cameo	$11,500	Private
1956, Type 1	PCGS	PF-68 Deep Cameo	$19,550	Auction
1957	NGC	PF-69 Ultra Cameo	$17,000	Private
1958	PCGS	MS-67 FBL	$15,275	Auction
1958	PCGS	PF-68 Deep Cameo	$27,000	Private
1958-D	PCGS	MS-67 FBL	$11,000	Private (2007)
1959	NGC	PF-69 Cameo	$19,000	Private
1960	PCGS	MS-67 FBL	$28,200	Auction
1960	PCGS	PF-69 Deep Cameo	$27,600	Auction (2008)
1960	PCGS	MS-65 FBL	$11,000	Private

Date/Variety	Certification	Grade	Price	Transaction
1960-D . . . . PCGS		MS-67 FBL	$27,000	Private
1961 . . . . PCGS		PF-69 Deep Cameo	$27,600	Auction
1961, Doubled-Die Rev . . . . NGC		PF-68	$23,000	Private
1962 . . . . PCGS		MS-66 FBL	$17,000	Private
1963 . . . . PCGS		MS-66 FBL	$28,200	Auction
1963-D . . . . NGC		MS-67 FBL	$22,000	Private

KENNEDY HALF DOLLARS

Date/Variety	Certification	Grade	Price	Transaction
1964 . . . . NGC		MS-67	$3,055	Auction
1964, SMS . . . . PCGS		MS-67	$54,000	Auction
1964 . . . . PCGS		PF-70	$9,400	Auction
1964, Accent Hair . . . . PCGS		PF-68 DCAM	$19,975	Auction
1964, Accent Hair . . . . NGC		PF-69 Ultra	$37,000	Private
1964-D . . . . NGC		MS-65 PL	$3,290	Auction
1964-D . . . . PCGS		MS-68	$23,000	Auction
1965, SMS . . . . NGC		MS-68 Ultra	$25,000	Private
1965, SMS . . . . PCGS		MS-67 DCAM	$12,650	Auction
1966 . . . . PCGS		MS-67	$9,987	Auction
1966, SMS . . . . PCGS		MS-67 DCAM	$3,220	Auction
1966, SMS . . . . PCGS		MS-68 DCAM	$16,450	Auction
1967, SMS . . . . PCGS		MS-68 DCAM	$17,625	Auction
1968-S . . . . PCGS		PF-70 DCAM	$10,575	Auction
1969-S . . . . NGC		PF-69 STAR ULTRACAM	$3,600	Private
1974 . . . . PCGS		MS-67	$3,290	Auction
1974-S . . . . PCGS		PF-70 DCAM	$7,931	Auction
1976-S, Silver . . . . PCGS		PF-70 DCAM	$2,760	Auction (2011)
1976-S, Clad . . . . PCGS		PF-70 DCAM	$3,290	Auction (2011)
1980-D . . . . PCGS		MS-68	$4,935	Auction
1982, No FG . . . . PCGS		MS-67	$2,820	Auction
1982-D . . . . PCGS		MS-67+	$3,525	Auction
1983-D . . . . PCGS		MS-68	$4,230	Auction
1984-D . . . . PCGS		MS-67+	$3,760	Auction
1987 . . . . PCGS		MS-68	$3,290	Auction

APPENDIX

PROOF LIBERTY WALKING HALF DOLLARS

Why did I include this appendix on Proof Liberty Walking half dollars, in a book devoted to Franklin and Kennedy half dollars?

I thought about this a long time.

First of all, they were the Proof half dollars that immediately preceded the Proof Franklin series. Many of the minting and packaging technologies used during the Proof Franklin era found their origins in those of the Proof Liberty Walking half dollar series. I have always thought of the two series as being related in that respect.

For the first time in its history of offering Proof coins to the public (1858 was the first year), the U.S. Mint saw serious increases in demand during the Proof Liberty Walking era. During the preceding Barber half dollar era, the typical Proof mintage for any given year was 500 to 1,000 coins. The final year of Liberty Walking Proofs saw more than 21,000 minted.

Second, the Proof Liberty Walking half dollars comprise a very short series. It's a great collector series! Though circulation-strike Liberty Walking half dollars had been minted since 1916, the Proofs weren't struck until 1936, and then they were discontinued prematurely after the 1942 production because of World War II. They were only struck for seven years.

For such a short series, it's impractical to write a whole book on so few coins!

The bottom line is that very little has been written on the Proof Liberty Walking half dollar series—certainly nothing covering these coins in a date-by-date analysis with high-quality pictures of finer known examples. And that is a shame, because they are such beautiful coins, true classics born during that wonderful Renaissance era in American coin design.

I see this series as a real opportunity for the collector of today. These beautiful Proof coins, *when found in their most pristine as-struck condition*, should be far more popular than they are today. I believe that, as with the Proof and Mint State Franklin and Kennedy half dollars, all that is about to change with the dissemination of information— beginning with this book!

This is a short appendix. This series deserves so much more. But I believe if you have never had the opportunity to learn about these rare and undervalued Proof coins, this section will provide much-needed insights.

1936 LIBERTY WALKING PROOF

PF-67

While circulation-strike Liberty Walking half dollars had been made since 1916, the first year of the series' Proof coinage was 1936.

The 1936 is the lowest-mintage issue of the series' Proofs. *A mere 3,901 examples were struck!* By previous production standards for the Liberty Seated and Barber half dollar series, from the 1850s to 1915, this was a high number; typically during those decades the Mint would issue only about 1,000 coins in a year!

As a point of interest, beginning in 1950 the Mint began to offer Proof coins only in complete sets that included the cent, nickel, dime, quarter, and half dollar. Prior to 1950, during the era of the Proof Liberty Walking half dollar, such was not the case. Collectors could order their coins individually, or buy all five issues. Typically the denomination the Mint received the most orders for was the Lincoln cent.

I have always thought of the Liberty Walking Proof half series as the U.S. Mint's entry into the modern era of Proof-making. Proof production for the Liberty Walking half dollar increased every year from 1936, with 3,901 coins, to the final year of 1942, when 21,120 were issued. The hobby of numismatics, once referred to as the "hobby of kings," began to experience significant growth in popularity among the middle class as economic prosperity slowly spread throughout the land during the era of the Proof Liberty Walking half dollar.

As the first year of issue, the 1936 is the king of Proof half dollars struck from 1936 to present, in terms of its rarity in superb gem condition. Hairlines pose the greatest problem, as the packaging used for shipping during this era was wholly inadequate (as it would later be during much of the Proof Franklin era!).

There are two primary characteristics I look for when acquiring Proof Liberty Walking half dollars: condition and eye appeal. I seek coins with relatively few hairlines, which grade at least Proof-64, and with no distracting spots or hazy toned fields.

Eye appeal is pretty simple: in my opinion the Proof Walkers with the greatest potential are those examples that represent the earliest strikes off new Proof dies, and have been preserved over the decades in a manner in which those deep-mirrored surfaces remain with their original brilliance and beauty!

The 1936 is extremely challenging in this respect. A quantity of 3,901 examples were struck. This was a much higher production total than previous Proof half dollar issues. Many 1936 Proof Walkers were struck from dies that were obviously quite worn, as even untoned examples can exhibit rather shallow mirrors, almost giving them the appearance of a Mint State circulation strike (much like some of the 1950 and 1951 Proof Franklins).

And then there is the method in which the Mint chose to package these delicate Proof coins. For much of this era, the packaging used was very similar to that used during the early Franklin years: brittle cellophane envelopes wrapped in tissue paper, and placed in a small cardboard box. Proof Walkers stored in this original packaging for a length of time typically develop a heavy, opaque, cloudy toning that totally obscures whatever deep Proof surface the coin may have originally exhibited.

Very few PF-65 and higher-grade 1936 Proof Walkers have survived without the aforementioned issues. Most examples either are late strikes with shallow mirrors, or exhibit the mottled haze so typical for the series.

PF-64–PF-66. As of our press date, 1,526 Proof Liberty Walking half dollars of 1936 have been certified in PF-65 or PF-66 by NGC and PCGS. *Perhaps only 5% exhibit the early-strike, clearly mirrored fields illustrated here.* Occasionally you can find one with some cameo contrast, though to date no 1936 Walker has been certified "Cameo."

Valuation—**PF-64** examples can be acquired for around $2,000 to $3,000. Average-eye appeal examples with the aforementioned opaque toning and/or shallow mirrors in **PF-65** and **PF-66** can be acquired in the $3,000 to $6,000 range. On the other hand, I would gladly pay double those numbers for superb deeply mirrored specimens with some cameo contrast! I am fortunate to get offered one per year.

PF-67 and higher. 134 have been certified in PF-67 and a single solitary example has been certified in PF-68. Most of these high-grade examples exhibit eye appeal no better than that of the typical survivor, with hazy-toned surfaces and shallow mirrors. Perhaps 10% to 15% of the certified PF-67 specimens exhibit superior eye appeal, deeply mirrored and problem-free. The finest example I have handled was certified by NGC as PF-67 Star, as the fields were crystal clear and deep as the day it was struck, with appreciable lovely cameo contrast on obverse and reverse. This was one of the few early strikes to survive exhibiting the original "as struck" beauty the Mint worked so hard to create! If only there were a few more survivors.

Valuation—I have seen a couple examples in PF-67 sell for as little as $6,000—a surprisingly low price for a Proof half dollar so rare. Then again, one has to consider the eye appeal of these "bargain" coins. Despite the PF-67 grade they were unattractive coins, their original Proof surfaces layered with grey/brown mottled toning. The finer deeply mirrored examples, featuring haze-free surfaces and some attractive cameo contrast, are far more valuable. The coin pictured above was acquired by me around 2016 for $16,000. Considering there was a time around 2001 or 2002 when unattractive PF-67 examples were selling for $15,000 to $30,000, superb deeply mirrored PF-67 Walkers at current levels, given their much greater condition rarity and their superior eye appeal, are in my opinion a real bargain at today's price levels.

1937 LIBERTY WALKING PROOF

PF-68

Production saw an increase to 5,728 coins in 1937. While this was an increase over the first year of issue, all Liberty Walking Proof mintages are incredibly low when compared to the mintages of today. When you then factor in the technology of the 1930s, and the poor packaging materials used by the Mint for shipment, it becomes easy to understand why these coins are so very rare in truly superb deeply mirrored Proof condition.

I love this date. It's a real sleeper! The quality of the 1937 is slightly improved over that of the first year of issue.

PF-65–PF-66. There have been 788 certifications in PF-65 and PF-66 by NGC and PCGS combined. As with the 1936, most examples are quite unappealing, featuring the usual unattractive toning, and most having been struck from worn dies resulting in coins with very shallow mirrors.

Valuation—The typical shallow mirrored or toned examples can currently be acquired for as little as $800 to $1,800 in **PF-65** to **PF-66** condition. I would gladly pay double for exceptional deeply mirrored 1937 Walkers with noticeable cameo contrast! Such survivors are *extremely rare*. They are beautiful!

PF-67–PF-68. 558 Walkers of 1937 have been certified in PF-67 and PF-68. Of these, 39 are PF-68s. There are no PF-69s. Perhaps 15% to 20% of this small quantity are early strikes that have survived in their original "as struck" look. Many of these are later strikes off the die, with very shallow mirrors. Very early strikes, with deep mirrors, even with a hint of cameo contrast, probably represent only 5% to 10% of the above populations. In other words, perhaps 30 to 60 Walkers of 1937 exist in virtually flawless condition, ranking among the earliest strikes, having also survived decades of storage to miraculously appear today as if they just came off the die!

Valuation—For a coin this rare in **PF-67**, with this *minuscule* mintage, one would think it would command more than $1,500 to $2,500 (what the majority of PF-67 specimens sell for), but the market is understandable given their fair eye appeal—the lackluster toning that obscures their original Proof brilliance. The few **PF-68** coins certified have sold for around $10,000—again, in average condition.

On the other hand, I have regularly paid double those figures and more for 1937 Proof Walkers in PF-67 and PF-68 that rank among the earliest die strikes, and that have been preserved in a manner where their magnificent deeply mirrored fields, complemented by a surprising dash of lovely cameo contrast, appeal to the viewer's eye.

1938 Liberty Walking Proof

PF-67★

There was another increase in Proof production in 1938, to a grand total of 8,152 coins. Imagine if a Kennedy half dollar Proof were released by the Mint today with only 8,000 examples struck! It would cost thousands of dollars as Kennedy collectors scramble to own one of the few. And consider: of those hypothetical 8,000 Kennedy half dollars, 7,995 would likely certify as PF-68 or higher. Most would be PF-69 or PF-70!

Despite their atrociously poor packaging, a small group of 1938 Proof Walkers have survived that are among the finest in the series. After two years of practice, the Mint's art of die preparation saw dramatic improvements. Many of these survivors display a surprising degree of cameo frost, contrasted against extraordinarily deep mirrored fields. A couple of these examples have actually received a Cameo designation.

Regarding the Cameo designation on Proof Walkers, there are many examples of the series I have handled that I felt deserved this designation. Both Miss Liberty on the obverse and the eagle on the reverse would display a high degree of cameo frost. However, the one portion of the device that typically would not have cameo frost was the sun, on the obverse. While it is my opinion that this small portion of a small obverse device should not be a determining factor regarding the Cameo designation, the grading services have a different opinion. Nevertheless, these phenomenal examples featuring a beautiful frosted portrait of Lady Liberty on the obverse and the American eagle on the reverse obviously rank among the most beautiful Proof Walkers in existence, and are obviously worth a significant premium over the typical shallow-mirrored variety.

PF-65–PF-66. Despite a small mintage of only 8,152 coins, 2,468 examples have been certified in PF-65 or PF-66 at the time of publication. As with all Walkers in the series, most are either heavily toned from decades of poor storage or very shallow mirrored. On the positive side, perhaps as many as 10% of the PF-65 and PF-66 examples have survived with very deep mirrors and light cameo contrast. This would translate to 70 to 100 examples—a very small number of coins!

Valuation—Toned examples trade in the $800 to $1,500 range; deeply mirrored examples may trade for $1,000 to $2,500.

PF-67–PF-68. A surprising number have been certified in PF-67 and PF-68: 533 in 67, and 74 in 68! None have graded higher.

Valuation—On occasion I have handled a spectacular **PF-67** 1938 Walker, including one that I have paid $6,500 for. It featured incredibly deep, "black" mirrored fields, and a surprisingly high degree of cameo contrast on obverse and reverse. This coin subsequently sold for $7,000. Some of the finest 1938 Proof Walkers are "Star"-designated coins graded by NGC. (The NGC Star designation is given to coins that exhibit exceptional eye appeal for their date and grade. Many times a coin will receive a star if it exhibits exceptional multi-colored toning. In the case of the Proof Walkers, on very rare occasions NGC will give the star for an example with very deeply mirrored fields and attractive frosted cameo devices. Star-designated Proof Walkers are *extremely rare*, and are usually worth a considerable premium!

There are six examples that have been certified in Cameo! One of these was a magnificent PF-67—one of only two Proof Walkers in the entire series to receive this grade in Cameo.

The typical hazy-toned or shallow-mirrored **PF-67** 1938 Walker may sell for as little as $1,500.

In **PF-68**, 1938 Walkers with average eye appeal typically sell in the $5,000 to $8,000 range. The finer known deeply mirrored wonder-coins exhibiting modest cameo contrast have been known to sell for upward of $15,000! In my opinion, these are actually something of a bargain. Very few such coins exist.

Putting a price on the Cameo-graded specimens is difficult, as it has been years since such a coin has appeared on the market. I do recall a fabulous PF-66 Cameo I placed with a client many years ago for around $8,000. This gorgeous Proof Walker would likely command far more today.

1939 LIBERTY WALKING PROOF

PF-68

There was only a very modest increase in Proof production in 1939, with 8,808 examples struck. This would be the final year that Proof mintage for the Liberty Walking half dollar was under 10,000 coins.

As with all Proof Liberty Walking half dollar dates, the great majority have appreciable toning that diminishes the original brilliant deep-mirrored Proof surfaces.

On occasion a clear-mirrored early strike will surface, and these rank among the most attractive coins in the series. A handful of examples have received NGC's coveted Star designation. Some of these Star coins exhibit lovely cameo contrast, and others display attractive color toning. Again, eye appeal is the factor determining whether a coin receives NGC's star. At this time, two 1939 Proof Walkers have even been certified in Cameo—one PF-64, and one PF-65!

PF-65–PF-66. 2,720 examples have been certified in PF-65 or PF-66 to date. Only about 10% to 15% exhibit the original as-struck deep-mirrored surfaces. On the positive side, many of this group, perhaps 200 to 300 coins, also display some attractive cameo contrast!

Valuation—**PF-65** and **PF-66** 1939 Walkers can be acquired for under $1,000—a great price no matter the eye appeal, for a coin with a total of less than 10,000 minted. Very attractive deep-mirrored specimens can be acquired for little more: $1,000 to $1,500.

PF-67–PF-69. At this writing, 799 1939 Walkers have been certified in PF-67, and 141 in PF-68, and 1 in PF-69! The lone PF-69 was an example I sold to a client 15 or 20 years ago. He has since passed away, and I sadly have not been able to track this coin down.

Valuation—Go after those lovely deeply mirrored coins with some of that gorgeous cameo contrast. They are a great buy at current levels: $2,000 to $3,500 for the occasionally seen **PF-67**. In **PF-68**, the price will be about double those numbers. These coins are getting more difficult to locate by the year. Get 'em while you can!

1940 LIBERTY WALKING PROOF

PF-68

For the first time in the Liberty Walking Proof series, in 1940 Mint production crept over the 10,000 mark. A total of 11,279 1940 Proof Walkers were struck. Although this was a record high for the time, by modern standards, if the Mint limited a modern Proof Kennedy issue to only 50,000 coins there would be a stampede to acquire the coin!   It's about time the Proof Walkers received the same level of interest, and more. Unlike the modern Proof Kennedy half dollars (those struck in the 1980s and later), so few of these tiny Proof Walker mintages have survived in attractive conditions.

PF-65–PF-66. In terms of eye appeal, the 1940 ranks among the toughest dates to locate in the series. 3,089 have been certified in PF-65 and PF-66. I would estimate 95% have either very shallow mirrors or unattractive toning. Deeply mirrored examples are few and far between. Specimens with a touch of cameo contrast are rarer still. Perhaps 5% of the 3,089 examples certified exhibit these most desired qualities.

Valuation—Most 1940 Proof Walkers in **PF-65** and **PF-66** can be acquired for less than $1,000. If you do happen across a very deeply mirrored specimen, with some cameo effect . . . buy it! I would go up to $2,000 for such a coin.

PF-67–PF-68. The 1940 is considerably tougher to locate in PF-67 and PF-68 than the previous year, 1939. Only 733 have been certified in PF-67, and 93 in PF-68. Though these coins are of higher grade than PF-65s, they are generally no more attractive. The 1940 must be considered a key acquisition when you can locate a true deep-mirror specimen in these higher grades!

Valuation—If you are looking for an attractive 1940 in **PF-67**, I would pay up to $3,000 for the right coin. I have seen only a few 1940 Walkers in **PF-68** that exhibited deep mirrored surfaces with any cameo contrast. The last example sold for $7,500.

1941 LIBERTY WALKING PROOF

With AW, PF-68

No AW, PF-68

A mere (small by modern standards) 15,412 Proof Liberty Walking half dollars were struck in 1941. This is a very interesting date, as there is a most popular variety, noted as the No AW. Normally on the reverse of a Liberty Walking half dollar, from the original master die, can be found the initials AW for Adolph Weinman at about 5 o'clock, by the rim. All Proof Liberty Walking half dollars bear these initials, except for those struck from one or two 1941 working dies which did not have the initials!

Why no initials? One of the die-maintenance procedures at the U.S. Mint throughout its history involved routine inspection of the dies during the course of operation. Typically when wear or slight damage became evident on a die, it would be removed for re-polishing of the surfaces. On rare occasions, a die would be over-polished, and some of the least recessed design details might be accidentally polished away. The 1937-D Three-Legged Buffalo nickel is an example of a coin struck from an over-polished die, where one of the legs of the buffalo disappeared from over-polishing of the die. Another example is the 1966 No FG Kennedy half dollar, where the initials of the designer, Frank Gasparro, no longer appear on the reverse. The 1941 No AW Proof Liberty Walking half dollar is another example.

No one knows the exact mintages for these varieties, as they are a type of mint error. If I had to make an estimate, after studying the Proof Liberty Walking series over the past 30 years, I would estimate 15% to 20% were struck without the AW initials. There are many more that have the remnants of the initials, but to qualify as a No AW and be certified as such by NGC, there can be no remnants of the original initials.

There was an improvement in quality for the Proofs of 1941 over those of 1940. A higher percentage of both varieties of 1941 can be found with deeply mirrored fields—perhaps 20% of surviving specimens of both the With AW and No AW varieties exhibit such fields, as struck. However, cameo-contrasted examples are few! Deeply mirrored 1941 Proof Walkers that also exhibit some cameo contrast on both obverse and reverse rarely surface. Given that the No AW represents only an estimated 15% to 20% of the total Proof mintage, this variety is especially rare.

At the time of this writing, NGC recognizes the With AW variety on the holder, and PCGS does not.

PF-65–PF-66. 4,135 have been certified of the With AW in PF-65 and PF-66; 303 of the No AW (these are, of course, all NGC coins). The noted With AW numbers do not account for the fact that many PCGS-certified 1941 Proof Walkers may be of the No AW variety, but not so recognized on the holder!

Valuation—Unattractively toned 1941 **PF-65** and **PF-66** Walkers of the With AW variety can be acquired for as little as $500 to $700. Currently, the No AW can be acquired for little more! That will surely change in the years ahead, as more collectors become aware of this highly desirable variety.

PF-67–PF-69. In PF-67, a total of 730 of the With AW have been certified, and 124 of the No AW. In PF-68, 83 of the With AW have been certified, and 25 of the No AW. There is 1 example certified in PF-69. It is the With AW variety. It is toned.

The 1941 Proof Walker in both varieties can be located in PF-67 without too much difficulty, but nearly all specimens display the usual hazy toned surfaces. Beautiful deeply mirrored examples with a hint of cameo contrast are very rare. They are especially rare in No AW. Only a handful of examples exist in both varieties in deeply mirrored PF-68!

Valuation—Unattractive PF-67 examples can be acquired for as little as $1,000 to $1,500 in either variety. Hold out for one of the few beautiful deep mirrors, especially if it exhibits some cameo. These are very rare! The finest PF-67 examples, with very deep mirrored fields and some attractive cameo contrast, have sold for more than $4,000. A couple examples in PF-68 have sold for more than $10,000!

1942 LIBERTY WALKING PROOF

PF-68

While the circulation-strike Liberty Walking half dollar series would continue for another several years, its last year of production being 1947, the final year for the Proof coins would be 1942. The Mint temporarily halted Proof production with the onset of World War II, and would not resume the making of Proof coins until 1950.

21,120 Proof Liberty Walking half dollars were struck in 1942. This was the high point for mintages of this short-lived series, and it also represented the zenith in quality!

The 1942 Proof Walker is generally speaking easily the highest-quality date of the series. A large percentage of surviving specimens are of gem quality, with a comparatively large percentage also reaching the highest grades of PF-67, 68, and 69.

Additionally, of these superb gem specimens, possibly as many as 20% may be of deep-mirrored quality, displaying some attractive cameo contrast as well!

PF-65–PF-66. To date, 5,919 Walkers of 1942 have been certified in PF-65 and 66. If the estimated 20% exhibit early–strike, untoned, deep-mirrored fields and a modicum of cameo contrast, that equates to approximately 1,000 to 1,500 coins! This is the highest population in the series. Comparatively speaking, though, this is still a very rare coin!

Valuation—You can acquire lovely deeply mirrored cameo-contrasted pieces for as little as $600 to $1,000. This is truly a great time to begin building that Proof Liberty Walking half dollar collection!

PF-67–PF-69. A surprisingly high number of 1942 Proof Walkers have been certified in the highest PF-67 to PF-69 levels. To date, 1,834 coins have been certified in PF-67, 251 in PF-68, and 9 in PF-69! These highest PF-68 and PF-69 grade populations surpass those of the early Franklin years. The 1950, 1951, 1952, and 1953 Franklins do not even come close to these totals, though they have higher mintages. The reasons why this is so is covered in the section on Proof Franklin half dollars.

Additionally, nine 1942 Proof Walkers have been certified in Cameo! Quite amazing, when you consider the Proof Liberty Walking half dollar dies did not receive the same acid-dipping procedure to create the cameo effect as did Proof coins of the 1950s through the early 1970s. The highest-grade Cameo 1942, a PF-67, belongs to a client of mine who owns one of the finest known Proof Liberty Walking half dollar collections. His 1936 is a PF-67 Star—an extraordinarily deep-mirrored specimen with gorgeous cameo contrast as well!

Valuation—The typical shallow-mirrored or toned 1942 Proof can be acquired for under $1,000. Of the approximately 200 examples estimated to exist in **PF-67** with deep mirrors and cameo contrast, these far more attractive specimens can be acquired for little more, usually in the $900 to $2,000 range. These represent a great value for this undervalued rarity!

Superb deeply mirrored cameo **PF-68s** I regard as a real bargain. Far fewer than 100 such coins exist, and they can currently be acquired for as little as $2,500 to $5,000. I was the underbidder on a beautiful 1942 in PF-68 Star that eventually sold for almost $15,000. **PF-69s** have sold for more than $30,000. The examples I have seen were toned.

The 1942 PF-67 Cameo was sold to my client about 10 years ago for more than $20,000.

EXCEPTIONAL CAMEO CONTRAST

For those who are unfamiliar, let me give you a brief background of cameo grading history. After the publication of my first book, *Cameo and Brilliant Proof Coinage of the 1950 to 1970 Era* (in late 1991), I sat down with David Hall, then president of PCGS, and we hammered out grading standards for Proof and Special Mint Set coins that were cameo-contrasted. Up until then, all PCGS had for Proof coins was the numeric grade, with no recognition regarding the fact that the coin was cameo. NGC, on the other hand, only had a Cameo designation, adopted in the late 1980s through some lobbying I had done in association with one of their graders at the time.

As one of the original architects of these grading standards, over the last few years I've felt compelled to weigh in again. After much thought, I decided to release a seal of Exceptional Cameo Contrast, reserved for those coins that I feel display only heavier levels of cameo contrast for their date and designation.

As all cameo collectors understand through experience, there can be a huge difference in cameo contrast between two coins of the exact same grade. Take a look at these two Kennedy half dollars, for example:

Coins without (left) and with (right) exceptional cameo contrast.
Note that although the reverses are not illustrated, coins must have
Cameo or Ultra / Deep Cameo mirrors to be considered for ECC selection.

While both coins received the exact same grade from the same grading service, it should be clear that there is a huge objective difference in the cameo contrast between them. The coin on the left is on the lower end of the Deep / Ultra Cameo standard, while the coin on the right is at the very top end. In this example there is a huge qualitative difference in eye appeal and cameo contrast between these two coins. This can often be the case with cameo-contrasted coins. Because of these differences, I've had many clients asking me to start my own grading service for cameo coins.

Because of my unique position, due in part to my help in the creation of the cameo grading standard and the sheer number of cameo coins I have handled over the years, I concluded the time was right for a personal endorsement seal of Exceptional Cameo Contrast (ECC selection). Only coins with exceptional obverse and reverse cameo contrast will make the cut for the ECC selection.

The ECC seal.

Both of the 1961 Franklins illustrated here have received the same grade of PF-68 Cameo from one of the two major grading services, NGC or PCGS, but they have significant differences in eye appeal. If you refer to my Cameo grading set, the coin on the left falls into the Cameo Minus category, while the coin on the right falls into the Cameo Plus category.

Two 1961 Franklin half dollars, each graded PF-68 by the same professional grading service.

Due to the myriad of differences for every date and designation, each coin has been personally selected by me, with only the finest-quality cameo examples receiving my ECC Selection. As I've said many times: "Buy the coin, not the holder." While in practice this may not always be possible, I feel that my selection and certification of exceptional cameo contrast gives you, as the collector, peace of mind that you are receiving some of the highest levels of cameo contrast and eye appeal available for each date and grade.

APPENDIX

REMARKABLE FRANKLIN AND KENNEDY HALF DOLLAR ERRORS

"*Errare humanum est*," wrote Richard G. Doty, curator of the Smithsonian's National Numismatic Collection, in his foreword to the book *100 Greatest U.S. Error Coins*. "To err is human. Errors on coins have been around as long as coinage itself. The reason is simple. Coinage is an industrial process, and coins were the first mass-produced objects in human history. Mass production of anything involves a number of simple, repetitive steps. During each of these steps, something can go wrong. Given the nature of human endeavor as summed up by Murphy's Law, something *will* go wrong, even if the manufacturing process is simple, requiring few steps for its completion. And the more sophisticated production becomes, the more individual steps it involves, the greater the potential for error. This is as true for coinage as it is for any other human product."

This appendix explores some of the most fascinating error and misstruck Franklin and Kennedy half dollars. As outlandish as they may seem, they are all real coins—each was personally examined by error-coin experts Nicholas P. Brown, David J. Camire, and Fred Weinberg as they wrote their book *100 Greatest U.S. Error Coins*. "In selecting the coins for this book," they said, "we felt it was crucial to have each in our possession to be able to confirm that it actually exists, to ensure the authenticity of each error coin being considered, and to capture high-resolution photographs."

PRICING ERROR COINS

It is challenging to price error coins, since many are considered to be unique and many trade privately. The factors in determining error-coin values are similar to those that determine the price for non-error coins, with some important distinctions. Brown, Camire, and Weinberg describe them thus:

- The "wow" factor. How excited does someone get viewing the coin? Error coins are often dramatic. The more dramatic an error, the higher the price usually is for the coin. It bodes well when someone says, "I have never seen this coin before." Even better is when someone says, "I never knew a coin like this existed."

- Rarity. How rare is the error? How many coins are known of its type and of the series? Is it the only known of that date? Does it even have a date? Is it the farthest off center? The list of qualities that can make an error coin unique is nearly endless. Rarity definitely plays a key role in determining the price.

- What is the condition of the coin? How much detail can be seen, and how well preserved is it? This is no less important a consideration for an error coin than for a regular coin.

- The popularity of a series is also an important factor in determining the price of an error coin.

A GALLERY OF REMARKABLE FRANKLIN AND KENNEDY HALF DOLLAR ERRORS

1965 Kennedy half dollar die cap. Instead of being ejected after being struck in the coining press, this half dollar was struck twice, essentially becoming a "die" itself, which caused the coin to spread out and split apart.

Kennedy half dollar die cap.

Undated Kennedy half dollar off-center mirror reverse brockage. A brockage is a mirror image of a coin's design impressed on the opposite side of the same planchet. This error was caused when the struck coin remained in the die after striking, impressing its image into the next blank planchet as it was struck, leaving a negative or mirror image. Off-center brockage coins are typically worth less than those with a full impression—but this still makes a visually intriguing coin. Its retail value is about $300.

Kennedy half dollar off-center mirror reverse brockage.

Off-center Kennedy half dollars. The 1995 coin, minted in Denver, was struck out its collar and incorrectly centered, with part of its design missing. Off-center coins with a readable date and mintmark are among the most valuable. This example is worth about $250.

Off-center Kennedy half dollar with a readable date and mintmark (1995-D).

Off-center Kennedy half dollar with its date missing.

Franklin half dollar struck on a dime planchet. An unusual error like this one can be valued up to $6,000.

Franklin half dollar struck on a dime planchet.

1951-D off-center Franklin half dollar. The Franklin half dollar is considered one of the scarcest 20th-century series for major mechanical errors. Off-center strikes are scarce, with fewer than a dozen known. This example is the only known from the Denver Mint. Used in the late 1990s as the *Guide Book of United States Coins* plate coin to illustrate misstrikes, it is graded MS-63, and was estimated to be worth $15,000 in 2010, when it was ranked no. 47 among the *100 Greatest U.S. Error Coins*.

Off-center Franklin half dollar (1951-D).

(1948) Franklin half dollar struck on a 1948 Lincoln cent. This first-year-of-issue Franklin half dollar was struck on a previously struck 1948 Lincoln cent. (It is assumed the half dollar is dated 1948, although the date does not appear on the coin.) Only four or so Franklin half dollars are known struck on struck cents. In this example, all of the details of the obverse undertype (the date, LIBERTY, the motto, and Lincoln's portrait) are visible. The reverse shows similar detail with visible wheat stalks and mottoes. It was ranked as no. 58 among the *100 Greatest U.S. Error Coins* in 2010, at which time it was valued up to $25,000.

Franklin half dollar struck on a Lincoln cent.

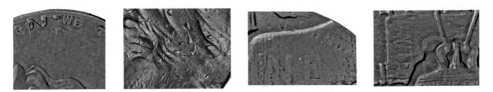

Details of the cent's design under the half dollar striking.

Franklin half dollars struck on wrong planchets. The first coin pictured here is from the Smithsonian Institution's National Numismatic Collection in Washington, D.C.—a unique example of a Franklin half dollar struck on a dime planchet, off center. It was ranked no. 62 among the *100 Greatest U.S. Error Coins* in 2010, at which time it was valued (in theory, since none of the Smithsonian's coins are for sale) at $20,000. There are fewer than a dozen Franklin half dollars known to be struck on dime planchets, and this is the only one struck off center.

Also pictured is a Franklin half dollar struck on a Washington quarter planchet.

Franklin half dollar struck off center on a dime planchet.

Franklin half dollar struck on a quarter dollar planchet.

Kennedy half dollar bow-tie scrap. After coinage blanks are punched out of a long coiled strip of the proper metal composition, that punched strip is fed into a machine and chopped into small pieces of scrap webbing to be melted and processed into another coil. These small chopped pieces can be bow-tie–shaped, the result of two holes being punched on either side of the chopped fragment. This phenomenon is explained in appendix A of *100 Greatest U.S. Error Coins*. Somehow, this error was created when a piece of scrap found its way into a coinage press and was struck as a coin. Its value was estimated in 2010 as $3,500 to $5,000.

Kennedy half dollar bow-tie scrap.

CREDITS AND ACKNOWLEDGMENTS

I would like to acknowledge the contributions of the following individuals in the team effort required for this project:

Sasha Bivin   Trish Portella-Wright
Jim Capper   Gary Tomaska
David W. Lange   Ron Workman
Brett Parrish

Thanks to Caitlin Tomaska for photography and to Mike Cannavino for research.

Alan Hager provided extensive support in editing and gathering data for the section on circulation-strike Kennedy halves, and provided several coins for photography in the first edition. Sean Couch provided additional new photography for the second edition. The Franklin and Kennedy half dollars pictured in the pages of this book and on the cover represent many of the very finest known examples from both series.

A very special "thank you" to the following individuals, who donated their coins for photography. Their contribution to numismatics will be appreciated by generations of collectors to follow!

Norm Aronfeld   Eddie Gerson   Paul Pelland
Brett Benham   Steve Heller   Bob Rosenthal
Stephen Borowko   Thomas Henderson   Larry Starkey
Steve Buford   John Hollow   Marshall Turner
Ray Daniels   "Little Jeffrey"   Donald Twito
Mark Dixon   Don Koziak   Erik Vitols
Alfred Dunatte   Tim Krajewski   West Park Collection
Russ Folkvord   Richard Lee
Helen Gates-Kirk   Graham Napier

A special "thank you" to the Mint personnel who provided invaluable insights into the Proof-making process:

- Mike Allphin: pressroom branch foreman, chief of coining division (1965–1995)
- Ed Fulwider: die setter trainee, die setter, senior die setter, work leader for Proof packaging (1966–1987)
- Mark Layfield: press operator, coin support branch foreman (1966–1996)
- Don Weaver: press operator, general foreman, production controller, chief of coining division (1960–1990)

Thanks also to the professional grading services. Without the contributions of PCGS and NGC in validating the rarity of Franklin and Kennedy half dollars in their finer Mint State and Proof condition, there would still be some dealers today claiming that no rarities were struck after World War II, as was the case back in the 1980s.

ABOUT THE AUTHOR

If you have ever seen or owned a Proof or Special Mint Set U.S. coin graded by PCGS that is designated cameo or deep cameo, or an NGC coin with the ultra cameo designation, the origins of those grades go back to Rick Tomaska's first book, published in 1991, *Cameo and Brilliant Proof Coinage of the 1950 to 1970 Era*.

Before that book there were no cameo and deep cameo designations for Proof coins on PCGS holders. There was no ultra cameo designation on NGC holders. There was only the Proof grade, with no reference to the coin's possible cameo contrast.

It was after publication of that book that Rick approached David Hall, then president of PCGS, to discuss the implementation of cameo designations for Proof coins. That was in early 1992. David Hall adopted his suggestions, and the rest, as they say, is history.

Immediately following this, he did the same with NGC. (NGC had instituted a "cameo" designation in the late 1980s, on Rick's advice, with the assistance of Yitzak Gedolowitz, a grader at NGC at that time.)

Six years later Rick published his second book, *The Complete Guide to Franklin Half Dollars*. Upon the publication of that book, he conferred with both PCGS and NGC on establishing a "Full Bell Line" (FBL) designation for Mint State Franklin series, which both services subsequently adopted. Rick has also been instrumental in assisting both organizations in designing the PCGS and NGC set registries.

In addition to his books, he has contributed articles to *The Numismatist* (receiving the Wayte and Olga Raymond Memorial Award for Distinguished Numismatic Achievement), *Numismatic News*, *Coin World*, *COINage*, *Coins*, and PCGS. He was honored to be among a handful of dealers asked by PCGS to contribute to their encyclopedia of U.S. coinage, for which he offered his expertise on cameo Proof coinage.

This book was the first published by Whitman devoted solely to the Franklin and Kennedy half dollars—two very important and increasingly popular collector series. More collector sets of Franklin and Kennedy half dollars listed in the NGC and PCGS set registries than any other half dollar series in U.S. numismatics.

Rick is proud of the fact that his company currently has over 240 clients with collections ranking among the finest known in both the NGC and PCGS set registries.

Today, Rick actively works with the PCGS Price Guide, NumisMedia, and Coin Values in setting accurate values for U.S. Proof coins and Mint State Franklin half dollars.

Coin collecting is a very personal experience. Rick's goal is to make the journey as enjoyable as possible for the collector by offering the finest possible quality and service and never second-guessing a client who chooses to return a coin. Rare coins are meant to be enjoyed.

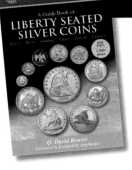

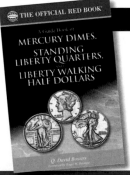